AF386525

Making for America

Making for America

*Transatlantic craftsmanship:
Scotland and the Americas in the
eighteenth and nineteenth centuries*

Edited by

VANESSA HABIB, JIM GRAY AND SHEILA FORBES

Michael K Brown, David H Caldwell, Edward J Cowan, George Dalgleish, Vanessa Habib,
George R Haggarty, Stephen Jackson, David Jones, Alexandra A Kirtley, Ann Smart Martin,
Jennifer A Thompson and Jill Turnbull

Edinburgh 2013
SOCIETY OF ANTIQUARIES OF SCOTLAND

Jacket image: Trustees of the National Museums Scotland

Published in 2013 in Great Britain by Society of Antiquaries of Scotland

Society of Antiquaries of Scotland
National Museum of Scotland
Chambers Street
Edinburgh EH1 1JF
Tel: 0131 247 4115
Fax: 0131 247 4163
Email: administration@socantscot.org
Website: www.socantscot.org

The Society of Antiquaries of Scotland is a registered Scottish charity no SC01044.

ISBN 978 1 90833 203 5

British Library Cataloguing-in-Publication Data
A catalogue record for this book is available from the British Library.

Society of Antiquaries of Scotland gratefully acknowledges funding towards the publication of this volume from the Winterthur Museum, the Center for American Art at the Philadelphia Museum of Art and Ron Haggarty

Design and production by Lawrie Law and Alison Rae
Typesetting by Waverley Typesetters, Warham, Norfolk
Manufactured in Great Britain by Berforts Information Press, Stevenage

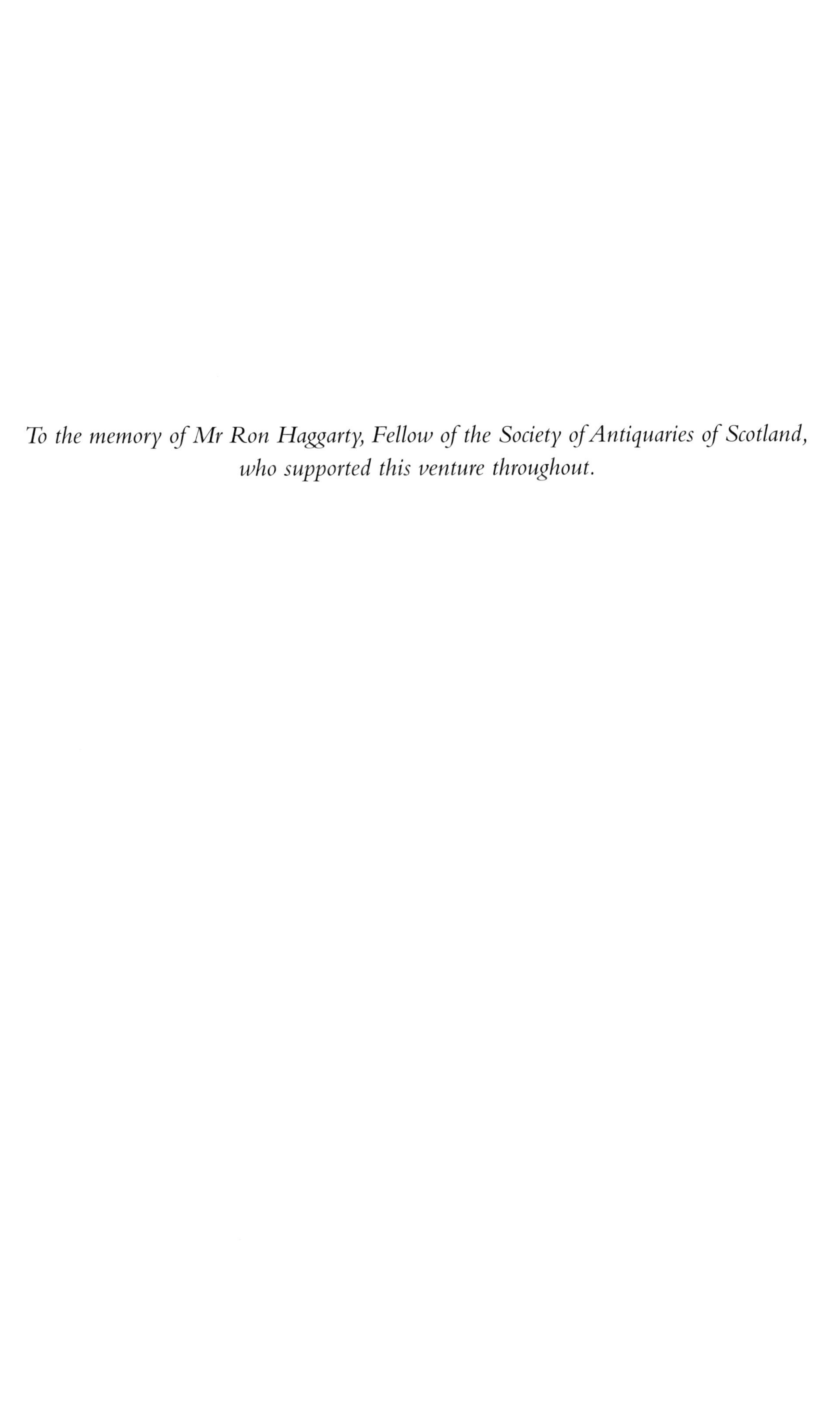

*To the memory of Mr Ron Haggarty, Fellow of the Society of Antiquaries of Scotland,
who supported this venture throughout.*

Contents

Foreword

BARBARA CRAWFORD

A highlight of my presidency of the Society of Antiquaries of Scotland was the Society's first international conference held in October 2009 on the theme of 'Transatlantic craftsmanship: Scotland and the Americas in the eighteenth and nineteenth centuries'. It was organised by the Society of Antiquaries of Scotland, National Museums Scotland and Winterthur Museum, and was held at Philadelphia Museum of Art, Pennsylvania, and Winterthur Museum, Delaware. Over 200 delegates attended the conference to listen to presentations by experts from both the United States and Scotland on early Scottish crafts and craftsmen in early America.

The first session of lectures was held in the Philadelphia Museum of Art; it included Jennifer A Thompson on 'The taste for Scottish painting in America' and David Jones on 'Scottish high-style furniture: the key types, 1750–1850' prior to the evening keynote lecture by Professor Edward J Cowan from the University of Glasgow, on 'Scots across the Atlantic'. Two full days of lectures followed: David Caldwell on 'Collecting Scottish weapons: identity and identification'; Alexandra Kirtley on 'A Scottish cabinetmaker in colonial Philadelphia: Thomas Affleck of Aberdeen'; Vanessa Habib on 'Kilmarnock carpets in the American colonies'; and Stephen Jackson on 'The influence of Scotland in American cabinetmaking, 1750–1850'; as well as lectures on Scottish furniture makers in the Early South (Robert A Leath), 'From Fife to Phyfe; or "the tale of one Scotsman's odyssey in early America"' (Michael Brown), 'Classicising the interior in eighteenth-century Scotland' (Ian Gow), 'Silver in Scotland' and 'The Scottish silversmith in the Americas' (two lectures by George Dalgleish), 'The trade in Scottish pottery to the Americas, c 1750–1850' (George R Haggarty), 'Scottish glass and the American trade' (Jill Turnbull), and '"The Channel … centring in Glasgow": Scottish merchants in eighteenth-century America' (Ann Smart Martin). These sessions were held at the beautiful and historic Winterthur Museum and Country Estate (www.winterthur.org), the former home of Henry Francis du Pont (1880–1969), of the chemical industry dynasty, an avid antiques collector and horticulturist, which has now become a centre for the interdisciplinary study of America's artistic, cultural, social and intellectual past.

The meeting ended with a session on the final morning when experts identified and discussed objects brought along by participants ranging from some very fine Scottish silver communion cups, through furniture, to a pair of swords! In addition Dr Rebecca Jones from the Royal Commission on the Ancient and Historic Monuments of Scotland introduced 'ScotlandsPlaces', an exciting new online resource being developed by the RCAHMS and the National Archives.

The whole visit, and the presentations by the topmost authorities from Scotland and the USA on the theme, was a most rewarding experience. It is therefore exceedingly important that the meeting of knowledge from both sides of the Atlantic can be enjoyed by a wide reading public and knowledge of this wonderful aspect of shared culture brought before a bigger audience with the book which has ensued. Not very much is known about the impact of the Scots on the cultural life of the newly independent American colony. Apart from their contribution to the development of crafts in eastern America Scots also played a very big role in the mercantile life of the early trading centres like Philadelphia. The delegates' visit to Mount Pleasant, the country seat of John Macpherson – a successful Scottish sea captain – built on the east bank of the Schuylkill River between 1762 and 1765, demonstrated to us the way in which successful Scots displayed their wealth and new-found status in elegant Georgian buildings. The means by which the architecture and the flourishing of different crafts were brought from Scotland and the way in which they developed in a traditional way, but often enriched and elaborated, shows vividly the pioneering spirit of many craftsmen in the new and vibrant independent nation. This book, with its array of colour images of the paintings, furniture and examples of *beaux arts* like glass and pottery, is a wonderful and permanent result of a conference which it is hoped may be the first of such meetings across the Atlantic. The long-term consequences of this pioneering conference will be closer connections between the Society of Antiquaries of Scotland and its North American Fellows.

Our thanks are due to the staff of Winterthur Museum and Country Estate, Delaware, to the staff of the Philadelphia Museum of Art, for their successful organisation of the conference, to the contributors for producing their written texts and illustrations, and to the staff of the Society of Antiquaries of Scotland, above all the Publications Committee and the book's editors, Vanessa Habib, Jim Gray and Sheila Forbes, for the production of this beautiful addition to the Society's publications series. Thanks are also due to the supporters of this publication and to those who contributed to speakers' expenses at the conference. Mr Ron Haggarty's generosity is remembered with gratitude, and this volume is dedicated to his memory.

BARBARA E CRAWFORD
OBE, PhD, FRSE, FSA, FSAScot,
Member of the Norwegian Academy.
Past President of the
Society of Antiquaries of Scotland
14 April 2013

Foreword

LINDA EATON

The staff at Winterthur were delighted to work with our friends and colleagues in Scotland and Philadelphia to hold the conference at which these papers were given: *Transatlantic Craftsmanship: Scotland and the Americas in the Eighteenth and Nineteenth Centuries.* Many people from both sides of the Atlantic were involved in the planning, but at Winterthur the person most responsible for making this conference happen is Patricia Halfpenny. Pat served as the director of collections during the initial planning and continued to play a central role as the idea grew into a reality after her retirement.

In addition to this important publication, the coming together of such an eminent group of transatlantic scholars resulted in an exchange of ideas that will inform the work of both speakers and participants for many years to come. One of the most significant effects of the conference was an increased awareness of the wealth of as yet untapped resources in both Scotland and the United States, including archival materials as well as objects in both public and private collections. In particular, it was a great pleasure to see the surprise and delight on George Haggarty's face as he examined examples of intact ceramic forms that he had previously only seen as excavated sherds.

Winterthur has been involved with the study of material culture for over six decades. Our focus on object-based research is an important part of the Winterthur Program in American Material Culture, a master's program run in conjunction with the University of Delaware since 1952. The Winterthur/ University of Delaware Program in Art Conservation has incorporated technical examination alongside treatment and preventive conservation since it was founded in 1974. Since 1977 Winterthur has welcomed research fellows from around the world to work with both our library and museum collections, and hosts a variety of conferences, lectures and workshops for both scholars and collectors. Despite the growing range of online resources and opportunities for virtual conferencing, for those of us engaged in object-based research this publication shows the importance of transatlantic collaboration and exchange in the real world.

LINDA EATON
John L and Marjorie P McGraw Director of
Collections & Senior Curator of Textiles
Winterthur Museum
23 May 2013

Minister for Culture, External Affairs and the Constitution
Ministear airson Cultair, Chùisean Taoibh A-muigh agus a' Bhun-reachd
Michael Russell MSP/BPA

T/F: 0845 774 1741
E: scottish.ministers@scotland.gsi.gov.uk

**The Scottish
Government**
Riaghaltas na h-Alba

homecomingscotland2009.com
An Tilleadh Albannach 2009

MESSAGE OF SUPPORT

August 2009

I am sorry not to be able to accept your kind invitation to attend the International Transatlantic Craftmanship Conference jointly organised by the Society of Antiquaries of Scotland, the National Museums Scotland and the Winterthur Museum.

I am heartened to hear of this international event with American colleagues and send this message in support of the work you are doing and the sustainable and mutually beneficial links we can build. Links that are all the more important, in this the Year of Homecoming. One of the key themes of Homecoming is great Scottish minds and innovations; a theme that resonates with many given that the Society was born during a period of intellectual energy and is the oldest antiquarian society in Scotland.

We are proud of the influence by Scots and by our Scottish Diaspora, estimated at around 40 million, and the legacy they have given. It is important to remember our history, our links to the past and how it can help form our future. It is also important to celebrate our rich culture, heritage, ancestry and the impact that our Great Minds and Innovators have brought to the world.

We in Scotland value our international links and are grateful for the work that organisations like yourselves are undertaking in promoting Scotland overseas. This conference gives us an opportunity to join together with overseas friends and colleagues. I hope this event will help develop bonds, new and old, which will strengthen Scotland's future.

MICHAEL RUSSELL

St Andrew's House, Regent Road, Edinburgh EH1 3DG
Taigh Naomh Anndrais, Rathad Regent, Dùn Èideann EH1 3DG
www.scotland.gov.uk

Acknowledgements

The Society of Antiquaries of Scotland would like to thank everyone involved in the organisation and smooth running of the Transatlantic Craftsmanship conference in 2009 and well as the subsequent work on this publication. In particular, we would like to extend our gratitude to George Dalgleish, George Haggarty and Pat Halfpenny who conceived the idea for the conference and helped bring the ambition to reality. David Caldwell ensured a fantastic collaboration with National Museums Scotland and was an enthusiastic advocate of the project throughout. Barbara Crawford, then President of the Society, actively championed the Society's first major conference in North America and acted as our ambassador, taking the Scottish Government's letter of support provided through the good offices of Linda Fabiani MSP and Michael Russell MSP.

Kathleen Foster of the Center for American Art in the Philadelphia Museum of Art hosted the conference in the PMA (including an excellent lunch!), organised the visit to Mount Pleasant and helped to arrange funding for this book. Both Alexandra Kirtley and Jennifer Thompson, also of the PMA, offered gracious hospitality as well. David Roselle, Tom Savage and Linda Eaton were our hosts at Winterthur. Linda has continued to support the project to its final publication, while Onie Rollins guided us through the generous funding from Winterthur Museum for this book. The conference would not have been possible without them.

Neither would it have been possible without the organisational assistance of Jody Cross, Janis Kraft and Susan Moqtaderi of Winterthur Museum and Jacqui Clabby of the Society. The conference in Winterthur was sponsored by Mr and Mrs James R Alexander. Kevin Hicks designed the Society programme for the event and the jacket of this book. ScotlandsPlaces provided free access to their website for conference delegates, and the Royal Commission on the Ancient and Historical Monuments of Scotland supported Rebecca Jones' attendance. Ron and Rosemary Haggarty supported the attendance of several of the Scottish contingent as well as helped to fund this publication. Our thanks to them all, and we have dedicated this book to Ron's memory.

Finally, a very special thanks must go to Vanessa Habib, who volunteered to edit this publication and who was ably assisted by Sheila Forbes and Jim Gray. Anyone who has tried to bring together a conference proceedings will understand the monumental effort involved!

List of maps and illustrations

Maps

Accurate maps and marine atlases were important in a period of colonial expansion and rivalry. As trade in commodities and the passage of people increased between Britain and the American colonies, safe navigation into and out of rivers and ports was essential for the captains and owners of merchant ships.

Cartouches engraved on some of the larger eighteenth-century maps often describe the riches possible from trade and exploration. Maps of Scotland also begin to show the growing centres of population, the development of Atlantic-facing ports and the roads, rivers and canals linking them to manufacturing areas.

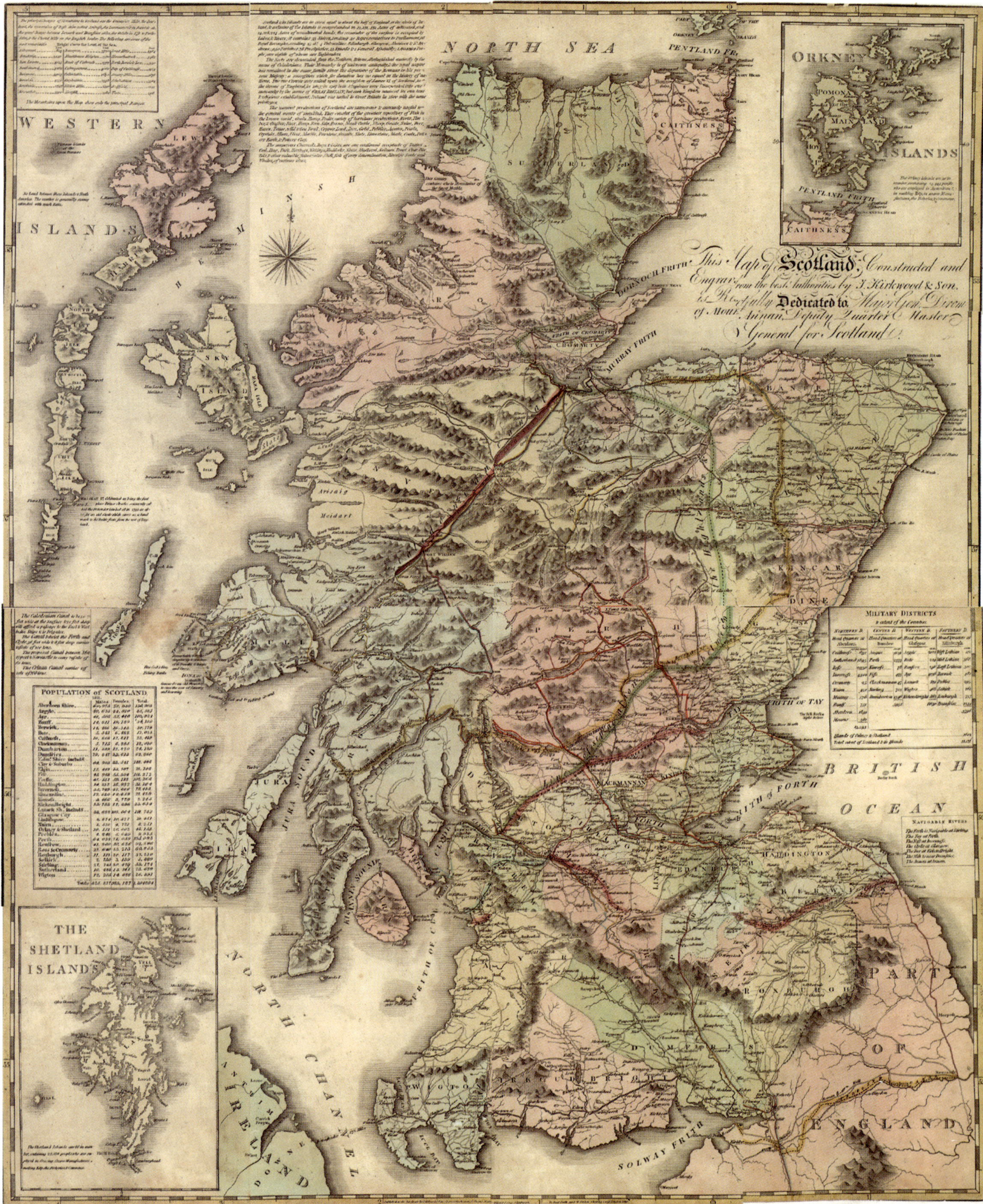

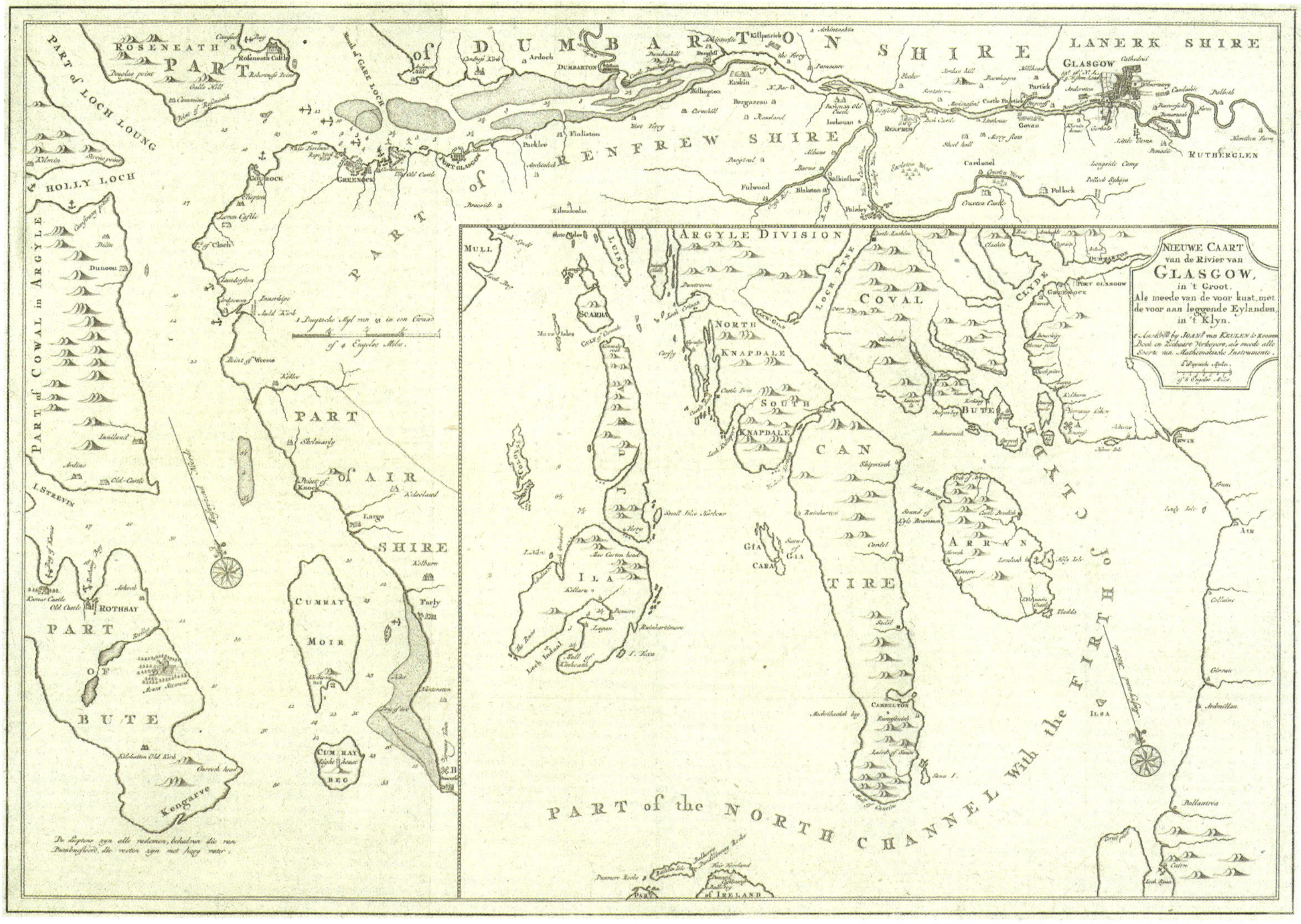

Map of the Clyde 1756.
Johannes Van Keulen ll, showing the outer approaches to the Firth of Clyde and the inner reaches leading to Glasgow.
[Copyright © Royal Scottish Geographical Society]

Map of Scotland 1810.
James Kirkwood.
[Courtesy of the National Library of Scotland]

Map of the West Coast of Scotland 1781.
Joseph Huddart, showing the inner reaches of the Firth of Clyde and the southern coast of Skye. Huddart indicates the dangers facing shipping around this coast. Atlantic-facing ports: Port Glasgow, Greenock, Irvine and Ayr are shown.
[Copyright © Royal Scottish Geographical Society]

A NEW CHART
OF THE
WEST COAST OF SCOTLAND
from THE MULL OF GALLOWAY to DUNAN POINT in SKY.
INCLUDING
THE WESTERN ISLANDS OF ILA,
JURA, MULL, TIRE-IY, COLL, RUM &c.
with THE OPPOSITE COAST OF IRELAND,
and THE NORTH CHANNEL;
Being a Continuation of the Hydrographical Survey made
BY CAPt JOSEPH HUDDART.
LONDON
Printed for R. Sayer and J. Bennett, No 53 Fleet Street,
as the Act directs 31, Octr 1781.
Scale of Nautic Leagues.
INVERNESSHIRE
KNOIDART
RUM ISLAND
ARASAICK
MOIDART
ARDNAMURCHAN
LOCHABER
WESTIR
MORVERN
MULL ISLAND
ARGYLLSHIRE
DUMBARTONSHIRE
COWAL
RENFREWSHIRE
CUNNINGHAM
ISLE OF ARRAN
CLYDE
FIRTH OF CLYDE
ILA ISLAND
LAGGAN BAY
CANTYRE
AIRSHIRE
CARRICK KYLE
LOCHRYAN
GALLOWAY
GLENLUCE BAY
O C E A N
N O R T H   C H A N N E L
COUNTY OF ANTRIM
PART OF IRELAND
COLERAINE
RED BAY
GLENARM BAY
CARRICKFERGUS
BELFAST LOCH
BELFAST

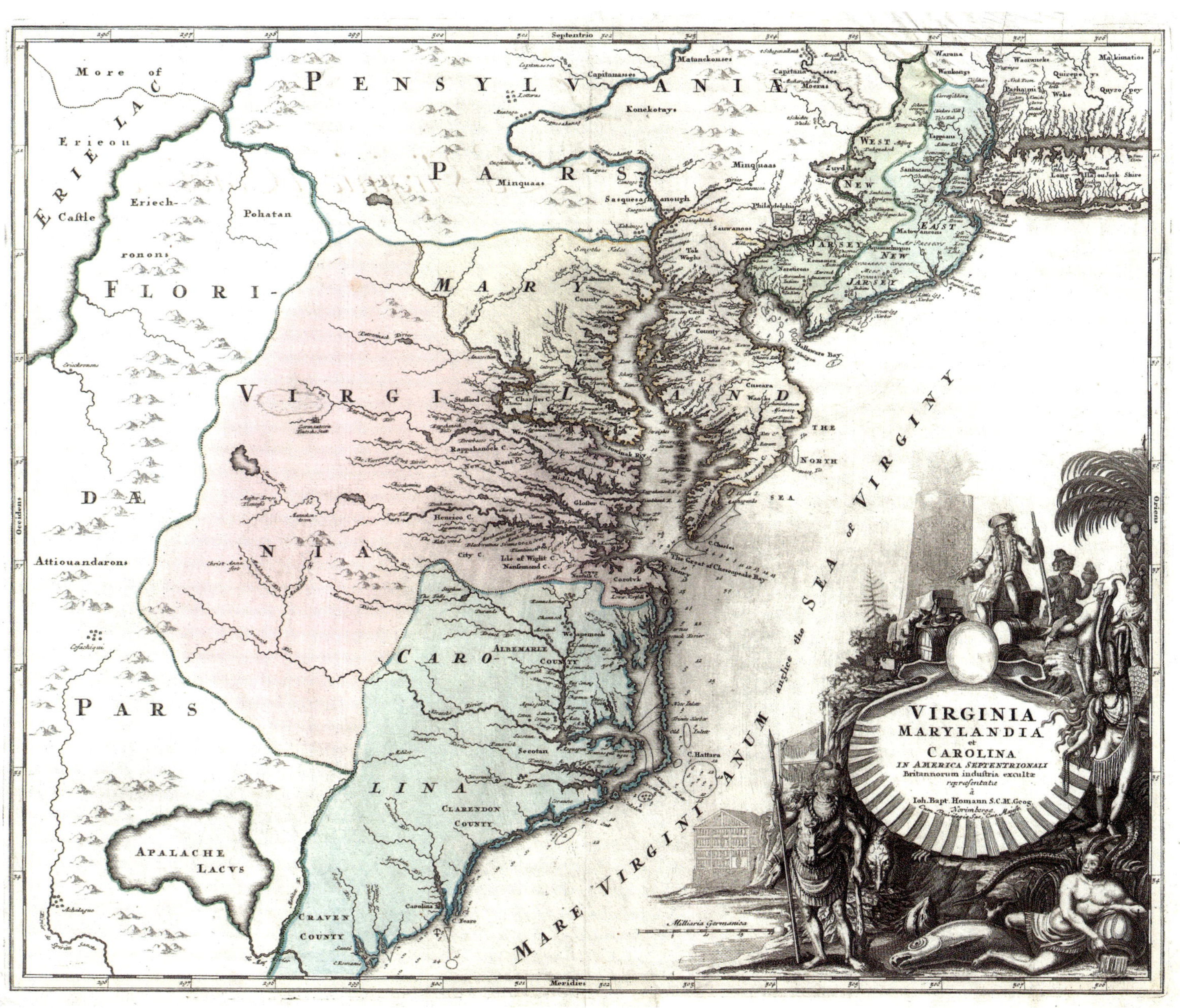

Map of Carolina, Virginia, Maryland and New Jersey 1715.
Johann Homann, showing the Atlantic coast from New York City and Long Island southwards as far as modern-day Georgia. This map was drawn in response to Alexander Spotswood's plan to settle the interior of Virginia with German immigrants. The Delaware Bay and the Chesapeake Bay are mapped in detail with depth soundings shown. The decorative cartouche shows American Indians trading with European merchants and the natural abundance of the country. [From Wikimedia Commons]

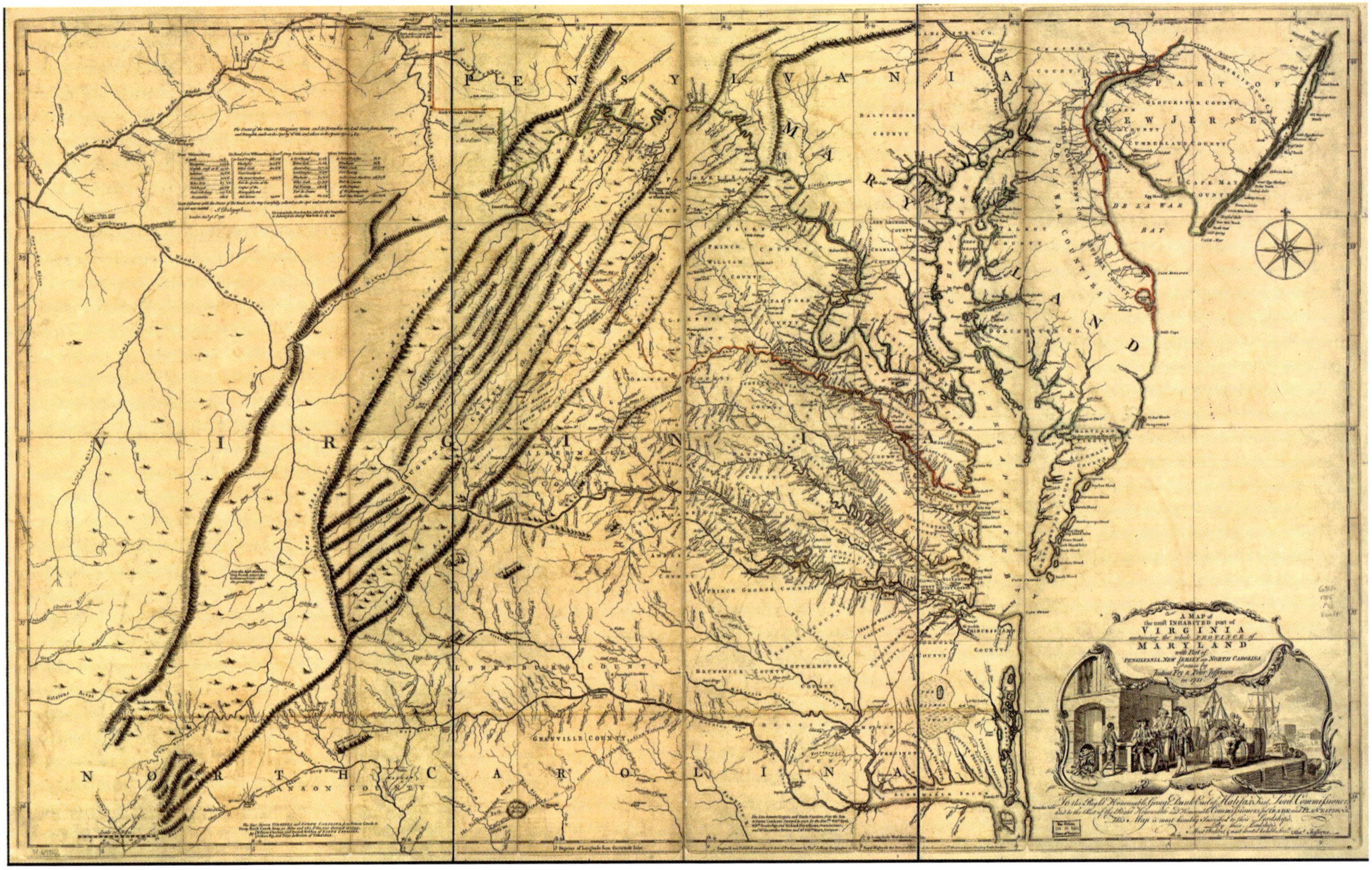

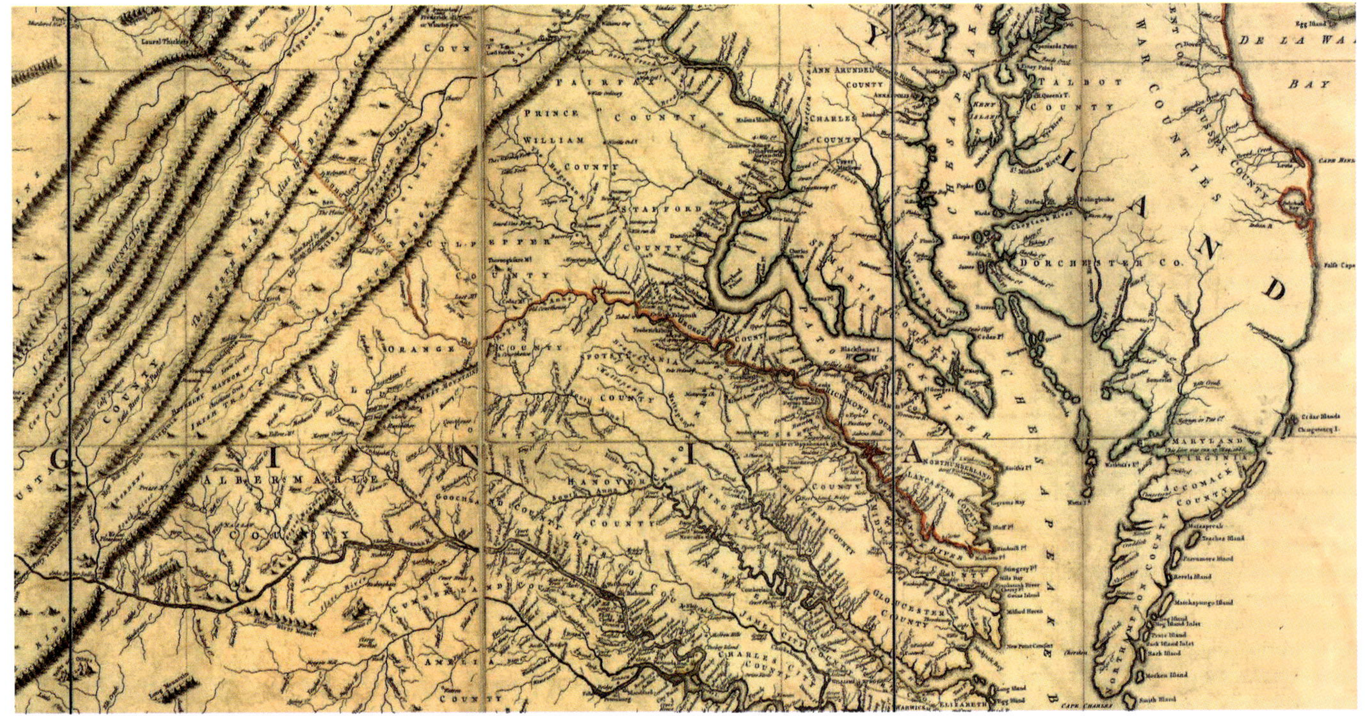

'A Map of the most inhabited part of Virginia containing the whole province of Maryland with part of Pennsylvania, New Jersey and North Carolina' 1751.

Joshua Fry and Peter Jefferson, 1751. The cartouche, designed by Francis Hayman, reveals a wharf scene, where a tobacco planter is negotiating with a ship's captain: the trade in tobacco was dependent on a slave economy. [From Wikimedia Commons]

Map of the West Indies, Florida, Mexico and the Caribbean.

Herman Moll, 1732. 'A Map of the West-Indies or the Islands of America in the North Sea; with ye adjacent Countries; explaining what belongs to Spain, England, France, Holland &c. Also ye trade Winds, and ye several Tracts made by ye Galeons and Flota from place to place. According to ye newest and most exact observations, by Herman Moll, Geographer'. In this informative map Moll comments on the natural resources of the mainland and islands which, among, a wealth of detail, include silver, indigo and cochineal.

CHAPTER 1

'Sober attentive men':
Scots in eighteenth-century America

EDWARD J COWAN

Since the conference which gave rise to this collection of papers took place during the 250th anniversary of the birth of Scotland's national bard, Robert Burns, it is appropriate to note, as I have suggested elsewhere,[1] his celebration of the symbiosis between the greatest heroes of Scotland and America. When Congress declared independence in 1776 George Washington addressed his troops with the following stirring words:

> The time is now at hand which must determine whether Americans are to be Freemen, or Slaves; whether they are to have any property they can call their own; whether their Houses, and Farms, are to be pillaged and destroyed, and they consigned to a State of Wretchedness from which no human efforts will probably deliver them … Our cruel and unrelenting Enemy leaves us no choice but a brave resistance, or the most abject submission … We have therefore to resolve to conquer or die … Let us therefore rely upon the goodness of the Cause …[2]

In 1793 the musician Pietro Urbani asked Burns to compose verses for the tune 'Hey Tutti Tatti', romantically known as 'Robert Bruce's March to the Battle of Bannockburn'. Burns wrote that he had no intention of troubling himself with the request 'till the accidental recollection of that glorious struggle for Freedom [ie the Scottish Wars of Independence] associated with the glowing ideas of some other struggles of the same nature, not quite so ancient, roused my rhyming mania'. Burns's editor, James Kinsley, and almost every other modern commentator have taken the poet's 'other struggles' to be referring to the French Revolution, but the republic was barely a year old at the time, and that cataclysmic event still had to run its course, its outcome quite unknown, whereas the American example was plain for all to see. It seems to me that there are parallels of lexis and sentiment in Washington's declaration and Burns's 'Scots Wha Hae' in the latter's reference to 'Chains and Slaverie' and the

'wretchedness' and 'abject submission' of Washington's address conveyed by such terms as 'traitor-knave', 'coward's grave', 'base slave' and the appeal of free men drawing 'freedom's sword':

> Now's the day, and now's the hour;
> See the front o' battle lour;
> See approach proud Edward's power.
> Chains and Slaverie.
>
> …
>
> By Oppressions woes and pains!
> By your sons in servile chains!
> We will drain our dearest veins,
> But they *shall* be free!
>
> Lay the proud Usurpers low!
> Tyrants fall in every foe!
> Liberty's in every blow!
> Let us Do – or DIE!!!

Eight months later Burns produced his 'Ode for General Washington's Birthday' in which he explicitly identified Washington with William Wallace:

> Dare injured nations form the great design,
> To make detested tyrants bleed?
> Thy England execrates the glorious deed!
> Beneath her hostile banners waving,
> Every pang of honour braving,
> England in thunder calls – 'The Tyrant's cause is mine!'[3]

So far as Scotland's greatest poet was concerned, George Washington was *both* Robert Bruce and William Wallace. He could have conferred no greater accolade on Washington than to compare him to the two finest heroes in Scotland's historical galaxy.

The year 2009 also marked the 200th anniversary of the birth of Abraham Lincoln, who has been described as a kindred spirit of Burns, for whose works, and their enshrining of equality and liberty, he retained a lifelong passion, reportedly reciting the poems with a Scottish accent. Indeed it could be said that Burns

Illustration 1.1
Part of Kirkcudbright and Dumfries from James Kirkwood's Map of Scotland, 1810. [Courtesy of the National Library of Scotland]

articulated the aspiration of many Americans of the new republic, just as he did for his fellow Scots. To some extent he was the bard of America, as of Scotland, until Lincoln's resonant speeches proved much more accessible, pertinent and, above all, more American, so replacing Burns in American hearts.[4]

Some of the most interesting aspects of migration are the ideas, assumptions, values and attitudes that people take with them. This chapter offers a brief survey of some Scots who went to America, for their own good reasons, mainly in the period before 1815, including some from Dumfries and Galloway in the south-west of Scotland. The ports of the Solway Firth on the region's southern border traded with the American colonies, which proved a magnet for many emigrants (illus 1.1). While the tobacco and sugar trades are generally associated with Glasgow and the Clyde, their impact upon Ayrshire, Wigtownshire, Kirkcudbright and Dumfries was also very significant since fortunes made out of these commodities, as well as the tragic obscenity that was slavery, fuelled the purchase of great estates, agricultural improvement and the founding of small burghs such as Newton Stewart and Castle Douglas. These links between the Scottish south-west and America have so far been overlooked in emigration studies.

It is truly remarkable that Scots, who were detested by some as a major cause of the American Revolution, were welcomed by Thomas Jefferson so soon after the war; 'from that country we are surest of having sober, attentive men'. Almost all were on the make and the take, as they had been a century earlier, seizing opportunities that were inconceivable at home. Most were intent upon repaying America for the bounty that it brought them, whether they were convinced loyalists or in favour of independence. Some, unbeknown to themselves, were stoking the fires that would furiously erupt in 1775, while others consciously and effectively embarked upon what was arguably the greatest and most exhilarating constitutional experiment in British history, one which would impact worldwide. For these developments the Scots were, of course, by no means solely, or mainly, responsible but their role was not insignificant. Long before the war Scots attempted to reflect their success in the physical environments they created for themselves – great houses, gardens, fine furniture, china, silverware and books – gradually favouring the production of many of these items in America rather than importing them expensively from Old Scotia or Europe. It took John Witherspoon, President of the College of New Jersey, later Princeton

University, three months to become an American and, like many of the fellow-countrymen who preceded him, he seems to have found the process painless, partly because he found much that was familiar.[5]

Crossing the Pond

It was from Galloway that the first recorded Scottish colonial venture was attempted. In 1621 Charles I granted Nova Scotia to William Alexander, Earl of Stirling, at this time a huge but ill-defined territory comprising large portions of New England and eastern Canada. Two years after the sailing of the *Mayflower*, Stirling entrusted Sir Robert Gordon of Lochinvar with the promotion of a colonial scheme in Cape Breton, renamed New Galloway. The affair did not reflect well on Scottish enterprise; the ships were forced to winter in Newfoundland. After further setbacks the Scots eventually discovered the joys of Cape Breton, reporting on what they considered its considerable potential, but the expedition was abandoned soon after. A notable concomitant was a pamphlet by Gordon, *Encouragements For such as shall have intention to bee Under-takers in the new plantation of Cape Briton, now New Galloway in America, by Mee Lochinvar* (1625), which is, quite simply, a short masterpiece in the literature of colonisation, anticipating most of the reasons for emigration which would be trundled out by later advocates and enthusiasts.[6]

During the seventeenth century many Covenanters were to find themselves in the Caribbean islands and the American plantations as a result of penal transportation. Their ideas were to play an important role in the formation of attitudes which culminated in the creation of the American republic, particularly those questioning the separation of church and state and the legality of resistance to tyrannical kings. There were also several other Scottish experiments in colonisation.[7]

The Lieutenant-Governor of Virginia from 1710 until 1722 was Alexander Spotswood, grandson of Sir Robert who was Scottish secretary of state at the outset of the Covenanting revolution (illus 1.2). He led the 'Knights of the Golden Horseshoe' expedition across the Blue Ridge Mountains to the Shenandoah Valley in search of settlement sites. He acquired huge mining interests, his Tubal Iron Works representing an ambitious pioneering venture in colonial America. In Spotsylvania he established the settlement of Germanna, on the Rapidan River, overlooking which he built his own 'enchanted castle', a large mansion

Illustration 1.2
'Portrait of Alexander Spotswood' by Charles Bridges, 1736. Oil on canvas, 52 x 39½ in (1321 x 1003mm).
Governor's Palace, Colonial Williamsburg, Virginia. [Courtesy of the Colonial Williamsburg Foundation]

house with a terraced garden. A fountain was part of the scheme and he also provided a church, a jail, a pillory and a courthouse which was later moved to Fredericksburg. Spotswood owned 80,000 acres (or 324 square kilometres), comprising no fewer than fifty-seven plantations when he was recalled to Britain, though he later returned to America as Postmaster-General, eventually dying in Annapolis. It was a Scottish surveyor, George Hume (1698–1790), who, in 1727, surveyed and laid out the fifty acres on which Fredericksburg was founded.[8]

One individual from north-east Scotland who was motivated to emigrate by Spotswood was Robert Rose, born at Wester Alves, Moray, in 1704. He arrived in Virginia, aged twenty, having been ordained as an Anglican parson. He decided to keep a diary, 'having frequently found the inconvenience of not keeping account of the most precious talent God had entrusted to Man', namely Time. Furthermore he hoped to refute accusations 'of asserting and advising what I never said or thought'. The surviving journal runs from 21 January 1746 to 13 June 1751. Invaluable though his record is, he wrote little that is memorable and, indeed, the diary would be less useful and meaningful without the voluminous editorial annotations and references.

Rose's family had Jacobite sympathies. He had some knowledge of medicine, as well as surveying, and he was a devoted land-speculator and tobacco-grower; he was also an assiduous chronicler of the weather. Described as 'a circuit-rider parson', he covered his 2,500-square-mile parish about six times a year, truly a 'ramblin' Rose'! We find him marking the bounds of his properties using terminology reminiscent of medieval charters. He has been celebrated as the developer of a special kind of large dugout canoe for the river transportation of tobacco, in which enterprise his associates were fellow countrymen John Harvie and Duncan Cameron.

Rose was not a high flyer and in a way that is part of his fascination. The number of Scots he encountered, usually in fairly mundane circumstances, suggests the unrecognised and unmeasured contribution of the inconspicuous, who generally fail to find a place in the history books, as indicated by a selection of random samplings from his diary:

> Heard news of Cornelius Sales's death which was like to his life, easy and quiet … this Day the wind blowd extremely hard and cold … brought home Wine, Rum & other Necessarys … wrote Mr Fitzhugh's will, he divided his Negroes, and assigned his 3 sons their shares … a hazy rainy day Everybody has got colds … wrote

sundry letters to Scotland in the morning … so hoarse I could not preach … spent the day with Mr John Harvie of Aberfoyle who is of opinion the Master is liable for the Negligence of his Slave … this morning we find the place justly named Aberfoyle, for of Eight horses we put in pasture last night not one to be seen … christened in Albemarle 31 persons … heard an account of my death which had over run the whole county … stayd with reapers … the last week was the hottest I ever travelled in … many horse & catell dropt dead at work & several Negroes and some sailors … Mr Anderson brought a Glasgow Journal of 25 May … heard of the *Anne* of Aberdeen, Capt. Ferguson arrival from the Orkneys in 2 weeks … Mr George Black from Aberdeen brought me letters from my Mother, Sister & Brother … went up into the mountains to look for land but found only Bears … married John Sheppard to Sukey Boulware about 9 months too late … my son Patrick, aged 31 moneth, by taking Jerusalem Oak seed has voided in four days 19 worms … visited Joseph Leman whom I orderd to be blistered yesterday … great number of people in prayers disturbed by a Retailer of Whiskey, one William Miller … I have drunk more whiskey than ever I did before, and find when a man is heartily fatigued any thing will do instead of claret.[9]

The diary demonstrates the degree to which Rose operated within, though by no means exclusively, a Scottish network. John Miller from Glasgow was a tavern-keeper at Brookes Bank; his brother William, who fought in the revolutionary war, was buried at Kinloch Farm (161).[10] John Finlason ran an inn at Germanna until killed by a falling tree (126). Scottish merchant Andrew Anderson had a shop nearby. In 1745 he advertised a recent delivery of 'best hairs and other materials for making all sorts of wigs … after the newest fashions' (116). Patrick Mitchell of Glasgow was an early merchant at Port Royal (120). James Gray, Archibald Ritchie and his kinsman Samuel Ritchie were merchants at Tappahannock. Duncan Graham from Perthshire listed his ancestors back to 1400 in his memorandum book. He originally acted as factor in Virginia for his brother John, a Glasgow merchant who, on emigrating, became one of the wealthiest merchants in Caroline County (132, 154). James Bowie was a merchant at Port Royal; his namesake operated a ferry on the Rappahannock River (328). There were thus Bowies in Virginia fully a century before Jim Bowie, inventor of the Bowie knife, died at the Alamo. Brothers Archibald and Alexander Campbell emigrated in 1730 to join their merchant cousin Daniel Campbell; Archibald later trained as a minister (174). James Crosby, yet another Glaswegian, set up at Williamsburg (168). Patrick Chalmers, a merchant from Edinburgh and possibly a Jacobite, gave Governor Spotswood 'a neat new-fashioned snuff-box' in an attempt to curry favour (173). Edward Brisbane from Ayrshire was a merchant at Petersburg (199).

Scottish ministers were a fairly common export, men such as Alexander Cruden who served at South Farham, Essex County (123) or Isaac Campbell who moved from near Germanna to Charles County, Maryland, where he was minister for thirty-six years, composing a tract on civil government (125). The Revd Robert Innes was born in 1720 at Wester Alves, the same parish as Rose, who witnessed his baptism. He had a charge in Drysdale parish for almost twenty years; a brother-in-law was the soberly named Mourning Richards (224, 282). Two Keith brothers, George and James, from north-east Scotland emigrated with their cousin, also James, who became minister of Hamilton parish (227). Dr Thomas Tulloh (*Scotice* Tulloch) was paid eight times by St Paul's parish to treat its destitute sick (281) (illus 1.3).

Physicians were also numerous, for Scottish universities tended to over-produce medical men. John Roy was engaged in the tobacco trade while his brother was a physician (131). William Alison was a medical doctor from Glasgow (136). Dr Alexander Mackenzie owned part of the land on which the University of Virginia at Charlottesville is now situated. It is thought he may have been related to Kenneth Mackenzie, a physician in Williamsburg (177). Robert Rose noted on 17 May 1748 that he buried 'an honest man Daniel Ferguson, an Eminent Instance of ye uncertainty of Life', described as a doctor and tailor in Port Royal (31, 169). Dr Robert Halkerstone practised medicine near Fredericksburg and then at Port Tobacco, Maryland (323). Dr Michael Wallace, who practised in the vicinity of Falmouth, a town said to have been founded by Scots (128–9), named his house Ellerslie, a place identified with the birth of Scotland's national hero. The doctor had been indentured to Dr Gustavus Brown (1689–1762), thought of as an enlightened man, who seems to have patronised a number of immigrants. A son of Dalkeith, he emigrated to Maryland in 1708 to become a physician. He married Frances Fowke by whom he had twelve children; his second wife produced a modest two. The minister Isaac Campbell married one of his nine daughters, John Graham another. Other sons-in-law were the minister John Moncur from Kincardineshire, and John Key, who may also have

been a Scot since Kay or Key are sometimes shortened versions of Mackay (125, 154, 143, 282–3).

Other Scots immigrants worthy of mention include John Somerville (d. 1798) who settled in Fredericksburg where his son was elected mayor three times. Archibald Macpherson (1705–54), 'a gentleman of education, refinement and wealth, and a friend to the poor and needy', endowed a trust fund for a charity school in the town.[11] Robert Gilchrist was another participant in the tobacco industry who arrived in Norfolk County where he built a fine house,

Illustration 1.3
Plaque commemorating the Scots Kirk at Charleston.
[Illustration courtesy of Padeapix]

Townfield, and later served as a magistrate and sheriff. He was one of the founders of Kilwinning Port Royal-Crosse Masonic Lodge No 2 in 1755 (270).

Not all immigrants were middle-class and well connected. The entry for 9 August 1750 in Rose's diary reads: 'John Marr came with two servts from Mr Andrew Anderson, one named Robt McCook, the other John McLachlan, five years to serve. Cost £27' (86). John Marr was the overseer on one of Rose's plantations. The two servants were indentured, their fares probably paid by Anderson who was reclaiming the £27 for same. It would take McCook and McLachlan five years to work off the debt (308). However, they were unusual among those Scots who could be described as members of Rose's circle, or who were fairly casual acquaintances, since most of his fellow-countrymen were conspicuous achievers with equally conspicuous consumption very much on their minds and a willingness to patronise the craftsmen and artisans with whom this book is concerned.

Robert Rose's acquisitiveness is impressive; he owned 35,000 acres and shared title to a further 80,000. He had at least eight plantations, four lots in Fredericksburg, four in Beverley Town and one in Richmond (140). He possessed just over a hundred slaves, two named Sawney, a Scottish diminutive for Sean, one Glasgow and a Tammie. His will listed much livestock and many agricultural tools. At the Bellivet Plantation he documented nine bedsteads, one 'scrutore', a desk, a book case, two walnut tables, two pine tables, sixteen leather chairs, much silver- and pewterware, Delft dishes and plates, six stone chamber pots and one of pewter, pots, pans and cutlery, among other things (340). Rose was a conscientious clergyman who appears to have taken his responsibilities seriously, but if the Virginians did well by him it must be admitted that he did well out of Virginia.

The nine daughters of the physician Gustavus Brown reportedly had a total of twenty-seven husbands between them (175). Four brothers and one sister of Robert Rose also emigrated to America. By his first marriage Robert had one son and two girls, both of whom died young. With Anne Fitzhugh he had six children, four of whom had offspring of their own. Robert had planted a veritable 'Rose garden', leaving forty-eight grandchildren, most no doubt aspirers like himself, eager to match his material accomplishments and perhaps even willing to commission immigrants of talent from the Auld Country, if indeed they had any knowledge of it. The trauma of revolution undoubtedly turned them into unrepentant Americans if they had not thought of themselves as such before.[12]

Scots in Fredericksburg and New York

John Graham of Dumfries went to Virginia in 1739 where he helped to found Dumfries on the Potomac at the centre of the tobacco trade. George Washington regularly dined or breakfasted there on his travels back and forth between Mount Vernon and Williamsburg, a journey of three or four days each way.[13] Young Washington received his first commission from Governor Robert Dinwiddie, originally from Dumfries, Scotland, who presided over the mismanagement of Virginia during the years 1751 to 1758. He was by no means the only Scot to alienate American colonists from British rule. At the outbreak of war Scots and Scots-Irish combined are estimated to have numbered some 250,000;[14] many proved to be loyalists, but significant numbers of Scots aligned themselves with the patriots.

Fredericksburg was to prove something of a magnet for Scots. Late in 1773 John Paul fled there to escape possible criminal prosecution, hoping to find refuge with his older brother William, who had emigrated to establish a successful business as a tailor. However, he had died; he is buried in the same graveyard as George Washington. His property in Fredericksburg was bequeathed to his beloved sister, Mary Young, and her two oldest children 'in Abigland [Arbigland], in the parish of Kirkbean, in the Stewartry of Galloway, North Britain'.[15] Thus John Paul Jones arrived in America; 'my favourite country from the age of 13, when I first saw it', to receive succour in Fredericksburg from a fellow-Scot, the highly educated Dr John Read, and congenial company in the comfortable and stimulating atmosphere of the local masonic lodge.

George Washington spent his formative years from the age of six to the age of twenty (1738–52) at Ferry Farm on the banks of the Rappahannock, later developed by his sister and her husband as a substantial plantation. The place was named Kenmore for Kenmure Castle, the caput of the Galloway Gordons, after it was purchased by Samuel Gordon from Lochdungan, Kirkcudbright, in Galloway, who emigrated in 1783. Another Galloway contemporary who found his way to Fredericksburg was the poet John Lowe (1750–98), whose father was the gardener at Kenmure Castle. Disappointed in love, he migrated to Fredericksburg in 1773 where he became tutor to the children of George Washington's brother, Charles, eventually opening a boarding school. An unhappy marriage drove him to the bottle. He is remembered nowadays, if at all, for his song, 'Mary's Dream', the refrain of which, 'Mary weep no more for me', was inscribed on his tombstone:

The moon had climbed the highest hill
That rises o'er the source of Dee,
And from the eastern summit shed
Her silver light on tower and tree,
When Mary laid her down to sleep.
Her thoughts on Sandy far at sea,
When soft and low a voice was heard
Saying, 'Mary, weep no more for me'.[16]

Other Scots who found themselves in Fredericksburg included General Hugh Mercer, a Jacobite veteran of Culloden, who set up a prosperous medical practice and 'the oldest drug store in America', as well as purchasing other properties in the city. He performed stalwart service for the patriot cause until his death at the battle of Princeton in 1777, tended at the end by Dr James Craik of Arbigland (see below). Another individual whose biographical details are scant was Colonel Gustavus Brown Wallace, the son of Dr Michael Wallace of Ellerslie, some five miles from Fredericksburg. He twice visited Scotland to deal with matters of inheritance. In between he fought for his country's independence. He was with Washington at Valley Forge and saw much service before he was captured at Charleston, though eventually paroled for 400 hogsheads of tobacco. In 1802 he died of a fever and was buried in the masonic cemetery of Fredericksburg.[17] The city's Lodge No 4, Ancient Free and Accepted Masons, was constituted on 1 September 1752. It can be assumed that good use was made of it by Scots, both residents and visitors, and Washington himself was a member. The master of the Lodge, Daniel Campbell, made a visit to the Grand Lodge in Scotland in 1758 to secure the charter for Fredericksburg.[18] Masonic fellowship may have served to somewhat blunt the Virginian antipathy towards Scots and to have partially eased the plight of prisoners on both sides of the conflict.

In New York a number of souwesters were involved in the prestigious St Andrew's Society founded in 1756 and still going strong.[19] The eleventh president of the society, William McAdam (1772–3), came from Carsphairn, Kirkcudbrightshire. At one point he invited his nephew, John Loudon McAdam, future engineer and inventor of macadamised road surfaces, to visit him in New York. John later became a close associate of James Fenimore Cooper. David Johnston's antecedents are uncertain but he died at his country residence, 'Annandale', in Dutchess County, New York in 1809. One of his descendants made the unlikely claim that he was offered the title and estates of the Marquis of Annandale but declined.

The fifteenth president, Robert Lenox (1798–1814), was one of the most interesting (illus 1.4, 1.5). Born in Kirkcudbright in 1759, he emigrated with his brothers to New Jersey on the eve of revolution to join his uncle, David Sproat, a merchant in Philadelphia. Sproat, a loyalist, became Commissary-General of Naval Prisoners in North America, in which capacity he was awarded some £550 towards the relief of American naval captives. William Lenox supported the loyalists, dying in Charleston in 1781. Another brother, David, fought for independence and survived, a wealthy merchant, in Philadelphia until 1828. Robert Lenox was to become one of the greatest American merchants of his day. Trading at 59 Broadway, New York, with his youngest brother, James, he eventually owned land between 4th and 5th Avenues, and 68th and 71st Streets. This valuable Manhattan property was bequeathed to his son James, who sold off portions to the value of three million dollars, leaving a further four million to endow various charities as well as the famous Lenox Library, now part of New York Public Library. James Lenox was a bibliomaniac who hoarded books by the thousand, refusing to lend them even to close friends.[20] Although his father's fortune funded his collecting habit, James had grown away from his Scottish roots. He turned down holographs, or as they were known at the time, 'autograph manuscripts', of 'Auld Lang Syne' and 'Scots Wha Hae', on the grounds of expense! Lenox's associate, sometime agent and memorialist, the bibliographer and fellow book-chaser Henry Stevens of Vermont, thought these 'two gems … would be better appreciated in America than even in Scotland'.

'Auld Lang Syne' was sent post-haste to Albany for the Burns Centenary Festival in 1859 at which the praeses requested 'all to rise, join hands and sing the song from the poet's own handwriting'. The effect was reportedly sublime and the price of ten guineas was not bad either. The story of the 'Scots Wha Hae' manuscript is equally interesting. Stevens had purchased a number of Burns items from the estate of the late William Pickering, another collector. His acquisition of the 'Bannockburn' piece was reported in *The Times*, where it was noticed by the prominent Edinburgh antiquarian David Laing. He informed Henry Stevens that some years before he had seen some papers belonging to the Earl of Buchan, 'the correspondent of Washington', including a letter from Burns with the song as an attachment. This, however, had become detached and Laing could never discover its whereabouts. 'Now I suppose you have the one

Illustration 1.4
'Portrait of Robert Lenox' by John Trumbull, 1806. Oil on canvas, 36¼ x 28in (920 x 711mm).
Bequest of Waldron Phoenix Belknap Jr. [Courtesy of the New York Historical Society Museum and Library]

Illustration 1.5
'Portrait of Mrs Robert Lenox' by John Trumbull, 1806. Oil on canvas, 36¼ x 28in (921 x 711mm). Bequest of Waldron Phoenix Belknap Jr. Rachel Carmer (Mrs Robert Lenox) was the daughter of Nicholas Carmer, cabinetmaker and hardware merchant in New York. [Courtesy of the New York Historical Society Museum and Library]

leaf and I the other. Pray send me the poem and I will send you many others in exchange.' It says something for Burns's reputation in America that, instead, Stevens sent Laing half a dozen of the bard's recently purchased poems and letters in exchange for the Buchan letter, 'for the two ought to come together again, never to be separated, and then go to America where they would be so highly appreciated'. The letter was duly sent, and Stevens, having reunited the pages, had them bound in red morocco. 'This done I reported the beautiful little volume to Mr Lenox at fifty guineas … he declined it as too dear'! For twenty years he was unable to sell it until he showed the item, 'the rejected of men', to Charles Sumner, the sometime Senator for Massachusetts and dedicated anti-slavery campaigner, who responded, 'What! Mr Lenox, a New York son of a Scotchman, a collector and a millionaire, decline that for a paltry half-a-hundred guineas! I had rather possess this "Scots wha ha" than anything else of the kind I can name.'[21] Sumner later bequeathed the holograph to Harvard but the story very well illustrates how Burns was falling out of fashion in the US during and after the period of the Civil War.

Other presidents of the Society included Archibald Gracie, born at Dumfries in 1755, who emigrated to New York where he became a lifelong business associate of Robert Lenox. John Graham, nineteenth president (1828–31), born at Burnswark near Ecclefechan about 1770, also made a fortune in business, leavened by a taste for literature and a fondness for composing verses to old Scottish airs. His successor, John Johnston, was born on 22 January 1781 in the parish of Balmaghie, 'Gallowayshire', Scotland. He was twenty-two when he arrived in New York to found an import/export business. Another presidential native of Kirkcudbright was David Kennedy, born there in 1791. His uncle was the oft-mentioned Robert Lenox, which illustrates how family and business networks overlapped. Many other 'doonhamers' would serve throughout the nineteenth century. The nickname came from natives of Dumfries and Galloway working in Scotland's Central Belt who went 'down home' for holidays and family visits.

Two contrasting transantlanteans: James Currie and John Paul Jones

When James Currie of Kirkpatrick-Fleming (1756–1805), later the biographer of Burns, was sent to the grammar school at Dumfries, he encountered American chums such as William Wells, born in Charleston, South Carolina, whose father had been a bookseller in Dumfries before he emigrated, and also a distant relative, Robert McMurdo, whose father was a merchant in Virginia. Another was William Cunninghame of the well-known Glasgow tobacco family. It was the weed that took Currie to Virginia, as it did John Orr, a planter, and James Currie's cousin, Dr James Currie of Dockenflatt who, as a qualified physician, moved to Richmond where he became the confidant of Thomas Jefferson. When young James's father negotiated his indenture the boy was fourteen. In preparation he took additional classes in accountancy; such was the secret of Scottish success: so many were numerate, as well as literate. By 1771 James Currie was on his way to Virginia, where he experienced the early and heady stirrings of the American Revolution.[22] One of his cousins, not of America but of London, became James's brother-in-law; he ran a slave ship named the *Dumfries* to Africa and the Americas.[23] Currie's acquaintance with slavery was to render him a lifelong abolitionist.

At the age of nineteen he was unimpressed with the world of commerce, stating in remarkably Burns-like sentiments: 'Show me the man who acquires a fortune, and in general I will show you a wretch devoid of every noble sentiment, dead to all sense of shame, who makes money his god, whose face cannot blush, whose heart cannot feel.' Though he might not enjoy personal success 'it shall not be owing to any blemish in my character or defect in my abilities; and whatever misfortunes I may go through, I will endeavour to behave under them with becoming fortitude, and to maintain the character of an honest man'.[24] James was abroad at a fascinating time, as the colonial system was beginning to collapse, largely due to the monopolies and aggressive business tactics of the Tobacco Lords.[25] Cynical Britons reported of Americans that 'the more a man is in debt, the greater the patriot he is'.[26] Currie actually published a defence of the Scottish merchants in the *Virginia Gazette* but he increasingly sympathised with the colonists. Indeed, he announced that he would return home to study medicine at Edinburgh with the ambition, unfulfilled, of eventually settling in Virginia.

The American legend, John Paul Jones, was born in 1747, son of a gardener on the Arbigland estate at Kirkbean, Kirkcudbrightshire, though some whispered that he was actually the offspring of the proprietor, William Craik. John Paul was a man who could, like Currie and Burns, rhetorise with the best of them. He immodestly rejoiced in his personal participation in the struggle for independence:

> I am not an Adventurer in search of Fortune, on the contrary I laid aside my enjoyments in Private Life and drew my Sword at the Commencement of this War only in support of the Dignity and Violated Rights of Human Nature.[27]

In 1778 he predicted that the American navy 'will rise as if by enchantment, and become, within the memory of persons now living, the wonder and envy of the world'.[28]

Jones was largely forgotten until 1905 when his body was exhumed from a pauper's grave in Paris for reburial at the Naval Academy in Annapolis on the orders of President Theodore Roosevelt. Many new legends about the Scot were created at that time to inspire young recruits, including the attribution of noble sentiments which he neither wrote nor uttered. These compounded the considerable degree of self-mythologisation in which Jones indulged in his own lifetime. Several authors have suggested that doubts about his paternity and a resentment of Scottish feudal attitudes drove him away at the age of thirteen,[29] but while the latter claim may have some merit, the former is not altogether convincing. Indeed, the illegitimacy claim, although still repeated in print to the present day, was rejected as long ago as 1830.[30] Those who have argued that he might actually have been fathered by William Craik betray something of a patrician attitude which held that a man of Jones's talents could not have sprung from his humble background. However, Craik did have an illegitimate son, James (1730–1814), who was educated as a doctor to become, in time, George Washington's personal physician and, in 1798, Physician-General. Towards the end of his life George Washington, driven by the westward urge, would undertake expeditions into the bush solely accompanied by his friend and confidant, Dr James Craik. If the rumours were true why would Craik treat one boy so favourably, funding a university education and presumably using his American contacts to advance his career, while alienating the other?

John Paul joined the merchant navy in Whitehaven in the absence of a commission to the Royal Navy. One of the keys to his future success was an association with the Masons. He joined the Kirkcudbright Lodge, a very Scottish action we might think, for the Masons had practically been invented in Scotland and they were rapidly gaining popularity in America.[31] In 1775 John Paul decided to throw in his lot with the revolutionaries in typical self-regarding style, linking his own destiny with that of the nascent republic. 'Since liberty hath chosen America as her last asylum every effort to protect and cherish her is noble and will be rewarded with the thanks of future ages.'[32] He found like-minded companions at the St Andrews Lodge in Boston, which has been described 'as a hotbed of revolutionary agitation',[33] where the Tea Party was planned and whose Grand Master, General Joseph Warren, was killed at Bunker's Hill.

Jones's main contribution to the American war effort was in his understanding of the potential of terror, though since he was not responsible for a single civilian death, he can hardly be deemed a terrorist. There were many atrocity stories about British attacks on America's eastern seaboard. John Paul shrewdly detected that the British were fearful of invasion, hence his motive for the attack on the Solway in 1778. He also had a notion that if he could capture some well-known figure he might be able to force the release of American prisoners. Edwin G Burrows' recent study describes the appalling treatment many of the prisoners received.[34] The famous attack on the Selkirk family at St Mary's Isle may have been potentially a good idea, but it was the gardener's son from Kirkbean who perceived the 4th Earl of Selkirk to be the man whose kidnapping would bring the British government to the negotiating table. In the event, the Earl of Selkirk was away from home. The correspondence between Jones and the Selkirks, with his ludicrous protestations of sympathy and gentility, still survives. Having missed out on the Earl, he tried to persuade his Countess to use her influence to end the war.

> Though I have drawn my sword in the present generous struggle for the rights of men, yet I am not in arms as an American nor am I in pursuit of riches … I profess myself a citizen of the world, totally unfettered by the little mean distinctions of climate or of country, which diminish the benevolence of the heart and set bounds to philanthropy. Before this war was begun, I had, at an early time of life, withdrawn from sea service, in favour of 'calm contemplation and poetic ease'. I have sacrificed not only my favourite scheme of life, but the softer affections of the heart, and my prospects of domestic happiness, and I am ready to sacrifice my life also, with cheerfulness, if that forfeiture could restore peace and good will among mankind.[35]

Illustration 1.6
The Galloway connection survives in South Carolina. [Illustration courtesy of Padeapix]

To the Earl he protested: 'I have endeavoured to serve the cause of liberty, through every stage of the American Revolution, and sacrificed to it my private ease, a part of my fortune and some of my blood.'[36] The Selkirk affair was a fiasco but the attack on Whitehaven was effective in creating a climate of fear among the local inhabitants.

After his stunning victory at Flamborough Head he was demonised by the British as a base traitor, though when he later met and conversed with Basil, Lord Daer, Selkirk's heir, in Paris, the latter reported that Jones was not the incarnation of evil so often depicted. A recent biographer concludes that he 'fought for a world in which men might advance by their merits and drive, and not be pegged by their birth or place. His pride would not allow him to see that, as most men measure success, he

won.'[37] The Scot was truly an American phenomenon (illus 1.6).

Revolution and reaction

On the eve of revolution, the architect and engineer William Mylne took ship for America. His correspondence illustrates that, initially at least, he considered emigration. He sailed to Charleston, settling for a time in a log cabin near Augusta, where he anticipated Henry David Thoreau's Walden Pond experience by living as a semi-recluse. He was tempted by the life of a planter: 'There is a tract of land of 300 acres finely situate on the River Savannah, this place I want much to buy … [it should cost £60] … The person who owns it lives at St Augustine in East Florida.' He reckoned that if he could buy the land and 'three or four negroes' he would be made for life. Material needs were to be supplied by his tailor and cobbler in Edinburgh as he contemplated ordering linen waistcoats and jackets, checked and white shirts, stockings, a duffle greatcoat, a hat and shoes. He craved Scotch snuff but in an early compromise learned to make his own. He required sheets, tablecloths and towels but thought he might buy a feather bed locally. He felt the want of reading material. He contemplated cutting down trees, removing roots, ploughing and planting such crops as corn, indigo and tobacco but realised he could not do this alone. A network of associates included Robert Mackay, Augusta merchant from Caithness by way of Cuba and Charleston, who assisted the passage of emigrants from Orkney; Alexander Cameron, related to, and deputy of, John Stuart, Superintendent of Indian Affairs for the Southern District; David Taitt, Scottish surveyor, sometime commissary to the Creek Indians and John Stuart's deputy superintendent; Andrew Robertson, relation of Mylne and long settled in South Carolina before moving to Georgia in 1773; and George Baillie from Haddington, Savannah merchant. James Gordon from Orkney was a land speculator, plantation owner and would-be coloniser, a loyalist who fled to Nova Scotia. He married one of his slaves and lived with her in the Bahamas. 'Their attachment was such that after her death he refused to bury her body and kept it, dressed and bejewelled, in a protective cage.'[38]

An outbreak of fever forced Mylne to move. At Wilmington he was told that 'many of our countrymen' lived locally, including Flora Macdonald of Bonnie Prince Charlie fame and her husband, part of the Cape Fear colony. He encountered Murray of Philiphaugh, who was moving down to Georgia, 'much hated on account of his pride'. Pennsylvania reminded him of England, 'a fine country if the people would be good', but then he reached Philadelphia, 'by far the finest laid out town I have ever yet been in'; it had the 'finest market in the world', praise from the rather gloomy Mylne. He wrote his journal from memory for fear that if he was seen taking notes he would be mistaken for a spy. 'As to politicks I think most of the people are mad.' Throughout his journey he saw troops mustering to fife and drum, often clad in new uniforms. Some were crack shots who could take the head off a hawk at a hundred yards. An old Irishman observed of the militias that one-third would run away, one-third be killed and the other hanged. In this climate trade had ceased and there

was no place for an architect. He still fancied the life of a planter, which promised independence 'but I am afraid it will not do'.[39] By September 1775 he was back in Britain.

One doonhamer who confused his contemporaries as he has baffled posterity was George Johnstone, brother of William Pulteney, 'the wealthiest man in England', who promptly changed his surname when his wife unexpectedly inherited the Earl of Bath's fortune in 1767. An older brother, James, was MP for Dumfries and the target of a couple of poems by Burns. George was described by contemporaries as one who 'does nothing feebly', who, 'in his whole character [is] active, decisive and bold'.[40] After a naval career he became Governor of West Florida, which he hailed as 'the emporium of the New World', immediately ordering a survey of the place, drawing up a programme for trade, increasing the number of immigrants and slaves, and attempting to establish good relations with the native people. He advertised Florida's opportunities in periodicals such as the *Scots Magazine*, blatantly lying about the climate and comparing the primitive settlement at Pensacola to Venice, no less. Lord Adam Gordon arrived there shortly afterwards to plan an emigration scheme from Scotland to Florida. He found the colony a miserable place, stressing the levels of sickness and fevers, though he recognised that it had potential, a view shared by Johnstone who bitterly lamented that recent immigrants represented 'the refuse of the jails of the great cities, and the overflowing Scum of the Empire'.

Though he displayed considerable leadership and acumen, Johnstone's governorship was largely an exercise in frustration. He was instinctively autocratic, so alienating the military garrison whose failure to accept his authority, he believed, would lead to anarchy or despotism. Previous commandants, such as Major Forbes and Captain Mackinnen [*sic*], had enjoyed little success in treating with the native peoples, but Johnstone made some progress, holding two congresses during his tenure. He was fortunate to recruit John Stuart, superintendent for Indian affairs, a navy man as well as a Scot. He also dispatched two other Scots, John Hannay and naval lieutenant Thomas Campbell, to reside with the Creek Indians for six months. The result was a temporary peace. Johnstone likened the native people to the Gaels, a fairly common ploy in British colonial discourse. 'Suppose the actors at an English election changed into shrewd, pawky, proud barelegged Highlanders, all armed and reeling. The wives are exactly the same. It is impossible to over-reach any of them, drunk or sober, or gain a point, without a present.'[41]

He also had good ideas, unrealised, about bypassing New Orleans, so channelling trade to Pensacola, which he vigorously attempted to transform into a worthy and increasingly self-sufficient colonial centre. He held very regular meetings of the colonial council and continued to extol the possibilites of West Florida. What brought about Johnstone's demise as governor was his volatility. More trouble with the Creeks led him to advocate something very like genocide. His battles with the military continued. To underline his own supposed authority he fired the colony's chief justice, but twenty-two colonists sent a petition to London to seek relief from Johnstone's 'unjustifiable, arbitrary and tyrannical principles'. He was given six months' leave and returned no more.

Johnstone had served on the peace-negotiating team sent by the British government to Philadelphia in 1778. Like Pulteney, for whom he deputised, he was prepared to make every possible concession to the Americans with the exception of independence. In many respects Johnstone had come round to the American point of view but he was nervous about the possibility of a Franco-American alliance. His ambition was 'that every subject of the empire might live equally free and secure in the enjoyment of the blessings of life; – not one part dependent on the will of another with opposite interests, but a general union, on terms of perfect security and mutual advantage'. Adam Ferguson, one of the foremost of Enlightenment thinkers, author of *Essay on the History of Civil Society*, was appointed secretary to the delegation, apparently on Johnstone's recommendation. It transpired that the British, well intentioned though they were, had very little understanding of the revolutionaries. Johnstone reportedly believed that his 'powers of argument' would suffice to convince the Americans. Another commentator considered that he exhibited 'a species of ardent, impetuous, half-savage eloquence, restrained by no delicacy of language, yet capable of powerfully affecting his hearers by the display of information, by his energetic appeals to their passions, and even his gesticulations'.

Johnstone's career was finally undone by Elizabeth Ferguson, the daughter of Dr Thomas Graeme of Graeme Park and the granddaughter of Sir William Keith, Governor of Pennsylvania. Her husband was Henry Hugh Ferguson, a loyalist who returned to Scotland in 1775 leaving her behind. Elizabeth, a poet,

also hosted a literary salon. She described Philadelphia as 'the Athens of North America', quite possibly in homage to Edinburgh.[42] She let it be known that Johnstone had raised with her the possibility of bribing prominent Americans, a suggestion perfectly believable in an eighteenth-century context. It has been plausibly suggested that she sought to ingratiate herself with the American authorities to save her fortune. Johnstone departed America, his Border blood inspiring a similar response to that concerning the Floridian Indians: British troops should be 'employed in Plundering and ravaging, laying waste, and burning all the accessible parts of America of Consequence to the Northward and Southward'.[43]

One of Johnstone's kinder letters, addressed to the Board of Trade, concerned George Gauld whose survey of the Bay of Pensacola had 'opened a new Light to us, both respecting the Nature of the country, and the Importance of it, which exceeds the most sanguine Expectations'. It was rare, he remarked, that 'Health, Inclination, Mathematical Exactness, and a proper Delineation are found to unite in the same person'. Gauld, from Botriphnie in Banffshire, was born in 1732 and much of his productive life was spent in East and West Florida. He studied at King's College, Aberdeen, and subsequently entered the navy as a schoolmaster charged with the education of young midshipmen at sea. He then graduated to the position of surveyor and cartographer. When he sailed on the *Tartar* to West Florida in 1764, under captain Sir John Lindsay and mate Robert Reid, George Johnstone should have been aboard but he was delayed. For the last leg of the journey Gauld was joined by Lord Adam Gordon. He later worked with many Scots, for example, Lieutenant-Colonel James Robertson, Captain George Murray, midshipman John Forbes, Captain Basil Keith, army surgeon Dr John Lorimer, David Ross, Governor John Eliot who committed suicide, army engineers James Campbell and Archibald Robertson, and Major Alexander Dickson. Little wonder that Lieutenant-Governor Montfort Browne detected a 'Scotch Party' in West Florida.[44] Gauld enjoyed a distinguished career during a period when Imperial Britain realised that accurate sea charts were necessary for maintaining naval power. Like most patriotic Scots who had the opportunity, he imposed some place-names from his native parish on Florida maps, such as Isla, Fiddich and Dullen.

With a symmetry imposed by history or Lord Bute, or both, a Scot was also appointed to govern Florida's eastern colony from 1763 to 1771 – James Grant of Ballindalloch Castle on Speyside. Many admired Grant's military prowess but he attracted many critics:

> Without abilities, or the least knowledge of his profession; he possessed a kind of cunning, invariably directed to the promotion of his own interest. Insensible to the ties of blood, incapable of friendship, or a generous action. He was a Gamester, a Glutton, and an Epicure. In short, it may be truly said that he lived only for himself.[45]

Like Johnstone, he called for surveys of his colony, pondered economic development and attempted to pacify the native population. Grant too had serious problems with civil and military authority, particularly with Major Francis Ogilvie, who was in command of the 9th Regiment. The governor personally favoured a colony on the Nova Scotia model whereby a sizeable number of settlers (500 in that case) would give the project a flying start, but he never succeeded in recruiting a critical mass. For a time Adam Gordon seemed to offer a solution through a syndicate of land speculators, who formed the East Florida Society of London which also included such Scottish peers as Buccleuch and Cassillis, but this came to nothing. A scheme devised by Dr Andrew Turnbull for a planned colony at New Smyrna on Mosquito Inlet collapsed after 1,500 Greeks and Italians rioted within a month of arrival. By 1771 the population of East Florida consisted of 208 whites and 900 slaves. Grant established a plantation which made him a small fortune from indigo, a crop heavily dependent on slave labour. Other Scottish plantations were owned by Richard Oswald, who possessed 100 slaves at Mount Oswald, by Lieutenant-Governor John Moultrie and by Captain Robert Bisset, while at least four others were in English hands.

Grant developed St Augustine as his capital, built around The Parade and established churches and schools there. All was quiet on the eastern front; the political struggles to the north did not impact much upon Florida, whose governor had no sympathy whatsoever with 'that spirit of Disunion, Discord, Dissension & Disaffection' prevailing in the thirteen colonies. He claimed his patch was 'the only Place of absolute Safety . . . in America'. Grant avoided problems with a council by seldom convening it; charges of acting as the autocrat he undoubtedly was did not emerge until after he had returned home. He pacified the native peoples, in partnership with John Stuart, by showering them with presents, claiming that this represented 'a new system never before practised in

any part of America', which was nonsense but probably well intentioned.

In 1771 he took overdue leave and although he had fully intended to return to America he became a Member of Parliament for Tain Burghs. He continued to enjoy as much as £2,000 per year from his indigo plantation. He had taken home with him his black slave and cook, Baptiste, shrewdly suspecting this would raise an eyebrow or two in London and Speyside. His views on Americans had not mellowed. In February 1775 he became embroiled in controversy for an ill-considered speech in which he dismissed them all as 'a weak and degenerate race', roundly traducing their military abilities. This lifelong bachelor once remarked that he thought more of America than of matrimony, but in the House of Commons his rhetoric had got the better of him. A retraction was demanded, but his utterances displayed no contrition when, recalled to the army, he was dispatched to Boston in 1775: 'tis high time to try how Severity will operate'. America would be 'lost if not conquered . . . there is no middle Path'. For four years he was heavily involved in the British campaigns before he returned home for good.[46]

At the battle of Long Island Grant faced an American who desperately wanted to be a Scot, and a Scottish earl no less, one William Alexander. Alexander's father, James (c 1691–1756) had been a lawyer, politician, newspaperman, scientist, Attorney General of New York, one of the founders of the American Philosophical Society, a trustee of what became Columbia University and, last but not least, a native of Muthill, Perthshire.[47] His mother came from a powerful mercantile family; thus William was raised in the ranks of New York's elite. He married Sarah Livingston, daughter of Philip, heir to the dynasty which originated with Robert Livingston the Elder (1654–1728) who was born at Ancrum, Roxburghshire. Robert Livingston had fled to the Netherlands because of his Covenanting sympathies, there learning Dutch, which was an obvious bonus when he emigrated to New Amsterdam. Sarah's brother, William, was governor of New Jersey during the revolutionary war.[48] Robert R Livingston, great-grandson of Robert the Elder, was one of the drafters of the Declaration of Independence. He was appointed first Chancellor of New York in which position he administered the oath of office to George Washington as first President of the United States in 1789 (illus 1.7). On that occasion the military escort was commanded

Illustration 1.7
'Inauguration of General George Washington, 30 April 1789'. J Clarence Davies Collection.
[Courtesy of the Museum of the City of New York]

by General William Malcolm, an officer of the St Andrew's Society of New York.[49]

During a five-year visit to Britain from 1756 to 1761, Alexander took it into his head to claim the lapsed earldom of Stirling and thus (he hoped) the vast territories of Nova Scotia granted to the Earl of Stirling back in 1621. This initiative probably resulted from the 'great respect shown, and court paid to him by the Scotch, particularly by Mr Alexander Wedderburn, Drummonds the bankers, Lord Aberdeen and others of Scotland', in which country he cultivated the Duchess of Gordon and the Duke of Argyll. Other eminent Scots encouraged his claim. A pedigree was manufactured showing him to be 'nearest male heir to the last Earl of Stirling'. He then pursued a futile, and expensive, quest to have his title recognised by the House of Lords while considering the purchase of either a Stirlingshire estate or Argyll's Lodging in Stirling, which had been built by the Earl of Stirling in 1630.

In the event he returned to America to be known thereafter as Lord Stirling, building himself a fine aristocratic mansion at Basking Ridge, New Jersey. He imported many material comforts from the Auld Country, as well as some of his indentured servants. He had a well-stocked library which included works by Smollett and Hume. His luggage included a six-horse crimson carriage bearing the Stirling coat of arms. His wardrobe consisted of '31 coats, 58 vests, 43 pairs of breeches, 6 powdering gowns, 2 pairs of trousers, 30 shirts, 17 handkerchiefs ... 119 pairs of hose, 16 nightcaps, 5 pairs of drawers, 2 pairs of gloves, 14 pairs of shoes and 4 pairs of boots'.[50] Here was a man whose patronage immigrant Scots might profitably seek.

Stirling remained a loyalist until the outbreak of war when he reclaimed some of his father's Whiggism, disgusted at his treatment by the House of Lords and permanently alienated by the British response to American petitions. As Colonel Lord

17

Stirling he was appointed chief commander of the New Jersey troops, rising to the position of general in Washington's Continental Army when he confronted General Grant at Long Island. He refused to surrender to Grant personally because of the latter's ill-considered Commons speech, opting instead for the Hessian commander, Von Heister. Although his captors ridiculed his aristocratic pretensions, his instincts were probably correct because Grant could have been expected to be particularly venomous towards a spurious Scottish peer. Stirling was soon exchanged, for Montfort Browne, formerly of Florida but now Governor of Providence Island in the West Indies. He continued to play a stalwart role in the campaigns, taking part in the battles of Trenton and Monmouth and trying to ensure, not always successfully, that loyalist prisoners were humanely treated. He died in 1783, 'full of not only honour but of good liquor'.[51]

For people like Stirling or for that matter Grant, the revolutionary struggle took on the characteristics of civil war, so often did they encounter acquaintances from an earlier era. British army lieutenant, John Peebles, for example, from Irvine, Ayrshire, first saw service in North America in 1758. His diary during the American War from 1776 to 1782 shows him meeting people from the pre-war years both of loyalist and patriotic sympathies. While he did not, like James Currie, convert to the American cause, he did develop a grudging admiration for the rebels and an early realisation that the British could not win.[52] I like to think that when he retired to Irvine he would sometimes yarn with John Galt, in whose novels, or 'theoretical histories' as he preferred to call them, *The Annals of the Parish* and *The Provost*, the war takes place off-stage.

Philadelphia

By the second half of the eighteenth century Philadelphia was developing into the cultural capital of America, and the Scots, though not great in number, were to make a disproportionate contribution to the intellectual life of that city. In a different time William Mylne might have become a second Robert Smith (1722–7), the architect and master builder from Dalkeith who carried out many important projects in Philadelphia.[53] The city also attracted Cadwallader Colden (1687–1776), son of the minister of Duns in Berwickshire (illus 1.8). A lifelong loyalist, he died in the 'Year of Independence'. Medical doctor,

scientist, botanist, tireless and talented politician, and correspondent of Carl Linnaeus, Colden was a true polymath of the old school, interested in everything under, and beyond, the sun. His good friend was Ulster Scot James Logan, agent of William Penn, and it was another Scot, Robert Hunter, Governor of New York, who lured him to that city and state, where he established his wilderness hideaway, study and laboratory at Coldengham, named after himself and the Scottish Border village. He was visited there by various luminaries including Alexander Garden, physician and plant expert from Edinburgh, after whom the gardenia is named. Until quite recently the role of scientific enquiry in the exploration and colonisation of the so-called New World has been surprisingly ignored,[54] though the subject is now receiving considerable scholarly attention.

One extraordinary naturalist, who made his way to Philadelphia in 1794 to escape political oppression, was Alexander Wilson, a weaver and chapman, or peddler, from Paisley, who was to produce the stunning *American Ornithology*, despite having previously shown little interest in either birds or illustration. He began his American career as a schoolteacher, mastering mathematics, German, music and drawing, but in 1803 he announced that he planned to 'make a collection' of America's finest birds, having been introduced to the science of ornithology by William Bartram. Another crucial contact was Alexander Lawson from Ravenstruther in Carstairs parish, Lanarkshire, who, like Wilson, had quit Scotland for political reasons. Denied entry to revolutionary France, he took the Atlantic route, settling in Philadelphia, where he became the foremost American engraver of his day. Wilson's great project consumed the rest of his short life. 'Few Americans have seen more of their country as I have done and none love her better,' he wrote. George Ord, his posthumous collaborator, described Wilson as of the *Genus irritabile*, like many of his countrymen, we may think, but one of the artist's great gifts was communication. His appetite for conversation was as great as his passion for birds. He deplored slavery and appears to have been blind to colour, creed or country of origin. He was certainly no idoliser of Scots. Brilliantly complementing his art, he was able to couch his descriptions, as humorous as they are evocative, in lay language, while expressing his sympathy and enthusiasm for the natural world. To quote one of his biographers, 'Wilson's aim was to discover the design of the world of birds as a link to an unspoiled past of nature. His creation in American

Illustration 1.8
'Portrait of Cadwallader Colden and his grandson' by Matthew Pratt, *c* 1772. Oil on canvas, 50 x 40in (1270 x 1016mm).
Morris K Jessup Fund, The Metropolitan Museum of Art. [Image courtesy of the Metropolitan Museum of Art, New York]

ornithology was so rare, strange and hauntingly beautiful that it transformed a work of science into a work of art'.[55]

Many Scots who ventured to Philadelphia were, like Wilson, involved in education. William Smith, a graduate of Aberdeen University, famously became provost of the College of Philadelphia. His deputy was Francis Alison, an Ulster Scot, who had studied at the Universities of both Edinburgh and Glasgow.[56] Andrew Hook has pointed to the foundation of the St Andrew's Society of Philadelphia in 1747 as an indicator of Scottish influence through a membership which included the Society's first president, Perthshire physician Thomas Graeme. Other members included James Hamilton, Governor of Pennsylvania, Alexander Alexander who taught at the College, as did Henry Beveridge and James Wilson, one of two Scottish signatories of the Declaration of Independence; Alexander Barclay, Philadelphia's controller of customs, and David Hall, partner in Benjamin Franklin's printing office. Graeme and Hamilton were both members of the American Philosophical Society founded in 1769. Scots probably benefited enormously, and perhaps undeservedly, from Franklin's great admiration for Scottish learning. He considered the professors of Edinburgh University 'to be a Set of as truly great men ... as have ever appeared in any Age or Country'. There were close connections between the medical schools of Edinburgh and Philadelphia, just as there were contacts between the musical societies of both cities.[57]

Such interaction between Scots and Philadelphians in the age of Enlightenment is undoubtedly significant, but much more tangible links have recently been demonstrated in the magisterial study by Richard Sher of Scottish publishers in Philadelphia. Robert Bell from Glasgow and Robert Aitken from Dalkeith specialised in American reprints of Enlightenment publications. Bell, who launched his American business with William Robertson's *History of Charles V* (1771), believed in 'a philosophy of natural improvement through print' and invoked a kind of economic nationalism by citing the cheapness of his books and the fact that they were produced in America. His shameless advertising might not surprise modern publishers, but he never doubted the serious value of his endeavours; literature would 'durably support the honour of that glorious vehicle of Knowledge and Liberty'. Robert Aitken published the first American edition of William Buchan's *Domestic Medicine* in 1772, a work that for long was to prove

invaluable in the self-treatment of pioneers out in the bush. Bell and Aitken collaborated on the publication of one volume of Kames's *Sketches of the History of Man* in 1776. American printings of Scottish books may have been rather scarce before the Revolution, but they positively flowed from the presses in the 1790s.

Later arrivals included Thomas Dobson from Galashiels whose employer, bookseller Charles Elliot, sent him to Philadelphia to open a branch of his business. He was to reprint the third edition of *Encyclopaedia Britannica* with some entries rewritten for American readers. William Young from Kilmarnock made a speciality of publishing works on Scottish Common Sense Philosophy. Like Bell he argued against the importation of clothes and books, considering them detrimental to 'the enjoyment of freedom and independence'. In 1788 one of his partners, Peter Stewart, produced the first American printing of the poetry of Robert Burns. Robert Campbell (1769–1800) from Edinburgh opened what became the largest bookshop in Philadelphia, his brother Samuel operating a similar business in New York. One of Campbell's great achievements was the publication of an ambitious Philadelphia edition of David Hume's *History of England*.

It will not be forgotten that if American independence had been conceived in Virginia, it was written in Philadelphia. It has been asserted that almost 38 per cent of those who signed the American declaration in 1776 were of Scottish descent.[58] One who did not sign but who certainly anticipated the Philadelphia document was Patrick Henry, whose father, John, from Aberdeenshire had studied at King's College. From 1771 to 1778 Patrick lived at his Scotchtown estate. On 23 March 1775 at Richmond he delivered the fiery speech which would later resonate with the ideas of a distant Scottish bard:

> There is no retreat but in submission and slavery. Our chains are forged; their clanking may be heard on the plains of Boston. The War is inevitable, and let it come. I repeat ... let it come! ... The war has already begun. The next gale that sweeps from the North will bring to our ears the clash of resounding arms. Our brethren are already in the field. Why stand we here idle? Is life so dear or peace so sweet as to be purchased at the price of chains and slavery? Forbid it, Almighty God! I know not what course others may take; but as for me, give me liberty or give me death![59]

Elsewhere I have briefly investigated the contributions to the debate made by the only two native-born Scots among the signers of the Declaration in Independence Hall, John Witherspoon the minister and James Wilson the lawyer. Witherspoon condemned the brutal actions of the British military, convinced as he was that 'the public mind is entirely on the side of liberty and for the independence of America'. In his victory sermon in 1783 he preached that 'in free States where the body of the people have the supreme power properly in their own hands and must be ultimately resorted to on all great matters … civil liberty cannot be long preserved without virtue'.

James Wilson in his *Address to the Inhabitants of the Colonies* (1776) stated: 'We wish for peace – we wish for Safety: But we will not, to obtain either or both of them, part with our Liberty. The sacred Gift descended to us from our Ancestors: We cannot dispose of it: We are bound by the strongest Ties to transmit it, as we have now received it, pure and inviolate to our Posterity.'

He it was who argued that 'all power was originally in the people – that all the Powers of Government are derived from them – that all power, which they have not disposed of, still continues theirs'. This to him was the 'Revolution Principle', 'the first and fundamental principle in the science of government'.[60] To loyalists such ideas were, of course, anathema, and most fled their consequences while retaining their regard for America herself. However, many Scots would have agreed with Witherspoon and Wilson, especially those with any Covenanting sympathies. For others these concepts were assumptions that extended all the way back to Scotland's own Wars of Independence in the thirteenth and fourteenth centuries. Personified by Scots, the Old World entered the New on the basis of shared assumptions which grew ever stronger in the liberating combination of enlightenment, enrichment and enfranchisement. A British province had become an independent nation and, as thousands of Scots were to demonstrate, so far as they were concerned, it was none the less attractive for that.

Notes

1 Edward J Cowan, *'For Freedom Alone': The Declaration of Arbroath*. Edinburgh, 2003, revd edition 2008, 116–17.

2 Frequently quoted but cited here for convenience from John Ferling, *Setting the World Ablaze: Washington, Adams, Jefferson and the American Revolution*. Oxford, 2000, 128–9.

3 *The Poems and Songs of Robert Burns*, James Kinsley (ed), 3 vols. Oxford, 1968, vol 2, 707–8, 732–4; vol 3, 1438–41, 1453–4. For discussion of resonances with Thomas Paine and the French revolutionaries, as well as with supporters of the Scottish Reform movement of the 1790s see Liam McIlvanney, *Burns the Radical: Poetry and Politics in Late Eighteenth-Century Scotland*. East Linton, 2002, 212–13, which, however, fails to mention Patrick Henry's Richmond address, see below.

4 Fred Kaplan, *Lincoln: the biography of a writer*. New York 2008, 59–70. See also Ferenc Morton Szasz, *Abraham Lincoln and Robert Burns: connected lives and legends*. Carbondale, 2008.

5 For some discussion of Scottish cultural influence in America see Edward J Cowan, 'Tartan Day in America', in Celeste Ray (ed), *Transatlantic Scots*. Tuscaloosa, 2005, 318–38, and 321–6 and 'Back-home and the Back-country, David Fischer's *Borderlands Revisited: the Appalachian journal*'. Winter 1992, 166–73. 'From that country we are surest of having sober, attentive men', a letter from Thomas Jefferson to Joseph C Cabell about recruiting a teacher for Albemarle Academy quoted in James Bryant Conant, *Thomas Jefferson and the development of American public education*. Berkeley and Los Angeles, 1962, note 73.

6 Edward J Cowan, 'The Myth of Scotch Canada', *in Myth, Migration and the Making of Memory: Scotia and Nova Scotia, c. 1700–1990*. Marjory Harper and Michael Vance (eds). Halifax and Edinburgh, 1999, 49–72.

7 George Pratt Insh, *Scottish Colonial Schemes 1620–1686*. Glasgow, 1922, now greatly superseded by Allan I Macinnes, *Union and Empire: the making of the United Kingdom in 1707*. Cambridge, 2007.

8 Ralph E Fall, *The Diary of Robert Rose: a view of Virginia by a Scottish colonial parson 1746–1751*. Verona, VA, 1977, 129.

9 Fall, *Diary of Robert Rose*, 3–30, 94, 105.

10 In-text references are to Fall, *Diary of Robert Rose*.

11 Silvanus J Quinn, *A History of the City of Fredericksburg, Virginia*. Richmond, VA, 1908 reprinted 2009, 131, 162.

12 For an informative account of a Scottish family in Alexandria see John D Munson, *Col. John Carlyle, Gent: A True Story and Just Account of the Man and His House 1720–1780*. Alexandria, 1986.

13 Paula S Felder, *George Washington's Fredericksburg*. Fredericksburg, 1988, 53–72.

14 For some discussion of population see David Hackett Fischer, *Albion's Seed: Four British Folkways in America*. Oxford, 1989, 608–10.

15 Quinn, *History of Fredericksburg*. Richmond, 1937, 163.

16 Malcolm McLachlan Harper (ed), *The Bards of Galloway: A Collection of Poems, Songs, Ballads etc by Natives of Galloway*. Dalbeattie, 1889, 8–9, 244.

17 Alvin T Embrey, *History of Fredericksburg, Virginia*. Richmond, 1937, 119–28.

18 Quinn, *History of Fredericksburg*, 149–50.

19 For what follows see George Austin Morrison, *History of Saint Andrew's Society of the State of New York 1756–1906*. New York, 1906, 70–92.

20 Henry Stevens, *Recollections of Mr James Lenox of New York and the Formation of his Library*. London, 1886, 3–4, 8–9.

21 Stevens, *Recollections*, 176–81.

22 Robert Donald Thornton, *James Currie: The Entire Stranger & Robert Burns*. Edinburgh and London, 1963, 13–32.

23 Thornton, *James Currie*, 43–4.

24 Thornton, *James Currie*, 39, 41

25 Thomas M Devine, *The Tobacco Lords: A Study of the Tobacco Merchants of Glasgow and their Trading Activities c. 1740–90*. Edinburgh, 1975.

26 Thornton, *James Currie*, 48

27 Mrs Reginald De Koven, *The Life and Letters of John Paul Jones*, 2 vols. New York, 1913, vol 1, 385.

28 Quoted in Evan Thomas, *John Paul Jones: Sailor, Hero, Father of the American Navy*. New York, 2003, 6.

29 See, for example, Thomas, *John Paul Jones*, 82, 113–14.

30 Robert C Sands, *Life and Correspondence of John Paul Jones Including His Narrative of the Campaign of the Liman from Original Letters and Manuscripts in the Possession of Miss Janette Taylor*. New York, 1830, 14. See also Samuel Eliot Morison, *John Paul Jones: A Sailor's Biography*. New York, 1959, Appendix 1.

31 See David Stevenson, *The Origins of Freemasonry: Scotland's Century*. Cambridge, 1988; and *The First Freemasons: Scotland's Early Lodges and Their Members*. Aberdeen, 1988.

32 De Koven, *Life and Letters of John Paul Jones*, vol 1, 89.

33 Thomas, *John Paul Jones*, 83.

34 Edwin G Burrows, *Forgotten Patriots: The Untold Story of American Prisoners During the Revolutionary War*. New York, 2008.

35 Sands, *Life and Correspondence of John Paul Jones*, 91.

36 Sands, *Life and Correspondence of John Paul Jones*, 99 note.

37 Thomas, *John Paul Jones*, 308.

38 Ted Ruddock (ed), *Travels in the Colonies in 1773–1775: Described in the Letters of William Mylne*. Athens, GA, 1993, Index.

39 Ruddock (ed), *Travels in the Colonies*, 25–77.

40 Robin F A Fabel, *Bombast & Broadsides: The Lives of George Johnstone*. Tuscaloosa, 1987, preface and 91. The extensive Johnstone of Westerhall family is the subject of the brilliantly insightful study, Emma Rothschild, *The Inner Life of Empires: an eighteenth-century history*. Princeton and Oxford, 2011.

41 Fabel, *Bombasts & Broadsides*, 42.

42 Andrew Hook, 'Scottish Thought and Culture in Early Philadelphia', *in* Richard B Sher and Jeffrey R Smitten (eds), *Scotland & America in the Age of the Enlightenment*. Edinburgh, 1990, 238–9.

43 Fabel, *Bombasts & Broadsides*, 24–57, 101–19.

44 John D Ware, *George Gauld: Surveyor and Cartographer of the Gulf Coast*. Gainesville, 1982, 119, 1–94 and passim.

45 Paul David Nelson, *General James Grant: Scottish Soldier and Royal Governor of East Florida*. Gainesville, 1993, 3.

46 Nelson, *General James Grant*, 45–86.

47 See Henry Noble MacCracken, *Prologue to Independence: The Trials of James Alexander, American 1715–1756*. New York, 1964, passim.

48 Paul David Nelson, *The Life of William Alexander, Lord Stirling*. Alabama, 1987, 7–9.

49 David Baillie Morrison, *Two Hundredth Anniversary of Saint Andrew's Society of the State of New York*. New York, 1956, 157–9.

50 Nelson, *Life of William Alexander*, 46.

51 Nelson, *Life of William Alexander*, 4.

52 Ira D Gruber (ed), *John Peebles' American War 1776–1782*, Army Records Society. Stroud, 1998.

53 Charles E Peterson, 'Robert Smith, Philadelphia Builder-Architect: From Dalkeith to Princeton', *in* Sher and Smitten (eds), 275–99.

54 Edward J Cowan, 'The Scots Imaging of Canada', *in* Peter E Rider and Heather McNabb (eds), *A Kingdom of the Mind: How the Scots Helped Make Canada*. Montreal and Kingston, 2006, 5.

55 Quoted in Joseph Kastner, *A World of Naturalists*. London, 1978, 192; for an excellent discussion of Wilson's achievement see 159–92. Also Clark Hunter, *The Life and Letters of Alexander Wilson*. Philadelphia, 1983. On his earlier life in Scotland see Edward J Cowan and Michael Paterson (eds), *Folk in Print: Scotland's Chapbook Heritage 1750–1850*. Edinburgh, 2007, 30, 41–3.

56 George S Pryde, *The Scottish Universities and the Colleges of Colonial America*. Glasgow, 1957, 16–25.

57 Hook, 'Scottish Thought and Culture in Early Philadelphia', *in* Sher and Smitten, 227–41. See in the same volume Deborah C Brunton, 'The Transfer of Medical Education: Teaching at the Edinburgh and Philadelphia Medical Schools', 242–58 and Anne McClenny Krauss, 'James Bremner, Alexander Reinagle and the Influence of the Edinburgh Musical Society on Philadelphia', 259–74.

58 Duncan A Bruce, *The Mark of the Scots: Their Astonishing Contributions to History, Science, Democracy, Literature and the Arts*. Secaucus, 1996, 32.

59 Quoted from Quinn, *History of Fredericksburg*, 197.

60 Cowan, *For Freedom*, 128–34.

CHAPTER 2

Scottish merchants:
sorting out the world of goods in early America

ANN SMART MARTIN

The antiquarian of the old school collected a heterogeneous group of articles together and valued them, simply because they were old. Now, the mere fact of an article, say a table, a watch, or a sword, being old, gives it no more interest than the mere fact of its being new. What does give it interest is, that the way in which it is fashioned, and the manner in which it was used, throw light on the way of life of the men who used it, and in it we see the germs of similar articles of a later growth. If this be true of a chair or a sword, it is true of a building and truer still of a custom, a trait of manners, or a phase of belief. In studying them, we see ourselves in the making, and unite ourselves to the far-off ages by the magic cord of sympathy.

Colin Dunlop Donald (1848–95)
Address at the Annual General Meeting,
Glasgow Archaeological Society
15 November 1894

Colin Donald's words over a century ago were a harbinger for a truly modern study of material culture. The idea that studying the chair, the sword, the building – 'the way in which it is fashioned, and the manner in which it was used' – tells new things about the men and women who used it is now accepted in multiple academic fields and is an avowed core belief for others. So too is the study of 'custom, a trait of manners, or a phase of belief'. This chapter takes on Donald's challenge of seeking the 'magic cord of sympathy' with Scottish peoples in their homeland or in their diaspora. It does so through the large net of Scottish commercial enterprise, seeking the objects and customs, words and traits that together helped define 'Scottishness' in its commercial boom and decline in the American Chesapeake colonies.

In seeking those essential clues, scholars are in essence asking questions about the Scottish and American character itself. One of the essential qualities of American society is the drama of a population from many places and the actual performance of

pluralism (immigrants standing apart) or a melting pot (becoming 'American'). The problem is not new: the wish to blend in with a dominant culture or keep apart as a special people vexed settlers long before we were a nation. Ned Landsman writes: 'American pluralism from the outset was particular rather than universal in its purposes and justifications; it served not only to include but also to exclude' (Landsman 1998: 106). This cultural frame is made more complex if we are looking for physical or material evidence of such individual, social and cultural choices in all their permutations. This is the large job of a material culture approach to the analysis of the Scottish people in a new land.

In the decades of study of the Scottish diaspora, scholars searching for Scottish influence mainly looked at mainland America and Canada for connection through language, religion and settlement patterns. But expanded study of all the Americas is more recent, especially the sugar islands of the West Indies where so many Scots followed prosperous trade routes at the end of the tobacco boom that contemporaries estimated one third of the white population was Scottish (Burnard 2004: 88–9; Hancock 1994: 28–9; Nelson 2005: 63–79; Robertson 2001: 73–95). Obvious material culture evidence that might mark Scottish identity has been more problematic. Ian Graham worried that a Lowland influence on North America would be difficult to find at all as 'many of them went to areas like western Pennsylvania where they mingled with and became almost indistinguishable from the Scotch-Irish'. He further asserted that the middle-class Scottish merchants were anxious to be considered like the more polished Anglo-Virginians who would find their home language 'somewhat uncouth' (Graham 1956: 110). Interests in geographic and folkloric techniques led to examination of the distribution of attributes like building types. The Scotch-Irish hardly invented log cabins, but the way many individuals notched their logs with a half dovetail at the buildings' corners and filled empty spaces with mud matched the patterns of their expansion over the Appalachians in the early nineteenth century (Evans 1969: 73–9).

The spread of Scots over the North American landscape and marks of Scottish identity and workmanship still interest scholars. A more multi-layered approach asks how and why such patterns occur and what is the best way to document them. If we think about ways of eye/hand-making skill – how, for instance, one is taught to frame a building or a chest of drawers – then we are asking about a form of craft practice. If we phrase it as a question of eye/brain attention and notice, we might ask what visual cues draw attention as an individual moves through an environment with multiple, sometimes conflicting clues. Are certain aspects of familiar Scottishness key signifiers? Other methods of study include using biographies to tell stories of individual artisans who learn and teach particular methods that are not merely repeated habits but can also be solving problems with new ideas and designs. The same biographies can attest to business practices, such as looking for commissions from a friendly local circle that might be loosely based on ethnicity.

This final method is of the greatest importance in this study. Indeed, scholars in the past too often have left the wishes of historical people to either differentiate or assimilate as a binary choice. A third way is how an individual associates with people who are willing to agree on *what looks right and works*. Hence, if someone of respect introduces a new fashion there is no need to evaluate it at all, simply join with others to like similar things. Once a commodity is affordable, available and, in some way socially agreeable to a given Scot, it may become desirable. Hence, a community may move in identifiable patterns as the merchant, object and buyer come together.

But how does that community of interest evolve? This chapter will further examine Scottish links and webs, how Scottish-made things moved to America and/or how the predominant Scottish storekeeper worked to move, manage and vend the international array of artefacts that American colonists, and soon American citizens, wanted. Two particular kinds of evidence are integrated below. One is a Scottish traveller remarking on his journey through America at the turn of the nineteenth century following the trail of the once mighty Scottish tobacco trade. His journal is personal, and through him we can see the essential importance of Scottish descent in America in terms of relationships. The second investigation is the integration of the Scottish mercantile system with Scottish manufacture, shipping and sales. It asks, for example, whether these Scottish merchants particularly vended Scottish-made things. Did the vaunted Scottish tobacco trade load Scottish artefacts on to Scottish ships aimed for Scottish merchants and perhaps Scottish customers? If so, does the common claim of Scottish 'clannishness' extend into the material culture of trade? Or were bloodlines diminished by the Scottish merchant's supposed love of a 'good pennyworth'? Together, these sets of Scottish people, habits and objects are seen through the documentation of merchants active in the Chesapeake.

The Scottish traveller

A Scottish accountant, Alexander Dick, was appointed by Parliament in 1806 to investigate outstanding unresolved pre-Revolutionary debts owed to British merchants. The domestic commission of Thomas MacDonald, Henry Pye Rich and John Guillemaid hoped to decide which claims were valid, a task made too difficult without the actual account books themselves.[1] The subject had befuddled presidents and diplomats since the ending of the war. Rather than try to ship thousands of scattered books of accounts, British lawmakers appointed Dick to go to America and examine them. He left Edinburgh in August 1806, began his journal in New York five months later, travelled as far south as Charleston, South Carolina, and returned to Edinburgh in September 1809. The personal journal of his trip is extraordinary; he is frank, observant and in several places laugh-out-loud funny. Like many gentlemen travellers of the time, he was interested in the natural world and so flying squirrels bemused, hummingbirds delighted and low-lying (unhealthy) places worried the observant Scot (Lewis 1984: 66, 167–8).

But most of all he is travelling and observing as a Scotsman, comparing people and lifestyles in the United States to those at home. Dick saw a 'good deal the appearance of one of our Highland Country girls' in a 'German-American' girl in the Virginia backcountry. He compared strawberries and found the ones at home more flavoursome. He contrasted deportment and furnishings, finding that the New York elite 'excel us in manners & address & they Seem to shew a great deal of attention to Strangers'. Yet, even if they were well mannered and kind, they had the less fortunate habit of 'indulging in greater Luxury and Shew than people of the same rank & fortune do at home' (Lewis 1984: 49, 101, 279).

Hardly a week passed when he did not meet fellow Scots and he nearly always noted some aspect of their connection to Scotland – whether family, home place or number of years away from that home. Dick and his wife slept at a tavern kept by a fellow Scotchman from Ayr, 'House of Robb', while another compatriot was from near Strathaven 'and has been 36 years from home'. Some were simply fellow-countrymen who invited him and his family to dinner or tea and helped wrangle accommodations when all were full. He was following a wandering path connecting sites of mercantile exchange that a half-century before stood new and prosperous. Some now, like Bladensburg, Maryland, stood vacant after the colonial tobacco boom ended. Thus, his travel reveals both the decay

of the Scottish store tobacco empire of the Chesapeake and the remaining large web of pre-Revolutionary debts (Lewis 1984: x, 87, 142).

While the large majority of Scottish merchants left the southern American colonies for Scotland, Canada, the sugar islands or other points of imperial trade when war broke out, thirty years later Dick found the remaining merchants lived in a variety of circumstances. Invited to the 'Country Seat' of David Williamson about seven miles outside of Baltimore, Dick admired his 'pleasant retreat' as he had 'improved it much & indeed it is with Stone dishes in the Scotch Style' (Lewis 1984: 87–8). But not everyone had succeeded in maintaining a previously flourishing lifestyle. 'Once in affluent circumstances', a Mr Drummond ran a tavern at his house. Dick marvelled that the structure was 'as handsome a One as almost any I have seen in this part of the Country'. Standing about a quarter of a

Illustration 2.1
Watercolour, 'View of Richmond from the south side of the James River', 1796. Benjamin Henry Latrobe (1764–1820).
[Courtesy of the Maryland Historical Society, 1960-108-1-1-36]

mile off the road in the midst of a large open lawn, it was 'regular with Wings &c & Comfortably furnished'. Drummond was home and Dick had a letter of introduction. Nonetheless, he never saw his host, for unlike many other tavern-keepers, Drummond did not appear at table to mingle with guests. Dick was irked: 'I suppose he [Drummond] *feels* having been under the necessity of Converting into a Tavern at a House built for his own use, &

which has indeed all the appearance of a Gentleman's Seat.' He hastened to add, though, that 'keeping a Tavern in this Country is not Considered as very derogatory' so Drummond had little excuse for refusing the bounds of civility and the web of Scottish ties (Lewis 1984: 87–8, 317).

He passed through hamlets and villages, spent time in and wrote at length about New York, Philadelphia, Washington DC and Charleston. He

Illustration 2.2
Engraving, 'St Andrews Parish Church', Robert Paul, 1759. Glasgow Museums.
[Reproduced with the permission of Glasgow City Council, Libraries Information and Learning]

seemed especially pleased with Richmond, Virginia, noting the city's important sites and relating them to those he knew in Scotland. (See illustration 2.1.) The Penitentiary was 'somewhat of the form of the New Bridewell at Edinb. But on a rather larger scale' (Lewis 1984: 248). The grand new state capital designed by Thomas Jefferson based on the classical Roman temple at Nîmes (La Maison Carrée) was a most notable sight. Dick described it as a 'building of mostly the genl Appearance of St. Andw Church Glasw but without any spire & stands by itself'. Drawing upon and perhaps symbolising the great wealth of early so-called Tobacco Lords in Glasgow, the St Andrew's Parish Church was built between 1739 and 1756 in a metropolitan style, borrowed from James Gibbs at St Martin-in-the-Fields, London (Williams et al 1990: 452) (illus 2.2). Seeming to loom over fields and woods at mid-century, the church was enclosed by a square in 1786–7, lined with houses favoured by merchants. Some would be home to wealthy transatlantic merchants.

It was not just buildings which caught his attention. An old Scottish community that lived in Richmond also attracted him. 'A good many Scotchmen reside here. Some of whom have attained to a very advanced age. – Mr. McCale 74 – Mr. Lyle 80 – Mr. Wm Huy, Mr. Warden & others upwards of 60.' Now at the age of eighty Mr Lyle was part of the highly competitive Scottish tobacco market before the American Revolution and represented the very debts and businesses that Dick was investigating. Mr Warden ('a great original') was the most remarkable, not from his age but his appropriate performance of Scottish identity. 'He entertained us the first time we Saw him with a long recitation from the Gentle Shepherd and other Scotch Poems with the genuine accent and pronunciation' (Lewis 1984: 256–7).

The old men gathered there that night knew the ballads, songs and poetry that Allan Ramsay first published in Scotland half a century before. Scots revered Ramsay's *Gentle Shepherd* as their own country's pastorale and demand for the stories

Illustration 2.3
Textile panel, copper-plate printed in red on bleached-cotton ground, 1790–1800. 48¼ x 27⅓in (1226 x 695mm). Six vignettes of scenes from Allan Ramsay's play and book, *The Gentle Shepherd*. [Photograph courtesy of the Winterthur Museum, Winterthur, Delaware]

remained high. A new edition was published that very year in Edinburgh. A cotton textile panel now found at the Winthertur Museum shows copper-plate printed vignettes from the play (Montgomery 1970: 275–7) (illus 2.3, 2.4, 2.5). Drawn from David Allan's 1788 aquatint illustrations, these scenes included dramatic and comedic depictions of everyday life,

Illustration 2.4
Detail, cotton panel, copper-plate printing in red, 1790–1800. In this detail, the youthful Patie, that is the 'Gentle Shepherd',
embraces his love, Peggy. Plate 5 in Ramsay's *Gentle Shepherd* of 1788

such as conflict (illus 2.3 top right: 'Madge and Bauldy': young woman assaulting man with distaff as older woman attempts to intervene), romance (next left: young man trying to embrace young woman) and reproach (below, on the left, scolding shepherd who fell asleep).

As Francisa Irwin reported in her study, *Scottish Eighteenth-Century Chintz and its Design*, the original aquatint print by David Allan depicted Patie in knitted knee-breeches, but the later copper plate changed the breeches to tartan plaid hosiery. That would no doubt aid foreign audiences in understanding the comical overtones of the actions of the poor Scottish lad (illus 2.4).

Illustration 2.5 shows a comic view of relaxed rural Scottish life. Sir William sits at the centre of the table, holding a mug, and to his right a man smokes a pipe. On the table rest a wine bottle, glass and perhaps an oatcake and pasties. The ground appears to be strewn with household objects. Patie is jauntily perched on the right, arms akimbo and tartan plaid stockings in prime view.

Ramsay's other publications of songs were also immensely popular in the colonies and the new nation. For example, his 1763 volume *Tea-table Miscellany: or, a Collection of Choice Songs, Scots and English* was stocked at the Scottish merchant John Hook's Virginia store before the Revolution. By his thirteenth edition Ramsay could write in its preface about how popular the collection of songs was around the world.

My worthy friend Dr. *Bannerman* tells me from *America*,
Nor only do your lays oe'r Britain *flow*
Round all the globe your happy sonnets go
Here thy soft verse, made to a Scottish air
Are often sung by our Virginian fair. (Ramsay 1763: xii)

Alexander Dick viewed part of the Atlantic world of Scottish trade. While he visited other cities north and south, his work to settle debts was particularly strong in the Chesapeake, more than thirty years after its pre-Revolutionary heyday. Scotsmen were not the only traders in tobacco in the larger mid-Atlantic but they soon became the majority. Working largely in systems of stores managed from Glasgow, they extended copious amounts of credit, particularly to small farmers in the backcountry regions of Maryland, Virginia and North Carolina where individual debts were often under £50. In the fifteen years leading to the Revolution, Scottish storekeepers became more common and undoubtedly more vilified.

But Dick is following not only the ghosts of Scottish trade, but of Scottish things. Scottish stores succeeded because they carried the small manufactured goods that American colonists wanted, and Glaswegian merchants had set up especially efficient ways to vend crops in return for credit at a local store. Ships sailed directly from Glasgow to Virginia ports to collect tobacco and return with a wealth of goods. While they also carried the new manufactures of Birmingham and northern England and the international imports from the East India Company in London, it was advantageous whenever possible to avoid shipping costs and increasingly choose from manufacturers in western Scotland or nearby ports. If there existed one inexorable way that Scottish and American material culture was blended, it was through that combination of Scottish merchants, British things and Anglo-American customers.

Illustration 2.5
Detail, cotton panel, copper-plate printing in red, 1790–1800. 'Sir William Worthy and Patie'.
Plate 6 in Ramsay's *Gentle Shepherd* of 1788

Travelling things

'All Commerce ends in the Consumption and with the Consumer', wrote Daniel Defoe in the *Complete English Tradesman* in 1727. Through the various retailers, 'the general Commerce of this Kingdom is carried on, the home made Manufactures dispers'd and circulated, and the foreign Importations handed about to the *last consumer*' (Defoe [1725–7] 1969: vol 2, pt 2, 75). Defoe stresses the variety of manufacturers, wholesalers, retailers and the complex route to the last consumer. The Scottish stores in Virginia were part of that final link in a long chain and part of their success lay in stocking, shipping and retailing innovation.

The Chesapeake store is probably the best-documented form of retail trade in the eighteenth-century British Empire. Because of a need to account for business for multiple partners or employers, a highly complex import/export trade with producers, and the long-term credit relations of customers who often exchanged crops for goods, bookkeeping was precise and more detailed than in many other commercial operations. Because, even as late as the 1770s, tobacco formed almost three-quarters of Virginia's exports, the movement of that crop to England in exchange for manufactured goods was of vital importance to colonial business, with little need to innovate for competing systems. Maryland's economy was more varied and the Glasgow trade was more closely limited to the Potomac River and the Eastern Shore. Finally, because these documents have often been curated in family papers and local archives, without the stresses of wartime paper drives and intense competition for space on archive shelves, the story of the retail trade in the Chesapeake becomes unusually vivid.

One result of this successful heightened competition was that, by the 1770s, prices paid for Virginia tobacco often approximated European prices and remittances went to England at a bookkeeping loss. Increasingly, the merchant's profits had to come from the goods he stocked (Price 1974: 108). John Mair's popular manual *Book-keeping Methodiz'd* urged a varied and complete stock for a Virginia or Maryland store and 'the greater variety … the better; for wherever planters find they can be best suited and served, thither they commonly resort' (Mair 1757: 333).

Thus the second key to success was the ever-improving selection of attractive, affordable goods. These stores were true emporiums, selling everything from nails to novels. Mair suggested fifteen different broad categories for Virginia merchants, merely to help organise the thousands of items they stocked. It is the breadth of kinds of objects for sale that is so remarkable. At the same time, textiles, notions and accessories formed the heart of the store's stock. About 40 per cent of the cost of setting up shop was in supplying textiles, and this number was remarkably consistent in the stocks of various Virginia merchants (Martin 2008: 78).

While there were many concerns at this size, three giant conglomerates headed by Alexander Spiers, John Glassford and William Cunninghame dominated the Scottish trade. These three men, each with combined capitalisation of over £100,000, overshadowed any comparable commission business in London, and no Scottish business of any kind could rival their size, with the exception of the Carron Ironworks (Devine 1982: x–xi; Price 1980: 28–9). These huge syndicates had chains of Chesapeake stores and imported over one-half of the tobacco landed at ports on the Clyde. Indeed, Scottish merchants as a group captured the lion's share of the Chesapeake trade. By 1769 more tobacco was imported into Scotland than all of the English ports combined, hence putting the institutional heart of the transmission of manufactured goods into Scotland. The merchants there had several key advantages: a shorter route, greater available credit, fewer expenses because of cheaper labour, and consolidation of purchasing by a few great Tobacco Lords. John Glassford was one such commercial titan and his renown for wealth in Glasgow certainly set other young Scots out in hopes of fortune. One English merchant wrote in exasperation that the Scottish 'Ships are perpetually coming – They never stop buying.' Their large shipments had 'thinn[ed] the Warehouses' (Bynum 1981: 51).

What effect did these Scottish men and Scottish things have on American material culture? Objects from foreign places are sometimes a bit like meteorites bringing information, values and personal meaning. Some ideas are lost or burned off and others are added en route and upon landing on foreign soil. But that attention to movement from maker to buyer helps focus on linkages and voyages. Arjun Appadurai, for one, reminds us that objects have biographies and urges us to tell their whole story (Appadurai 1986: 3–4). If consumer goods traded in the Atlantic basin don't hold quite the drama of a journey through cosmic space, they are certainly complex, tangible bundles of ideas, meanings and values, some shared and some personal.

Buying and selling things builds relationships formed on the triangulation of merchants, customers and objects. Scottish products were often valued because of their lower cost. Originally sourced from Germany, Scottish osnaburgs (coarse linens) were popular because there was huge demand for inexpensive textiles to clothe enslaved men and women in the Chesapeake. While linens were often still part of a web of outsourcing to householders, other Scottish industries were moving to a single point of manufacture, requiring huge outlays of capital. Carron Ironworks, for example, and Delftfield Pottery grew quickly to supply the commodities desired by American tobacco planters. At the same time, a more efficient internal trade system developed between makers and consumers. The manner in which individual storekeepers in Virginia matched partners in Britain and the nature of that business relationship most often predicted the use of particular centres of British trade. Some merchants in the consignment trade marketed tobacco for their clients and supplied the goods that they ordered. In essence, those London-based merchants served as long-distance shoppers for their well-heeled clients. Others, like the merchants in the direct Scottish store trade, bought household goods and textiles at the cheapest cost to ship outward in their own company's vessel to be filled with tobacco for the return voyage. In either case, the more senior merchant on the British side of the Atlantic usually dictated what was purchased and where.

An extremely difficult part of the trade was the unstable flow of goods on hand in Britain available to ship to the colonies. German osnaburgs often seemed to be in short supply. Prices for textiles might fluctuate wildly, as in 1759 when the raw material of skin wool went up 20 per cent. Englishman Joshua Johnson removed from Maryland to England to get better goods and better prices for his business. But his disgust grew as he travelled to manufacturing towns, the most 'capital' being 'Gloucester, Tewkesbury, Bromsgrove, Birmingham, Coventry and Woodstock'. Hoping to gain a better supply at a cheaper price, he was disappointed to find that the system of manufacture precluded any break in the established chain. For instance, he found that an agent usually provided working materials such as iron to poor workers, mostly women and children, who returned finished products in a week. That agent then shipped the goods off to a principal in London or Birmingham. Well aware of changes in prices and in an established network, these agents had little incentive to deal with independent small buyers like Johnson (Price 1979: 33).

So how can a scholar track Scottish manufacturers in the trade to North America? One way is to look at overall patterns of trade while continuing to seek information on specific wares and potteries. Scottish historian Jonathan Delham, for one, counted all the ceramics shipped out from Glasgow between the years 1742 and 1774 and found that over half went to Virginia. In 1770 seven bales and a cask of Delftfield wares were dropped off at a Virginia inland river town (Austin and Hunter 1994: 15–16). A year later, the Delftfield pottery near Glasgow exported a massive number of wares, including 2,600 pieces of delftware to Philadelphia; 12,828 to Virginia; and 19,000 pieces of delft and stoneware to Maryland (Lange 2001: 82; Fleming 1923: 252–3).

Although such sources do not describe individual vessels, merchants' invoices sometimes do. A large research project from 1984 to 1988 entitled 'English Ceramics in America' by George L Miller and this author (funded by the National Endowment for the Humanities) allows detailed study of the export of British ceramics and other food storage and serving wares. The result of an exhaustive archival search, business records for nineteen Virginia and Maryland merchants in business between 1740 and 1800 were coded in a database and together give a broad view of the supply of ceramics to early America (Martin 1988).

Of those, three Scottish merchants trading in the Chesapeake in the two decades before the Revolution have detailed enough records to help in delineating patterns of manufacture and sale in the Atlantic trade basin. Understanding this supply system can answer some key questions about Scottish trade success, including additional land transport of commodities. The Delftfield Company of Glasgow received early capitalisation by several Scots with Virginia connections, including Lord Dunmore, Governor of Virginia. Knowledge of that management connection to the Chesapeake has encouraged archaeologists, curators and historians to scrutinise eighteenth-century Scottish production of tin-glazed (delft) ceramics for half a century, and there has also been a more recent investigation of the developing salt-glaze technologies (Archer 1966: 17–22, 1971: 238–46; Austin and Hunter 1994; Edwards and Hampson 2005; Skerry and Hood 2009).

Scottish potteries were certainly making the kinds of wares shipped to Virginia from various ports. By utilising documents and known sherds from Delftfield archaeological investigations and matching them to excavated sherds in the Chesapeake, John Austin and Robert Hunter demonstrated a strong commercial connection of early Delftfield wares with Virginia

(Austin and Hunter 1994: 13–15). Janine Skerry and Suzanne Findlen Hood similarly have sought a Scottish connection for explaining the many fine white salt-glazed stoneware artefacts in Virginia. Larger-scale archaeological investigation at the Delftfield site is impossible due to later extensive development, and excavation of a small drainage area revealed artefacts but no stoneware. With this preclusion to analysis as well as conflicting terminology in documentation of sales, they have been left wistfully concluding that 'we may never definitively answer the question of whether or not Scottish-made stoneware was present in early America, but the evidence certainly suggests its likelihood' (Skerry and Hood 2009: 181).

William Allason, John Semple and John Hook were all Scottish merchants who supplied household goods, textiles, foodstuffs and tools to colonists in Virginia and Maryland. Their short biographies of business practice highlight the variety of methods and sources of acquiring goods for sale in America. They enable the study of the path of Scottish and English ceramics to colonists who valued objects that were well made, well priced and fashionable. They were also three Scots who developed different strategies for being Scottish and *buying* Scottish in the late eighteenth century.

William Allason of Falmouth, Virginia

For more than twenty years, William Allason was a travelling supercargo for Baird & Walker of Glasgow, peddling their stocks in Virginia, St Kitts and Antigua. With backing from Scottish relations, by 1760 he ended his days on horseback and opened his own store in Falmouth, Virginia. On the fall line of the Rappahannock River, his store drew a large number of customers from the piedmont and the upper Shenandoah Valley, and he and his brother opened a satellite store farther west before a feared Indian attack ended their venture. He remained in business until the Revolution when his profits as a merchant enabled him to retire to a large estate in Faquier County. The majority of his goods – about two-thirds of the wares he stocked between 1760 and 1774 – were pewter. He ordered tin-glazed earthenwares in the 1760s, and they were sold in small but constant quantities until he introduced creamware in 1770. After that time, the leftover tin-glazed wares lingered on his shelves until the closing of the store (Martin 1994: 25).

Who were the manufacturers of the many ceramics and other tablewares that Allason supplied to his customers? Evidence is sketchy, but a long run of invoices and inventories shows the nature of the process. For instance, James Dunlop sent a large shipment valued at £1,260 from Glasgow to William Allason's store in Virginia on 19 December 1759. The ceramics are shown in Table 1.

Dunlop does not reveal in his invoice the source of these wares, but Delftfield was certainly a possibility. With the exception of supplying tortoiseshell teapots, Robert Allason's order from Glasgow in 1761 was nearly identical to Dunlop's a year earlier. But Allason also received ceramics from throughout Britain. Robert Bogle of London sent a similar large order from London, with the added variety of 'Dutch' probably Westerwald stoneware mugs and earthenware gorges (or pitchers).

In the decade ending in 1771 Allason received fourteen different shipments of ceramics from London, Bristol, Liverpool and Glasgow. Do the orders suggest detailed local priorities or preference for Scottish ceramic production? London merchants provided the greatest variety in porcelain as well as large shipments of more general wares. Bristol merchants were more likely to send only bottle jugs and other more protean wares like butter pots, but they too sent some more generic supplies of ceramics. Merchants in Liverpool tended to send the greatest variety of both coarse and fine wares. Wares shipped from one Allason brother in Glasgow to the other in Virginia most often included delftware bowls, but overall his shipments included fewer and fewer ceramic wares.

Even so, beginning in 1766 William Allason's invoices and inventories clearly demonstrate that the overall variety of available ceramic ware types and forms exploded. Different British merchants included porcelain tea and tablewares in two shipments in that year and 'white flint ½ best and blue Dutch-best' chamber pots arrived from Liverpool. The merchant thus asked for a variety of chamber pots, both newer and more fashionable white salt-glazed stoneware (best and seconds) and the still popular Westerwald wares. Allason's store inventory that year included two sets of white stoneware oval dishes – seven to a set – and Nottingham brown jugs. Nonetheless, once the most fashionable cream-coloured wares were available, little else was sold as tablewares. Delft bowls continued, many large enough to be generous punch bowls. While his business location is unclear, Henry Parry sent sixteen dozen plates, six sizes of dishes and multiple other more cosmopolitan table forms of 'Queen's stone china' to Allason in 1770.

Table 1
James Dunlop to William Allason, 19 December 1759

Qty	Form	Size	Colour and description	Price/dozen £ s d	Total price £ s d
6 doz	Plates		Delph ware	0 3 0	0 18 0
1 doz	Bowls	2 qt	„		0 7 0
4 doz	„	3 pt	„	0 5 0	1 0 0
6 doz	„	1 pt	„	0 3 0	0 18 0
8 doz	„	1 qt	„	0 4 12	1 12 0
18 doz	Tea ware	Lg	„	0 2 00	1 16 0
18 doz	Tea ware	Sm	„	0 1 06	1 7 0
3 doz	Milk potts		„	0 3 0	0 9 0
½ doz	Tea „	Lg	„	0 8 0	0 4 0
1 doz	Tea „	sml	„	0 8 0	0 4 0
2 doz	Sugar boxes		„	0 6 0	0 12 0
3 doz	Coffee Cans		„	0 2 0	0 6 0
4 doz	Chamber pots			0 5 0	1 0 0
4	Milk pans		Earthenware	0 0 03	0 1 0
12	„		„	0 0 2	0 2 0
14 + 6	„			0 0 1¾	1 3 9
12	Butter mugs		„	0 0 1¾	1 3 9
2	Jugs	Qt	„		
3 doz	Mugs	„		0 1 6	0 4 6
1½ doz	„	pt		0 1 0	0 1 6
3 doz	„	½ pt	„	0 0 6	0 1 6
1 doz	Bowls-				

William Allason Invoice and Inventory Books 1760–96, and Loose Papers, Library of Virginia, Richmond.

The new cream-coloured wares were clearly taking the field.

So where are the Scottish ceramics? Relying on Allason's detailed records of shipment location, they seem to be surprisingly underutilised in the tobacco trade. Even Scottish firms with close Scottish buyers in Glasgow relied mostly on a variety of British firms for their ceramic supply after perhaps favouring Glasgow firms before 1760. Of course, there may have been supply problems in the 1760s as Delftfield was forced to declare bankruptcy and re-emerge under a different set of owners. As this shortage may have occurred, various Liverpool firms were actively shipping the new and perhaps more highly regarded Staffordshire wares. The advertisement by the potter John Cadell in the Edinburgh newspaper *Caledonian Mercury* on 8 September 1770 gives us new insights as manufacturers on the edge of empire (Scotland) had to compete with the more prestigious ceramic wares of Staffordshire. In announcing ceramics for sale at his business outside Edinburgh, Cadell proclaimed that he had a variety of 'the best English Cream Coloured stoneware from the first makers in Stafford-shire'. He pointedly added, however, 'he continues to sell all sorts of White, Cream, Black and Tortoise-shell ware of the Prestonpans Manufactory'. His announcement becomes a plea that his own firm's ware 'will give equal satisfaction to those who wish to encourage the industrious among ourselves' (Skerry and Hood 2009: 174). Cadell's appeal to those who might want to 'buy Scottish', that is, encourage Scottish manufacturing, may be just the kind of 'magic cord of sympathy' imagined by Colin Donald.

John Semple and John Lawson

Surviving correspondence between business associates sometimes reveals how storekeepers obtained goods, but only a rare few name the suppliers and allow a view of the complex chain of distribution linking British goods and Virginia consumers. Most Scottish firms treated the partner in Scotland as the source of their shipped goods and offer no further details. The firm of John Lawson of Glasgow and John Semple of Port Tobacco, Maryland, however, stand as an important exception, for often they list the name of specific suppliers or manufacturers next to the list of goods shipped to the Chesapeake ventures. That simple fact may have been due to the firm's bankruptcy and long court proceedings. Sloppy in his accounting – mixing personal and store business, for example – and a profligate spender of the company's money on himself, Semple drove the firm to bankruptcy. Semple was what Allan Karras in his important book *Sojourners in the Sun* dubbed 'the Tobacco Factor Run Amok' (Karras 1992: 93).

Lawson and Semple's business stood in the town of Port Tobacco at the edge of a broad creek flowing to the Potomac River with further egress on to the Chesapeake Bay. The town, enacted in 1732, flourished from the tobacco business. By the 1770s at least eight merchant companies had made their base there, including John Glassford, the largest Scottish firm trading to the entire Chesapeake. A court, tavern and stores surrounded a busy square in a typical small county town. But local tobacco land was overused, the creek began to silt up, and major tobacco plantations moved westward. Already in decay in 1796, eighty houses still stood. Only three houses from the colonial period – one built by an English merchant – still stand, and one, the Burch House, is currently under archaeological investigation (Lee 1994: 34–5; Reps 1972: 241–3, Gibbs 2011: 15–20).

From the beginning Lawson took extreme care in selecting goods for the firm. He purchased rugs and white cottons from Mary Wakefield & Sons in Kendal, light gowns from Manchester warehousemen Robert and Nathaniel Hyde, and cotton gowns from Kennedy & Bell of Glasgow. Scottish manufacturing

firms benefited greatly from this export trade: ropes went from the Port Glasgow ropeworks, delft from the Delftfield House of Glasgow, sugar from the King Street Sugar House, woollens from the Kilmarnock Wooling Manufactory, and agricultural tools from the Smithfield Factory. Lawson visited dozens of Scottish craftsmen to fill his orders: at least three shoemakers (who supplied different kinds of shoes and pumps), cloth calenderers, stay-makers and silversmiths. From London he acquired glass, china, looking-glasses, spices, silks, guns, furred hats, and other fine goods. In all, for a single shipment in the ship *Charming Sally* in December 1757, Lawson dealt with forty different manufacturers, craftsmen and merchants to supply the goods for an invoice totalling £1,808. This assortment included a vast array of goods from prosaic ropes and house brooms to 'one dozen dressed babies'.

Most specifically Semple ordered ceramics from two different sources for that winter shipment on the *Charming Sally*. The first pottery sent to Port Tobacco was made by the Delftfield Company (see Table 2). Though called different names ('Delftfield, Delft House' etc) and written with different spellings, five different orders of one hogshead ceramic each were placed by Semple.

But the December order was clearly already a small catch-up from the much larger spring shipment in April from the Delftfield potteries. That detailed invoice dated 12 April lists a massive number of tablewares: 30 dozen fine plates, and eight dozen 'butter slight dishes', dishes by size (a dozen each of great, main, or small), bottle and basins 'painted', small or butter middle basons along with different size cans, chamber pots, and 'flour horns'. The last vessels, probably wall pockets in a cornucopia shape – are a quite cosmopolitan form that has not previously been attributed to Delftfield.

Compared to the prodigious output of the successful Delftfield factory, the other supplier was a little-known potter, John Holden. No place of business is listed for him in the December 1757 shipment of goods (see Table 3). He was married in the St Andrews Episcopal Church in Glasgow where he was listed as a potter and an Englishman in 1760. Other potters listed at St Andrews were described as Delph-makers or Stoneware-makers or even particularly noted as living 'at the Delft-house', but Holden is more broadly sketched (Hallen 1888: 91).

John Holden and his business appear to be a cipher. According to a nineteenth-century history of Scottish

Table 2
Delftfield Company to John Semple, Port Tobacco, Maryland. December 1757

Qty	Form	Size	Price/dozen £ s d	Total price £ s d
6	Bowl	Small middle	0 12 0	0 6 0
2 doz	„	2 quart	0 7 0	0 14 0
3 doz	„	3 pint	0 5 0	0 15 0
5 doz	„	2 pint	0 4 0	1 0 0
5 doz	„	Pint	0 3 0	0 15 0
5 doz	„	½ pint	0 2 0	0 10 0
6 doz	Teaware	Lg	0 2 0	0 12 0
1 doz	Tea pots		0 6 0	0 6 0
1 doz	Milk pots			0 3 0
1 doz	Sugar boxes		0 6 0	0 6 0
2	Coffee cans		0 2 0	0 4 0

Currie-Dal Misc. Bundle 20, Box 243, National Archives of Scotland. Microfilm, Colonial Williamsburg Foundation

music, John Holden was indeed a potter and living in Glasgow by 1757. He was made a Guild-brother by purchase and also listed as a merchant. Described as an 'able scholar and eminent as a music theorist', Holden wrote music, published a collection, and was heavily involved in the music of Glasgow College (Love 1891: 171). That his pottery continued alongside his gentlemanly musical pursuits can be seen when, at his death, his wife advertised in the *Glasgow Mercury* on 17 April 1781 the sale of that pottery 'adjoining the Gorbals Church' owned by John Holden, now worked by Andrew Boag (Reid 1884: 85).

Compared to the ubiquitous tin-glazed earthenware from Delftfield, Holden's shipment of a hogshead of ceramics included different wares or decorations. The wares are distinguished as white (table and tea wares), black (coffee pots or ink jacks) or 'stone' (soup plates). Black wares were probably what is often termed 'Jackfield' today. The term 'carved' remains ambiguous to contemporary scholars. Earlier in the century they might have been a kind of globular stoneware vessel, containing a multi-layered outer wall with one layer pierced or carved out to create visual lightness (Edwards and Hampson 2005: 286–7; Hughes 1960: 38). Nonetheless, stoneware sauceboats and plates like those in Holden's list here were listed in other documents in the 1760s and could easily be

enamelled and relief-moulded white salt-glaze or other mid-century patterns and rims delineated by Angelika Kuettner (2009: 228–39).

John Semple made thirteen other distinct shipments of ceramics to Maryland between 1757 and 1768. As in Allason's business, ceramics came from large wholesalers in the cities of London and Liverpool. (No Bristol firms were listed in this sample.) But an additional five orders between 1757 and 1762 came from the Delftfield Company. Nearly all were orders for bowls and tea wares, each filling a hogshead, although vessels were sorted in each container somewhat differently.

If ceramics flowed from Glasgow in 1757, John Lawson also turned to Staffordshire for a 1760 order, to John Baddeley at Shelton near Newcastle-under-Lyme. Among Semple and Lawson's papers, written orders are far less common than invoices, suggesting that Semple may have ordered most of his wares in person. He wrote to Baddeley that he wanted 'second' stoneware, sent to Liverpool ('to Mr. Walker Merchant') and quickly ('be there by ye last of the month at farthest (or don't send them)'). His list was specific in terms of categories ('well sorted'), but oblique in terms of describing vessels: £4 value of Tea ware, Ten pounds value of table ware in Setts 'well sorted. Equall quantities of Soop & Table Dishes & Equal quantities

Table 3
John Holden to John Semple, Port Tobacco, Maryland. December 1757

Qty	Form	Size	Colour and description	Price/dozen £ s d	Total price £ s d
4	Mugs	Qt	Enameled		0 5 4
8	Sauce boats		Enameled and carved	0 8 0	0 5 4
24	Mustard pots		Enameled	0 2 6	0 5 0
10	Mugs	Qt	White		0 6 6
12	Mugs	Pt	„		0 2 2
12	Tea pots	Pt			0 2 2
12	„	½ pint			0 1 1
12	Baking dishes	Qt			0 4 4
12	„	Pt			0 2 2
24	„	½ Pt			0 2 2
15	„	Smaller			0 1 1
4	Bowls	3 pt			0 1 1
24	„	Pt			0 2 2
15		½ pt			0 2 2
36	Coffee cups and saucers	Double			0 2 2
4	Sauce boats	Mid	White	0 0 2½	0 0 10
3	Coffee pots	Quart	Black	0 0 7	
4	Sauce boats	Small	Carved	0 0 2	0 0 8
36	Tea cups and saucers	Large			0 1 9
36	Tea cups and saucers	Smaller			0 1 6
3	Coffee pots	Pint	Black		0 0 10½
24	Milk Jugs		White		0 2 2
Doz	Soup plates		Stone carved stone		0 3 6
Doz	„		Stone carved stone		0 3 2
Doz	Ink jacks	Quart	Black		0 12 0
Doz	Bottles Mustard	¼ lb			0 5 0

Currie-Dal Misc. Bundle 20, Box 243, National Records of Scotland. Microfilm, Colonial Williamsburg Foundation

of Soop & Table Plates'. Finally, he wanted hollow wares: '£6 value of mugs, Cans, Bowls & Custer [*sic*] Dishes'. Semple wanted the wares to be 'neat and genteel' although as cheap as possible to 'encourage future dealings'. If Baddeley needed a reference for his business, he could enquire at any of his 'acquaintances' at that place. Semple's letter to Baddeley intimates that the business of shipping Staffordshire wares in the Glasgow trade was not unusual, as Baddeley would certainly have 'acquaintances', that is, other merchants in Glasgow that could allow him into the mercantile web of credit and compliance between Staffordshire and Glasgow.[2]

Baddeley's account books in turn place the orders of Semple and Lawson in the context of their supplier's business on the other side of the water. Between 1753 and 1767 this successful potter shipped more than 100 crates every few months to Amsterdam, in addition to the sizeable local trade he maintained in surrounding towns and, occasionally, with local nobility. He also sold crates of pottery to middlemen in Glasgow, Edinburgh and Liverpool, some of which probably ended up in the American colonies. By 1771 even rival Josiah Wedgwood acknowledged Baddeley's products as 'the best ware perhaps of any of the potters'. Wedgwood marvelled that the Shelton potter had made an 'ovenfull of it Per Diem' and had led the way in lowering prices (Mallot 1967 (2): 124–66; 1967 (3) 181–247). Perhaps this reputation had spread to Glasgow so that Lawson specifically ordered these cheap and well-made tea and table wares for his Virginia and Maryland customers. Baddeley followed Semple's request to ship his wares through Mr Walker, and in September 1760, the *Sally* at Liverpool sailed with a cargo from the firm Rumbold & Walker containing Baddeley's wares to Maryland. The invoice included the categories ordered by Semple: dishes and plates (flat and soup), tea ware, custards, mugs, cans, bowls ('bassons') and, as important, listed the ceramics in potters' formulaic pricing language, suggesting it may have been simply copied over from a factory invoice.

Individual invoices are uncommon from an English or Scottish middle-man or wholesale merchant. Particular orders from specified potters are rare; archaeological investigation of merchants' sites in combination with those documents is highly unusual. But the colonial town of Port Tobacco is remarkably well preserved and archaeological investigation has recently begun. Thousands of sherds from common eighteenth-century wares have been unearthed by archaeologist James Gibbs.[3] The immediate environs of the eighteenth-century Burch House are currently being tested yielding a plethora of ceramic evidence. In one square (Unit 91, Stratum 11) archaeologists uncovered eighty-three ceramic sherds of table and teaware fragments. The ceramic sherds were quite small, but over two-thirds were tin-glazed earthenware, 12 per cent white salt-glazed stoneware, and 8 per cent Chinese porcelain.

Archaeologists also discovered small quantities of black and brown ware. Together, these artefacts roughly mirror contemporaneous ceramic shipments to Semple and Lawson. One clue is particularly enticing. Lawson's request for white salt-glazed wares from John Baddeley and the 1760 shipment from Rumbold & Walker of white salt-glazed plates included details like 'mosaic' or 'basket' and artefacts with these border patterns blanket mid-century sites. There are also two specific references to a moulded pattern called 'China

Rail'. In Cask 46 of the consignment of white salt-glazed stoneware shipped in the *Sally* from Rumbold and Walker were two dozen plates and a dozen soup bowls described as china rail. This pattern remains obscure and is rarely found in potters' records; the only mention in Diana Edwards and Rodney Hampson's *White Salt-Glazed Stoneware of the British Isles* notes that John Harrison supplied Thomas and John Wedgwood with 'mosaic breakfast plates and China rail table plates' in 1759 (2005: 259). Angelika Kuettner at the Colonial Williamsburg Foundation has identified and published multiple patterns of relief-moulded white salt-glazed plates, including the Chinese rail pattern (see illus 2.6). (In total forty-eight different borders from twenty-two different categories of decorative motifs are found on white salt-glazed stonewares popular in the middle of the eighteenth century. The Chinese rail/basket plan was found at a number of sites at Colonial Williamsburg, including taverns. At least three slight variations of the pattern have been found in the Virginia colonial capital. It seems far less common on colonial Maryland sites.) Only a single sherd recovered from the Port Tobacco site, or from many others excavated by Gibbs, was ornamented with that specific moulded design (see illus 2.7). In that one small field of the plate border's rococo abundance, straight lines mimicked Chinese railing patterns published in

Illustration 2.6
Plate, white salt-glazed stoneware, 'Chinese rail/basket' plan. Colonial Williamsburg Foundation, 1972-214, 5. Museum purchase. [Courtesy of Colonial Williamsburg Foundation]

Table 4
Casks 41–4: sample variety of white salt-glazed stoneware shipped in the *Sally* from Rumbold & Walker, Liverpool. September 1760

Qty	Form	Size	Colour and description	Price/ dozen £ s d	Total price £ s d
36 doz	Cups and saucers		White 36 to ye dozen	0 0 12	1 18 0
2 doz	Bassons	Pint	White, Best (12 lathed)	0 1 6	0 3 0
1 doz	„		Seconds	0 1 2	0 1 2
2 doz	„		„ 30 to ye dozen	0 1 6	0 3 0
1 doz	Bassons	Pint	„ 30 to ye dozen	0 1 2	0 1 2
2 doz	Teapots		Best „ 12 „	0 1 6	0 3 0
2 doz	„		„ 16 „	0 1 6	0 3 0
1 doz	„		„ 24 „		0 1 6
1½ doz	Cream Jugs		„ 24 „	0 1 6	0 2 3
1 doz	Coffee Cans		„ 30 „		0 1 6
½ doz	Tea Pots		„ 24 „		0 0 7
4 doz	Mugs	Qt	Best White 6 „	0 1 6	0 6 0
6 doz	„	Pt	„ „ 12 „	0 1 6	0 9 0
2 doz	„	½ Pt	„ „ 24 „	0 1 6	0 3 0
3 doz	Bassons	Pint	12 to ye dozen	0 1 6	0 4 6
2 doz	„	½ Pint	24	0 1 6	0 4 6
1 doz	„	½ pint	30	0 1 6	0 3 0
6 doz	Mugs	Qt	'Second' 6	0 1 2	0 7 –
6 doz	„	PT	„ 12	0 1 2	0 7 –
3 doz	Bassons	„	„ 12	0 1 2	0 3 6
3 doz	„	½ pint	„ 24	0 1 2	0 3 6
1 doz	„	„	„ 30	0 1 2	0 1 2
17 doz	Plates	'Flate'	"Best" 12	0 2 –	1 14 0
9 doz	„	'Soop'	„ 12	0 2 –	0 18 0
3 setts	Dishes	'Flate'	„ 5 in a sett	0 3 –	0 9 0
2 setts	Dishes	'Soop'	„ 3 in a sett	0 1 3	0 2 6
10 doz	Plates	'Flat'	„ 12	0 2 3	
5 doz	„	'Soop'	„ 12		
8 doz	„	'Flat'	Second	0 2 0	
4 doz					…
2 setts	Dishes	'flate'	Best 5 in a sett	0 4 7	0 9 2
1 sett	Dishes	„	Second „	0 3 0	0 3 0
2 setts	„	Soop	Best 3 in a sett	0 1 10	0 3 8
1 sett			Second „	0 1 3	0 1 3

Currie-Dal Misc. Bundle 20, Box 243, National Records of Scotland. Microfilm, Colonial Williamsburg Foundation.

Illustration 2.7
White salt-glazed stoneware sherd, William Burch site,
unit 91, stratum 11. Port Tobacco, Maryland.
[Photograph courtesy Gibbs Archaeological Consulting]

numerous eighteenth-century books of chinoiserie designs and most commonly seen in furniture and stair passages in modish Anglo-Chesapeake houses. Multiple shipments from Scottish potteries flowed to Virginia and Maryland through the businesses of Scottish merchants. This single sherd is identifiable because of a precise request from a Staffordshire potter. Nonetheless, scientific examination of body type from Scottish factories will enable more precise matching of those Scottish wares in America. The excavation at the town – and perhaps some day the site – of the Scottish firm of Lawson & Semple will continue to open up the world of Scottish material culture in America.

This intimate look at several manufacturers' shipments may seem to take us far away from our question of Scottish material culture in America. But this is one significant way to ascertain the complex actions of Scottish merchants in Scotland and America and the ways in which Scottish – and British – goods flowed to the mid-Atlantic colonies. The final merchant examined here tells less about the wares he sold and more about the man himself. John Hook was perhaps the quintessential contemporary stereotype of a North Briton to his Virginia neighbours. Commercial success through craft and cunning and political alliance with the British proved it.

John Hook and David Ross

Virginia merchant John Hook ordered a clock with 'Moon Age to Shew the Days of the Month with Mahogany Case' from the maker John Barr of Port Glasgow in 1772.[4] Here, finally, we find a Scottish merchant ordering a specific product from a known Scottish maker, perhaps in the kind of business relationship that might express some 'magic cord of sympathy' between merchant and homeland or, perhaps the insularity and clannishness of Scots in America. But it was William Mead, a wealthy German immigrant customer, who had specifically asked for John Barr; John Hook was merely fulfilling the request.

John Hook's story is one final twist in the study of Scottish material culture in America. The son of a small-scale soap manufacturer in Glasgow, he and his three brothers took advantage of their father's connections to gain employment in Virginia, Jamaica and India, and therefore were like so many Scottish sons who followed trade routes and business opportunities across the empire.

Through his long Virginia career Hook had a variety of business relationships. He began at the bottom, sweeping floors, before moving up to keep books and manage a store, including working for the well-known house of Robert Donald (see illus 2.8). Hired by Robert Donald, who later became Provost of Glasgow, John Hook shared his home at Pages Warehouse, Virginia. It was about that time that Donald shared hospitality with a young George Washington. Much later, Donald corresponded with the newly elected President Washington, asking him to remember those happy times some forty years before and seeking help with a position for his nephew. When the merchant John MacDougall came to the Donald firm looking for an assistant, Hook was essentially passed on to a different part of the company to keep books for one year with the promise of his own store in the backcountry in twelve months' time.

But the backcountry store position did not transpire when a family member, Andrew Donald, did not return home as planned. Hook never quite recovered from these disappointments – the time wasted working with McDougall and Andrew Donald with no advancement, the missed promotion and ability to sell his own goods on his own for side profit, and having to struggle to find other capital and arrangements with a Scottish partner. Finally, by 1771 he realised that the business could not support both William and James Donald and himself. Robert,

the younger brother of James, was also ready to assume more responsibility. Family always trumped promises.

But it was always to Scotland, family and Scottish merchants that Hook turned. He hoped to begin an import/export trade with his brother in Jamaica, assuring his father that imported soap could not be sold in Virginia because everyone made their own with lye. At the loss of a junior employee, he sought 'one or two clever young men from home that could write well for four years each'.[5] He urged his father to seek capital for his trade from a distant relative.

But did this wish to use Scottish connections extend into the supply of goods from Scottish manufacturers? In 1768 Hook urged William Donald to settle upon a correspondent in Liverpool or Bristol to send 'Cotton Cards, Grind Stones and Sack Salt', but would prefer Bristol for cotton cards and sack salt.[6] When he later became partner with the Scottish merchant David Ross, he was careful to set up some conditions for their business. For instance, Hook wanted to 'know what Ports my Goods come from for a guide to me hereafter in sending for goods'.[7] Ross's regular partner, however, was not in the busy Glasgow, Liverpool or London ports, but in Whitehaven whose early Chesapeake tobacco business was slowly being drained away to Glasgow. As Hook grew more dissatisfied with the Whitehaven partner, he supervised his shipments more closely. Even so, there was no mention of caring about Scottish goods or Scottish ships.

Although John Hook's records tell little of particular Scottish goods they reveal much about his life. By all evidence he was a quarrelsome man, difficult to please and always ready to press for debts in Virginia and complain to partners in Glasgow. He, like many Scottish clerks and factors, was repeatedly disappointed at his inability to return home 'genteely'. Yet he ended his career in the Scottish store trade an extremely wealthy Virginia planter.

In one other particular way he was a good Scot. Like so many of his countrymen, he supported Britain in the American Revolution (Colley 1992: 132–46). Accused of English sympathies before the war, prints of 'George III and his queen' still hung in his house at his death in 1809 (Martin 2008: 196).

Illustration 2.8
'Robert Donald of Mountblow' (1724–1803). Oil on canvas, 762 x 635mm. Artist unknown. The Glasgow Donalds were Scottish merchants with connections deep and wide in Virginia. [Image courtesy of Culture and Sport Glasgow (Museums)]

The political crisis in the Chesapeake had deep economic roots. When Robert Cowan, James Callaway, Robert Donald and John Hook, the four merchants in Bedford County, met in 1772 to stave off ruin by setting prices for tobacco and goods, Bedford planters howled in protest. If Scots were too generous with planters when trying to woo their business, many of the planters felt the opposite had occurred; the Scots had taken advantage. The merchants had extended liberal credit but encouraged their consumer desires and overcharged for goods. Furthermore, they saw immense fortunes being made. Resentment had been simmering for years. In October 1771, for example, 'Junius Americanus' wrote a letter to the *Virginia Gazette*, scorning the 'junto of North Britains, whom the favor of the Virginians had raised from beggary to affluence'.[8]

The Scots merchants had gone too far. Bedford planters met in 1773 to protest the 'destruction and total combination of the merchants against the people and inhabitants of this colony'. They agreed not to sell their tobacco under a set price and suggested a cooperative arrangement under local planter Richard Stith to market their own tobacco. This was not a local or temporal problem, but one that cast a light on the whole trading system. A blistering letter in the *Virginia Gazette* recounted the doleful history.

> The Scotch nation about fifty years ago, being informed of this valuable Country, and of the weak and blind side of its inhabitants, chose some of them to quit their packs, and leave their poor fare, and baren country, and make an experiment in the tobacco trade which by a little industry, and the mechanik turn of mind and the artful craftiness and cunning natural to that nation, they soon not only raised great estates for themselves, but found a plan to enrich their countrymen and raise Glasgow from being a small petty port, to one of the richest towns and trading points in his majesty's Dominions, and all by Fawning and Flattery and outwitting the indolent and thoughtless planters.
>
> *Virginia Gazette*
> 25 November 1773: 2

'Let us Bedfordsmen lead the way to liberty and renown,' they continued, 'and turn the channel from centering in Glasgow (richly overflowing all Scotland, and aggrandising all Scotchmen) to center in Virginia.' This could easily be done if other Virginians would join them in not dealing with any merchant who did not reside in the colonies and spend their riches here. They were chafing for commercial liberty from the 'craft and cunning' of Scottish merchants.[9]

William Allason, James Semple and John Hook were just a few of the many Scots who had helped 'set a channel to Glasgow'. Indeed, controlling Scottish–American trade helped Scotland as national wealth rose sharply after Scottish and English trade joined in the eighteenth century. Colonists – wherever there was commercial empire – might need delftware bowls or iron hoes. Such needs and desires placed Scotland firmly on the worldwide stage of Britain's colonial empire.

Conclusion: 'Stone dishes in the Scotch Style'

Have we found a 'magic cord of sympathy' that united the Scots in the New World and was part of the grand venture of becoming American? Alexander Dick found that poetry, house furnishings, habits, ritualised hospitality and social bonding all made the remaining pockets of Scottish people in Virginia happy. His experience of new things was quite often not of *the thing itself*, but of the way the thing connected with a picture in his mind. Thomas Jefferson's majestic capital of Virginia was not an extraordinary reprisal of a Roman temple but bore the appearance of a church in Glasgow. Location, family and length of time in this country compartmentalised every Scot that he met, hence tying them to Scottish places and people.

Linda Colley has alerted us to the difficulties of defining Britons; there were as many differences between Highland and Lowland Scots as between Scottish and English merchants (1992). 'The junto of North Britons' was the scornful term of angry Virginians when they discovered that the channel from Glasgow had flooded them with consumer goods that they later regretted purchasing. To them, the Scots were clannish and conniving, and excluded other Americans from their economic success. But they were the outsiders looking in – the Scots as a group were held apart. The evidence for the transatlantic connections between Scotland and America is both material and ephemeral. Economic definitions of Scottish goods are surprisingly elastic: Scottish or English manufactories filled orders from Scottish merchants as needed. Scottish place-names – and family names – dot the landscapes of the mid-Atlantic and the Caribbean yet identifying some 'pure' form of Scottish material culture has proved elusive.

A single man embodies the very conundrum of sorting out the transatlantic Scottish world of goods. The enslaved man Harry ran away from his Virginia owner in 1775. The advertisement searching for him in the *Virginia Gazette* noted that Harry could read and write, had suffered the smallpox and carried several changes of clothes. He could also 'speak *Scotch*, and sings some *Scotch* songs' (see illus 2.9). His previous owner, James Donald, 'had taken him to Scotland where he resided for many years'. Why had James Donald raised the young man in Scotland and later returned him to Virginia? Did Harry run

JAMES CITY county, *November* 1, 1775.

RUN away from *Drummond*'s neck, the 27th of laſt month, a young negro man named HARRY, who can read and write, and carried with him ſeveral ſuits of clothing. I purchaſed him of mr. *James Donald*, who brought him from *Scotland*, where he had been many years. He has had the ſmallpox, can ſpeak *Scotch*, and ſings *Scotch* ſongs. Whoever brings him to me ſhall have 20 s. reward, beſides what the law allows.

JOHN AYLETT.

Illustration 2.9
Virginia Gazette, 1 November 1775. [Courtesy of Special Collections, John D Rockefeller Jr Library, Colonial Williamsburg Foundation]

away in the chaos of wartime to join the English fight against the American rebels?[10]

Like so many things sold by Scots in America, Harry was part of the multiple webs of debt and credit twining them together. The same commercial frame of mercantilism and capitalism sent Alexander Dick on his travels collecting decades-old bills from Virginians and pushed the Donald family in Glasgow into bankruptcy. Scottish manners linked Harry to other Scots, yet, sadly, fond and familiar words and tunes became the very markers that could aid his capture.

The stamp of Scottish merchants on American soil is hence inestimable. 'Round all the globe your happy sonnets go' opined the author of the foreword to Allan Ramsay's *Tea-table Miscellany*. Scottish merchants, Scottish objects, Scottish debts and Scottish songs were all part of the global eighteenth-century transatlantic world.

Alexander Dick visited with dozens of Scottish families in his journeys between 1807 and 1809. But he only listed one specific thing that signalled his pleasure: 'stone dishes in the Scotch style'. Ironically, hunting the elusive meaning of those dishes (stoneware? natural stone?) or 'dishes in the Scotch style' as a common shorthand for traditional Scottish foodways obliquely links all the evidence of the search for Scottish material culture in the Chesapeake. The 'magic cord' of sympathy continues to tug.

Acknowledgements

Special thanks to the many people who helped me bring together such a broad swathe of research materials. George Miller was the progenitor of the huge 'Ceramics in America' project for which I gathered the merchants' data here found almost two decades ago. James Gibbs and Anne Hayward responded to my excited interest in the ceramics from Port Tobacco. Angelika Kuettner and Janine Skerry provided ceramic insight and the image from the Colonial Williamsburg Foundation. Following Vanessa Habib's suggestion, Linda Eaton found and Heather Hanson helped with the research into the marvellous textile illustrating Allan Ramsay's *The Gentle Shepherd* at the Winterthur Museum. Vanessa Habib helped with editing my draft and Simon Gilmour was our own gentle shepherd of wandering authors. Pat Halfpenny did the heroic job of putting together the earlier conference at the Winterthur Museum.

Finally, James Donald contacted me after publication of my book *Buying into the World of Goods* four years ago, and his dogged work has helped clear up the 'endless Donald connections' that had so long frustrated me and located the portrait of Robert Donald. He also provided me with the extraordinarily prescient definition of material culture used by his great-grandfather Colin Donald and hence the felicitous phrasing of the 'cord of sympathy'.

Notes

1 Alexander Dick Journal, 1806–9, Albert and Shirley Small Special Collections Library, University of Virginia, Charlottesville, VA. Due to the fragility of this volume, a transcript is most often used. Helen Beall Lewis, 'Journal of Alexander Dick in America, 1806–09', MA Thesis, Dept of History, University of Virginia, 1984. References here are to date recorded and page number of her thesis.

2 James Lawson to John Baddeley at Shelton near Newcastle-under-Lyme, Glasgow, 2 January 1759. Semple-Lawson papers, John Baddeley sales book, 1753–61, vol 101, Aqualate Papers, Staffordshire Record Office.

3 Anne Hayward, Gibbs Archaeological Consulting, personal communication, 26 May 2011.

4 Memorandum of Goods for Mead, 9 September 1772. John Hook papers, Duke University, Durham, North Carolina.

5 John Hook to David Ross, New London, 10 March 1774, John Hook Miscellaneous Papers, Library of Virginia.

6 John Hook to William Donald, New London, 29 May 1768, John Hook Letter Book, Duke University.

7 John Hook to David Ross, New London, 7 November 1771, John Hook Letter Book, Library of Virginia.

8 *Virginia Gazette*, Purdie & Dixon, 17 October 1771.

9 *Virginia Gazette*, Purdie & Dixon, 25 November 1773.

10 *Virginia Gazette*, Purdie & Dixon, 1 November 1775.

Bibliography

Appadurai, A (ed) 1986 *The Social Life of Things: Commodities in Cultural Perspective*. Cambridge.

Archer, M 1966 'Delftware Pottery made at the Glasgow Pottery of Delftfield', *The Connoisseur*, September, 1966, 17–22.

Archer, M 1971 'Delftware made at the Glasgow Pottery at Delftfield: a starting point for research', *The Connoisseur*, April.

Austin, J C & Hunter, R 1994 *British Delft at Williamsburgh*. Colonial Williamsburg Foundation.

Burnard, T 2004 *Mastery, Tyranny and Desire: Thomas Thistlewood and His Slaves in the Anglo-Jamaican World*. University of North Carolina Press.

Bynum, W 1981 'Roger Atkinson, Merchant-Planter in Revolutionary Virginia'. MA Thesis, University of Virginia.

Colley L 1992 *Britons: Forging the Nation 1707–1837*. New Haven: Yale University Press.

Defoe, D [1725–7] 1969 *The Complete English Tradesman* (2 vols). London. Reprint Augustus M Kelly, New York.

Devine, T M (ed) 1982 *A Scottish Firm in Virginia, 1767–1777*. Scottish History Society.

Edwards, D & Hampson, R 2005 *White Salt-Glazed Stoneware of the British Isles*. Woodbridge, Suffolk.

Evans, E E 1969 'The Scotch-Irish: Their Culture Adaptation and Heritage in the American Old West', 69–86 in *Essays in Scotch-Irish History*, Green E R R (ed), London.

Fleming, J A 1923 *Scottish Pottery*. Glasgow: Maclehose Jackson & Co.

Gibbs, J 2011 Phase III Archaeological Data Recovery at the Burch House Site (18CH765) Port Tobacco, Charles County, Maryland. (restoreporttobacco. org/page5/files/Burch House Phase lll.pdf).

Graham, I C C 1956 *Colonists from Scotland: Emigration to North America, 1707–1783*. Ithaca, New York.

Hallen, Revd A W 1888 *Cornelius, The Scottish Antiquary, or Northern Notes and Queries 1891–1903*.

Hancock, D 1994 'Trade' *in Scotland and the Americas, 1600–1800: Rare Books, Maps and Prints from the Collection of the John Carter Brown Library*. Catalogue of an Exhibition at the John Carter Brown Library and the Forbes Magazine Galleries.Providence, RI.

Hughes, G B 1960 *English and Scottish Earthenware 1660–1860*. New York: Macmillan.

Karras, A L 1992 *Sojourners in the Sun: Scottish Migrants in Jamaica and the Chesapeake, 1740–1800*. Ithaca, NY.

Kuettner, A 2009 'Appendix A: White Salt-glazed Stoneware Plate Patterns', *in Salt-Glazed Stoneware in Early America*. Colonial Williamsburg Foundation.

Landsman, N C 1998 'Pluralism, protestantism and prosperity: Crevoceur's American farmer and the foundations of American pluralism', *in* Katlin, W F, Landsman, N C & Tyree, A (eds), *Beyond Pluralism: The Conception of Groups and Group Identities in America*. Urbana.

Lange, A E 2001 *Delftware at Historic Deerfield, 1600–1800*. Historic Deerfield, Deerfield, MA.

Lee, J B 1994 *The Price of Nationhood: The American Revolution in Charles County*. New York.

Lewis, H B 1984 'Journal of Alexander Dick in America, 1806–9', MA thesis, University of Virginia.

Love, J 1891 *Scottish Church Music: Its Composers and Sources*. Edinburgh.

Mair, J 1757 *Book-keeping Methodiz'd: A Methodical Treatise of Merchant-Accompts, According to the Italian Form*, Edinburgh.

Mallot, J 1967 'John Baddeley of Shelton: an Early Staffordshire Maker of Pottery and Porcelain', *English Ceramic Circle Transactions*, no 6 pt 2 and 3.

Martin, A S 2008 *Buying into the World of Goods: Early Consumers in the Virginia Backcountry*. Baltimore.

Martin, A S 1994 '"Fashionable sugar dishes, latest fashion wares": the creamware revolution in the eighteenth-ventury Chesapeake', *in The Historic Archaeology of the Chesapeake*, Shackel, P & Little, B J (eds). Washington.

Martin, A S 1988 'To supply the real and imaginary necessities: the retail trade in table and tea wares, Virginia and Maryland, *c* 1750–1810.' Final Report of research funded by the National Endowment for the Humanities, 'English Ceramics in America 1760–1860; Marketing, Prices and Availability', Miller, G L, Martin, A S & Dickinson, N.

Montgomery, F 1970 *Printed Textiles: English and American Cottons and Linens, 1700–1850*. New York.

Nelson, L P 2005 'Anglican Church Building and Local Context in Early Jamaica', *Perspectives in Vernacular Architecture*, vol 10, Building Environments.

Price, J 1980 *Capital and Credit in British Overseas Trade: The View from the Chesapeake, 1770–1776*. Cambridge.

Price, J (ed) 1979 'Joshua Johnson's letterbook: Letters from a London merchant to his partners in Maryland'. London Record Society.

Price, J 1974 'Economic function and the growth of American port towns in the eighteenth century', *in Perspectives in American History*, (eds) Fleming, D & Bailyn, B. Cambridge.

Ramsay A 1760 *Tea-table Miscellany: or, a Collection of Choice Songs, Scots and English*. London.

Ramsay A 1788 'The Gentle Shepherd', A Scotch Pastoral Comedy', with 13 plates, David Allan, Glasgow: A & R Foulis.

Reid, R 1884 *Glasgow Past and Present* (3 vols). Glasgow.

Reps W J 1972 *Tidewater Towns: City Planning in Colonial Virginia and Maryland*, Williamsburg VA: Colonial Williamsburg Foundation; distributed by the University Press of Virginia, Charlottesville.

Robertson, D 1891–1903 *The Scottish Antiquary, or Northern Notes and Queries*. Edinburgh.

Robertson J 2001 'Jamaican architectures before Georgian', Winterthur Portfolio vol 36, no 2/3.

Skerry, J E & Hood, S F 2009 *Salt-Glazed Stoneware in Early America*. Colonial Williamsburg Foundation.

Williams, E, Riches, A & Higgs, M 1990 *The Buildings of Scotland: Glasgow*. London: Penguin.

CHAPTER 3

Thomas Affleck: Philadelphia cabinetmaker – 'late of Aberdeen'

ALEXANDRA ALEVIZATOS KIRTLEY

Thomas Affleck's reputation as the pre-eminent cabinetmaker of colonial and early federal Philadelphia is unsurpassed in the literature on American furniture. When the prodigious researcher William MacPherson Hornor Jr published the still relevant *Blue Book of Philadelphia Furniture: William Penn to George Washington* in 1935, he presented Affleck – his career, his stature and his furniture – without documentation. While so much of what Hornor wrote about Affleck has stood the test of time, new research provides concrete evidence about Affleck's family and background in Scotland, his apprenticeship and how he attained his reputation in the cabinetmaking community of 1760s Philadelphia. The brilliance of Affleck's career in Philadelphia, a city with a deeply rooted cabinetmaking tradition and a substantial number of competent native-born and newly émigré cabinetmakers, is remarkable and makes his meteoric rise all the more extraordinary.

Thomas Affleck was born in the city of Aberdeen, Scotland, in 1740. Aberdeen lies on the north-east coast of Scotland, 127 miles north of Edinburgh. Affleck's Aberdeen of the mid-eighteenth century existed in the shadows of Edinburgh, Scotland's capital city and the centre of commerce and culture. However, Aberdeen's active eighteenth-century port fuelled its independence from Edinburgh's dominance. Aberdonian merchants carried on an international trade in agricultural goods gathered from the hinterlands of northern Scotland. Trade between Philadelphia and Aberdeen had begun at least by September 1735 when *The American Weekly Mercury* noted the arrival of the ship *Diligence* of Aberdeen, which was registered with Captain Alexander Gordon. The next month, the same paper announced that the ship had cleared out of the port of Philadelphia. The *Diligence* made at least two annual trips in and out of Philadelphia for the next decade.[1]

Aberdeen furniture makers, or 'wrights' as they were called in Scotland, united in 1527. The Incorporation of Wrights and Coopers were, and still are, recognised as members of that city's ancient organisation of Seven Incorporated Trades and used their alliance to wield power. In 1768 the journeymen wrights announced in the *Aberdeen Journal* that they wished to receive a two-shilling increase in their day wages after the 10th of June. Although Aberdeen was geographically remote, it was 'not remote from fashionable ideas, nor were they [the wrights of the city] dependant [*sic*] upon Edinburgh for ideas of "present taste"'. There, the wrights cultivated the prosperous merchants as their patrons. Local mercantile wealth and patronage attracted the attention of London and Edinburgh cabinetmakers and upholsterers who, looking to expand their markets, advertised furniture for sale in Aberdeen newspapers. Wrights comprised a privileged class of tradesman in eighteenth-century Scotland, as Scottish furniture historian David Jones noted: 'cabinetmaking in eighteenth-century Scotland was a gentleman's trade, witness Francis Brodie who was the scion of an aristocratic family, for example'.[2]

In 1754 Thomas Affleck Sr, a tobacconist, put out his fourteen-year-old son Thomas as an apprentice to Alexander Rose, cabinetmaker of Ellon, Scotland. He paid Alexander Rose £8, which covered the first five years of the apprenticeship; in 1759 he paid £2 for the final two years of young Thomas's training. This final payment made the total cost of Affleck's apprenticeship the customary £10.[3]

Ellon is a small town twelve miles north of Aberdeen. In 1754 it was a considerably smaller town than Aberdeen, but both were active ports. Situated on the Ythan River, Ellon was famous for salmon fishing and pearl mussels, and the port's proximity to the North Sea made it relatively convenient to export agricultural products (illus 3.1). Along with Rosehearty and Newburgh, Ellon conducted a healthy and profitable trade along the north coast of Scotland. Ellon Castle, now in ruins, was occupied by the Constables of Aberdeen; when Affleck lived there,

Illustration 3.1
Part of Aberdeenshire including Ellon from James Kirkwood's Map of Scotland, 1810. [Courtesy of the National Library of Scotland]

George Gordon, the Earl of Aberdeen, owned the castle and housed his mistress there.[4]

Little is known about the cabinetmaker Alexander Rose, and no furniture has been documented to him or his shop. Rose may have sought out his clientele from the numerous landed noblemen in the area. Like cabinetmakers from nearby Banff, Cullen and Inverness, Rose advertised periodically in the *Aberdeen Journal*, for example, in 1759, 1760 and 1769. While Affleck was apprenticed to him, Rose listed an extensive inventory of 'good and fashionable' furniture for *roup*, or auction: mahogany desks, desks with book cases, beds, clothes presses, women's drawers, tables for dining, breakfast, tea, card and claw tables, game boards, tea chests, wash stands, dumb waiters, fire screens, clock cases, wainscot escritoires, chests of drawers with writing surfaces, brackets and a wide-ranging inventory of chairs of various woods and form.[5] In 1769 Rose advertised that 'he intends giving up Business' and has 'all Kinds of Furniture, finished, the Particulars would be too tedious to mention'. However, when he died in April 1774, his executors advertised a sale in the *Aberdeen Journal* for the same broad assortment of furniture as well as wright's tools, wood and upholstery materials. All suggest that Rose operated a comprehensive cabinetmaker's business.[6]

Given the traditional length of seven years for an apprenticeship, Affleck completed his time in 1761 at the age of twenty-one. It was customary in Britain, and in colonial America, that on completion the newly minted cabinetmaker (or wright) would seek work as a journeyman. There is no record of Affleck ever going to Edinburgh or even sailing out of Edinburgh on his way to London, where Quaker meeting records document him as having arrived by 1761. That the ambitious Affleck left Rose's tutelage and ventured to London to gain experience in the world's most prolific and fashionable furniture-making centre is natural. Records document an astounding number of furniture exports; the pace of furniture production in eighteenth-century London was brisk. Unfortunately, no information has yet surfaced about where Affleck resided or the cabinetmakers with whom and for whom he was working in London in the 1760s. Affleck did not apply to be a freeman (or member of the guild) – a fact that seems consistent with an intention to emigrate to America.

Potential family ties between Affleck and London cabinetmaker James Affleck or London upholsterer John Affleck remain to be substantiated. James and John may have descended from a different line of the Auchinleck family, which is the root of the surname *Affleck*. James Affleck, who was at least a generation older than Thomas, was a subscriber to the 1754 first edition of Chippendale's *Director*. Unlike Thomas, James and John Affleck are not recorded as Quakers.[7]

While the network of fellow cabinetmakers with whom Affleck (through Rose or others) fraternised in London is not known, he took advantage of his Quaker and Scottish connections. He attended the London Two Weeks Meeting, where he met Thomas Fisher (1741–1810), the son of Joshua Fisher of Philadelphia. As noted by previous scholars, Joshua's son Thomas Fisher wrote to his father from London in July 1763: '7th month, 20th, 1763: Honour'd Father, The bearer Thos Affleck intended to settle in Philadelphia, & knowing the satisfaction of being introduced to some acquaintance there shall I just say he is a friend of David Barclay and a person from whose character I have reason to esteem. Our friends the Barclays as well as several others & myself in particular will take it kind thou will render him thy world civility & any advice & assistance that may be necessary …'

While ambition as a cabinetmaker may have been part of the impetus to go to Philadelphia, Affleck had family contacts there as well as newly established Quaker contacts in the Fisher family. The Fishers were prominent there, politically and socially, and members of the Quaker community. Affleck's friendship with them was not fleeting, and he remained a close confidant of theirs for his entire life, even serving as a family guardian.

In November 1763 Joshua Fisher welcomed the Proprietary Governor of Pennsylvania, John Penn, to Philadelphia with a public address. The date of Thomas Fisher's letter (20 July 1763) and Affleck's introduction at the Arch Street Meeting (25 November 1763) suggest that he arrived around the same time as Penn. Hornor's claim that Affleck was on board the same ship as Penn has become tradition over the years but that legend cannot be substantiated and seems implausible. However, less tenuous connections do link Affleck to Governor John Penn and his brother Richard Penn, and these will be discussed later.[8]

When Affleck arrived in Philadelphia, he knew how to navigate through and within the tightly woven networks of cabinetmakers, other woodworkers, Quakers and Scottish émigrés. Affleck was a cousin to John Elsmlie, the prominent Philadelphia turner 'at the Sign of the Screw and Spinning Wheel, near the South End, in Strawberry Alley'. Elmslie had arrived from Aberdeen in 1759. Even though turning was not as lucrative or socially acceptable a trade as cabinetmaking, Elmslie more than eked out a living. As a competent, well-trained young cabinetmaker himself, Affleck would have been able to introduce himself to other tradesmen in need of his skills such as house-builders and master cabinetmakers with whom his cousin may already have forged and established relationships. As his cousin's career progressed, Elmslie received business from Affleck's patrons, and Elmslie provided turned elements for Affleck's furniture. By 1771 Elmslie described his shop as 'in Second Street, near the Bridge', which was close to Affleck's Second Street shop, just below the Bridge. Shop proximity and kinship probably account for Elmslie's receipt of money on Affleck's behalf in September 1773.[9]

The Quaker community, including 'kin' as Affleck called his Scottish relatives, provided a second network for him. The letter of introduction from Thomas Fisher to his father Joshua Fisher described Affleck as a friend of David and John Barclay, important men in the Quaker circles of Aberdeenshire, London, New Jersey and Philadelphia. Affleck's acceptance into the circle of London Quakers immediately endeared him to the extended Fisher family of Philadelphia and to the wider circle of Philadelphia Quakers. Joshua Fisher's youngest son, Miers (1748–1819) became one of Affleck's closest friends. The reference to Affleck being associated with the Barclays in London suggests a connection to the Barclays of Philadelphia and northern New Jersey. A close friendship developed between Affleck and architect Robert Smith (1722–77) of Philadelphia, who was both a Quaker and a native of Scotland. Smith trained as a carpenter but gained experience in Scotland working on the Duchess of Buccleuch's Dalkeith estate. He was encouraged to come to America by Philadelphian William Hamilton and immediately showed an affinity for applying William Adam's designs. Affleck's close and instantaneous working relationship with Smith – preordained through Scottish and Quaker connections – indicates that Affleck was closely aligned to the building trades.

THOMAS AFFLECK

Cabinet-maker

Takes this method to acquaint the public, and particularly those who have been pleased to favour him with their custom, that he has re-moved from his late shop in Union street to Se-cnd-street, a little below the Bridge, and oppo-site Henry Lisle's, where he carries on the cabinet-making business in all its various branches. He takes this opportunity of returning thanks to his customers for their past favours, and assures them that they may depend he will continue to do every thing in his power to give them intire satisfaction.

His standing in the Quaker community offered him extraordinary opportunity as he situated himself as a cabinetmaker in the Philadelphia region.[10]

Affleck also benefited from the connections he made with fellow Scots like Smith and others. In America the Scots' insistence on education furthered their reputation for industriousness. In Philadelphia Affleck became conversant with Scottish merchants, lawyers, real estate speculators and doctors who had already established their fortunes, many of whom were not Quakers. On 30 May 1769, the secretary of the St Andrew's Society of Philadelphia, a charitable organisation of elite men of Scottish extraction, recorded that 'Mr. Thomas Affleck being proposed was unanimously admitted as a Resident member'. At that time, Affleck joined only a small number of tradesmen who were members – the painter Cosimo Alexander, the architect Robert Smith and the printer Daniel Kennedy. Affleck's inclusion shows that he was recognised as a significant enough Scottish émigré to be invited to join the leading social club that offered (and still offers) support to Philadelphia Scots. Affleck's earliest patrons were concentrated among those two groups – the Quakers and the Scots.[11]

All evidence suggests that Affleck worked without a business partner in the 1760s. During that time, Quaker merchant Charles Wharton paid Affleck for cabinetwork in 1766 and listed Affleck as 'of this city Joiner' in his receipt book. He may have worked for other cabinetmakers, such as fellow Quaker Henry Clifton. Or he may have received work through his close friend, the Scottish

Illustration 3.2
Charles Willson Peale, 'Portrait of John and Elizabeth Lloyd Cadwalader and their daughter Anne',
signed beneath table: C W Peale/pinx 1772.
Oil on canvas, 50½ x 41¼ in (1283 x 1048mm).
[Purchased for the Cadwalader Collection with funds contributed by the Mabel Pew Myrin Trust and the gift of an anonymous donor, 1983, Philadelphia Museum of Art]

architect Robert Smith. The only advertisement Affleck ever produced for his cabinetmaking business appeared in *The Pennsylvania Chronicle* in December 1768, which continued to run through to March 1769. It does not enumerate any furniture forms made (or specialised in) by Affleck and it mentions no partners or the dissolution of a partnership; rather, it suggests that he had operated another shop, had received enough patronage to continue in the business, and gives the new address.

The Gordon family

Research now shows that the most important thing Thomas Affleck did for his career as a cabinetmaker was marry the right woman. Isabella Gordon was the daughter of Lewis Gordon (d. 1783), the *prothonotary* of Northampton County, Pennsylvania. As such, he served as the Penn family's financial and legal agent for a lucrative area of their proprietary lands. Thomas and Isabella (1752–82) were married in Easton, Pennsylvania, in late February 1771. Her family's large network and considerable wealth and influence seemingly earned Affleck the credibility and connections he needed to distinguish himself as the premier cabinetmaker of colonial Philadelphia.

Lewis Gordon had arrived in Philadelphia by 1742 and registered ownership of land warrants in Bucks County in 1745. That same year he secured an appointment as clerk to a prominent Philadelphia lawyer, Richard Peters (1704–76). Peters served the Penns as their private councillor, secretary of their land office and secretary of the Provincial Council, which was the executive branch of the colony's government. Gordon probably acquainted himself with Peters, a defrocked priest of the Church of England, through Gordon's brother, John (1717–90). By that time, the Reverend John Gordon was ordained. He became the rector of the largest parish in colonial Maryland, St Anne's Parish in Annapolis, which was that colony's

Illustration 3.3
Charles Willson Peale, 'Portrait of Benjamin Randolph' (1737–92), *c* 1775–80. Watercolour on ivory, 1¼ x 1 in (32 x 25mm). This miniature on ivory is the only known image of the celebrated cabinetmaker Benjamin Randolph (active 1762 to 1785). [Gift of Mr and Mrs Timothy Johnes Westbrook, 1990, Philadelphia Museum of Art]

governmental capital as well as the region's fashion and social capital. In 1749 Maryland Governor Samuel Ogle appointed Reverend Gordon as the rector of St Michael's Parish in Talbot County on Maryland's eastern shore, where the fertile land produced that colony's great wealth and where the most prestigious families maintained large, manorial seats.[12]

In 1747 Lewis Gordon was among the twenty-five gentlemen of Philadelphia who formed the St Andrew's Society of Philadelphia. Gordon married Mary Jenkins (1729–63), the daughter of Philadelphia merchant Aaron Jenkins and his wife Mary Jenkins on 4 January 1750 at Christ Church in Philadelphia. Lewis and Mary Gordon had two daughters, Elizabeth (b. 1750) and Isabella (b. 1752), before moving to Easton in Northampton County in 1752, where they had four sons.[13]

Other Affleck–Gordon ties

How or when Affleck met Lewis Gordon and his daughter Isabella is not known. Isabella Gordon was born a Scottish Episcopalian and raised in wealthy households in Easton, Pennsylvania, and Bordentown, New Jersey, where she lived a privileged life. Affleck may have known of Lewis Gordon and his family while growing up in Aberdeen. Ellon, where Affleck was apprenticed, was one of the seats of the Earls of Aberdeen, Lewis Gordon's family. While Affleck was in London, he was well acquainted with the Barclay family, who were powerful landowners and relatives of the Gordons. In Philadelphia Affleck's friendship with the Fisher family may have put him in contact with Richard Peters, Lewis Gordon's legal instructor and business associate. Another possibility is that Affleck accompanied Robert Smith, his close friend and fellow Scottish Quaker, to Easton when Gordon commissioned Smith in 1765 to design and build the Northampton County Courthouse. Gordon oversaw the entire project. Affleck could also have met Gordon through the St Andrew's Society.[14]

Illustration 3.4
Attributed to Benjamin Randolph, side chair, 1768–9. Mahogany, white cedar 37 x 24¼ x 22½in (940 x 616 x 572mm); Seat: 17¾ x 22 x 19½in (451 x 559 x 495mm). [Gift of the McNeil Americana Collection, 1991, Philadelphia Museum of Art]

The Cadwalader commission

In the autumn of 1770, Thomas Affleck landed the most prestigious cabinetmaking commission in colonial Philadelphia. This was to make the remainder – which added up to more than two dozen pieces of elaborately designed and lavishly carved mahogany furniture for the house of John Cadwalader, a merchant from an old Philadelphia family with Welsh and Quaker roots, and his new wife, the Maryland heiress, Elizabeth Lloyd (illus 3.2). By receiving this commission, Affleck effectively displaced Philadelphia's predominant cabinetmaker Benjamin Randolph (1737–92) who had already made furniture for the Cadwaladers (illus 3.3). Affleck's relationship with the Gordon family explains the Cadwaladers' sudden switch from Randolph to Affleck, a move that has not previously been explained. Randolph, a native of New Jersey and a former Quaker with familial ties to the Gordon

family, had been paid £94 15s for furniture for the Cadwaladers' house before 10 October 1769, when John Cadwalader reimbursed his brother Lambert for this expense. Unfortunately, a description of the furniture is not known. Several scholars have suggested that the £94 15s corresponds not only with the documents but also physically to a pair of straight-railed card tables, and set of saddle-seat, ribbon-back chairs and set of straight-railed, trapezoidal-seat chairs. Furniture attributed to Randolph shows him to be a masterful cabinetmaker in design and execution, employing – and perhaps scouting out and subsidising the careers

Illustration 3.5
Attributed to Benjamin Randolph, side chair, 1768–9. Mahogany, white cedar 38⁷/₁₆ x 23¾ x 21⁵/₈in (977 x 603 x 549mm). Purchased with the Fiske Kimball Fund, the John T Morris Fund and with funds contributed by Marguerite and Gerry Lenfest, The Richard Chilton Foundation, H Richard Dietrich Jr, Robert L McNeil Jr, Fitz Eugene Dixon Jr, Mrs E Newbold Smith, Charlene Sussel, Anne H and Frederick Vogel III, Andrew M Rouse, and Dr and Mrs Robert E Booth, Jr 2003. [Philadelphia Museum of Art]

of – the best London-trained carvers in Philadelphia (illus 3.4, 3.5).

The low back, the intricate ribbon-carved splat, the saddle-shaped seat, the upholstery that extends half-over-the-rail, and the hairy paw feet on the chair seen in illustration 3.4 distinguish it as an extraordinary design, not typical of the Philadelphia canon. It is likely this chair was made after an English prototype inherited by the Cadwaladers from Elizabeth Cadwalader's father, Edward Lloyd III (1711–70) of Maryland. When not in use, the silk seat was protected by a furniture check cover that tied in the back.

The side chair seen in illustration 3.5 was one of a set commissioned by John and Elizabeth Lloyd Cadwalader for their opulent Philadelphia house. Much of their furniture reflected Mrs Cadwalader's preference for the English rococo style. This chair's proportions, the design of the carved splat, and the shape of the seat all adhere to the prevailing Philadelphia style of the mid-eighteenth century, while the hairy paw carved feet and over-the-rail upholstery suggest the special nature of the commission. The chairs had two sets of loose covers – a common cover in 'furniture check' or gingham, and the blue silk cover with long silk fringe reproduced here. In CW Peale's portrait of the Cadwaladers and their daughter, Mrs Cadwalader is seated in one of the chairs from this set; the splat is visible underneath her left arm.

The £180 24s paid to the carver John Pollard, who was a full-time employee in Randolph's shop at that time, suggests that the furniture was ornamented with lavish carving. The frames for the Cadwaladers' marble slabs, which they purchased from C Coxe for £30 during the time Randolph was making them furniture, probably represent solely the art of the London-trained carver, John Pollard, and account for a significant amount of that invoice.[15]

Affleck's commission included two desks, a bed, card tables, a tea table, sofas, an easy chair, fire screens and sundry other furniture for the Cadwaladers' house just before October 1770. The furniture he made closely followed the prevailing (though perhaps *retard à taire*) British aesthetic for baroque furniture in the French, or rococo, taste. Its proportions and excessive carved ornament fundamentally steps outside and beyond the bounds of the more restrained Philadelphia paradigm. The Affleck furniture served as a pendant to the first-rate, London-made 1750s furniture the Cadwaladers had recently inherited from her deceased parents, Edward and Anne Lloyd of Wye House.[16] However, the Cadwaladers were

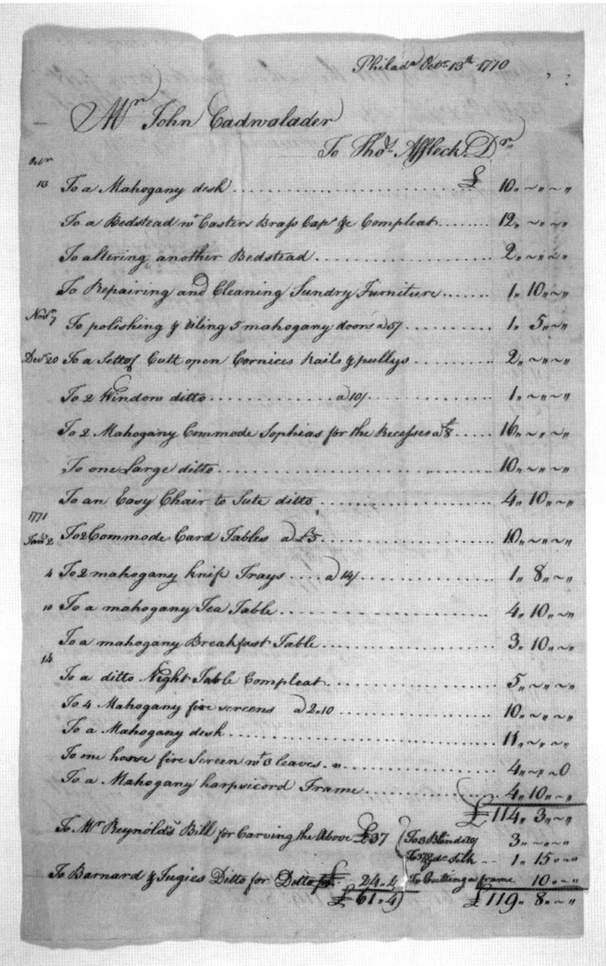

Illustration 3.6
Affleck invoice to John Cadwalader, October 1770.
[Courtesy of the Historical Society of Pennsylvania, Cadwalader Papers]

neither Scottish nor Quaker nor tradesmen – the usual categories for Affleck's patrons. While Affleck's shops – both the old one and the new one advertised in 1768 – were located near their house, strong familial ties through Affleck's wife may link him more securely to the Cadwaladers.

From the time they were married on 25 September 1768 to the late spring of 1770, John and Elizabeth Cadwalader lived at Wye House on the Eastern Shore of Maryland, where they had tended to her ailing parents. After Elizabeth's father urged Cadwalader in June 1769 to set up house in Philadelphia, Cadwalader closed on the house of real estate speculator Samuel Rhoads on Second Street between Spruce and Pine. The house was a

Illustration 3.7
Workshop of Thomas Affleck, card table, 1770–1. Mahogany, yellow pine, yellow poplar, oak, 28⅞ x 39 x 19¾in
(733 x 991 x 502mm). Purchased for the Cadwalader Collection with funds contributed by the Mabel Pew Myrin
Trust and with the gift of an anonymous donor, 1984. [Philadelphia Museum of Art]

commodious pile, and the young, aspiring couple made plans to outfit it in a grand manner befitting their means and taste. Builders promptly stripped the interior down to the walls to ready the structure for a particularly stylish update. By May 1770 all of the best Philadelphia architects, plasterers, painters, carvers, ironworkers and upholsterers had been commissioned to outfit the interiors.[17]

Ultimately, Affleck's connection to the Cadwaladers eclipsed the reputation of his well-established colleague Randolph as Philadelphia's finest cabinetmaker. At the 1768 marriage of John and Elizabeth Cadwalader, the priest who officiated was the

rector of the parish church, called St Michael's Parish, near Wye House, Talbot County, the Reverend John Gordon, the brother of Lewis Gordon and a dynamic man of great local popularity and notoriety. The Lloyds' relationship with Gordon was not perfunctory or cursory. When Elizabeth Lloyd Cadwalader's father, Edward Lloyd III, wrote his will in 1750, twenty years before his death, he stipulated that Gordon be given £50 to buy a suit and, about the 'dear little son', Edward Lloyd IV, that Gordon examine and oversee the child's progress as a person. Though the need for implementing this latter instruction never came to pass, the Lloyds' closeness with Reverend Gordon continued over the years. After the Cadwalader wedding, he officiated at the burials of Elizabeth's parents – Anne Rousby Lloyd on 6 May 1769 and Colonel Edward Lloyd on 1 February 1770. Both were interred in the family's private burial ground in their garden at Wye House. The relationship between the Cadwaladers and the Gordons was so close that it is possible that the Gordons introduced John Cadwalader to Elizabeth Lloyd.[18]

A 1771 letter provides evidence that the Reverend Gordon and his wife Sarah continued the friendship after the Cadwaladers moved to Philadelphia in late 1770. Returning from Easton to Philadelphia, Thomas Gordon, a brother of Isabella Gordon Affleck, brought a letter of greeting from the Gordons to the Cadwaladers. Taking advantage of the 'free postage' to have their nephew Thomas deliver the letter directly to the Cadwaladers, the tone of Reverend Gordon's letter is chatty, noting that he is pleased to have heard from Mrs Cadwalader's brother, Richard Bennett Lloyd, that they are in good health.

John and Sarah Gordon also left records that establish their friendship with their niece, the wife of Thomas Affleck. When Sarah Gordon died in 1774, she had only been married to Reverend Gordon for seven years. Sarah owned only one asset, the slaves who in the eighteenth-century agricultural economy were chattel. She gave ten slaves whom she listed by name, age and skill to her daughter by her first marriage. The next named beneficiary is her niece 'Isabella the wife of Thomas Affleck Cabinet Maker in Philadelphia one Negro child named Cato ...'[19]

In Philadelphia the Cadwalders became re-engaged in directing the outfitting and furnishing of their house and awarded the lion's share of the furniture commission to Thomas Affleck. The sudden transfer of the furniture commission from Randolph

Illustration 3.8
Made by the workshop of Thomas Affleck. Carving attributed to Nicholas Bernard and Martin Jugiez. Easy chair, 1770–1. Mahogany, yellow pine, white oak, white cedar, black walnut, tulip poplar, 46 x 36½ x 34in (1168 x 927 x 864mm). [Gift of H Richard Dietrich Jr, 2001, Philadelphia Museum of Art]

to Affleck suggests that the Gordons recommended Thomas Affleck as a cabinetmaker for the house of his friends, the Cadwaladers. After this commission was completed Thomas Affleck (then aged thirty-one) married Isabella Gordon (aged nineteen) in Easton, Pennsylvania, in February 1771. While, conversely, it could be suggested that Affleck met Isabella Gordon through the Cadwaladers, the numerous intersections between Affleck and the Gordons support the chronology that Affleck met the Cadwaladers through the Gordons and not vice versa.[20]

Affleck's invoice to the Cadwaladers is dated 13 October 1770 and outlines the work he performed from then to January 1771 (illus 3.6). Based on the invoices of carvers, upholsterers and other craftsmen, this period represents the peak moment for work on the Cadwaladers' interiors, moveable furniture and fittings. Gregorian names of the months rather than the expected Quaker numeric references appears on this Affleck invoice and others, including that of Quaker James Pemberton. Affleck's hand is elegant, steady, even – a style called 'copperplate'; the idea being that he learned to write by copying letters from a copperplate print.

In October and November Affleck put up beds, repaired and cleaned furniture, and oiled mahogany doors. By December he completed the frames for the upholstered furniture – the bed cornices, the window cornices, two large mahogany commode sofas for the recesses, the single large commode sofa, and the easy chair. Finally, in January, he delivered the remainder of the furniture, including a mahogany tea table, a mahogany night table and breakfast table, four fire screens, a horse fire screen, a mahogany desk, a mahogany harpsichord frame and a pair of commode card tables (illus 3.7). (These exceptional card or gaming tables – with their strong curves, sharp knee angles and hairy paw feet – appear on the invoice to John Cadwalader from Affleck dated 13 October 1770: 'commode card tables @ £5 … £10'. One of the pair is on loan to the Philadelphia Museum of Art.) The pace and ordering pattern suited the needs of the other craftsmen, such as the carvers and upholsterers who had to embellish it.

Noted on the invoice is the work of London-trained carvers James Reynolds, Nicolas Bernard and Martin Jugiez. It is unusual to see the names of the carvers on an invoice, and it is unique among Affleck's surviving receipts. In London and Edinburgh, designers included the names of their craftsmen but rarely did the craftsman include names of carvers or ornamenters. While competition among cabinetmakers was steep, especially without the type of protective guild system with which Affleck would have been familiar, the number of carvers capable of executing material at this level in Philadelphia was limited.[21]

Here, Reynolds charged £37 and Martin and Jugiez charged just over £24, all for 'carving the above' furniture. This included the easy chair seen in illustration 3.8, part of a suite of furniture for their Second Street house in Philadelphia. With its curved rails, sharply angled knees, hairy paws and

sensuous carved ornament, it closely corresponds to the other pieces of Cadwalader furniture in the Museum's collection. The upholstery and trim was a lavish display of wealth and taste. Affleck presented the cost of the carving but did not add their totals to his, suggesting that the carvers were paid directly by Cadwalader. Such an arrangement makes sense, given that the carver also worked on the architectural fixtures of the house. The carving firm of Bernard and Jugiez submitted an invoice for £28 for work completed from October 1770, which covered the carving of pilasters, trusses, leaf grass, ribbons, flowers and other small details of the architectural ornament. The enormous expense for the work of James Reynolds, which came in at over £175, covered carved and gilded frames for pier and oval glasses,

Illustration 3.9
Attributed to Thomas Affleck, possibly carved by the shop of James Reynolds, side chair, 1763–72. Mahogany, white cedar, cherry. [Gift of Mrs William Macpherson Hornor, 1946, Philadelphia Museum of Art]

Illustration 3.10
Chest on chest, Thomas Affleck, *c* 1775. Mahogany, tulip poplar and white cedar. Mr and Mrs Lewis B Rumford II.
[Courtesy of the Colonial Williamsburg Foundation]

a dressing glass, a picture frame and over 500 yards of elaborate scrolls – Palmyra and Leaf and Reed. A side chair with a sophisticated splat design which is almost mannerist in its origins is not repeated on any other chair splats made in Philadelphia (illus 3.9). This chair descended in the family of Miers Fisher (1748–1819) and his wife Sarah Redwood Fisher. The Fishers were the Afflecks' closest friends. Reynolds also carved frames for Charles Wilson Peale's series of Cadwalader family portraits, on which the scrolls and flourishes were sadly cut off in the nineteenth century. Affleck's employ of these two carving firms suggests that he was working within a known set of specialist carvers working simultaneously on the interiors and that of the carved furniture, which must have corresponded seamlessly with the architectural ornament. For the Cadwaladers, this was ideal – an assurance of having a truly carved room. What does not appear on Affleck's invoice is the upholstery work; for that, Cadwalader hired Plunkett Fleeson and the London-trained John Webster. Affleck's easy chair, two small sofas and one large sofa, and several of the beds are easily discernible on both Webster's and Fleeson's invoices.[22]

The Cadwalader commission marked a watershed moment in Affleck's cabinetmaking career. The elaborate furniture displayed a rococo aesthetic fashionable in 1750s and 1760s London when Affleck was training and working there. As the Cadwaladers began to entertain, their furniture was admired by the many guests and dignitaries who called on them, including Silas Deane, the Connecticut delegate to the Continental Congress, who famously remarked that he 'dined yesterday with Mr. Cadwallader, whose furniture and house exceeds anything I have seen in this city or elsewhere'.

Other notable commissions

During the decades of the 1770s, 1780s and 1790s, Affleck remained at the forefront of the furniture-making world in Philadelphia and became a leading citizen. In 1775 he made £117 worth of furniture for James Pemberton, including an upholstered easy chair and two elbow chairs.

David Deshler of Germantown paid Thomas Affleck £108 13s in May 1775. Though furniture is not enumerated on the receipt, a monumental chest-on-chest that descended through Deshler's family is firmly linked to this receipt (illus 3.10). Inscriptions inside the case beginning in 1814 record the chest's

Illustration 3.11
Attributed to Thomas Affleck, carving attributed to Nicholas Bernard and Martin Jugiez, armchair, 1765–70. Mahogany, oak, 40½ x 28¾ x 28½in (1029 x 730 x 724mm); Seat: 15¾ x 27¾ x 23⅝in (400 x 705 x 600mm). [On loan from the Commissioners of Fairmount Park, Ryerss Museum, Burlholme Park, Philadelphia, Philadelphia Museum of Art]

descent through the Deshler family until it was given to the Colonial Williamsburg Foundation in 1983. It is solidly constructed and elegantly proportioned, and while it is especially notable as among the most London-inspired of Philadelphia chests-on-chests, elements of it follow a Philadelphia paradigm and show Affleck working confidently on a familiar type which had taken the place of the high chest, outmoded in Britain by the 1750s.

The set of French or elbow chairs (presently numbered at thirteen) that scholars have attributed to Thomas Affleck because of their association with the Penns presents a quandary (illus 3.11). Benjamin Chew and others acquired them in sets of two after 1771, the year that Governor John Penn (1725–95) returned to London. These armchairs conform in design, proportion and construction to London-made examples of their time; the dispersal two by two of the elbow chairs to people close to Penn helps tie them together. However, the connection between Penn

Illustration 3.12a
Attributed to Thomas Affleck, sofa, 1768. Mahogany, oak, yellow pine; mattress insert: woven wire, 38 x 95 x 37in
(965 x 2413 x 940mm). [Gift of Mr and Mrs James Wood, 2006, Philadelphia Museum of Art]

Illustration 3.12b
Detail of the original yellow Moreen upholstery

and Affleck is beyond what Hornor conjectured (or perhaps conjured); the relationship between Affleck and Penn probably rested in his close friendships with Gordon (Penn's prothonotary), in Joshua Fisher, or in Benjamin Chew, himself a Quaker with close Lloyd-family connections.[23]

Quaker merchant Levi Hollingsworth (1739–1824) purchased furniture from Affleck beginning in the late 1760s and through the 1780s. This is often not enumerated in the accounts, though furniture that descended from him is often attributed to Affleck based on the payments. Two high chests, two dressing tables, chairs, a tea table and a sofa survive from the Hollingsworth set. Remarkably, the sofa survives with a considerable amount of its original upholstery and the obverse of the crest rail is marked 'Mr. Hollingsworth' in an elegant, self-assured script (illus 3.12, 3.12a). The hand is closely related to Affleck's and, combined with Hollingsworth's unwavering patronage, helps to strongly attribute the sofa to Affleck.

Exile

Along with a group of leading Philadelphia Quakers, Thomas Affleck was exiled to Virginia for a period of nine months from 9 September 1777 to May 1778. The *Pennsylvania Gazette* accused them of 'unpatriotic behavior' and described them as men who 'have uniformly manifested by their general conduct and conversation a disposition highly inimical to the cause of America'. But this had more to do with Quaker nonconformism than support for Britain and King George III. Affleck would neither pick up arms against the British nor support the cause by paying a tax. The names were listed in the following order:

James Pemberton, Henry Drinker, Israel Pemberton, John Pemberton, Samuel Pleasants, Thomas Wharton, Senator Thomas Fisher, son of Joshua, Samuel Fisher, son of Joshua, Myers Fisher, Elijah Brown, John Hunt, Phineas Bond, Rev. Thomas Coombe, Charles Jervis, William Drewett Smith, Charles Eddy, Thomas Pike, Owen Jones, Jun, Edward Pennington, William Smith, Owen Gilpin and Thomas Affleck.

Affleck was among only three tradesmen (Thomas Pike was a dancing instructor and Charles Jervis was a hatter) in a list of merchants and politicians with long-standing prominence in Philadelphia. Though it is not known who selected the names and no reasons were stated, the announcement by the Council was political muscle-flexing to encourage other Philadelphians to

support the cause for independence. That Affleck was included, places him among the most stalwart members of Philadelphia's Quaker community. Though well respected on his own, Affleck was also the son-in-law of Lewis Gordon, well known to be loyal to King George III after having served him and the Penns for so many years. Gordon held out his loyalty to the Crown until the last possible minute – his deathbed in April 1778, an act many historians believe was insincere and done to protect his estate in Northampton County from being confiscated by the rebelling Americans. That date coincides with Affleck's return from exile.[24]

In her diary Elizabeth Drinker Biddle recorded with poignancy Affleck's personal trials while he was imprisoned in a still extant house near the Quaker burial ground on Apple Pie Ridge Road just outside Winchester. The Quaker community there welcomed 'Tommy Afflick', as she described him, particularly members of his kin. These included the clockmaker

Illustration 3.13
Thomas Affleck, armchair for the United States Senate, 1790–3. Mahogany, oak, 34¼ x 24 x 24in (870 x 610 x 610mm), seat: 15 x 24 x 19½in (381 x 610 x 495mm). [Gift of Henry P McIlhenny, 1977, Philadelphia Museum of Art]

JUST PUBLISHED,

[NUMBER I. Price FIVE SHILLINGS]

Containing Ten Copper-Plates, with Explanations in Letter-Press, to be continued Monthly, and published, on the first Wednesday of each Month, until the Whole of the 120 Designs are compleated.

A

COLLECTION

OF

DESIGNS

IN

ARCHITECTURE,

CONTAINING

New PLANS and ELEVATIONS of HOUSES,

FOR GENERAL USE.

WITH

A great Variety of Sections of ROOMS; from a common Room, to the most grand and magnificent.

THEIR

DECORATIONS, viz. Bases, Surbases, Architraves, Freezes, and Cornices, properly inriched with Foliages, Frets and Flowers, in a new and grand TASTE.

WITH

Margins and Mouldings for the PANELLING.

All large enough for Practice.

To which are added,

Curious Designs of Stone and Timber Bridges,

Extending from 20 Feet to 220, in one Arch.

Likewise some SCREENS and PAVILIONS.

IN TWO FOLIO VOLUMES.

Each containing Sixty PLATES, curiously engraved on COPPER.

Designed, by ABRAHAM SWAN, Architect:

And Engraved, by JOHN NORMAN.

An Engraving of the New Goal, of Philadelphia, and another of the Carpenter's Hall, both elegant Modern Buildings, will be given gratis, to the Subscribers, in the Twelfth and last Number.

N B. Subscriptions for this Work, are received by Robert Bell, Printer and Bookseller, next Door to St. Paul's Church, in Third-Street, Philadelphia.

Goldsmith Chandlee, the son of Mary Hallowell, who was a cousin of Mary Hallowell Elmslie (1728–91), the wife of Affleck's cousin, the turner John Elmslie. Affleck was also well connected to Sarah Zane of Winchester, whose sister Hannah was married to John Pemberton.

While in Winchester Affleck was able to further the iron forge business of his brother-in-law James Taylor. Taylor was an attorney who was married to Elizabeth Gordon and the son of George Taylor, Signer of the Declaration of Independence. The Taylor family owned and operated a prominent Philadelphia iron furnace and through Affleck established ties with the Quakers in Winchester. After his return to Philadelphia, the Continental Congress hired Affleck to outfit their chambers. In late 1790, when President Washington and the Congress moved to Philadelphia, they legislated the policies of the newly formed government from Congress Hall in Philadelphia. Affleck may have had a strong hand in the design of those chambers and is documented as having made the armchairs for the Senate Chamber in Philadelphia (illus 3.13). He received the commission to make the tables and chairs for the United States legislatures in the city, chosen as the first capital of the United States and remaining so for ten years, as put forth in the Residence Act of 1790. While often viewed as unexciting and mundane, such a public commission allowed Affleck the opportunity to fashion the visual language of the young government, and thus the nation.

In 1784 the noted Scottish bookseller and friend of Affleck, Robert Bell, died. Affleck was a co-executor of his estate with Francis Bailey, originally of Lancaster, Pennsylvania, and the founder and publisher of the *Freeman's Journal*. Bell was arguably the most important bookseller in colonial and early national America. He supplied books (mainly British) to dealers in every urban centre in colonial America. Affleck's friendship with Bell would have put him at the forefront of every popular literary phenomenon in Philadelphia and put him in contact with learned people and those

who had mercantile ties. One title they sold off in the Affleck estate sale is particularly noteworthy, Swan's *British Architect* (illus 3.14). American patrons, architects, house-builders and carvers drew inspiration for architectural treatments, frets and carved ornaments from Swan's designs. The two arts – architecture and furniture – benefited from overlapping fashions and techniques in the trade of an eighteenth-century cabinetmaker.

Affleck died on 5 March 1795 'after a severe and tedious illness, which he bore with Christian fortitude and resignation … [he was] in the fifty fifth year of his life'. Of significance, Affleck's will made absolutely no mention of the succession of his shop or cabinetmaking business. It is a fairly short, uncomplicated document, much of it urging a fair course of action by his eldest son, Lewis Gordon Affleck, as he manoeuvred the ongoing affairs of his father-in-law's and wife's estate. (See Appendix 1.) The personages mentioned in the will are 'my cousin' Barbara Evans and her husband ('my kinsman') John Evans, 'my friend' Owen Jones, 'my kinsman' John Elmslie Junior (son of his cousin John Elmslie, the turner), 'my friends' Sarah Redwood Fisher and Miers Fisher.[25]

The nature of Affleck's shop is revealed only through his inventory, taken by cabinetmaker Daniel Trotter and merchant William Rigby and dated 1796. (See Appendix 2.) The inventory opens with the back best parlour furnished as a dining-room and parlour – it held the clock and case (£13), eight chairs (two of them arms), a gilt frame looking-glass, four pictures and a family picture. The parlour had two closets with crockery, shaving utensils, a spy glass, a chamber organ and backgammon board and sundry smalls. The kitchen was stocked with furniture and cooking equipment. Upstairs, there were several bed chambers. The one with the most valuable bedstead (£11 5s) had a mahogany double chest of drawers (or chest on chest) and a desk and book case. The books were valued together at £22. Separately valued were the following two books: *An Atlas* at £2 5s and *Shippendale's Designs* [*sic*] at £1. A fine, 'homely' house, and not extravagant in any way – no china (porcelain) or wrought silver.

According to the probate inventory, Affleck's shop was a place of active cabinetmaking at the time of his death. A pair of square bureaus remained unfinished and more than ten other pieces of furniture were completed and ready for sale. The cabinetmaking business dominated his house. There was a shop where the furniture was made, a wareroom, probably facing the street (Elmslie's Alley) where furniture was

Illustration 3.14
Advertisement for Abraham Swan's *A Collection of Designs in Architecture* first published by Robert Bell in Philadelphia, 1775. *The Freeman's Journal* or *North American Intelligencer*, 16 March 1785, vol IV, issue CCIV. Published by Mr Francis Bailey, one of Robert Bell's executors, and a close friend of Thomas Affleck. [Courtesy Avery Architectural and Fine Arts Library, Columbia University]

showcased, and a shed in the yard for storage. Given the six workbenches, the shop had room for six to ten cabinetmakers to work there. Though many contend that late eighteenth-century cabinetmakers did not maintain stocks of timber, this one did. He owned an extraordinary 5,443 feet of mahogany at 8/yd £192 15s 6½d (over a mile of mahogany board!). Such a quantity of timber suggests he was supplying it to fellow cabinetmakers.

Thomas Affleck of Aberdeen, Scotland, arrived in Philadelphia in 1763 with a solid education, a sound moral compass guided by the principles of his Quaker beliefs, and good hand skills in the art of cabinetmaking. He still identified himself as 'of Aberdeen in Scotland' more than three decades after leaving there. He spun his talent as a cabinetmaker and his familial and social connections into a prosperous career in a burgeoning young American city. An intensive study of his furniture (now in progress) will hopefully identify the idiosyncrasies of his art.

Acknowledgements

For assistance with this study, the author thanks the late Robert L McNeil Jr of Barra, David deMuzio, Nan Goff, L W S Petznick, George and Marjorie Haggarty, Sheila Forbes, David Jones, Stephen Jackson, Roger Kirtley, Robert F Trent, Tom Savage, Jeanne Solensky, Jean Russo, Jim Gergat, Tara Chicurda, the staffs of the Guildhall Library, London, the London Metropolitan Archives, the National Archives at Kew, the National Archives of Scotland, the Winterthur Library and the Philadelphia Museum of Art Library.

Notes

1 His father, also named Thomas Affleck, was a Quaker and was listed in the Quaker records as a tobacconist. He and his first wife Lilias had three children before she died in 1724. Thomas Affleck Sr married Jane Elmslie, another Quaker, in 1725. The Elmslie family was of English extraction but had settled in the central Highland town of Kinmuck, where the Scottish Society of Friends (Quakers) was founded. As a tobacconist, Affleck's father was at the forefront of trade in Aberdeen. The tobacco trade put him in close contact with Glaswegian merchants who traded with colonial America, which was the source of Scotland's tobacco. See Beatrice B Garvan, 'Thomas Affleck', *in Philadelphia: Three Centuries of American Art* (Philadelphia: Philadelphia Museum of Art, 1976). The Quaker records for Aberdeen were transcribed in the early 1970s by A Strath Maxwell, a volunteer. For a bibliography of Quakers in Scotland, see Paul F Burton, 'Quakers and Quakerism in Scotland: A Bibliography' at http://personal.cis.strath.ac.uk/~paulfb/ScotBibl.htm. The author is grateful to George Haggarty for sharing this link with her.

2 The Seven Incorporated Trades of Aberdeen are the Weavers (founded before 1222), Bakers (1398), Shoemakers (1484 and 1520), Tailors (1511), Hammermen (1519), Wrights and Coopers (1527) and Fleshers (1534). Still in existence, their meeting building is Trinity Hall on Holborn Street in Aberdeen. See Janet Brinsden, 'Furniture Makers in Eighteenth Century Aberdeen: An Introduction', *Regional Furniture: The Journal of the Regional Furniture Society* (ed) David Jones, vol XVIII (2004): 38, 45. E-mail with author, 25 September 2009.

3 *Index of Apprentices of Great Britain*, Guildhall Library, London. Index to Apprenticeship Records of Great Britain, 1710–82; vol 25486, Inland Revenue Department, vol 52, 46 reads '1754. Affleck, Thos. to Alex. Rose of Ellon, Scotland, cabinetmaker. £8'. An additional notation dated 13 May 1759, records another £2 paid. Affleck's apprenticeship with Rose was first published in 1989 by Morrison Heckscher in 'Philadelphia Furniture, 1760–1790: Native-Born and London-Trained Craftsmen', *in The American Craftsmen and the European Tradition, 1620–1820*, (ed) Francis J Puig and Michael Conforti (University Press of New England, Hanover, NH, for the Minneapolis Institute of Arts, 1989): 95. The source was not cited in that publication or by Deborah Anne Federhen in 'Politics and Style: An Analysis of the Patrons and Products of Jonathan Gostelowe and Thomas Affleck', *in Shaping a National Culture: The Philadelphia Experience, 1750–1800*, (ed) Catherine E Hutchins (Winterthur, Delaware: Winterthur Museum, 1994): 294. Both Mr Heckscher and this author located the apprenticeship information from the same British apprenticeship records.

4 See Dennison, P E, Lynch, M and Ditchburn, D 2002 *Aberdeen Before 1800: A New History*. East Linton: Tuckwell Press, 153.

5 The National Library of Scotland, *Aberdeen Journal*, 10 April 1759. The author thanks Sheila Forbes of Edinburgh, Scotland, for finding this advertisement.

6 Brinsden, 47, 48 (Appendix). The wrights who advertised in these cities are Piper, Oughton, Dott in Banff; Duffus in Cullen and Monro in Inverness. The National Library of Scotland, *Aberdeen Journal*, 5 June 1769; and 18 April 1774. The author thanks Sheila Forbes of Edinburgh, for finding this advertisement.

7 Guildhall Library, MSS 8051/5 Freedoms 1750–1804. London was Aberdeen's most active trade partner and the majority of ships were bound for London. See also Chalmers, K 1994 'The lives of the Scottish subscribers to Thomas Chippendale's 1754 edition of *The Director*', MA thesis, University of St Andrews, 1994, 14.

8 Joshua Fisher (1707–83) was a native of Sussex, Delaware, and self-trained as a surveyor. In the 1730s and 1740s, he surveyed the region's waterways and the three lower

counties of Pennsylvania – New Castle, Kent and Sussex – which eventually seceded from Pennsylvania to form the colony of Delaware. Once in Philadelphia in the 1750s, Fisher pleaded with the Penns to publish his charts, corresponding with the Proprietors through their attorney Richard Peters. Fisher simultaneously established a thriving merchant house called Joshua Fisher & Sons in Philadelphia by 1753 that supported him and his sons (Samuel, Thomas and Miers) well for several decades. See Peter J Parker, 'Joshua Fisher', *in Philadelphia: Three Centuries of American Art* (Philadelphia: Philadelphia Museum of Art, 1976): 125. Lawrence C Roth, 'Chart of Delaware Bay and River', *Pennsylvania Magazine of History and Biography* vol 74 (1950): 95–9. Historical Society of Pennsylvania, William Logan Fox Papers, Thomas Fisher Diary, 1763, 171.

9 *The Pennsylvania Gazette*, 10 January 1765. Elmslie had moved to Second Street below the bridge by 1771, when he advertised a stray brindle and white cow in *The Pennsylvania Gazette*, 31 January 1771, . This is close to Affleck's shop. Elmslie received a payment from John Dickinson for Thomas Affleck in 1773. See Logan Papers, vol XLI, Dickinson Papers Estate of William Hicks, #379, Folder 42.

10 See Charles E Peterson, *Robert Smith: Architect, Builder, Patriot 1722–1777* (Philadelphia: The Athenaeum of Philadelphia, 2000): 21. See also Isabella Affleck's will.

11 Brock, W R 1982 *Scotus Americanus: A Survey of the Sources for Links between Scotland and America in the Eighteenth Century*, Edinburgh University Press, 17, 111–18, 182–3, 216–17. See *An Historical Catalogue of The St. Andrew's Society of Philadelphia, 1749–1896* (Philadelphia: Printed for The Society, 1896).

12 In the 1750s, Peters' work on behalf of the Penns was extensive and autocratic. He gauged the political pulse of the people settling in their lands. Naturally, the Quakers' inclusive manner and existence contradicted this type of government, and Peters reported this to the disavowed Penns. Along with James Hamilton, William Allen, William Plumstead and others, the Pennsylvania government was forced to radically alter their proprietary government to be in accordance with the classless democracy for which the Quaker-German alliance lobbied. During this ideological contest for political control, Peters maintained a close correspondence with Joshua Fisher. Fisher advocated for the more egalitarian style of government preferred by the Quakers, who had befriended the Germans and now represented their interests. Fisher's initial and continued promotion of Affleck as a citizen and cabinetmaker beginning in 1763 could also have placed Affleck in the position to meet noteworthy Philadelphians like Gordon, Peters and Penn. Francis S Fox, *Sweet Land of Liberty: The Ordeal of the American Revolution in Northampton County, Pennsylvania* (University Park, Pennsylvania: Pennsylvania State University Press, 2000): 37. See http://www.archives.upenn.edu/people/1700s/peters_rich_rev.html. Herman Wellenreuther, 'The Quest for Harmony in a Turbulent World', *in Pennsylvania Magazine of History and Biography*, vol 107 (October 1983): 552–9. Affleck witnessed Fisher's will in 1782. City of Philadelphia, S.222, Will of Joshua Fisher, written 4 mo. 24, 1782 (proven 7 March 1783). Mary M Starin, 'The Reverend Doctor John Gordon, 1717–1790', *Maryland Historical Magazine* vol 75, No 3 (September 1980): 170–4.

13 The Gordons' four sons were John (b. 1755 at Easton), Aaron (b. 1757 at Bordentown), Thomas [William?] (b. 1760 at Bordentown), and George Alexander (b. 1762 at Easton). Lewis Gordon was the first man to pass the bar in Northampton County and, accordingly, is considered the Father of the Northampton legal system. After witnessing a horrific Indian massacre at a Moravian mission called Gnadenhuetten in 1755, Gordon feared for his family's lives. He removed them to Bordentown, New Jersey, and gained admittance to the bar and advertised himself as a lawyer in April 1756. In New Jersey, Gordon connected with Gordon cousins, who were related through marriage to the Quaker Barclay family. Gordon served as the secretary of the St Andrew's Society and dined monthly with the colony's Governor Hamilton in Philadelphia at the Philadelphia meetings. By 1758, Gordon had been named prothonotary, a prominent position in which he acted on behalf of the Penns, and so the family returned to Easton.

14 Peterson, 95–7, 'A summer Jaunt in 1773', *Pennsylvania Magazine of History and Biography* vol 10 (1886): 208.

15 See Beckerdite and Graves, *American Furniture* (2000): 153–61. See Andrew Brunk, 'Benjamin Randolph Revisited', *American Furniture* (2007): 30–8. When the Cadwaladers sent their chairs to the upholsterers, they numbered 76. This is more than the Cadwaladers inherited from her parents and probably represents the Philadelphia-made chairs designed after her family's London chairs. See Alexandra Alevizatos Kirtley, 'Survival of the Fittest: The Lloyd Family's Furniture Legacy', *American Furniture* (2002): 10–11. For the importance of the carver's art, see Beckerdite and Miller, 'A Table's Tale: Craft, Art, and Opportunity in Eighteenth-Century Philadelphia', *American Furniture* (2004): 2–45.

16 See Kirtley, 1–53.

17 For the most comprehensive overview of the building of the Cadwaladers' house, see Nicholas Biddle Wainwright, *Colonial Grandeur in Philadelphia: The House and Furniture of General John Cadwalader* (Philadelphia: The Historical Society of Pennsylvania, 1964). For reference to letter, see page 3. The Cadwaladers owned Shrewsbury Farm near Galena, Maryland, on the Sassafras River near Delaware. For comparative purposes, it is interesting to note that in Annapolis at exactly the same time (1770), Mrs Cadwalader's younger brother, Edward Lloyd IV (1744–96), and his wife Elizabeth Taylor Lloyd, were building and outfitting their three-storey, five-bay house in Annapolis, which, unlike the Cadwaladers' house, survives.

18 Starin, pages 170, 174. The will reads 'in the meantime, and until he arrives to the said age of twelve years, I

desire my Worthy Friend The Rev'd Mr. John Gordon to, as often as he sees him [EL IV], to examine the Child, and Observe the progress he makes in Learning, and to report his thoughts to my executors, and advise them what may be best for the Child's Benefit. And it is my Express Will and request that they do pay due Defference to his opinion, and follow the Advice he may give. Item, I Give and Bequeath unto the said Mr. John Gordon Fifty Pounds Sterling, which he will be pleased to accept, and lay out in a Suit of Mourning, and such other things as he may be most Suitable to his fancy to be worn in remembrance of me.' See The Maryland Historical Society, The Lloyd Papers, MS 2001, reel 41.

19 Maryland Prerogative Court, Wills 1774–5, vol 40, 76, written 26 July 1773. It is not known what became of Cato; however, a slave would certainly have been an unwelcome inheritance for a Quaker. There are no references to him in the Quaker records and therefore, they probably manumitted him. The only two other beneficiaries for Sarah Gordon were two of Isabella Affleck's brothers, John and Thomas, who also inherited one slave each.

20 When Affleck married Isabella Gordon in Easton in late February 1771, it represented a major transgression of his Quaker bonds. He was read out of his Quaker meeting for it, but after confessing twice, was reinstated. See Garfinkel, S 2003 'Quakers and high chests: the plainness problem reconsidered', *in* Lapansky, E J and Verplanck, A A, *Quaker Aesthetics: Reflections on a Quaker Ethic in American Design and Consumption*, Philadelphia: University of Pennsylvania Press, 58.

21 Discussions with Scottish art historians Stephen Jackson, Simon Gilmour, George Haggarty, Ware Petznick and David Jones, Scotland, August, 2009.

22 See Wainwright, 40–1, 43, 51, 64.

23 Benjamin Chew of Cliveden, in Germantown was born in Maryland and studied law at the Inns of Court in London and returned to Philadelphia where he eventually became the Chief Justice of the Supreme Court of the Province of Pennsylvania until 1777. Chew was married to — Bordley, a native of Easton who knew the Revd John Gordon well. Chew purchased the Fourth Street, Philadelphia, house of John Penn for £5,000, a high cost that was, for many years, thought to have included the furnishings, including this sofa and a set of back stools. However, this story has been questioned, and in my opinion rightly so. That the upholstered furniture was probably made by Affleck, however, still stands in my opinion. Chew, like Affleck, was a Quaker, though Chew became an Anglican. Both men were expelled from Philadelphia during the same period of time for their possible loyalty to the Crown. This set of furniture is guilty of being made by Affleck until proven otherwise.

24 See Robert F Oaks, 'Philadelphians in exile', *Pennsylvania Magazine of History and Biography*, vol 96, 298–323. See Fox, *Sweet Land of Liberty*, 50. Fellow exile Owen Jones is mentioned in Affleck's will.

25 Thomas Affleck strongly desired the fair recompense of Affleck's children as equal beneficiaries in the sizeable estate. That would have refuted Lewis Gordon's will, which instructed that Lewis Gordon Affleck received double what his siblings inherited. By the time of Affleck's death, the estate of Lewis Gordon had been in probate for over fifteen years.

Appendices

I. Affleck's Will

Will 144 … 1795
Be it remembered that I Thomas Affleck heretofore of Aberdeen in
Scotland Son of Thomas Affleck late of Aberdeen dfs^d Merchant &
Jane Elmslie his Wife, now of the city of Philadelphia Cabinet Maker
Being mindfull of the uncertainty of the time of my Death & being
Favored with a well disposing Mind Do make and declare my Testament
& last Will in Manner & Form following that is to say

Whereas my late father in law Lewis Gordon Esquire by his Testa-
Ment & last Will devised his Estate to be equally divided among
His five children whereby my late beloved Wife Isabella his Daughter became entitled to one equal fifth part thereof; and she dying I am advised that
my eldest Son Lewis Affleck will be entitled to a double
Portion of his said Mothers Real Estate; but my Intention is that my children should take equal Proportions of all & Whatsoever belonged to myself & my said beloved wife as if the same were one aggregate Estate;

I do therefore hereby declare that the Devise hereinafter contained is upon the exprefs Condition as to my eldest Son that he renounce the double Portion to him belonging of his Mothers Estate and take but an equal
Share with his Brother and Sisters; & Should he refuse so to do the Difference is to be made up to with my other Children by deducting an equal Amount from his Share in their Favor so as to reduce them all to an exact Equality in both Estates – And my will is that whatsoever Sums I have
heretofore advanced for my said eldest Son or shall hereafter advance for him
or either of my other Children and which shall be found charged to
him or them respectively in my Books shall be considered as & for Part of
his or their Respective equal Shares of the said Estates & shall be accordingly deducted from his or their Portions thereof

I give and bequeath to my beloved Sons Lewis G. Affleck & William Affleck all my
Wearing Apparel of every kind to be divided between them by my Executors in such
Manner as will be most usefull for their own Use & Wear having regard as near
Ly as they can to equality in Value, but without being obliged to tender an Acc-
ount of the Distribution

I give & Bequeath to my beloved Daughters Mary and Margaret all the Wearing
Apparel late their Mothers and all her Rings, Trinkets, & Paraphunalia
to be equally divided between them by my Cousin Barbara Evans & my Friend Sarah Redwood Fisher according to their best Direction without any
account there to be tendered –

I authorize & impower my Executors hereinafter named & the Survivors & Survivors of them to Sell & dispose of all my Real Estate whatsoever & wheresoever for such reasonable Prices as can be obtained & to Receive the
Purchase Monies & relieve the Purchases therefrom & to place the
Fame at Interest for the Benefit and at the Risk of my Devises herein-after named &
to make & to execute good & perfect Deeds for the same ves-
tıng the same titles thereof in the Purchaser or Purchasers thereof in Fee
Simple and in the mean time to enter into & take Possession thereof & demise
the same for Life, Years or at Will in such Manner & Form as they shall think most beneficial to my said beloved Children

All the Rest Residue & Remainder of my Estate Real, Personal & mixed
Whatsoever & wheresoever which I have Power to dispose of I give devise &
bequeath to my beloved Children Lewis G. Affleck, Mary Affleck, Margaret Affleck & William Affleck and their Heirs Executors Administr
ators & Afsigns to be equally divided between them as Tenants in Common
_____________________________ [illegible] mentions as to my eldest Son, but if
either of them should die under age, unmarried, without issue, the share
of him or her so dying to be equally divided among Survivors –
I do revoke all former & other Wills by me at any time heretofore made
I do declare this only to be my Testament & last Will thereof I do constit-
Ute & appoint my Kinsman John Evans of this City Hatter & John Elmslie
Junr Merchant with my Friend Owen Jones Junr Executors thereof & I do Req –
uest my Friend Meirs Fisher to assist them with his advice in whatever

may occur in the Execution thereof, as having consulted him in drawing
as he may be the best able to explain any doubtful expressions used in con
veying my meaning

    In Witness whereof I have hereunto set my Hand and
Seal this 7th day of September in the year
Of our Lord One Thousand Seven Hundred
& Ninety Three

Signd Seald & Publishd as
& for his last Will & Testament
by Thomas Affleck in presence
of

Isaac Willis … affirm'd   Two of the Witnesses and the Executors are Affirmed
John Stillas … dead   the 10th day of March 1795…Before
Jnº Morton … affirm'd   Geo Campbell Regʳ

II. *Affleck's probate inventory (a portion of which is below):*

A pair of square bureaus (unfinished) £9
A pair of circular bureaus £13
A pair of Circular card tables £6
A Circular Side Board Table £9
6 Mahogany Chairs £7..10
1 Marble Slab and Frame £2..5
8 Mahogany Chairs £3..12
1 Easy Chair £1..2..6
A Desk and Bookcase (second hand) £3..15
Stringing and Shades £2..10
A Chest of Drawers £2..5
2 Night Tables £1..17..6
A Mahogany Stand £0..7..6
A Traveling Desk £0..15
5 Picture Frames £0..18..9
2 Fire Buckets Bag and Basket £1
A Lott Sundries £0..10
A Lott of Bees Wax £2..5
A Curcular Bureau £6..10
6 Work Benches £3..15
20 hand screws [vices] £1..17
A Lott Cuttings £4..10
An old Chest of Tools £1..10
A common Stove and Pipes £1..10
1 Old Saw £0..7..6
A Lott of Cutting in the ware room £6
Scantling £1..2..6
Poplar and Pine £2..12..6
The Shed in the Yard £3..15

A Grind Stone £0..15
The Shop £22..1..0
A Magnifying Glass of Time £5..15
78 ½ oz silver at 8/ pr gr [bag of silver, unwrought] £31
A Small Magnifying Glass and Box £1..15..
5443 Feet of Mahogany @ 8/yd £192..15..6 ½
[over a mile of mahogany board! stockpiling it, work coming in,
active space, selling it]

Total: £4396..63 ½
Wm Rigby the other appraiser   Daniel Trotter affd
Died since the foregoing   The 30th day of July
Inventory   1796

CHAPTER 4

Across the broad Atlantic:
Scottish glass and the American trade

JILL TURNBULL

Glass is one of those materials that everyone takes for granted. We literally look through it, and do not give it a second thought as we drink a glass of wine, open a jam jar, tap a barometer, or admire our reflection in a mirror. It is, however, a remarkable substance, which has transformed our lives in ways that few other materials can equal; we only have to think of architecture to understand the significance of window glass, for example. Our ancestors did not take glass for granted. It was expensive, owned by very few people in the seventeenth century and only the relatively wealthy in the eighteenth century. For those who collect glass, on both sides of the Atlantic, it is a tantalising subject, because of all the artefacts discussed at the Winterthur conference, glass is the least identifiable. With the exception of pressed glass, very little of it was marked

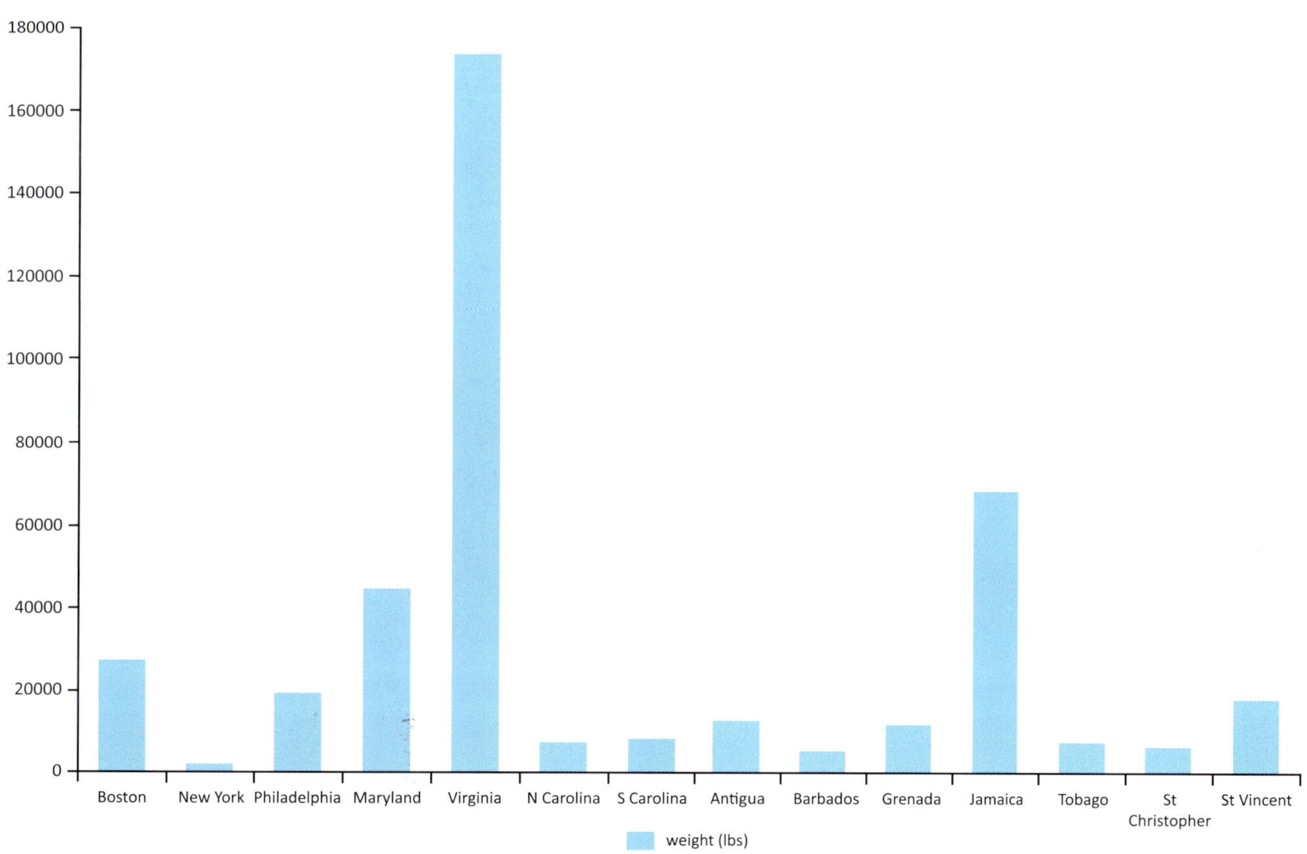

Illustration 4.1
Graph showing the destinations in North America and the West Indies to which glass was exported from Glasgow in 1771.
[Jill Turnbull]

until the twentieth century, unlike hallmarked silver or pottery which, even if not marked, can often be identified from the millions of sherds left on production sites. Glass, on the other hand, quite apart from being infinitely breakable, is also usually anonymous. It is notoriously difficult to attribute securely and even when there has been an archaeological investigation at a glassworks, very little is left behind, because broken and waste glass has always been recycled and re-used in the glass ingredients. It is rarely possible, therefore, to point out glass in American collections and identify it as Scottish, and it is even more difficult to ascribe it to a particular factory. Indeed, the same situation applies to Scotland itself, unless the glass was produced after the 1920s.

Documentary evidence for Scottish glassworks is plentiful, but patchy. The history of the glassworks at Leith, for example, is quite well recorded; the cones appear in paintings and we know fine glass was made there, but we have virtually no idea what it looked like. The products of other companies are much more accessible, however. There is a remarkable archive of material about the Holyrood Flint Glass Works belonging to descendants of the owners, which is housed in the Museum of Edinburgh, while pattern books from the Edinburgh & Leith Flint Glass Company, which later became Edinburgh Crystal, are in the care of the National Museums Scotland. This paper will, therefore, concentrate on the glass which can be identified from these archives.

For most collectors and museums interest lies in acquiring fine, decorative glassware, but bottles, although sought only by specialist collectors, are of considerable interest in the context of this paper. They formed an important part of the transatlantic trade, and a commercially successful arm of the glass industry, and must, therefore, be included in any discussion. It is also worth remembering that evenings spent around elegant dining tables laden with fine china and glass would not have been so enjoyable without the wine to drink with the meal – and that required bottles.

The 'English' bottle was developed by French Huguenot immigrants in the first half of the seventeenth century, after coal took over from wood as fuel for glass furnaces. Previously, bottles were thin-walled and fragile; they could be used as decanters but were not suitable for the storage of wine. Once the robust, dark green or black bottles, like those we use today, began to appear, the wine could be matured in them. The applied 'string rim' round the neck of a bottle enabled the cork to be tied

down securely and sealed with wax, ensuring the exclusion of air. The invention of these bottles not only transformed the wine trade but ensured a steady, and growing, demand in both the home and overseas markets for the bottles themselves. Some idea of the relative importance of bottles to the Scottish glass industry can be gained from household inventories. One fairly typical example of glass ownership in the early eighteenth century was a minor Scottish laird who, in 1708, owned just seventeen drinking glasses, a tumbler and two decanters, but in his cellar were 590 bottles containing a whole variety of alcohol.[1] It is little wonder that bottle production was the mainstay of the Scottish glass industry.

There was clearly a considerable demand, too, in North America. As Olive Jones points out in her book *Cylindrical English Wine and Beer Bottles 1735–1850*, 'hundreds of thousands of fragments of the cylindrical bottles are found on archaeological sites in Canada and the United States'.[2] Inevitably, the literature tends to describe bottles imported into America in the colonial period as 'English', as many of them were, but a large number were also exported from Scotland, particularly from Glasgow, where bottles were produced from 1700. A graph showing glass exports from Glasgow to North America and the West Indies in 1771 illustrates very clearly the

Illustration 4.2
Seal found on the site of the Verreville glass furnace in Glasgow. John Geddes was the manager, and later the owner, of the glassworks. [Courtesy Culture and Sport Glasgow (Museums)]

Illustration 4.3
A chip-engraved bottle made at the Alloa Glass Works.
[Courtesy National Museums Scotland]

connections between those areas and Scotland (illus 4.1). By far the most glass was exported to Virginia, which had, between 1751 and 1757, been governed by Scot Robert Dinwiddie, who was also a shareholder in the Delftfield pottery in Glasgow. He was one of many Scottish expatriates who either settled in North America in the eighteenth and especially the nineteenth centuries, or who went there on business. The emigrants tended to maintain contact with their families in Scotland, some of them setting up import businesses to provide goods to other settlers.

One popular, but expensive, service offered by the manufacturer to the purchaser was that his bottles could be 'marked' (commonly called 'sealed' today), by paying for a die depicting initials, a coat of arms or a date, to be pressed into a blob of hot glass, which had been added to the shoulder or body of the bottle. The seals were, therefore, of double thickness, so tend to survive better than the rest of the bottle, and can sometimes be useful for identification. Dated examples are often used to create a typology of bottle shapes, as they changed over time. Seals found on archaeological sites can sometimes raise more questions than answers – the significance of the date on the Verreville seal, for example, has yet to be discovered (illus 4.2). John Geddes was first

Illustration 4.4
'Portrait of Patrick Colquhoun' hanging in the boardroom of the Glasgow Chamber of Commerce in George Square, Glasgow. [Courtesy Glasgow Chamber of Commerce]

The export trade was always vital to the survival of the Scottish glass industry, and America was an important destination. In 1824 the Alloa Glasshouse Company advertised that they had 'warehouses established for the last ten years, in Glasgow, Dublin and New York, where there is always a regular demand for bottles to a great extent'.[3] The company certainly would not have maintained a warehouse in New York for that long unless sales of their bottles justified it. Bottles are not glamorous, but they are important because they maintained the Scottish glass industry throughout its 400 years of existence. In the twenty-first century over two million bottles a day are being made at Alloa, on the site where the original glassworks was founded in 1767.

Until the last quarter of the eighteenth century, it was difficult to sell enough domestic glass to make a

the manager and then the owner of the glassworks, so was in a good position to have his own bottles marked as he wished.

Identifying Scottish bottles is obviously very difficult, although capacity is a possible indication. Until well into the eighteenth century, by far the most common bottle made in Scotland was the chopin, with a capacity of one and a half imperial pints; far fewer of the smaller mutchkin bottles, containing three-quarters of a pint, were produced. More traceable, at least in theory, are the bottles decorated with chip-engraving which are attributed to Alloa, although this form of decoration, created by chipping away the glass with something sharp like a nail, is really a type of folk art which can easily be faked, so caution is required (illus 4.3).

Illustration 4.5
The base of a blue scent bottle, found on the site of the Verreville Glass Works in 2005. [Courtesy Culture and Sport Glasgow (Museums)]

Illustration 4.6
Parts of the stems of 'seahorse' scent bottles, found on the site of the Verreville Glass Works
[Courtesy Culture and Sport Glasgow (Museums)]

glass manufactory profitable. The Scottish market was small, it was difficult to obtain expert workmen, the start-up costs were high, and cash-flow was always a problem, so the production of fine glass was spasmodic during the seventeenth and early eighteenth centuries, and no evidence has been found that any was made in Scotland between 1734 and 1777, although bottle manufacture continued.

Glassworks in Glasgow and Edinburgh

It was the flourishing trade with the Americas which eventually led to the establishment of the glassworks, later known as Verreville, at Finnieston in Glasgow, where table glass was made, and exported, for some sixty-five years. It is surely no coincidence that the prime movers behind the setting up of the business were three Glasgow merchants, Patrick Colquhoun

Illustration 4.7
William Ford's trade card for his first glassworks in Edinburgh, dated between 1810 and 1815.
[Ford-Ranken Collection, City of Edinburgh Museums and Galleries]

and brothers John and Alexander Ritchie, who ran a shipping company trading with North America, the perfect outlet for the glass they planned to produce. Patrick Colquhoun actually went to Virginia in 1761, when he was just sixteen, and remained there for five years, developing a good head for business while working with traders in the Chesapeake Bay area. He later established the first Chamber of Commerce in Glasgow, also serving as Lord Provost of the city (illus 4.4).

There is no doubt that Verreville glass was exported to America, but identifying it is another matter. Most of the sherds found on the site during excavation of the glass furnace in 2005 give little indication of the range of products and show merely that the company was making the same type of glass as all the other British glassworks. There are, however, two notable exceptions. In their book *American Glass*, George and Helen McKearin illustrate scent, or smelling, bottles which are identical to two types of sherd found on the Verreville site.[4] The excavation yielded the bases of blue diagonally ribbed bottles (illus 4.5) and pieces of what the McKearins call 'seahorse' bottles in both blue and clear glass, which are identical to the American examples (illus 4.6). The authors suggest that these little bottles were made in England, but it is now clear that they were certainly produced in Glasgow, from where they may well have been exported to Virginia and elsewhere in the Americas.

Among the numerous Scottish families with members on both sides of the Atlantic were the Crawfords who traded in a range of merchandise between Glasgow and St Johns, Newfoundland. In 1808 the *Countess of Bute* sailed from Port Glasgow carrying five identical parcels of glass from Verreville. Each cask contained goblets, tumblers, decanters with stoppers, finger cups, butter basons with stands and covers, wines, oval flat salts and some huge rummers: '3 quart Rummers & Covers @ 4/–' and '3 Half Gallon ditto @ 6/–'.[5] Sadly, it is not possible to illustrate any Verreville products which match that shipping list, nor to put images to the items on the firm's price list of 1811, but an extant trade card used to advertise the wares of William Ford, in his newly established Caledonian Glass Works in Edinburgh, shows examples of similar wares in the fashion of the time (illus 4.7).

There is one certainty about the manufacturers of consumer goods such as glass and pottery: they made anything that would sell, and if one of their rivals produced something that sold well, they copied it. It was crucial that the owners of both the Verreville and the Caledonian glassworks should keep up with changes in fashion, so it is reasonable to assume that Verreville glass production in the early nineteenth century would have been similar to the glass made by William Ford in Edinburgh at about the same time, although the exported glass might well have been slightly plainer.

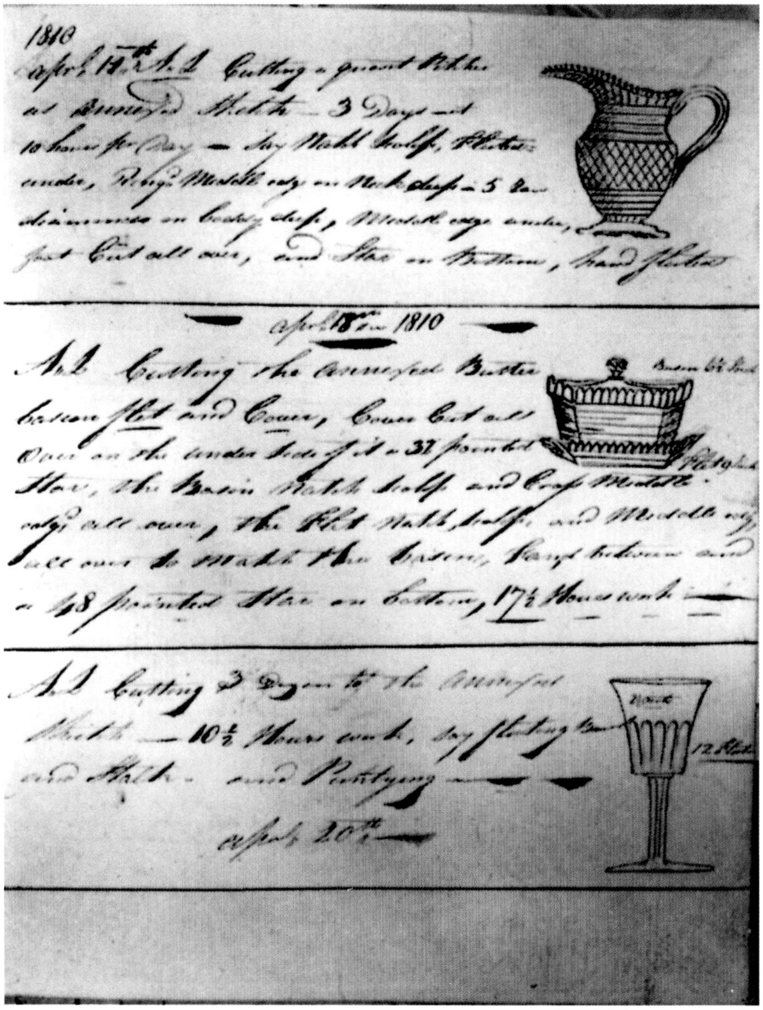

Illustration 4.8
Page 1 of a booklet titled *Account of Time on Work Done in the Cutting Shop*, 1810. [Ford-Ranken Collection, City of Edinburgh Museums and Galleries]

Illustration 4.9
A rather sanitised view of the cutting shop at the Holyrood Glass Works, Edinburgh, in 1836. The image appears on a large banner from the late nineteenth century, now in the National Museum of Scotland, and is based on an earlier engraving. [Courtesy National Museums Scotland]

William Ford started his business in 1810 and moved to new premises in 1815, so we have a precise date for the products illustrated on his trade card. They were deeply cut in the Regency style, which was highly fashionable at that time. The card also illustrates the importance of glass in lighting, including as it does a hanging oil lamp. After 1815 William Ford added to the card the information that his wares were for wholesale, retail and exportation.

Those ornately cut wares were expensive, but the Verreville list implies that the Canadian merchants were aiming at fairly wealthy purchasers, who would have wanted fashionable goods. A document in the Museum of Edinburgh shows why the Regency style glass cost so much. In April 1810, shortly after the foundation of the glassworks, a list was made of the times taken to cut some of their products. It shows that it took a skilled cutter seventeen and a half hours

Illustration 4.10
'Regency' designs in pattern book FR9, in the Museum of Edinburgh.
[Ford-Ranken Collection, City of Edinburgh Museums and Galleries]

to complete a butter dish with lid and stand, while an ornately cut jug took a full thirty hours (illus 4.8).[6]

The reason that the ornate Regency style cutting could be done at all was the introduction of steam engines to turn the cutting wheels. Until the 1780s they were turned by hand or by a horse-driven wheel, which meant that only shallow cutting was possible. After the introduction of steam engines capable of driving shafts attached to whole rows of cutting wheels, more elaborate and deeper cutting became possible (illus 4.9). Drawings belonging to descendants of the owners of the glassworks are currently on loan to the Museum of Edinburgh and provide a rich source of information about the Regency designs (illus 4.10).

The Caledonian Glass Works was not the only one in the east of Scotland making table glass in the nineteenth century. The Edinburgh Glass House Company at Leith added table glass to its bottle production in 1785. Once again, there is very little glass which is certainly attributable to the company, although an engraved jar on display in the Museum of Edinburgh is known to have been made there and subsequently buried in the foundation of the jail. It is, however, highly likely that the glass in a box belonging to one of Edinburgh's more exclusive clubs, the Whin Club, was also obtained in Leith. 'Whin' is the Scots word for gorse, their motto being 'Semper viret' meaning 'evergreen'. The club was founded by twelve young Edinburgh lawyers in 1799 and in the early nineteenth century they put together a baize-lined wooden box containing all the requisites for drinking the claret which they bought and stored in the house of one of the members. The two wine decanters and

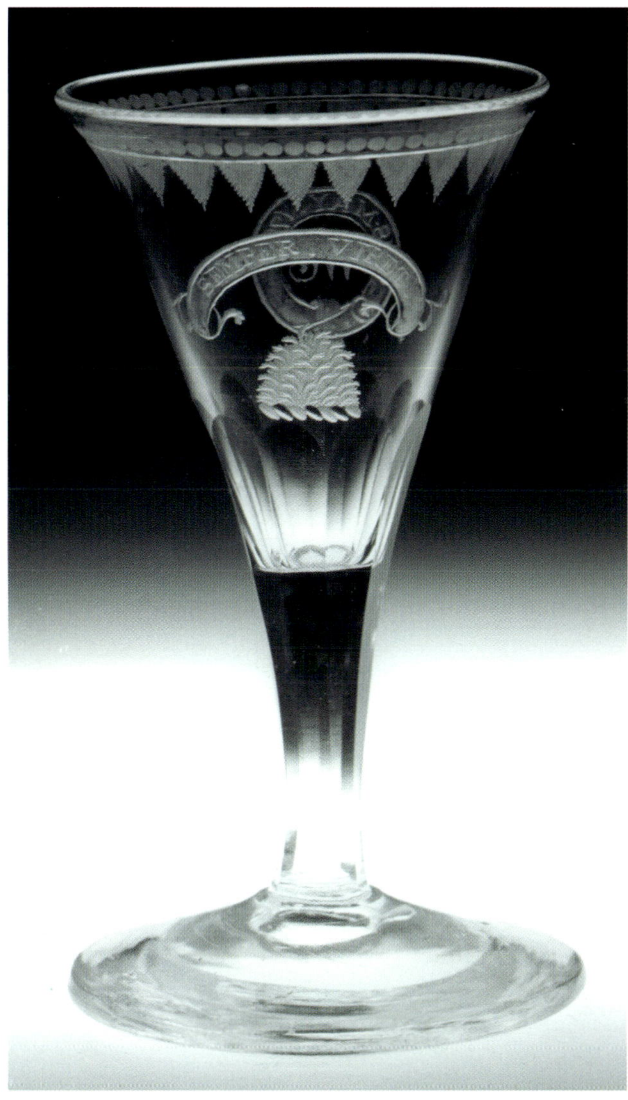

Museum of Glass, has confirmed that they had a major influence on American glass production. That view is supported by Lura Woodside Watkins who, in her history of the New England Glass Company, wrote: 'The early success of the New England Glass Co. may be largely attributed to the skilful management of Thomas H. Leighton' and later that 'it is impossible to outline the history of the works without mention of the Leighton name.'[7]

Thomas Leighton was born in 1786 in England, where he completed his apprenticeship, but in 1810, at the age of twenty-four, he started work, probably in charge of the glass-making, at William Ford's newly established glassworks in Edinburgh. He stayed there until, in 1826, he left without notice to take up a position as 'gaffer' with the New England Glass Company in Cambridge, Massachusetts.[8]

Leighton had been head-hunted by the American company. Poaching workmen was common practice, particularly when a new works was being established, although it was illegal for indentured workers to leave. Fortunately for Leighton, he was not in a legally binding contract, but his loss must have been a considerable blow to the Scottish glassworks, especially as he went on to recruit twin brothers George and Robert Dale, who had served their apprenticeships in Edinburgh and were therefore well known to him. George Dale became one of the New England Glass Company's best blowers, so the Cambridge glass industry benefited considerably from the training and experience such men had gained in

Illustration 4.11
Wine glass from the Whin Club box, decorated with an engraved gorse bush, the club's insignia and their motto, *Semper viret*. Private collection. [Photograph courtesy of the National Museums Scotland]

the wine glasses all reflect the shallow cutting of the eighteenth century, before the advent of steam engines (illus 4.11).

Atlantic connections

It is impossible to know what Scottish glass crossed the Atlantic, but it is certain that one important glass-making family, the Leightons, did. Jane Shadel Spillman, Curator of American Glass at The Corning

Illustration 4.12
A 'jasper' wine glass, made at the Holyrood Glass Works, belonging to descendants of the owners. [Ford-Ranken Collection, City of Edinburgh Museums and Galleries]

Illustration 4.13
Venetian revival glass made by Alexander Jenkinson's glassworks, later known as
Edinburgh Crystal, and purchased by Kelvingrove Museum in 1876. Acc. 1876.100.n.
[Courtesy Culture and Sport Glasgow (Museums)]

Scotland. Thomas Leighton was clearly aware of the loss to his old employers, but two years after arriving in Massachusetts, he plucked up the courage to write to John Ford, nephew of the founder William Ford, who was by then the joint owner of what had become the Holyrood Flint Glass Works, to apologise for the way he had left.[9]

In 1838 Leighton returned to Edinburgh and visited the glassworks. While he was there, John Ford gave him the recipe for his best flint glass – a very valuable gift – containing the sort of information which was usually jealously guarded. John Ford was just a boy when Thomas Leighton came to Edinburgh and clearly thought very highly of him. Leighton later wrote to Ford saying, 'I believe that I make the best metal [glass mixture] in this Country, we have received one gold medal and two silver ones at three exhibitions – but I think you beat me.'[10] Since the New England Glass Company was one of the best in America, this was high praise.

Thomas Leighton did not just take his glass-making expertise with him to Massachusetts; he also took seven sons. All possessed, or acquired, valuable skills. John took over when his father died in 1849, Peter, Robert and Thomas II were glass-blowers,

Illustration 4.14
A paperweight containing a ceramic cameo,
known as a sulphide.
[Courtesy National Museums Scotland]

Oliver was a cutter, James worked in the mould shop and William was a glass chemist. Deming Jarves, the company's first manager, acknowledged the family's importance, writing that, as well as the best practical knowledge, 'they had also artistic taste, which enabled them … to introduce new and more beautiful patterns'.[11] Bearing all that in mind, it is not unreasonable to assume that some of the production of the New England Glass Company in the 1830s was influenced by the Scottish glass the Leightons were used to making, although direct comparisons are not possible.

One type of glass produced by both companies was coloured by oxide of uranium, known in America as 'vaseline glass', and at the Holyrood Flint Glass Works as 'canary'. The first known uranium glass in Britain was made by Whitefriars of London in 1836.

The following year they made twelve finger bowls for the 1837 Corporation of London Banquet for Queen Victoria, to celebrate her coronation. They called the colour 'topaz'.

Just two years after the coronation Thomas Leighton wrote to John Ford at the glassworks in Edinburgh saying, 'You … informed me that to make your Canary Metal you used nothing but the Oxide of Uranium in your flint Batch. You did not give me any quantity but [said] that I can find out by small experiments.'[12] Leighton was clearly having difficulty in discovering the correct proportions by trial and error and asked Ford for more help. John Ford's reply is not known, nor whether Leighton succeeded in making uranium glass in the 1840s, but there is a recipe for canary glass, dated 1848, in his recipe book, and the company was certainly making it by

Illustration 4.15
An advertising card for the Holyrood Glass Works, showing a range of cut glass enclosing sulphides.
[Courtesy City of Edinburgh Museums and Galleries]

Illustration 4.16a and 4.16b
Pages from a Holyrood catalogue showing a range of pressed glass designs.
[Courtesy City of Edinburgh Museums and Galleries]

the 1860s. It is intriguing to wonder whether Thomas Leighton and the New England Glass Company were the first American manufacturers to make uranium glass, using a Scottish recipe.

Thomas Leighton's recipe book was added to by his son John after he became gaffer and it contains a long and very varied list of colours made at the works. One of the best known was gold ruby, the recipe for which was perfected by another of Thomas Leighton's sons, William. Lura Watkins has written that 'the two gaffers, father and son, and the brother, William Leighton, were constantly experimenting in the laboratory to create new and beautiful colours'.[13]

William went on to work for glass manufacturers in Wheeling, West Virginia, where he invented the recipe for lime glass, which was considerably cheaper than lead glass, and which had a huge influence on American glass production.

All the glasshouses experimented with new recipes and Holyrood was no exception. Pieces of their experimental glass are still in the Museum of Edinburgh. Two rods of reddish-brown colour are particularly significant, because numerous trials eventually resulted in the production of what was known at the glassworks as 'jasper' ware. Five pieces of this ware remain with the descendants of the owners

of the glassworks, including a small wine glass (illus 4.12). This type of opaque marbled glass is usually assumed to be lithyalin, which had been patented in Bohemia by Friederich Egermann in 1828, but it was also made in Edinburgh over quite a long period. The marbled effect could also be made in green. It is not known whether this particular recipe or these products crossed the Atlantic.

A great deal of coloured glass was made in Edinburgh in the nineteenth century by both the Holyrood Glass Works and the Edinburgh & Leith Flint Glass Company (later to be Edinburgh Crystal), but most of it is not identifiable. One exception, however, is a group of Venetian revival glass, examples of which were bought directly from the latter factory by museums in Edinburgh, Glasgow and Dublin. The company made a wide variety of this style of glass, inspired by the Italian revival of old Venetian glass, particularly the work of Antonio Salviati, examples of whose glass are in the National Museum of Scotland and Kelvingrove Museum in Glasgow (illus 4.13).[14]

The information which was shared between Thomas Leighton in Cambridge, Massachusetts, and John Ford in Edinburgh certainly benefited them both. Leighton suggested items that could profitably be made in Scotland and sent John Ford samples, which were often taken to Edinburgh by Scottish immigrant glass-makers who were visiting their relatives. In 1838, for example, Leighton sent some glass doorknobs, and a dozen 'heads for putting into knobs'.[15] It is not known what he meant by 'heads' to put into the knobs, but later on in the century doorknobs containing ceramic cameos of the heads of famous figures, *were* made in Edinburgh (illus 4.14). The Holyrood Glass Works made a whole range of similar wares containing ceramic cameos, known as sulphides (illus 4.15).

Until the 1830s table glass was too expensive for most of the population, but the development of a system for pressing glass in America changed all that. Pressing was much used at the New England Glass Company, from where Leighton sent some examples to John Ford in Edinburgh, doing his best to encourage Ford to embrace

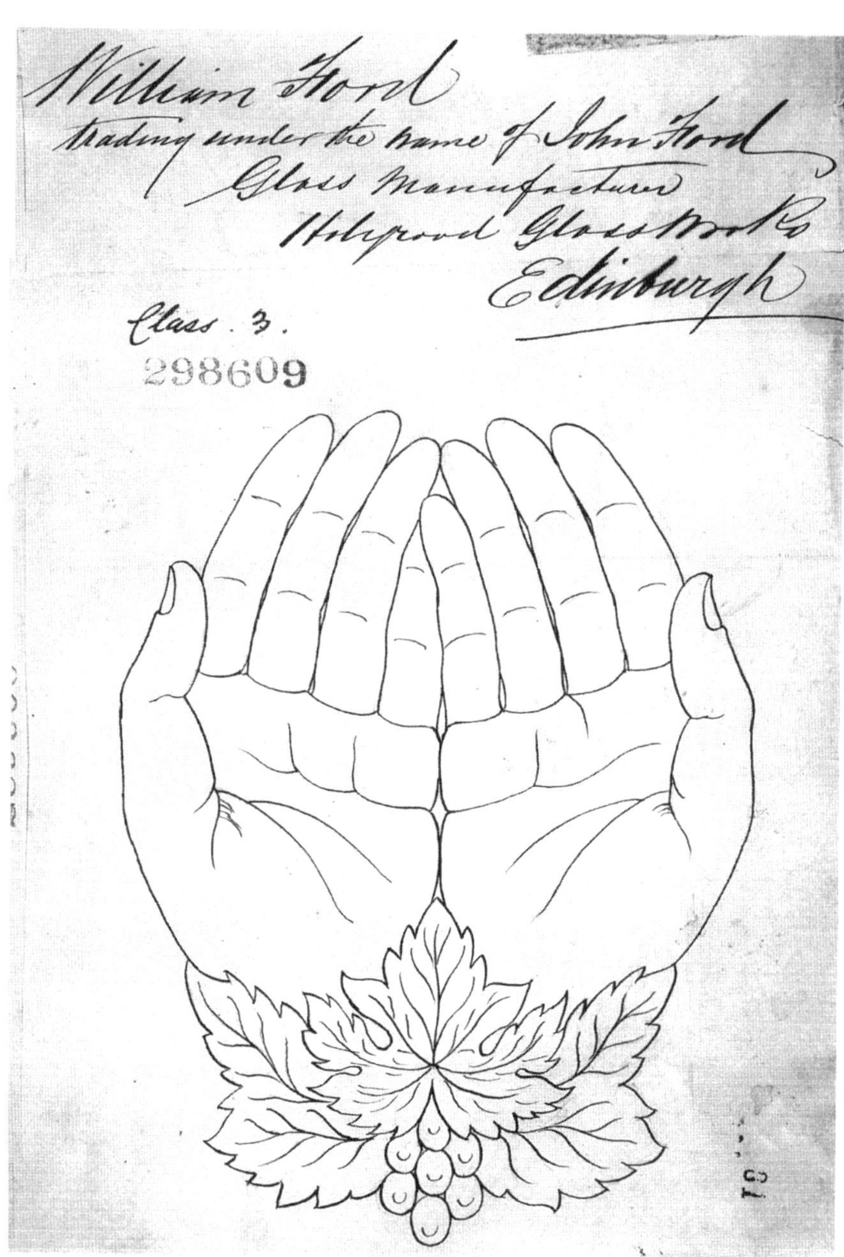

Illustration 4.18
Design for bowl in the shape of hands, registered in London by the Holyrood Glass Works in 1876. [The National Archives, UK]

the new technology. Eventually the Holyrood glassworks did make a range of pressed items (illus 4.16a, 4.16b) but their more distinctive wares were moulded, rather than pressed.

Some of the moulded wares were versatile as well as decorative. The shepherdess, for example, could be bought as a plain candlestick, or a highly elaborate candelabra, or carry a bowl in a variety of designs on her

head as a comport. Her companion was a woodman, who could be used in a similar fashion (illus 4.17). One of the best-known models was a moulded dish in the form of cupped hands. It is intriguing that this design was actually patented first in America by the New England Glass Company in 1875, and it was then registered in London by the Holyrood Glass Works in 1876 (illus 4.18).[16] So, nearly thirty years after Thomas

Illustration 4.19
A set of musical glasses made by James Smith of Edinburgh, now in the Museum of Edinburgh.
[Courtesy City of Edinburgh Museums and Galleries]

Leighton's death in 1849, we have a continuing direct connection between the two companies 'across the broad Atlantic', as he had described it in one of his letters.

One of the more unusual products advertised in 1829 by the Midlothian Glass Manufactory (another name for what later became the Holyrood Glass Works), were glass armonicas, or sets of musical glasses. They were described as: 'Musical glasses diatonic and chromatic, fitted up in Mahogany and painted cases, which for accuracy of tone and power of tone, are allowed to be infinitely superior to any offered to the public.'[17] They consisted of rows of glasses, tuned to different notes, which were played by running a wet finger round the rim. Each glass was ground down to tune it and the foot was held in a clamp.

Musical glasses like this were drawing-room instruments which were originally tuned by putting the appropriate amount of water into each glass, but an officer in the Perthshire militia, Daniel Menzies, was one of several people who devised a method of tuning by grinding away the glass, a big step forward. The cover of a verbose treatise written by Menzies described his version of the 'Angelica or Musical Glasses' as being 'without water'.[18]

James Smith took up the idea and produced sets which appeared to be nothing more than a mahogany side table, giving no clue as to its function when the lid is closed. A set made in 1823 and originally presented to Edinburgh City Library, is now in the Museum of Edinburgh (illus 4.19). Among the twenty-four tuned glasses are two which are footless, and are designed to hold the water for wetting the player's fingers. Another set in private hands in San Diego, also made by James Smith, contains glasses arranged exactly as set out by Daniel Menzies in his treatise.

In America a Francis H Smith of Baltimore, who described himself as 'sole patentee', advertised a very ornate pedestal table containing a set of musical glasses or 'Grand Harmonicon'.[19] In 1831 he also wrote a preceptor to accompany it, just as James Smith had published a 'tutor' in 1829. Both men included tunes such as 'Robin Adair', 'Kinloch of Kinloch' and 'Rousseau's Dream'. Whether they were related is not known.

On a more serious note, one of the best-known, and most expensive, types of glass produced in Scotland, was engraved glass. Jacobite glass will not be discussed here because there is no evidence that any flint glass was made in Scotland between 1734 and 1777, suggesting that all the Jacobite glasses made during that crucial period must have been produced in England or Europe. Engraved glass was always costly because of the degree of highly skilled hand work involved. The technique and equipment have changed very little over the centuries, the only real difference being that the lathes are now powered by electricity, rather than a foot pedal. The basic shape, the leather strap carrying oil to lubricate the wheel, and the copper wheels themselves are just the same, and the skills take just as long to acquire (illus 4.20).

The most renowned engravers came to Britain from Bohemia and were working in Scotland

Illustration 4.20
A plate from the service made by the Holyrood Glass Works and presented to the Duke and Duchess of York by the citizens of Edinburgh, on the occasion of their marriage in 1893. [Courtesy City of Edinburgh Museums and Galleries]

from the start of flint glass production in the late eighteenth century – men like Anthony Strobach, an engraver with a drink problem, who worked at Verreville in Glasgow. Unfortunately, although we know something of his private life because of litigation, we know none of the patterns he engraved.[20] During the second half of the nineteenth century, a considerable number of Bohemians settled in Edinburgh, establishing their own workshops, as well as engraving in the glassworks themselves, where they had a considerable influence on the designs. In America Thomas Leighton's grandson Henry was an engraver, and his work too shows a Bohemian influence, one of his designs illustrating dogs chasing a rabbit. Similar motifs appear in the Ford pattern book, in use in the late nineteenth century (illus 4.21).

During this period there are plenty of identifiable examples of Scottish engraved glass, such as a goblet from the Holyrood Glass Works decorated in 1858 with a view of the new Royal Museum, in the presence of the director. Another glass reflecting Scottish patriotism is one engraved with the 'Honours of Scotland', depicting the Scottish regalia of crown, sword and sceptre, with a finely engraved thistle

Illustration 4.21
A design from the Holyrood pattern book, showing a strong Bohemian influence.
[Courtesy of The Corning Museum of Glass]

Illustration 4.22
A 'regalia' goblet, engraved with a thistle border
and the Regalia of Scotland. [Private collection]

Illustration 4.23
Celery glass in the fern pattern, Holyrood Glass Works. The
design appears in the firm's catalogue and in the Corning
pattern book. [Collection of the Author]

border. Evidence for its provenance is contained in a letter from one of Queen Victoria's household at Balmoral, requesting replacements for two which had been broken, and illustrating the glasses required (illus 4.22).[21]

Not all the glass was fine and fragile. Designs for hotels and ships needed to be both practical and robust. In 1840 John Ford was trying to fulfil an urgent order for a large American steamboat, which was due to sail from Liverpool. Despite every effort, the glass-

makers just could not get the colour of the glass clear enough, so the decanters and other glass had to be bought in from another manufacturer, a serious loss

Illustration 4.24
A decanter and wine glasses in the 'ribbon and wreath' pattern, part of a large service made at the Holyrood Glass Works in the late nineteenth century, illustrated in the firm's catalogue and pattern book. [Collection of the Author]

to the company. Shipping companies and hotels could have their insignia engraved to order on the standard designs.

Somewhere in the centre of the price range came suites of glasses, often engraved and aimed at the middle-class market. The fern pattern tends to be associated with the Holyrood Glass Works, and certainly a great deal was made there, but it was also produced in England – and in America (illus 4.23). Also popular were suites which combined cutting and some engraving, the 'ribbon and wreath' pattern being a good example (illus 4.24). This design is identifiable from the Holyrood pattern book, now housed in The Corning Museum of Glass in New York State, otherwise there would be no way of knowing who produced it. There are hundreds of engraved designs in the book, most of which would be attributed to Stourbridge in England if they appeared at auction. Holyrood was not, of course, the only Scottish glassworks making fine engraved glass; beautiful examples were also created at the works of John Baird in Glasgow and elsewhere.

There is little doubt that some of the Scottish glass discussed in this paper would have found its way to the Americas in the late eighteenth and nineteenth centuries, and it is likely that some of it remains in private and public collections, but the extent to which it influenced the style of American glass is open to question. There is, however, no doubt about the importance of the expertise, training and experience of the skilled workmen who went there, some from England, but others, most notably the Leighton family, from Scotland.

Acknowledgements

I am particularly grateful to David Scarratt and Helen Edwards of the Museum of Edinburgh, Dr John Cruikshank, Jane Shadel Spillman of The Corning Museum of Glass, Al Rice, Curator of the Fiske Museum of Musical Instruments, Claremont, California, and Alison Brown of Culture and Sport Glasgow (Museums) for their help in preparing this paper. I am indebted to Glasgow Chamber of Commerce for allowing me to take, and permission to publish, the photograph of the portrait of Patrick Colquhoun. Thanks are also due to the staff of the National Archives of Scotland, the National Library of Scotland and the Signet Library in Edinburgh.

Manuscript sources

NAS National Archives of Scotland
NLS National Library of Scotland
SL Signet Library
Museum of Edinburgh

Notes

1 Dunbar, E 1865 'The Inventor of plenishing in Thunderton's Lodging in Duffus, Moray, 15 May 1708', *Social Life in Former Days*. Edinburgh, 205–13.

2 Jones 1986, 9.

3 *The Scotsman*, 18 December 1824.

4 McKearin 1941, 448–54, plate 240.

5 NAS CS39/107/1/25 Records of John Crawford & Co. Merchants, Port Glasgow. Invoice book 1790–1815.

6 Museum of Edinburgh FR10, 'Account of time on work done in the cutting shop', 1810.

7 Watkins 1930, 15.

8 'The word "gaffer" in this connection means the superintendent of the glass-house … Deming Jarves has defined the status of the gaffer when he says that he must have a knowledge of chemistry in order to mix the materials in such a way as to produce the best and clearest glass, and that his personal character shall be such as to command the respect of the workmen. Mr. Leighton filled both of these requirements.' Watkins 1930, 163.

9 Museum of Edinburgh, FR2/20, Thomas Leighton to John Ford, 1 April 1828.

10 Museum of Edinburgh, FR2/20, Thomas Leighton to John Ford, 28 November 1839.

11 Watkins 1930, 162. There are a number of glass notebooks and batch books, formerly belonging to the Leighton family, in the Rakow Library at The Corning Museum of Glass.

12 Museum of Edinburgh, FR2/20, Thomas Leighton to John Ford, 28 November 1839.

13 Watkins 1930, 52.

14 Turnbull, J, '"Scotch Venetian Glass" – Edinburgh's contribution to the Venetian revival', *Journal of the Glass Association* 9, 2011.

15 Museum of Edinburgh, FR2/20, Thomas Leighton to John Ford, 1 April 1838.

16 Morris 1978, 202. She writes that the design was patented in the United States by W L Libbey & Sons, who leased the New England Glass Company in 1878.

17 *The Scotsman*, 18 April 1829.

18 NLS, Mus.E.t.30, *A Treatise on the Angelica or Musical Glasses without water Arranged in a new & approved Manner.* Edinburgh nd.

19 A photocopy of part of Francis H Smith's preceptor and his advertisement were given to the author by Al Rice, Curator of the Fiske Museum of Musical Instruments in Claremont, South California. He also gave me details of the musical glasses in San Diego and some pages of James Smith's 'Tutor'. A book of tunes and an instruction booklet

accompany the set of musical glasses held in the Museum of Edinburgh.

20 SL, Court of Session Papers 171;14, Petition of Gilbert Hamilton and John Geddes.

21 Museum of Edinburgh, Ford-Ranken archive, E Lawley, Balmoral Castle to John Ford, 23 September 1887.

Bibliography

Jones, O R, 1986, *Cylindrical English Wine & Beer Bottles 1735–1850*. Ottawa: Studies in Archaeology, Architecture and History, National Historic Parks and Sites Branch Environment Canada – Parks.

McKearin, G S, Helen, 1941 *American Glass*. New York: Crown.

Morris, B 1978 *Victorian Table Glass and Ornaments*. London: Barrie & Jenkins.

Watkins, L W 1930 *Cambridge Glass 1818 to 1888*. New York: Bramhall House.

CHAPTER 5

The Scottish silversmith in the Americas

GEORGE DALGLEISH

This chapter sets out to present a preliminary investigation into the numerous Scottish silversmiths who ventured across the Atlantic.[1] The position of the silversmith within Scottish society in general and in particular at the top of the crafts elites has been discussed elsewhere (Dalgleish and Fothringham 2008, 5, 6). We are concerned here rather with the reasons why many made the journey west and, to a lesser extent, their impact on the Atlantic world. The period under discussion could be called the 'long' eighteenth century, bleeding into both the preceding and succeeding centuries, while the geographical area corresponds with the modern Caribbean, the USA and Canada.

Modern historiography frequently emphasises that a considerable number of Scots migrants, particularly in the eighteenth century, came from what could be characterised as the 'middling sort' of society; often well educated, literate and highly motivated, and not the poor, downtrodden, landless labourers of other waves of emigration (Devine 1999: 26–7; Devine 2003, passim). They came to better themselves, often with the intention of returning homeward with a fortune in their pockets; this was particularly true of many Scots 'sojourners' who journeyed to the sugar plantations of the Caribbean (Karras 1992, passim), were involved in the tobacco trade of the Chesapeake (Devine 1975), and in the fur trade farther north. These highly lucrative ventures were heavily populated with that most impressive of creatures: 'the Scotsman on the Make'. It is not surprising, therefore, that several Scottish silversmiths sought to hitch their wagons to these success stories and travelled across the Atlantic to make use of the extensive kin-based networks that were an essential characteristic of this early Scottish diaspora.

Before looking at the migration of the craftsmen themselves, it might be worth reflecting on the impact of the export of examples of Scottish-made silver to the Americas and whether this had any effect on encouraging its makers to follow suit. Unfortunately, while many Scots presumably took examples of silver wares with them, either as functional requisites, portable sources of wealth, or as heirlooms of the old country, it has proved exceptionally difficult to trace many surviving examples that were taken over in the eighteenth century. Most of the large quantity of Scottish-made silver that is currently in both private and public collections in the USA and Canada is the result of twentieth-century collectors, rather than earlier migration. There are, however, a few important extant pieces which suggest that much more must have been taken, but then presumably melted down and recycled.

Two will serve to make the point. A rather curious-looking teapot now in the Museum of Fine Arts, Boston, was made by Robert Cruickshank, a silversmith in Old Aberdeen, about 1710 (Dalgleish and Fothringham 2008: 5.6). It is of interest for two reasons. First, it has an impeccable provenance (partly engraved on the teapot itself in the nineteenth century) (illus 5.1). It seems to have been made for Alexander Middleton, Collector of Customs in Aberdeen. He married an Aberdeenshire lady, Elspeth Burnet, in 1705. Their son, also Alexander, left the north-east of Scotland for Boston in 1735, taking the family teapot with him. The teapot descended to his daughter Mary, who married a James Lovel, a fairly prominent rebel against the Crown in 1776. The teapot remained within the family until it was donated to MFA in 1991 by Mrs Eleanor Lowell (information provided by MFA). Second, it is potentially the earliest Scottish teapot in existence, although its current form suggests it has been altered or 'improved' at some point in the past. Its maker, Robert Cruickshank, was one of the most important silversmiths in Old Aberdeen. He was admitted as a freeman of the Hammermen's Incorporation in 1699 and continued working until at

Illustration 5.1
Boston teapot, by Robert Cruickshank, Old Aberdeen, *c* 1710–20.
[Courtesy of the Boston Museum of Fine Arts]

least 1731 (James 1981: 53–4). It is currently on loan to National Museums Scotland and forms an important part of their displays on the Scottish diaspora.

The second piece is a 'thistle' cup, made by Hugh Ross, a silversmith in Tain in Ross-shire, about 1710, and used in Canada by James Thompson, also from Tain (illus 5.2). Thompson was a remarkable man. Born in 1733, he went to Canada in 1757 as a volunteer with the 78th Regiment of Foot, or Fraser Highlanders, to fight in the French and Indian War. The Fraser Highlanders were raised by Simon Fraser, son of the executed Jacobite peer Lord Lovat, in an area which had a few years previously been 'out' in the '45 on the Jacobite side. The 78th was one of the loyal Highland regiments that became a major instrument of the Hanoverian government's imperial expansion (and a means of cementing the rehabilitation of old Jacobites). In this instance Thompson's silver cup was definitely seen as a family heirloom of the old country. He did not take it with him originally, but had his sister send it on to him. He later told his son: 'This is one of the cups which each of my grandmother's children received and it was her rule to make them take a small dram of whisky on New Year's morning … In order not to break the family rule I have made a point to take a drop of whisky out of it every New Year's morning since it has been in my possession' (Quick 2009: 22). Thompson became a significant figure in Canada and remained there until his death in 1830, aged ninety-seven. He was one of the last survivors of the young Highland soldiers who had left home seventy years previously to become part of the spearhead of Empire (Quick 2009: 45–7). This little cup is therefore a witness to the Scots' crucial involvement in the development of the British Empire. However, it did not have any impact on the development of

Illustration 5.2
Montreal Thistle cup, by Hugh Ross, Tain, *c* 1710. [Courtesy of the McCord Museum, Montreal]

silversmithing in Canada, and eventually was collected from Thompson's family by David Ross McCord, and ended up in the museum that bears his name in Montreal. Because of its provenance it is one of the most important pieces of Tain-made silver in existence.

It is curious that two of the most important surviving examples of early Scottish provincial silver found their way across the Atlantic. This perhaps says something about the accidents of survival, where 'heirlooms' of the old country were treasured in a way they would not have been at home, where most likely they would have been melted down to create something more fashionable. Doubtless there are other examples of the early export of Scottish silver types, but survivals seem to be rare.

If, as seems likely, exported Scottish silver types had very little direct impact on styles or production techniques in the Americas, it might be instructive to look now at whether the migration of the craftsmen themselves could have had a greater effect on the material culture of the transatlantic world.

One must first consider the scale of this migration. The following, very incomplete survey was compiled from existing secondary sources and is merely suggestive rather than exhaustive. It does, however, bring to light a number of craftsmen identified as goldsmiths, silversmiths or jewellers migrating across the Atlantic within the period of our discussion.[2] There are references to about forty craftsmen who went to what is now the US, in the eighteenth century, arriving mainly in North and South Carolina, while those in the early nineteenth century mostly shipped in to the port of New York. A considerable number presumably travelled on to other destinations in the Americas. About twenty-five went to what is now Canada, mainly to Halifax, Nova Scotia, Quebec City and Montreal. Many also went to the Caribbean, all in the eighteenth century; at least sixteen of whom went to Jamaica, and one each to St Kitts, St Eustatius, Cuba and Tobago.

This is clearly not a huge migration, but it is still reasonably significant, and may have had some discernable impact on the production of silver wares in these areas. Like all other emigrants, Scottish silversmiths crossed the Atlantic for a variety of reasons. Dr Ross Fox has identified four basic categories into which most emigrating craftsmen fell (Fox 2008: 86).

First, apprentices who failed to complete their required 'time', usually seven years followed by one to three more as a journeyman. Such a lengthy training involved a heavy outlay. Initially, apprentices were not paid by their master, being given board and lodgings only. Costs were normally paid for in advance either by the apprentice's family or charity. Failure to complete their training would prevent them legitimately setting up in a Scottish burgh. Haphazard application of such rules in less-regulated or unregulated colonies therefore held some hope for a 'failed' apprentice to become established.

Second, even a 'time-served' journeyman might not have the necessary financial means to set up as a master/freeman with a workshop of his own. The resources needed were substantial. For example, the fees required by the Incorporation of Goldsmiths of Edinburgh before a qualified journeyman could gain entry as a freeman were heavy; and, of course, considerable capital was required for setting up in business (*EGM*: 119, A423 & 424). Many journeymen (particularly those from families outwith the existing goldsmiths' elites) simply could not afford this outlay and remained journeymen throughout their careers, working for 'meat and fee'. In Edinburgh they were the backbone of the workforce, outnumbering the freeman masters. It is from these first two groups that most Scottish silversmiths who went to the Americas came, with the hope of establishing a thriving business in less constricted circumstances.

The third category were others seeking their fortunes who came from the smaller provincial towns where demand for luxury goods and therefore prospects were limited. Indeed, this was also true of the larger centres in times of economic downturn in the regular cycle of boom and bust. Many Edinburgh-trained apprentices went south to Newcastle and London in an attempt to make a living (Dietert and Dietert 2007: 168–72). One can argue that a move to North America or the West Indies was simply a move to a more far-flung destination, given the economic factors pushing some craftsmen out of Scotland. Equally, Aberdeen was the source of many goldsmiths who found their way to the Indian subcontinent (Wilkinson 1987: xvii).

Fourth, there were also freemen/masters who had got into personal financial difficulties at home, who sought to improve their fortunes on the other side of the Atlantic.

I would add a further category. There were several goldsmiths who were amongst those unfortunate enough to be forced to leave Scotland for political reasons; that is, being on the wrong side of the prevailing political establishment.

I now propose to look at a few illustrative examples of craftsmen who fell into one or other of the above categories.

One of the earliest known transatlantic goldsmith emigrants is a good example of the last group – a political victim. Alexander Kerr was the younger son of a laird, Archibald Kerr of Graden in Roxburghshire in the Scottish Borders. He was apprenticed to William Law, goldsmith in Edinburgh on 22 December 1708 (IoG Reg Archive). Kerr does not seem to have completed his time, and is not recorded as either a journeyman or a master. This is unusual for a goldsmith of his social position. Several successful Scottish goldsmiths of the seventeenth and eighteenth centuries were younger sons of the gentry (Dalgleish and Fothringham 2008: 56). Kerr's failure to prosper in Edinburgh was a result of his involvement with the Jacobite Rebellion of 1715–16. He was captured as a rebel at the battle of Preston in 1715, convicted of high treason at Chester and sentenced to transportation to Virginia as an indentured servant. He was shipped out on the *Elizabeth and Anne* from Liverpool to Yorktown, Virginia, where he was 'signed for' by the Lieutenant-Governor of the Colony, Alexander Spotswood (Calendar of Virginia State Papers, vol 1, 1652–1781: 185–6). In a perfect illustration of the strength and penetration of Scottish kinship networks, Kerr seems to have had a rather easier time of adjusting to his new abode than many other transported rebels. Governor Spotswood was a distant relative, whose family were originally Border lairds as well. The Governor's cousin, John Spotswood, who lived in Scotland, corresponded with him regularly, and in a series of letters of 1716–17 he says: 'I recommend to your protection Alexander Ker, a younger son of the Laird of Graden in Teviotdale, a jeweller by trade, who has sett up a shop in Williamsburg. His mother is a daughter of Sir Harry of Roslin & again her mother

Illustration 5.3
Sauceboat by David Downie, Edinburgh, 1783–4.
[Courtesy of the Trustees of the National Museums Scotland]

95

and grandmother were Spotswoods of our family' (*Virginia Magazine*, vol 60, no 2, April, 1952: 234–5). Kerr seems to have prospered, first leasing then buying the house which originally bore his name on the corner of Capitol Square and Duke of Gloucester Street in Williamsburg. He died on 20 October 1738, and was recorded as a 'A Jeweller and Silversmith … Proficient in his Business and well respected'. His estate was put up for sale the following November including 'a large parcel of very saleable Store-Goods, Diamond and other rings, Gold, Silver, and other Snuff-boxes, Gold and other tooth-pick cases, and other silver Work; together with the furniture of his House' (Helen Bullock, Colonial Williamsburg Foundation Library Research Report, series 1133 and 1938, 1990). Clearly, Kerr's unfortunate political dalliance with rebellion ultimately did not hinder his success in business. Doubtless this was aided by being part of a kinship network that included the Deputy Governor of the colony.

At the end of the eighteenth century we have evidence of another goldsmith exiled for political reasons. David Downie from Edinburgh ended his days in Augusta, Georgia. Downie was unusual in the Edinburgh goldsmiths' fraternity, being both a Roman Catholic and a political radical. The son of a watchmaker, he was apprenticed to William Gilchrist in 1753, becoming a freeman of the Incorporation in 1770 (IoG Reg Archive) (illus 5.3). Although little of his work remains, records make it clear that he did a considerable amount of business within the small Scottish Catholic community.

He became involved in the radical politics of the 1790s, influenced by the spirit of republicanism, the events of the American War of Independence and the more recent French Revolution, and, of course, by the restrictions under which he and his co-religionists had to labour. Many sought, if not a republican nirvana in Britain, then certainly a greater measure of political representation and extended suffrage, especially in Scotland where the government was in hands of a very small self-perpetuating elite.

Downie joined the Friends of the People and in 1794 became involved in a conspiracy to overturn the Edinburgh city government known as the Pike Plot. Caught stockpiling weapons, including pike heads, he was tried for high treason along with the ringleader Robert Watt. In October 1794 both were convicted and sentenced to death, in the particularly grisly manner reserved for traitors; hanging, drawing and quartering. In the end Watt was simply hanged, but even this

caused an outcry, forcing the government to become more lenient. Downie's sentence was commuted to 'exile from Britain for life' (Fortescue 2012: 50). He fled to Augusta, Georgia, where he took up his former profession. Unfortunately, it is not known how well he fared, but it is clear that he took on at least two apprentices, so presumably business was reasonably good. He died there on Christmas Day 1816 (*Augusta Chronicle*, 1 January 1817). In a curious postscript, one of his daughters, Peggy, married a Paisley weaver and one of their descendants was President Ronald Reagan (*The Scotsman*, 7 June 2004). There seems to be no surviving example of Downie's work made in the United States, so it is impossible to speculate about whether he brought any Scottish stylistic influences to his new homeland.

Neither Kerr nor Downie left any examples of their wares made while in the Americas, but the following examples of migrant craftsman certainly did. Having looked at political motivation for goldsmiths migrating, we will now consider some of the financial and social factors. Moving down the eastern seaboard, the West Indies provides further examples.

Before investigating a few individual cases it is worth making some general comments about the Scottish experience in the Caribbean.[3] Across the area, throughout the eighteenth century, but especially after 1763, when the British made huge territorial gains from the French, the number of plantations growing sugar cane, coffee, indigo or cotton increased. Many were owned by Scots and provided employment opportunities for other Scots from the home country. Utilising kinship and local connections, or networks, Scots on plantations extended their links throughout the West Indies, buying land, and engaging lawyers, managers and bookkeepers. Many so-called 'adventurers' were from landed families and developed a whole series of networks based on pre-existing bonds; they were consciously transatlantic. Scots in the Caribbean drew heavily on these networks for support and patronage. Such 'spheres of influence' had characterised Scottish society for generations, the 'sojourners' simply transplanted them to wherever they settled.

Scots and their firms also contributed to the extension of credit and mercantile facilities which fostered an increase in the production of Caribbean staples. As these grew so did the demand for enslaved Africans. Scots were heavily involved in both the use and supply of slave labour. Key Scottish politicians, from the Dukes of Argyll to Henry Dundas, used government-sponsored colonial posts to extend their patronage, and they made astute use of this in distributing such patronage to 'useful' individuals. These connections were essential bonds that held together the Atlantic world and, as such, certainly played a role in the careers of several Scottish silversmiths seeking their fortunes in the West Indies.

During this period, Jamaica witnessed the immigration and settlement of Scots from virtually the whole of the country. Many came from landed families with well-established transatlantic networks; Campbells, Grants, Gordons and Grahams to name but a few. Charles Allan (1710–62), goldsmith in Edinburgh, London and Jamaica, was able to make extensive use of some of these connections to further his career.[4]

Allan was born in 1710, son of Benjamin Allan, an Edinburgh lawyer, and Sarah Campbell. Having been orphaned, he appears to have been apprenticed, *c*1724, without indentures, to Colin Campbell (who in turn had been the apprentice of one of the most talented Edinburgh goldsmiths of the early eighteenth century, Colin Mackenzie (IoG Reg Archive)). Campbell was probably related to Allan's mother; yet another instance of the importance of kinship links within the goldsmiths' profession. Unfortunately, there is no record of Allan finishing his 'time' with Campbell, which would have been about 1731, but it is fairly certain that he would have continued in his master's workshop as a journeyman until the mid-1730s. At some point he left Edinburgh for London, like so many other Scots at this time, presumably in order to better his career. It is possible that he worked in London as a retailer, or as a journeyman in another goldsmith's workshop, as he doesn't seem to have registered his mark with the Goldsmiths' Company there. However, the Allan family was connected through business with the notable legal family of Dalrymple of North Berwick, and Charles Allan was therefore able to draw on this connection to borrow significant sums from Sir Hew Dalrymple MP and his brother Dr Robert Dalrymple. This allowed him to establish himself in London, and then in the early 1740s to proceed to Kingston, Jamaica, where he set up a goldsmith's business in partnership with his former master's son, Archibald Campbell (Barker 2007: chapter 3, passim).

Here it is perhaps worth investigating another one of the connections which might have helped Allan's business. We have already seen he was well connected with the Dalrymples, a significant group

in both Edinburgh and London. However, through both his mother and his master, Charles Allan was intimately connected with a Campbell network, and this is perhaps just as significant for his Jamaican venture.

The first Campbell to become involved in Jamaica seems to have been Colonel John Campbell, leader of a band of some of the survivors of the Darien adventure, who drifted across to Jamaica in 1700 and settled in the west of the island. Many other Campbells were to be born there or to follow from Argyll. Before his death in 1740, John Campbell established an enormous network in Jamaica, formed largely of people from Argyll, and consequently 'through his extreme generosity and assistance, many are now possessed of opulent fortunes' (Hamilton 2005: 56). While it is difficult to be certain how closely related the various Campbells in Jamaica were, it is reasonable to suppose the existence of a powerful Campbell network in the island. In 1774 the planter turned historian Edward Long mentions a 'computation … of no fewer than 100 of the name Campbell … actually resident in [Jamaica], all claiming allegiance with the Argyle family' (ibid). John, 2nd Duke and Archibald, 3rd Duke of Argyll, were the political masters of Scotland for most of the first half of the eighteenth century. They were instrumental in furthering the early commercialisation and, indeed, industrialisation of Scotland, impelling many of their own and other clansmen to seek their fortunes overseas and creating a pool of migrants, many of whom settled in North America but a significant number of whom ventured to the Caribbean.

With the help of these connections, it was clear that Charles Allan had grand ambitions and hoped to supply luxury goods to the planter gentry of Jamaica.

Here it is perhaps worth recalling that goldsmiths and silversmiths were businessmen first and foremost and so were driven by their clients' demands, both financially and artistically. Allan obtained credit from both the Dalrymples and another Scottish merchant in Jamaica, and began by importing a large amount of highly fashionable rococo silver from London, to retail in Kingston. Unfortunately, this did not go as well as planned; he found it difficult to sell for cash. At some point about 1745 he started to manufacture in his own extensive workshop, producing a wide range of wares from spoons, bowls, salvers, cruet sets through to very substantial covered cups. All were characterised by good, heavy-gauge metal and well-executed chasing in the current rococo fashion, presumably reflecting

Illustration 5.4
Cup and cover, by Charles Allan, Jamaica, *c* 1750.
[Courtesy of the Trustees of the National Museums Scotland]

both the tastes and wealth of his customers (Barker 2007: chapter 3, passim) (illus 5.4).

Significant examples of his output have now been identified, particularly since we have been able to differentiate it from the work of Coline Allan of Aberdeen. For many years, prior to Robert B Barker's pioneering work, most pieces with a 'CA' maker's mark were confidently ascribed to Coline Allan, one of the most gifted and prolific mid-eighteenth-century Aberdeen silversmiths. This misidentification was further complicated by the facts that Coline was also a master of rococo chasing and that many such pieces appeared with an additional 'AD' mark, which some silver enthusiasts suggested was a hitherto unknown contraction of the 'AberDeen' town mark. In fact, this mark relates to Anthony Danvers, one of the Jamaican assay masters whom Charles Allan was instrumental in having established on the island in 1747 (Barker 1984: 134–5) (illus 5.5). He and another goldsmith from Edinburgh, William Duncan, successfully lobbied the Jamaican Assembly to introduce a local assaying system, in order to ensure the quality of metal used in the island. Significantly, this system looked to Edinburgh rather than London for its model; hence the assay master's initials were stamped on wares to identify the assayer who had tested and passed the silverware as being of sterling standard. The island's mark was an alligator's head. Charles Allan undoubtedly became the largest and most prolific goldsmith in the colony, but his success was short-lived – principally because it was entirely based on credit, and he was unable at crucial periods to obtain hard cash from his customers in order to pay his own debts. His creditors began to close in on him, demanding payment, and his business suffered dramatically in the early 1750s. He died in 1762.

Jamaica was not the only island in the Caribbean to attract Scottish craftsmen. Tobago, in the Windward Islands, was captured from the French and ceded as a British colony in 1763. The French later invaded and recovered it in May 1781 and held it until 1793, when it was finally retaken by the British. At the time of the French invasion, Tobago was under the governorship of a young Scottish lawyer and plantation owner, George Ferguson of Pitfour, but he was not to hold the position long. Despite conducting a valiant and

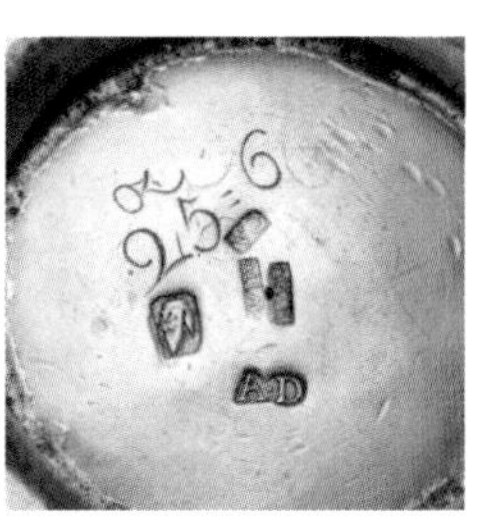

Illustration 5.5
Marks on a covered bowl, showing Charles Allan's maker's marks, assay master's mark for Anthony Danvers and the alligator's head Jamaica mark. [Courtesy of a private collection]

cunning defence, Ferguson was overwhelmed by the French forces (Gilchrist 1999: 4). He was not the only member of his family to have military skill: his older brother Patrick is famed for his invention of a breech-loading musket and for his heroic death at the battle of Kings Mountain, South Carolina, where he led a group of American Loyalists against the rebels in the war of American Independence (Gilchrist 2003: passim). The family also had an earlier connection with the island of Tobago; for Patrick, while serving in the West Indies, bought a sugar plantation in 1768 for the family at Castara. George Ferguson looked after this when Patrick returned to Britain for health reasons in 1772 (Gilchrist 1999: 6). He was still in the West Indies in 1795 when he fought a duel on the island of Grenada, but he was certainly recorded, at the time of his death in 1821, as being one of the last members of the gentry to remain living in the Old Town of Edinburgh. He was buried in the family vault in Greyfriars Churchyard on 15 January 1821 (ibid, 4, 12).

Ferguson was a man of considerable taste and commissioned several examples of excellent quality, highly fashionable silver. A pair of candlesticks, hallmarked Edinburgh 1814–15 and originally from a much larger set of eight or twelve, are of particular importance to this study.[5] They are formed of plain columns set on domed bases, with capitals formed from three boars' heads supporting screw nozzles and rising prickets. They are of a highly unusual design for Scottish candlesticks, which usually followed fashionable London patterns. Their almost severe plainness, combined with very heavy-gauge metal, are characteristic of this maker's work. The domed base and the use of an element from the engraved coat of arms (three boars' heads, for Ferguson) as part of the capital are, in my experience, a unique feature in Scottish sticks. The ingenious use of a rising pricket is also rare. Obviously, however, it is the maker that is of most importance for the present discussion; they have the maker's mark 'GF.Tobago', for George Fenwick (illus 5.6). There are, however, full hallmarks for Edinburgh 1814–15, clearly suggesting they were made in that city. The reasons for the inclusion of the word 'Tobago' in the maker's mark are presently unclear, but certainly indicate a fascinating connection with the island.

Illustration 5.6
Pair of candlesticks with 'George Fenwick, Tobago' mark, hallmarked in Edinburgh 1814–15.
[Courtesy of the Trustees of the National Museums Scotland]

Two silversmiths called George Fenwick, father and son, were working in Edinburgh at about the same time and it is not clear which is which at any given time. Fenwick senior was admitted as a freeman of the Incorporation of Goldsmiths on 20 September 1810, having previously been working in the city as an unfreeman. He was in a productive partnership with George McHattie between 1800 and 1807, and continued in business until his retirement in 1853 (IoG Reg Archive). He took his son, also George, as an apprentice in November 1811. George junior in turn was admitted as a freeman of the Edinburgh Incorporation on 23 May 1820, and very shortly afterwards emigrated to Tobago. It now seems clear that both Georges had some connection with the Fergusons of Pitfour and Tobago, as the mark on both these candlesticks and numerous other pieces of silver made *before* the younger George headed for the West Indies proves. Unfortunately, like so many Europeans, he succumbed to the climate and died at the Fergusons' plantation of Castara on Tobago on 4 September 1821. Surviving examples of the Fenwicks' work indicate that they were productive and talented craftsmen, not always following the set conventions of the day. Many of their pieces display bold design and the use of particularly heavy-gauge metal, something noted earlier with the Scots silversmiths in Jamaica. Unfortunately, there is not yet a complete answer to this story, and more research is still to be done, but these candlesticks are a remarkable piece of evidence for the Scots' links with the West Indies. They tie together the experience of a younger son of a laird who returned to Scotland with a fortune and a craftsman who did not.

For the final example of a Scots migrant goldsmith in this short study, we must turn to Canada, and the career of a fully time-served master goldsmith who possibly migrated because of a downturn in his financial affairs at home. Robert Cruickshank moved to Montreal in 1773 and became one of Canada's most prolific and influential silversmiths of the late eighteenth and early nineteenth centuries.[6]

The son of George Cruickshank, a Presbyterian minister in Arbroath, Cruickshank was born in April 1743 and at the age of sixteen was apprenticed to Alexander Johnston, goldsmith in London. Johnston was also a Scot, who had originally worked in Dundee, served in the Jacobite army in the 1745–6 rebellion, and had been forced to seek his fortune in London. Cruickshank was connected to Johnston through an extended kinship bond and became a freeman of the London Company of Goldsmiths on 9 April 1766, taking over his master's business when he retired to a Scottish estate in July 1766. Recorded as a plateworker (a maker of larger objects, such as cups, tureens, sauceboats etc) in Old Jewry from 1766 to 1773, Cruickshank seems to have pursued a successful career in the capital (Fox 2008: 83). Dr Ross Fox has convincingly reattributed numerous London-made pieces to Cruickshank, and from this evidence he was clearly a talented craftsman (ibid, 84). He certainly had links with the transatlantic trade, supplying James Craig, another silversmith of Scots descent, active in Williamsburg (ibid, 85). It is likely, however, that Cruickshank's fortunes took a turn for the worse during the extreme credit crisis that hit Britain in 1772, bringing on a widespread economic depression. It was presumably this that prompted him to emigrate to Montreal in 1773, one of the major centres of the burgeoning fur trade (ibid, 86). Scots were at the centre of this trade, occupying prominent positions in the management and operation of the North West Company.

Cruickshank was obviously a talented and adaptable craftsman and a skilled businessman. Very soon after his arrival he was producing a wide range of domestic and ecclesiastical silver for a range of customers. It is perhaps ironic that this son of a Scottish Presbyterian manse found himself producing large numbers of sacramental vessels for the growing Roman Catholic congregations of Montreal. While his forms follow standard French prototypes, one can argue that Cruickshank brought a measure of Calvinist simplicity to them in the form of restrained use of chased ornament. His domestic wares also echo the current neoclassical tastes demanded by his French- and English-speaking customers (Fox 2008: 87; Villeneuve 1988: 60).

However, it is in his production of so-called 'trade silver' that we can most see his Scottish roots. The use of silver goods for barter within the fur trade grew in the second half of the eighteenth century, especially by those traders operating out of Montreal. Many types of silver ornament were traded with Native Americans, particularly medals, gorgets, brooches and crosses. All helped to 'brighten the covenant chain', as the strengthening of the links between European traders and native peoples was described. However, one particular piece of jewellery found favour with native peoples in the east of the country – the heart-shaped brooch. So popular were these small brooches with the Iroquois that the style became something of a national badge.

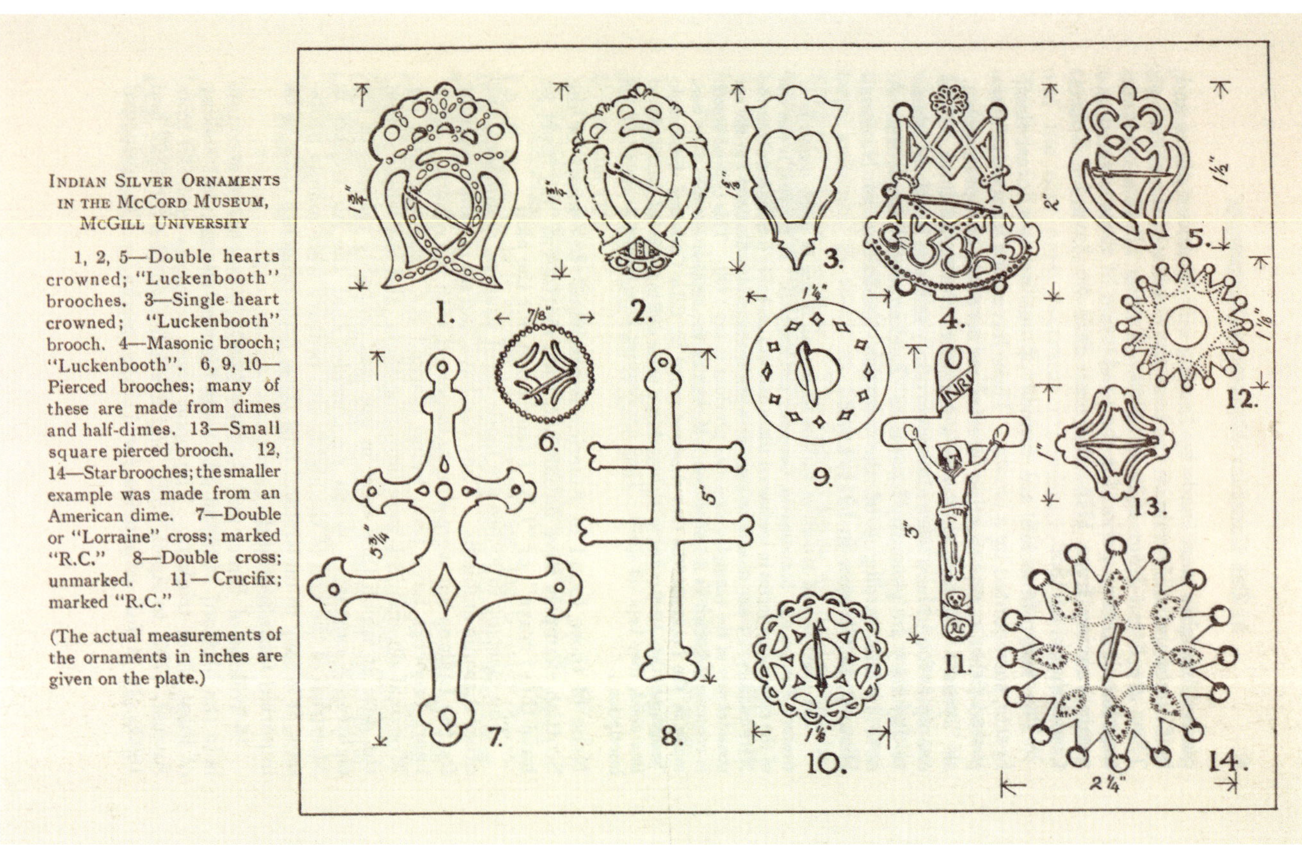

Illustration 5.7a
Trade silver, illustrated in Ramsay Traquair's 1938 article, compared with Illustration 5.7b, a selection of
Scottish heart brooches in the NMS collection, eighteenth and nineteenth centuries.
[Courtesy of the Trustees of the National Museums Scotland]

It is now accepted that the design of these very distinctive brooches had its origin in Scotland, where it later became known as a 'luckenbooth' brooch. The first scholar to suggest this and to discuss its significance was Ramsay Traquair (1874–1952), the influential Professor of Architecture at McGill University. His article on 'Montreal and the Indian trade silver' was published in 1938 (Traquair 1938: 4). The physical similarities between Scottish brooches and Montreal-made ones are obvious, from the use of the basic heart shape, through the addition of open-work crowns to the complex shapes arrived at by intertwining two hearts. How and why this example of Scottish folk-jewellery made the transition to become Canadian-made trade silver, sought after by native peoples, are complex and only partially answerable questions (illus 5.7).

Native American interest in these brooches may have started with seeing Scots settlers – women and children – wearing them. The numbers of Scots settler families in the east of the country increased after the end of the French and Indian War, and, of course, again in the aftermath of the American Revolution. It is quite probable that women wore the brooches as a reminder of emotional links with their home country. As many Scottish heart brooches were either made or used in the north-east of Scotland, it is certain that Robert Cruickshank, who hailed from that area, would not only be very familiar with their design but would also know of their cultural significance (Dalgleish 2006: 125). He became one of the largest suppliers of trade silver to the Montreal-based fur traders, many of whom were Scots or of Scots descent.

Illustration 5.7b

Trade silver both in Canada and the continental United States of America was a considerable commercial enterprise, and merchants ordered many tens of thousands of silver items. This trade saw its height during the days of bitter conflict between the Hudson's Bay Company and the North West Company.

We get some idea of its sheer scale from an order placed with Robert Cruickshank in May 1800, by Angus Mackintosh, an agent working for Mactavish, Frobisher & Co. The order included 12,000 small brooches at 6/6, 6,000 small brooches at 8/– and 5,000 large brooches at 15/– (Langdon 1966: 18–19).[7] This account was by no means exceptional in terms of total numbers of items ordered, as other bills and accounts confirm (Fredrickson and Gibbs 1980: 43–8).

One can perhaps see why in the wonderful painting of an unknown native woman with her son, erroneously titled *Pocahontas and Her Son* (illus 5.8). The portrait clearly dates to the early part of the nineteenth century. The woman's dress is lavishly decorated with alternating lines of heart and 'council square' trade silver brooches. Whoever painted this picture was aware of the cultural and ethnic complexity of the interaction between Native Americans and Europeans involved in the fur trade. In Scotland heart brooches were normally only worn by women or children, and usually one at a time. Native American women seem to have preferred to wear them in large numbers, as did Native American men with other forms of trade silver. One can get some idea of the value of the brooches in the fur trade from a list of 'Equivalents for barter of goods and skins' dated 1765. This indicated that one silver brooch (although unfortunately the list does not stipulate if it was a heart type) was to be exchanged for one racoon or musquash skin (Dalgleish 2006: 126).

Trade in silver ornaments decreased dramatically after the amalgamation of the North West Company and Hudson's Bay Company in 1820, as the Hudson's Bay Company did not favour the use of trade silver in their business. By this time, however, Robert Cruickshank

was no longer on the scene. In 1805 he had moved over to being a hardware merchant and in 1807 passed the business to his son-in-law Arthur Webster – another Scot, from near St Andrews in Fife, and yet further evidence of the importance of kinship ties in our story. Cruickshank died in 1809 on board ship,

Illustration 5.8
Portrait of an unknown woman, once thought to be Pocahontas and her son Thomas Rolfe, American School, *c* 1800. Photo: D C Pitcher. [Courtesy of the Borough Council of King's Lynn and West Norfolk]

just as he was returning to Canada from a visit to Britain (Fox 2008: 93). He was undoubtedly one of the most successful transatlantic Scottish silversmiths in our period. He also brings to an end this brief look at the careers of a few of the silversmiths who made the journey across the sea in the eighteenth century.

Conclusion

Assessing the impact of Scots craftsmen on the transatlantic silver trade is clearly problematic. While significant quantities of silver made in Scotland were doubtless carried overseas by emigrants, little has survived; certainly not enough to form the inspiration for identifiably Scottish styles in their new homelands. Nor did the reasonable number of migrant craftsmen themselves seem to develop particularly 'Scottish' products. With the obvious exception of the heart-shaped brooches so favoured by the North West Company's fur traders, one does not find large numbers of American-made quaichs or Jamaican egg-shaped coffee urns.

Like most other Scots émigrés, goldsmiths, silversmiths and jewellers left the country for a variety of reasons: economic, social and political. Equally, as part of the 'middling sort', they made particular use of the range of pre-existing kin- and area-based networks to further their careers. They were primarily businessmen geared to supply what their clients wanted and undoubtedly willing to adapt to the demands, taste and pockets of their customers. The use of heavy-gauge silver by West Indies silversmiths is probably a reflection of this. Some settled for good and integrated into their host societies, while some returned home, with or without a fortune. What is clear is that they were an integral part of the huge economic and social impact that the Scots had on the developing transatlantic world and, as such, I hope this short survey will prompt further research into the Scottish silversmith in the Americas.

Notes

1　My original conference paper owes a great deal to the pioneering work of Robert B Barker, Dr Ross Fox, Rene Villeneuve, Henry Fothringham OBE, Julianne Berger and William Fortescue, people I am privileged to call friends and colleagues, and whose work I relied on throughout.

2　I am grateful to Ms Julianne Berger, an intern from the Centre for British Studies, Humboldt University, Berlin, for painstakingly preparing a survey of Scottish silversmiths culled mainly from existing published sources.

3　Much of the following section is based on Douglas J Hamilton's detailed survey of the Scots in the Caribbean (Hamilton 2005: passim).

4　I am immensely grateful to Robert B Barker for generously allowing me to draw on unpublished material from his MPhil thesis (Barker 2007), as well as quoting heavily from his many published articles. He also kindly read this

article in draft and made many helpful and constructive comments.

5　These two candlesticks were acquired by National Museums Scotland in 2003.

6　Much of what follows is based primarily on the work of two Canadian scholars, Dr Ross Fox and Dr Rene Villeneuve; both have very kindly allowed me to use their recent research, published and in discussion, on George Cruickshank. The following theory about Cruickshank's inspiration for the use of heart brooches as trade silver is, however, my own interpretation.

7　I have not been able to consult the original account quoted in Langdon (1966: 18–19) and at first sight the prices, if quoted for individual brooches, look unrealistically expensive. As he emphasises elsewhere that the trade goods were to consist of 'inexpensive silver trinkets' (ibid, 18) it seems probable that the prices were actually per *dozen* items. I am grateful to Robert B Barker and Wynyard Wilkinson for alerting me to this apparent anomaly.

Bibliography

Barker, R B 1984 'Jamaican goldsmiths and assayers, 1665 to 1765', *in Proceedings of the Silver Society*, vol III, no 5 (1984), 133–7. London.

Barker, R B 2007 'Style transmission: rococo silver and colonial Jamaica', unpublished MPhil Thesis, Royal College of Art.

Dalgleish, G 2006 'Aspects of Scottish-Canadian material culture: heart brooches and Scottish pottery', *in* Rider, P E & McNabb, H (eds) *A Kingdom of the Mind: How the Scots Helped Make Canada*. Montreal & Kingston: McGill-Queen's University Press, Studies in Ethnic History Series.

Dalgleish, G & Fothringham, H S 2008 *Silver Made in Scotland*. Edinburgh: NMS Publishing.

Devine, T M 1975 *The Tobacco Lords: A Study of the Tobacco Merchants of Glasgow and their Trading Activities, 1740–90*. Edinburgh: John Donald.

Devine, T M 1999 *The Scottish Nation*. London: Penguin.

Devine, T M 2003 *Scotland's Empire 1600–1815*. London: Penguin.

Dietert, R & Dietert, J 2007 *The Edinburgh Goldsmiths I, Training, Marks Output and Demographics*. Private publication.

Dobson, D 1994 *Scottish Emigration to Colonial America 1607–1785*. Athens: Georgia.

Dobson, D 2006 *Scots in the West Indies, 1707–1857*, vol II. Baltimore: Genealogical Publishing Company.

EGM Edinburgh Goldsmiths Minutes 1525–1700, Steuart Fothringham, H (ed) Scottish Record Society new ser V 29. Edinburgh, 2006.

Fortescue, W 2012 *Edinburgh Goldsmiths and Radical Politics, 1783–4: The Case of David Downie*. Book of the Old Edinburgh Club, vol 9.

Fox, R 2008 'Robert Cruickshank (1743–1809), Silversmith in London and Montreal', *in Silver Studies. The Journal of the Silver Society*, no 23 (2008), 83–95. London.

Fredrickson, N J & Gibb, S 1980 *The Covenant Chain: Indian Ceremonial and Trade Silver*. Ottawa: National Museums of Canada.

Gilchrist, M M 1999 *The Fergusons of Pitfour: A Hero and His Family*. Edinburgh: Society of Friends of the Kirk of Greyfriars.

Gilchrist, M M 2003 *Patrick Ferguson: 'A Man of Some Genius'*. Edinburgh: NMS Publishing.

Hamilton D J 2005 *Scotland, the Caribbean and the Atlantic World*. Manchester: University Press.

IoG Registration Archive Incorporation of Goldsmiths of the City of Edinburgh Online Hallmarking Archive.

James, I E 1981 *The Goldsmiths of Aberdeen, 1450–1850*. Aberdeen: Bieldside Books.

Karras, A L 1992 *Sojourners in the Sun: Scottish Migrants in Jamaica and the Chesapeake, 1740–1800*. Ithaca and London: Cornell University Press.

Langdon, J E 1966 *Canadian Silversmiths, 1700–1900*. Toronto.

Quick, E 1997 *A Balance of Silver: The Story of the Silversmiths of Tain*. Tain.

Quick, E 2009 *James Thompson: A Highlander in Quebec*. Tain and District Museum Trust.

Traquair, R 1938 'Montreal and the Indian Trade Silver', *in The Canadian Historical Review*, vol XIX, March 1938. Toronto.

Villeneuve, R 1988 'English influences on Quebec silver', *in Antique Collector*, October 1988.

Villeneuve, R 1998 *Quebec Silver from the Collection of the National Gallery of Canada*. Ottawa: National Gallery of Canada.

Villeneuve, R 2006 'A Scottish-born silversmith in Montreal: Robert Cruickshank', *in A Kingdom of the Mind: How the Scots Helped Make Canada* (eds) Rider, P E & McNabb, H (eds). Montreal & Kingston: McGill-Queen's University Press, Studies in Ethnic History Series.

Wilkinson, W R T 1973 *Indian Colonial Silver: European Silversmiths in India (1790–1860)*. London: Argent Press.

Wilkinson, W R T 1987 *The Makers of Indian Colonial Silver: A Register of European Goldsmiths, Silversmiths, Jewellers, Watchmakers and Clockmakers in India and their Marks, 1760–1860*. London: private publication.

CHAPTER 6

From Fife to Phyfe;
or 'the tale of one Scotsman's odyssey in early America'

MICHAEL K BROWN

While still virtually unknown in his native Scotland, Duncan Phyfe (1770–1854) was proclaimed in 1817 by one enthusiast in his adopted land, 'Mr. Phyfe is so much the United States rage.'[1]

Within his own lifetime Duncan Phyfe's name and reputation extended far beyond his cabinet shop and showrooms in lower Manhattan to the banks of the Mississippi River in the west and well outside American borders to Saint Croix and Guadeloupe in the Caribbean. Furthermore, his renown did not die with him. By the 1880s Phyfe became one of the first American cabinetmakers to attract the attention of scholars and collectors. In the intervening years his life was researched and his superb furniture studied, once again making him the United States rage. While more than a century has passed since these nascent studies were undertaken, the name *Duncan Phyfe* remains iconic to a cadre of curators, collectors, antiques dealers, auctioneers, designers, manufacturers and woodworkers.[2]

Who better qualified to understand the contribution of one of the nation's pre-eminent cabinetmakers than a fellow cabinetmaker? In 1847, as Ernest Ferdinand Hagen (1830–1913), a recent immigrant to New York City from Hamburg, was apprenticed to Ernest Krieg and Augustus Dohrmann at 106 Norfolk Street, Duncan Phyfe was in the process of shuttering his long-established Fulton Street business only blocks away.

While Hagen never attained the stature that Phyfe had achieved, still he could boast of patronage by many prominent New York families including the Roosevelts and Havemeyers, as well as a clientele that included numbers of the city's leading furniture and decorating firms, such as Louis Comfort Tiffany, Leon Marcotte, the Herter Brothers, and Sypher & Company. Over time, Hagen's repertoire evolved and expanded to encompass the sale of antiques, responding to the

Victorian vogue to integrate them into the domestic interior while fuelled by an ever-growing fascination with the nation's historical past.

On the threshold of the twentieth century, Ernest Hagen, like Duncan Phyfe, had been active in the cabinet trade for more than a half century. By 1908, with his sons Frederick E (1868–1948) and Henry A Hagen (1877–1927), now overseeing the family concern, Hagen assumed the guise of an antiquarian. Looking back over the changes that defined his tenure, he drafted an account of this transformative age, *Personal Experiences of an Old New York Cabinet Maker* (1908), which examined its leading personalities, manufactories and their production. The immense worth of this manuscript has long been acknowledged by scholars as the singular, first-hand account of the cabinet trade in New York City over the second half of the nineteenth century.[3]

A year earlier, in 1907, Ernest Hagen completed his *Memorandum on Phyfe*. Hagen was probably the first to discover the New York cabinetmaker price books, published volumes that either codify the retail prices established by the master craftsmen, or else agreed to by them and the journeymen they employed. Over the next quarter century he continued his research tracing Duncan Phyfe's career through the city's directories, scrutinising his will, and successfully tracking and interviewing a number of the craftsman's descendants. His timing proved serendipitous, completing his *Memorandum* on the eve of a statewide observance of the 300th anniversary of Henry Hudson's discovery of the great waterway that bears his name, as well as the centenary of Robert Fulton's invention of the steamboat, the vessel that is credited with revolutionising travel and trade along the Hudson River, and, for that matter, well beyond it. A variety of celebratory events were scheduled across the state, while in New York City plans were well underway for a nine-day regatta, a grand procession along Broadway, and for Wilbur Wright and Glen Curtis to pilot the first flights over Manhattan Island.

At the Metropolitan Museum of Art these dual anniversaries were observed with not one, but two major exhibitions. In homage to Hudson, it brought together what was deemed the greatest collection of Dutch painting that the country had ever witnessed and, to complement it, Fulton was celebrated by an installation of early American painting and decorative arts – the first ever organised by an art museum. In the preface to an impressive two-volume catalogue, Robert W de Forest, a trustee of the museum who also chaired the Committee on Art Exhibitions for the Hudson-Fulton Celebration Committee, acknowledged the collector, Richard Townes Haines Halsey, 'for the complete showing of furniture by Duncan Phyfe', and Ernest Hagen for contributing his pioneering research on Phyfe, 'our earliest New York cabinetmaker'.[4]

The impact of the Hudson-Fulton exhibition created the impetus for the Metropolitan Museum to form a collection of early American decorative arts. Within the year it had purchased 434 objects from the pioneering collection formed by the Bostonian, Eugene Bolles, and by 1924, with generous support from Robert de Forest, then the Museum's president, it opened an entire wing dedicated to the arts of America. Furthermore, the 1909 exhibition, by publishing Ernest Hagen's *Memorandum on Phyfe* and the dozen entries on furniture that it ascribed to his shop, provided the genesis for a new generation of researchers and, in turn, a plethora of articles. In 1914 Harold Donaldson Eberlein and Abbot McClure contributed 'Duncan Phyfe & American Empire Furniture', to *Good Furniture* and the following year James Collier Marshall wrote 'Duncan Phyfe, American Cabinet Maker', for *Country Life*. Concurrently, Walter A Dyer authored 'Duncan Phyfe Furniture', for *House Beautiful* and dedicated a chapter, 'The Exquisite Furniture of Duncan Phyfe', to his volume *Early American Craftsmen*. In 1921 *Country Life* published his article, 'Rare Old Furniture of Duncan Phyfe'.

With Phyfemania on the rise, Charles Over Cornelius, the assistant curator of decorative arts at the Metropolitan Museum, organised the groundbreaking exhibition, 'Furniture from the Workshop of Duncan Phyfe', in 1922, the first time an American art museum dedicated a show to the work of a single cabinetmaker. Cornelius authored an accompanying catalogue, *Furniture Masterpieces of Duncan Phyfe*, as

well as submitting articles to *Country Life*, the *American Magazine of Art* and a brand new publication, *The Magazine Antiques*.[5]

In the midst of this growing adulation, scant attention was paid to the artisan's Scottish origins. What little was known had been gleaned by Ernest Hagen from his conversations with Duncan Phyfe's grandsons:

> In 1783 or 1784 just after the close of the revolutionary war, a Scotch family by the name Phyfe left their home of Loch Fannich, 30 miles NW of Inverness with 6 or 8 children of whom 2 died on the long voyage in the old, slow sailing vessel and coming here settled in or near Albany N.Y.[6]

Exactly two decades later, in 1929, Thomas Hamilton Ormsbee published his research into the family's Scottish origins. He established that the name of the family matriarch was Isabel Fife, a resident of Albany, New York, in 1790. Over time Ormsbee's discovery would prove a pivotal addition to the genealogical information supplied by the descendants.[7]

Nancy McClelland's (1877–1959) vision proved far more expansive. In 1939 she published *Duncan Phyfe and the English Regency*.[8] McClelland was passionate about early American decorative arts, yet she lived at a time before it was an established scholarly discipline with formal training and accreditation. McClelland belonged to the first generation of women decorators in America and she also gained recognition as a respected author and expert in antiques and historic wallpapers.

With Ernest Hagen's account of Phyfe's childhood and migration as a starting point, McClelland relates how her friend 'Mr. Frank Donald of Dundee offered to undertake an expedition into the Fife country'. Then, as today, his quest began in Edinburgh at Register House (now the National Archives of Scotland) and from there north to Loch Fannich. McClelland lauds Donald for his diligence, paying calls on the local clergy, the gamekeeper at Loch Fannich Lodge, the registrar for the district, and personally surveying the ancient graveyard – all without success. Further enquiries, made in Strathpeffer and Edinburgh, also proved futile. With nothing to augment Hagen's 1907 research, all that McClelland could contribute was to explain to her readers her efforts and introduce a genealogical table that charted seven generations of the Phyfe family.[9]

The surname Fife, however, is uncommon, and the names of only three individuals emerge from mid-eighteenth-century registers.[10] Two baptisms

Illustration 6.1
'Portrait of Sir James Grant and Jean Duff, Lady Grant' by David Allan, 42 x 51in approx (1067 x 1295mm).
Private collection. [Courtesy the Earl of Seafield]

are recorded in 1769. The first of these is to Mary and John 'Fyfee' of Tannadice, Angus, and the other is a son of Alexander 'Fyfe' of Scone, Perth. The third is registered a year later in the Abernethy and Kincardine parish to Donald and Isobel Fife of Inverness-shire. The latter is more consistent with the locale related by the Phyfe grandsons in their account and corresponds to the given name of Duncan Phyfe's mother, while an earlier citation to this family refers to the christening of his older brother John. As one delves deeper into the Phyfe genealogy, it becomes increasingly apparent that oftentimes the family account differs from the official records. For instance, John and Duncan's births and baptisms, in 1767 and 1770 respectively, are at variance with the dates that the family had traditionally registered, 1765 and 1768.

The Abernethy and Kincardine archives also document the nuptials of Isobel Grant and Donald Fife on 8 January 1767.[11] Albeit one of nineteen marriages recorded in Scotland between 1750 and 1775 which specifies that the bride is named 'Isobel' and her groom bears the surname 'Fife', the union between Donald and Isobel is the only one recorded in Inverness-shire.[12] Donald Fife's marriage to Isobel Grant appears to have been a propitious one as his bride's maiden name implies kinship with one of the most prominent Scottish clans in the north-east. By 1773 the Grant lands were under the administration of Sir James Grant, the 8th Baronet of Colquhoun, who, as clan chief, would serve as overseer for the next thirty-eight years (illus 6.1).[13] At Grantown-on-Spey Sir James created a manufacturing village which included linen and woollen mills to provide employment for the local

Illustration 6.2
Grantown and the district of Speyside. Detail from the Map of Scotland by James Kirkwood, 1810.
[Courtesy of the National Library of Scotland]

population, drawing Strathspey into an increasingly industrialised world (illus 6.2). Concurrently, a systematic reclamation of derelict land was initiated by reintroducing the indigenous Scots Pine forests. Yet, in spite of the success of the baronet's efforts, many, such as Donald and Isobel Fife, eventually chose to quit their native land.

Today, there is scant documentation of the exodus of these émigrés to North America prior to 1820. The earliest known manuscripts are a small cache spanning the period between February 1774 and September 1775. In spite of their obvious time limitations, they offer precious insights into the character of these people and the circumstances which caused them to leave their homeland.[14]

Categorised under seven headings, these papers list the passengers' names, their former residence, the age of the individual, 'Occupation and Employment', 'To What Port or Place Bound', 'On what account and for what purpose they go', and the name of the ship they were to travel on. During the twenty-month period covered, passages were recorded to Philadelphia, Pennsylvania; Wilmington, North Carolina; Charleston, South Carolina; Savannah, Georgia; and Salem, Massachusetts; as well as to St John's, Newfoundland, Quebec, and the Caribbean island of Antigua. However, by far the greatest number of voyages, eleven, were destined for New York City, more than double that of the next most frequented ports.

Among the vessels bound for New York was the *George* which departed Greenock on 13 May 1774. Included amid its 224 passengers were 140 from Strathspey, fifty-nine bearing the surname Grant. When questioned about their departure, they confided that it was driven by their need to find employment or else in response to the escalation of land rents, as most were involved in farming.[15] These reasons are consistent with those registered by other Highlanders, and the same concerns and circumstances may have prompted Donald and Isobel Fife to migrate.

A targeted survey of the extensive Seafield archive yields little information about Donald Fife, his family and profession. Receipts for land rents imply that he too gained a living from agriculture. However, given his son's later famed proficiency with woodworking, it would be tempting to link the family to the timber industry for which Strathspey had long been known. The Phyfes were still in residence there in 1773 when Donald 'Fyfe' is recorded paying for the rental of land, but no later citations have been located.[16]

Within the year another departure for New York City is recorded from Greenock. This time it was aboard the *Lilly*, which included among its passengers 'Isobell Fife', described as a twenty-seven-year-old from Paisley. Accompanying her is 'a Child' and the reason for her travel is 'Going to Her Husband'. The citation is intriguing but not specific enough to be sure that this is indeed Duncan Phyfe's mother.[17] Within five months, in September 1775, the British government prohibited any further emigration to America due to the growing strife there. Between April 1775, as the *Lilly* set sail from Greenock, and 1790, when the first United States census lists 'Isabel Fife', as a resident of Albany, New York, there are no further citations of the name Fife throughout New York State.[18]

The 1790 Census identifies Isabel Fife as the head of a household situated in Albany's first ward. The census taker did not specify other members of the household by name but would simply count and categorise them by their sex and age. Residing under Isabel Fife's roof were two 'Free white males of 16 years and upwards'. It seems reasonable to assume that these youths were her youngest sons, James and Laughlin, although, once again, the question of their exact ages makes it challenging to be absolutely certain about their identification. There being no mention of Duncan Phyfe in the census returns, it is likely that by 1790 he was residing elsewhere. Depending on whether he asserted 1768 or 1770 as his date of birth, either he was about to satisfy the requirements of his apprenticeship, an apprentice's twenty-first birthday marking the legal conclusion of his indenture, or else had just completed it and was now in the midst of embarking on a professional career.

Typically, the amendment of one's age is induced by a desire to expunge rather than add a few years; yet, there are discernible motivations for Duncan Phyfe to augment his. Claiming that he was slightly older than he actually was might have helped his career. If he was now gainfully employed then he was also in a position to provide needed fiscal support to his widowed mother and younger siblings. Granted, the question of Phyfe's exact age can be perceived as a seemingly minor matter, perhaps simply dismissed as an error in record-keeping; however, it is the first in a succession of signifiers that contribute towards developing a profile of someone who is ambitious and determined to succeed.

Whether Duncan Phyfe was apprenticed in Albany or New York City, the latter place possessed a greater allure. At this precise moment Albany's population was less than one-tenth of New York's, and, while little is known of its cabinet industry, it is believed to have been modest in size and not very distinguished. By contrast, New York City was beginning to emerge from seven devastating years of revolution and occupation. For its residents, this post-war period was defined by a spirit of optimism as the town was about to embark on an age of phenomenal growth. Before long it had outgrown its colonial boundaries and advanced steadily northward as the Collect Pond was filled, streets were extended, and an overall grid plan began to be implemented. The population swelled from 18,000 at the cessation of the war to 33,000 in 1790, with up to an additional 30,000 in each successive decade through to 1820.

In 1789 New York, functioning as the seat of the newly created federal government, celebrated the inauguration of George Washington as the nation's first president. Before long, it gained recognition as the nation's leading economic nexus. Old trade routes were expanding farther and farther into the American South and the West Indies, and with the completion of the Erie Canal in 1825, an inland water route provided direct access to the Great Lakes and burgeoning populations in the West. This resulted in an environment that spurred on the trades and prompted one British visitor to comment, 'I would remark, that the cabinetwork executed in this city is light and elegant. Indeed, I am inclined to believe, that it is superior to English workmanship.'[19] It is at this time and in this place that the earliest reference to Duncan Phyfe in America is recorded.

In 1792 Phyfe joined the ranks of the General Society of Mechanics and Tradesmen. This benevolent organisation was founded seven years earlier with the intent 'to promote mutual fellowship, confidence and good understanding among various descriptions of mechanics; as far as possible to prevent litigation and disputes amongst tradesmen; to promote mechanical knowledge; afford relief to distressed members; and to establish funds to enable the society to carry their

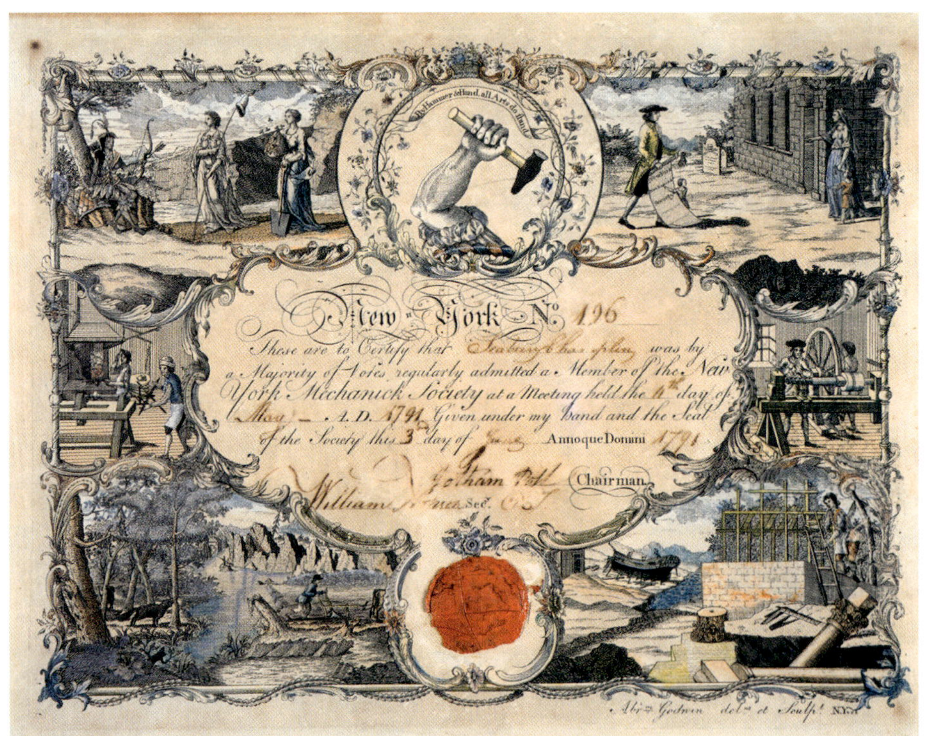

Illustration 6.3
Certificate from Mechanics Society of Seabury Champlin, designed and engraved by Abraham Godwin (1763–1835). The General Society of Mechanics and Tradesmen of the City of New York, 1791. Seabury Champlin was one of two members who nominated Duncan Phyfe for membership in the Society. Engraving with watercolour and wax on laid paper, 8½ x 11⅛in (216 x 283mm). [Courtesy, Winterthur Museum]

laudable designs into effect'. In addition, it rendered a form of personal assurance, lest anything should happen to its members, so that their families were guaranteed assistance (illus 6.3).[20]

Duncan Phyfe's decision to join this Society was seemingly his first priority as a young professional and must have been in anticipation of his marriage in February 1793 to Rachel Louzada (c 1781–1851) at the First Presbyterian Church. In the same year, his name appeared for the first time in the New York City Directory and would continue to appear for the next sixty years. However, it is the 1793 entry, in combination with the two subsequent editions, that are the most revealing about the young artisan and his aspirations.

The 1793 Directory denotes Duncan Phyfe's occupation as a 'joiner', a term that implies a role in the construction and finishing of residential and commercial structures. While this vocation was one deemed as intermediary between carpentry

Illustration 6.4
Unidentified artist. 'Shop and warehouse of Duncan Phyfe', 168–172 Fulton Street, New York City, 1817–20.
Watercolour, ink, and gouache on white laid paper, 15⅞ x 19⅝in (403 x 498mm). Rogers Fund, 1922, 22.28.1
[Image © The Metropolitan Museum of Art, New York]

Illustration 6.5
Detail from Illustration 6.4.

and cabinetmaking, at the time it was generally understood that the joiner possessed the ability to move freely between both vocations. Phyfe was then working from 2 Broad Street, a space he shared with Vincent Tillou, a turner and rush-bottom chairmaker. At its western extremity, Broad was dominated by Federal Hall where, four years earlier, George Washington was administered the oath of office for President. Although the government had since relocated to Philadelphia, this imposing classical structure stood out as the architectural focal point of a streetscape populated by a jumble of buildings ranging from traditional Dutch crow-stepped gable façades to modest Georgian-style residences occupied by prosperous merchants, gentlemen, and numbers of craftsmen, including cabinetmakers and chairmakers.[21]

Within the space of three years Phyfe subtly transformed his persona in print, and by doing so he discreetly shaped the public's perception of him. By 1794, he and Tillou had relocated directly across the street to 3 Broad Street and his occupation was now listed as 'cabinet-maker', signifying that he was concentrating his talents on the design and production of furniture. A further alteration to this entry, and a compelling one, was the modification of his surname from 'F-i-f-e' to 'P-h-y-f-e'. While careful to preserve

the phonetics, he adopted a name far more suitable for the new Republic. An elegant and sophisticated expression, it suggested a classical derivation that was clearly intended to elevate and benefit Duncan Phyfe's reputation and commerce.[22]

By 1795 Phyfe had parted Broad Street for 35 Partition Street which in 1816 was renamed Fulton Street in honour of the late inventor. This address would prove both fashionable and enduring. It was not far from the venerable St Paul's Chapel, and within the decade a refined new City Hall would become the signature building of Republican New York. For the next half century Fulton Street retained the unique distinction of traversing Manhattan Island from east to west – this facilitated access to ships arriving with raw materials and departing loaded up with furniture and other finished goods. From this vantage point Phyfe would survey a home and business complex over the course of the next six decades.[23]

Initially renting both residential and commercial properties by 1802 Phyfe began to acquire real estate. Within the space of five years, he became the owner of four adjacent properties along Fulton Street, three of which functioned as his shop, sales and showrooms. These are shown in the well-known streetscape in the collection of the Metropolitan Museum of Art which dates between 1817 and 1820 (illus 6.4, 6.5).

Illustration 6.6
Duncan Phyfe. Side chair, 1807. Mahogany,
33 x 19⅞ x 21in (838 x 505 x 533mm).
Bequest of Henry Francis du Pont, 1957 57.719.8.
[Courtesy Winterthur Museum]

The anonymous artist who depicted Duncan Phyfe's shop façades portrays not only the scale of the operation but suggests to the viewer the function of the trio of adjoining structures. The composition is centred on the open doorway at 170 Fulton Street which frames a figure, presumably Phyfe, discussing his signature forms, in this case elegant side chairs, with two stylishly attired ladies (illus 6.5, 6.6, 6.7). To the left, a group of journeymen are discreetly exiting from 168 Fulton Street. To the right an elegant three-and-a-half-storey brick structure, number 172, has the appearance of a characteristic New York townhouse. Peering out from the garret window, a figure, perhaps an apprentice, surveys the scene below. Eventually, Phyfe would amass no fewer than fourteen properties in lower Manhattan,

principally ones that were in close proximity to his residence and place of business.[24]

The expansion of Duncan Phyfe's real estate holdings coincided with his appointment to the city's volunteer fire department. The threat of fire was never far from a mechanic's mind, especially in a trade such as cabinetmaking, which utilised highly combustible materials such as seasoned wood, sawdust, varnish and glue pots. Between 1806 and 1813 he belonged to the Third Ward's Fire Engine Company No 16 which, in addition to combating fire, could yield business and social *entrées*.[25]

In 1810 Phyfe also became a member of the Washington Benevolent Society. While founded with the worthy goal of providing an education for underprivileged boys, this pro-British organisation became involved with the Federalist Party's attacks

Illustration 6.7
Curule side chair, 1815–20. Mahogany, ebony; secondary woods: mahogany, ash, 32 x 20 x 19¾ (813 x 508 x 502mm). Collection of George M* and Linda H Kaufman (*deceased). [Image © The Metropolitan Museum of Art, New York]

on President Thomas Jefferson and his Democratic-Republican Party. At this time American commerce was suffering from the effects of the British and French blockades, the initiation of Jefferson's embargo in 1807 and the passage of the Non-Intercourse Act of 1809. While the Embargo Act was designed to protect trade and foster domestic manufactures – it proved disastrous for the entire country, having a devastating effect on commerce and ultimately failing to keep the nation out of war.[26]

Immediately following the war of 1812, coastwise trade, between northern furniture makers and a southern clientele, was expanding and finished goods were regularly shipped to the principal coastal towns situated between Annapolis, Maryland, and Savannah, Georgia.[27] By the beginning of the nineteenth century an industrialised North was emerging, with Salem, Boston, Providence, Philadelphia and especially New York City becoming the predominant centres for the export of furniture.

Concurrently, the South's agrarian-based society was undergoing transition as the traditional staples of tobacco, rice and indigo were no longer very profitable. As a cotton agronomy began to develop, planters began moving inland and westward to establish substantial plantation communities which, in turn, caused the South's urban centres to experience an economic, as well as social, downward shift.

To survive, the merchants and artisans who were concentrated in the principal coastal towns adopted other means of trading, for example, through venture or speculative cargo or by 'warehousing'. In the former, the northern chair- or cabinetmaker would consign his goods to a southern merchant who, almost immediately upon arrival, would arrange to auction them off on or near the wharves. The success of this method could lead to an alternative process, warehousing, whereby the local merchant stockpiled northern-made speculative cargo for retail. This might, however, create competition between the merchant class and members of the local cabinet industry, with the former being in the position to offer the public a greater range of cabinetwares at a more economical

price. In response, an alternative developed, referred to as 'supplementary warehousing', whereby the local chair- and cabinetmakers replaced the vendors and by doing so augmented their own manufactures with imported goods.[28]

Savannah, more so than any other southern port, lent itself to the process of 'supplementary warehousing'. Due to its geography, it was more strategically located to serve as one of the principal ports of call for vessels before they entered the waters of the Caribbean and, conversely, for those ships en route to New York and Liverpool, England. Also, the city's small population, with a long history of relying on imports for many of its household goods, had never encouraged the development of a sizeable

Illustration 6.8
Label used at 33 and 35 Partition Street, Phyfe's business address from 1811 to 1816.
[Courtesy Winterthur Museum]

community of furniture makers. The fact that there were so few individuals employed in the trade must have entered into the decision by Duncan Phyfe to concentrate much of his commercial interest there. And, he was not the only one to recognise the city's attributes and potential, for by 1820 more than thirty cabinet warehousing concerns were established, many of them by furniture makers from New York City.[29]

Although Duncan Phyfe had begun to conduct business in Savannah as early as 1802, he cautiously avoided a more active role until after peace had been declared with Britain in 1815. His initial forays into the coastwise export trade there occurred by the autumn of 1817, when he consigned to the *Ariadne* a half dozen boxes and a bundle destined for the mercantile firm, George Anderson & Son. In December 1820 Calvin Baker advertised 'a large and elegant assortment of Cabinet Furniture just received from New York, and manufactured by the experienced workmen of Mr. D. Phyfe' implying that these goods were venture cargo which he would be offering at public auction.[30] In 1821 Phyfe appears to have contracted an arrangement with Isaac W Morrell (active 1811 to 1865), a cabinetmaker in his employment since 1812, if not earlier. By February 1811, Morrell was in Savannah and presumably established a shop there. Evidently, he would return to New York every year in order to

Illustration 6.9
Label used at 170 Fulton Street, the address of Phyfe's cabinet warehouse from 1817 to 1826. [Image © The Metropolitan Museum of Art, New York]

escape the summer heat, avoid the threat of yellow fever, and to procure additional stock while continuing to maintain his relationship with Phyfe. In May 1821 Morrell advertised himself as 'agent for D. Phyfe. New York'. In spite of its great promise, their collaboration was short-lived, and by 1825 Phyfe's presence in Savannah had come to an end.[31]

Sometime between 1806 and 1811, the first of at least three distinct personalised labels appeared which acted as advertisements on Phyfe's exported pieces of furniture. The second version was published between 1811 and 1816 (illus 6.8), and the third is dated August 1820 (illus 6.9). Indicative of their fragility

and vulnerability, the first two are only known by a single example. The third is recorded on seven pieces of furniture which when viewed as a group show how his styles evolved, with classically inspired designs being substituted by bolder, monumental forms. The fact that no later example has surfaced is probably explained by Phyfe's withdrawal from the export trade by the mid-1820s.[32]

For an individual possessing great ambition, Duncan Phyfe did not embrace many of the principal institutions and societies that could have benefited his career. For instance, although he was married at the First Presbyterian Church, he never seems to have taken a prominent role in the affairs of the kirk.[33] It is more challenging to explain his absence from the membership of the New York Society of Cabinetmakers, the Masons and the St Andrew's Society.

The St Andrew's Society, founded in 1756, functioned in a variety of capacities – as a conduit for the latest news from Scotland, a gathering place for the exchange of commercial information and a reliable source for services and goods that could be provided by merchants, shippers and craftsmen with a Scottish background. Phyfe's elder brother, John, joined in 1817, and some of his nephews, as well as numerous other individuals, both Scottish-born or else descended from immigrant Scotsmen.[34]

This mutually beneficial network included some of the city's prominent immigrant Scotsmen, such as the scholar and financier George P MacCulloch, who arrived in New York in 1806 and promptly placed an order for a sideboard, a set of dining tables, pairs of bureaus and bedsteads, including a key for the latter, all totalling $172.[35] Phyfe also had other customers who were of Scottish descent, for example, Lewis Stirling of Saint Francisville, Louisiana.[36] It seems that Phyfe also had business dealings with a fourth-generation American of Scottish descent, Fenwick Lyell (1767–1822). Lyell dealt intermittently with Phyfe between 1802 and 1809, and his surviving ledger gives details of the intricacies of the cabinet and related trades. For instance, in 1802 Lyell purchased an easy-chair frame from Phyfe, added a set of castors and then sold it to John J Post, an upholsterer, who had joined the General Society of Mechanics and Tradesmen at the same time as Phyfe.

By contrast, in 1805 Lyell billed Duncan Phyfe for a pine table – an object so mundane that it is inexplicable why Phyfe would commission this piece when it could have been supplied by anyone in his own employ with even the most rudimentary skills.[37]

Several prominent members of the New York furniture trade were also Scottish, including Benjamin Crookshank, a cabinetmaker, joiner and architect; John Mowatt, cabinetmaker and chairmaker; and James Ronalds, who described himself at various times as a joiner, carpenter and builder, as well as a cabinetmaker; Thomas Wallace, a cabinetmaker; Andrew Gifford, who found employment as a lumber dealer as well as in cabinetmaking; Thomas Gibson, a piano maker; Hugh McDougall, a cabinetmaker, house and sign painter, gilder and glazier; Robert Walker, a cabinetmaker; William Dove, a cabinetmaker and upholsterer; Thomas Gillespie, a carver; and probably Charles Watts, who was employed variously as a cabinetmaker and musical instrument maker, and a retailer of lumber, hardware, upholstery materials and other goods, as well as a real estate speculator.[38] Of these individuals, Watts is the most recognisable today, known from a half dozen of his account books dating from 1802 and concluding on his death in 1815.[39]

Charles Watts is thought to have emigrated to New York City by way of London, about 1789. That same year his name appears in the city directory, which gives his occupation as that of a 'cabinet and musical instrument maker'. By 1790 he had relocated to Charleston, South Carolina, but continued to enjoy substantial business in New York City. In Charleston he formed cabinetmaking partnerships with Scotsmen Thomas Wallace and Robert Walker who had followed a similar route, having briefly settled in New York. Watts met with phenomenal success in Charleston, in fact, so much so that he posted an advertisement in the *New York Diary* in an effort to lure upwards of fifteen journeymen cabinetmakers and chairmakers south, assuring them that 'they will receive generous encouragement'.

His clientele consisted of cabinetmakers, upholsterers and turners in New York and Charleston, and also in Scotland. There he conducted business with Hugh Law & Son of Leith and the Inverness cabinetmaker James Munro. In 1803 and 1805 Watts made return trips to London and Liverpool, and travelled extensively in Scotland, visiting Leith, Musselburgh, Carmunnock, Falkirk, Fife, Glasgow, Greenock, Kelso, Lanark, Melrose, Peebles, Perth and Kirkcaldy. His business records reveal a vigorous

trade, buying and selling virtually anything and everything related to the furniture industry – from Santo Domingo mahogany to upholstery fabrics.

The survival of the Watts and Lyell accounts underscores the paucity of business records from this dynamic age in the history of New York City's cabinet industry. For the fifty-five years that Duncan Phyfe was active, manuscripts are known only from seven furniture makers, including Lyell, and also James Ruthven, a turner, and Charles Watts, a cabinetmaker who, as noted earlier, also functioned in various capacities.[40] It is revealing and thought-provoking that four of these seven individuals conducted business with Phyfe and the fifth, John Hewitt, was profoundly influenced by him.

The arrival of the Staffordshire-born Hewitt in New York is marked by his appearance in the 1805 directory. Hewitt's records reveal much about the trade, particularly the production and reputation of his contemporaries, Duncan Phyfe and the talented Parisian *émigré* Charles-Honoré Lannuier. Hewitt clearly recognised the distinctiveness, as well as the marketability, of each craftsman's furniture, so much so that he made careful measurements of their work to replicate it, that he too might benefit from their success.[41]

It has only been in recent times that the contributions of immigrant Scottish furniture makers in early America have received greater recognition and scholarly attention.[42] Decorative arts historians are just beginning to research and assess their effect on the design and construction of American furniture. The process is complicated by the predominance of London design on the industry in both Edinburgh and America. In Scotland the majority of craftsmen who are identified and their origins traced back to their native land came from the Lowlands, rather than the Highlands. Typically, they came through Edinburgh and, perhaps after a spell working in London, subsequently migrated to the United States. Duncan Phyfe is an exception to this rule. Although he conducted business with Scottish-born craftsmen, merchants and patrons, as well as with Americans of Scottish descent, there is nothing recognisable in his cabinetwork to suggest his origins. Whether he migrated in 1775, 1783 or 1784, at most he was fourteen and hardly old enough to have had access to any skilled training. One tangible expression of his Scottish heritage is a diminutive silver and cowrie shell snuff box, engraved 'D. Phyfe' centred above an embossed thistle, a beguiling object which dates from

Illustration 6.10
Snuffbox. Possibly New York City, 1827–40. Silver, cowrie shell, 3 x 2⅜ x 1¾in (76 x 60 x 44mm).
Collection of Glorianna H Gibbon. [Image © The Metropolitan Museum of Art, New York]

the latter, rather than the initial period of his career (illus 6.10).

The lack of account books hinders a precise understanding of the organisation and operation of Duncan Phyfe's enterprise. However, more than forty invoices, receipts and bills of lading survive, making it possible to suggest a profile of his clientele, a range of the shop's production and what the forms retailed for, as well as record the mundane ancillary activities such as mending furniture, putting up and taking down bedsteads, the installation of light fixtures and, when necessary, supplying a coffin of accounts

hinders a precise understanding of the organisation and operation of Duncan Phyfe.

Now and then, an invoice has survived with the very objects that it references. The earliest of these was one of Phyfe's most extensive and important commissions. This was for furniture ordered by William Bayard, then one of New York's leading merchants, for his recently remodelled State Street residence with its commanding views of the Battery and harbour. The two invoices, dated November 1807 and totalling in excess of $1,700, include the renowned suite of chairs with their elegant 'sprung' legs that

Illustration 6.11
Peremptory and Extensive Auction Sale of Splendid and Valuable Furniture ... at the Furniture Ware Rooms of Messrs Duncan Phyfe & Son, Nos 192 & 194 Fulton Street, West of Broadway, Embracing Their Entire Stock, and of Their Own Well Known Manufacture, of Fashionable and Seasonable Furniture. Sale catalogue. Halliday & Jenkins, New York, 16–17 April 1847. [Courtesy of the Winterthur Library: Joseph Downs Collection of Manuscripts and Printed Ephemera]

herald the arrival of the Grecian aesthetic in Federal New York (illus 6.6).[43]

Other important clients included John Jordan Morgan, a Representative for New York in the United States Congress, Luman Reed, the entrepreneurial merchant who is heralded as one of the earliest collectors and patrons of American art and artists, Oliver Wolcott, the President of the Bank of America, and Thomas Worthington. A former governor of Ohio, and one of its first senators, Worthington had the misfortune to die while in New York City on business in June 1827, but the good fortune to be returned to Chillicothe in a coffin supplied by Phyfe.[44]

Beginning in 1836, a series of events marked a downturn in Phyfe's life and career. The premature death of his eldest child, Michael (1794–1836), a cabinetmaker by trade, was a severe blow. Presumably

apprenticed to his father, he seems to have struck out on his own by 1817. He is listed at 68 Chapel Street but within the year had transferred to Church Street which ran perpendicularly to Fulton Street; its southern extremity was almost directly opposite the Phyfe shop and showrooms. But by 1819 Michael was living in a property owned by his father that abutted the rear of 172 Fulton Street. In spite of there being no documentation for Michael's employment in the family concern, it seems highly likely that they collaborated during these years. The directory continued to list his occupation as a 'cabinetmaker' until 1828 when he is cited as the operator of a mahogany yard partnered with John Turnbull. Their enterprise proved short-lived, and Michael had left the city by 1830 and relocated to Rahway, New Jersey, where he died. Later, his children were sent to live with their grandparents on

Illustration 6.12
Duncan Phyfe. Pier table, 1834. Mahogany veneer, marble, looking-glass plate, 35½ x 42¼ x 18⅛in
(902 x 1073 x 460mm). The White House, Washington DC, White House Acquisition Fund, 1961.
[Image © The Metropolitan Museum of Art, New York]

Fulton Street where the eldest (b. 1818), named after his grandfather, was affiliated with the cabinet shop.[45]

For Duncan Phyfe, the ordeal of losing his eldest son, combined with the physical reality that now he was aged sixty-seven, may have prompted him to reconsider the staffing and structure of his business. In 1837 the name of the firm was amended to 'D. Phyfe & Sons', signalling the increased influence of two of his surviving sons, William (1803–75) and James Duncan (1814–87). William left the company in 1840. James, however, remained by his father's side, both at work and home, until his father's death fourteen years later.[46] As these changes were occurring at Fulton Street, the American economy was facing financial collapse, referred to as the Panic of 1837, which prefaced a depression in trade that would last for the next six years.

In 1840 when James Henry Hammond, a planter and politician from Columbia, South Carolina, visited Duncan Phyfe's shop, he commented to his wife, Catherine, that 'There is no sofa in New York to compare with ours in the drawing room & the highest priced one at of [*sic*] Phyfe's is $70, the single one & lounges are going out of fashion, so says every one but Phyfe who is as much behind the times in style as he is in price. He thinks it is still 1836.'[47]

Hammond's criticism was twofold, implying that Phyfe was oblivious of the economic downturn in the country and at the same time unaware of the dramatic transformation that was then taking place in furniture design as the Grecian plain style gave way to an aesthetic entirely developed and driven by Paris.[48] It may have had some bearing on Phyfe's decision to run a series of promotional advertisements in the newspapers from April 1843 and into the following year: 'D. PHYFE & SON offer for sale at greatly reduced prices, their large and fashionable assortment of Mahogany and Rosewood Cabinet Furniture. The reputation of the subscribers at home and abroad is too well appreciated by the public to need any commendation.' Yet, it seems that this enticement did little to spur commerce, reduce stock or generate income, for in April 1844, the auctioneers Edward C Halliday and Edgar Jenkins announced that they were representing 'Messrs. Duncan Phyfe & Son, who are closing their business'.[49]

Within the month an article appeared in the *New Mirror of Literature, Amusement and Instruction* which discussed the changes taking place in furniture style and manufacture: 'So marked is this change of taste, and the new school of furnishing, that the oldest and most wealthy of the cabinet warehouse-men

Illustration 6.13
D Phyfe & Son. Dining table, 1841. Mahogany, mahogany veneer, 28¾ x 65⅞ x 65½in
(730 x 1673 x 1664mm) closed; 187in (4750mm) extended with five leaves.
Collection of Richard Hampton Jenrette. [Image © The Metropolitan Museum of Art, New York]

Illustration 6.14
D Phyfe & Son. Sofa, 1841. Rosewood veneer, rosewood, rosewood grained mahogany;
secondary woods: ash, white pine, 37 x 87½ x 25in (940 x 2223 x 635mm).
Columbia Museum of Art, Columbia, South Carolina, gift of Mr and Mrs W R Clark.
[Image © The Metropolitan Museum of Art, New York]

in this city has completely abandoned the making of English furniture. He sold out an immense stock of high-priced articles last week at auction.' The unnamed cabinetmaker, most certainly Phyfe, had purportedly 'sent to France for models and workmen to start new with the popular taste', for 'the fashion of French furniture has come in lately with a rush, and the nabobs are selling out, from sideboard to broom, and furnishing anew, *à la Française*, from skylight to basement'.[50] And yet, for some reason, the substantive effort that the *New Mirror* reports by D. Phyfe & Son to adopt the latest Parisian fashions proved wholly unsuccessful. The venerable firm persisted for merely three more years before finally closing its doors in May 1847.

In a twist of irony, it was in preparation for this occasion that the most detailed and extensive record of the cabinet shop's production was generated. Once again, the Phyfes turned to Halliday and Jenkins to conduct the dispersal and, in anticipation, a twenty-page catalogue was compiled: *Peremptory and Extensive Auction Sale of Splendid and Valuable Furniture … at the Furniture Ware Rooms of Messrs. Duncan Phyfe & Son, Nos. 192 & 194 Fulton Street, West of Broadway, Embracing Their Entire Stock, and of Their Own Well Known Manufacture, of Fashionable and Seasonable Furniture* (illus 6.11).[51]

The lots were organised and numbered room by room, according to which floor and interior at 192 and 194 Fulton Street they were located. It is possible, therefore, to see which articles were considered the most important based on their placement. Furthermore, in addition to fully describing Phyfe's stock, the cataloguers offer some insight as to how these structures and spaces were configured and utilised in 1847. It becomes apparent that the cavalcade of revivals that would define nineteenth-century aesthetics was well underway. Although the furniture illustrated here by D Phyfe & Son is not the ones intended for sale, they hint at the styles offered at auction. The Grecian plain style, inspired by the restrained French Restauration introduced at the beginning of the 1830s, continued to endure, as shown for example in illustration 6.12. The most recent manifestation of the Gothic was flourishing (illus 6.13) while a 'rosewood Sofa, style of Louis XIV, serpentine front, covered with rich fig'd crimson plush', along with eight matching chairs heralded the onset of the rococo, a term which in this period seems to be used interchangeably with 'Old French' (illus 6.14). Throughout, the term 'French' is used to denote style and some forms have French names such as *escritoire* and *secretaire*, as well as upholstered seating including the *Voltaire* and the *cabriolet*.[52]

The extensive array of furniture can be divided into several distinct groups. The largest of these consisted of chairs, although two others, tables and stands, were almost as profuse. The remainder, listed here in order of their quantity, comprised bureaus, desks and bookcases, sofas and couches, stools, beds, wardrobes, cheval and toilet glasses, and sideboards. In addition, there was a miscellaneous category of disparate household items including bed steps, bidets, cabinets, cellarettes, fire screens, knife trays, music canterburys, a tambourette, a teapoy, and two mahogany refrigerators.

In most instances, Halliday and Jenkins specify the primary cabinet woods used. Predictably, mahogany and rosewood were the most fashionable and popular, comprising more than 80 per cent of the stock. The remainder consisted of either maple or curly maple, exotic imported varieties such as amboyna from South-east Asia and Brazilian zebrawood. At the other end of the spectrum, just off the street at 'No. 194, 1st Door on Entrance', was assembled a group of 'Painted Ware' items grained to resemble rosewood, mahogany, oak or simply painted white, the latter consisting of toilet tables and washstands.[53]

Detailed descriptions record the show covers for seating furniture, bed coverings and drapery, decorative backings for cheval glasses and fire screen frames, and curtains intended for the glass doors of sideboards and bookcases. Approximately 40 per cent of these were for silk, 23 per cent for plush and 20 per cent for haircloth respectively, whereas the remainder consisted of morocco leather, satin, a worsted moreen or caning which, if the customer so wished, could be supplied with cushions. The entries are composed in such scrupulous detail that frequently they specify the colours of these coverings, generally registering a preference for bold, strong tints. Slightly more than 20 per cent of the furniture was upholstered in crimson, followed by purple or striking contrasts of blue and buff, or orange and maroon, the latter perhaps a damask weave.

Lot number 357 in the catalogue was unusual: '1 rosewood reclining chair, richly carved with foot board on castors, made in Calcutta'. While there may never be a satisfactory explanation for the spectre of an Indian chair in the Phyfe showrooms, it imparts that the provincial town which Duncan Phyfe had settled

in as a mere lad six decades earlier had subsequently become the nation's pre-eminent urban centre, and presently was on the verge of international recognition when it hosted the New-York Exhibition of the Industry of All Nations.[54]

In July 1853 Phyfe must have been fascinated as the exhibition opened to the public. The world's fair derived its inspiration from, and in many respects was patterned after, the Great Exhibition of 1851, held in London. The 'Crystal Palace', Joseph Paxton's innovative cast-iron and glass-domed structure, was recreated to showcase industrial achievements from across the globe.[55]

Hopefully, Duncan Phyfe had an opportunity to attend the fair – and return more than once. In particular, he would have been drawn to the section dedicated to American furniture. There was showcased the work of Thomas Brooks (1811–87), the French *émigré* Alexander Roux (1813–86), Julius Dessoir (1801–84) and Erastus Bulkley (1798–1872), one of Duncan Phyfe's long-time rivals. More recently, Bulkley had taken on a twenty-three-year-old immigrant artisan, Gustave Herter (1830–98). Herter's extraordinary oak buffet with its grandiose scale and sculptural tableau symbolising the hunt was shown to wide acclaim. In many respects the newly formed partnership of Bulkley and Herter coalesce New York City's long-established cabinetmaking tradition with its ambition for a new generation of furniture craftsmen.

On 16 August 1854, at the age of eighty-four, Duncan Phyfe died at his Fulton Street residence. Within the month, the estate appraisers arrived and began making their way through the old house, methodically compiling an inventory of Phyfe's personal effects which chronicled a long life and brilliant career. When they reached the open garret, adjacent to an old rosewood and gilt pier table, they uncovered a lot of 'Cabinet Makers Books & Drawings', to which they assigned a value of 50 cents each, thinking them insignificant. In the upper hall they came across further remnants of the cabinetmaker's profession: a chest filled with many of Phyfe's woodworking tools, collections of imported French gilt furniture mounts and, by contrast, an accumulation of mundane locks, screws and castors – even a box of glue. Here, they also discovered a lot of mahogany veneers which were in the process of being purchased from the estate by Erastus Bulkley for $100. Seemingly a princely sum for the time, these veneers, along with '1 set Satin Damask Window Curtains (for 3 windows)' and a silver pitcher by Garret Eoff, were the most valuable possessions inventoried.[56]

Recalling his old competitor's ability and reputation, Bulkley must have fully understood and appreciated the quality of these veneers and as he left Phyfe's house with them was perhaps already contemplating the stylish piece of furniture that they would be reserved for. Would it pay homage to, or perhaps challenge, the memory of the great Phyfe?

Notes

1 McInnis, M D & Leath, R A 1996 'Beautiful Specimens, Elegant Patterns: New York Furniture for the Charleston Market, 1810–1840', *American Furniture* 147.

2 The most recent and comprehensive addition to the extensive Duncan Phyfe bibliography is Kenny, P M et al 2011 *Duncan Phyfe: Master Cabinetmaker in New York*, New York: Metropolitan Museum of Art.

3 Ralston, R 'A New York Cabinetmaker's Reminiscences', *Antiques*, December 1943, 284–5. Ingerman, E A 'Personal Experiences of an Old New York Cabinetmaker', *Antiques* 84, no 5 (November 1963): 576–80. The 'original draft' of Ernest Hagen's semi-autobiographical manuscript, 'Personal Experiences of an Old New York Cabinet Maker', is now in the Winterthur Library: Joseph Downs Collection of Manuscripts and Printed Ephemera, Collection 32, Ernest Hagen Papers. Additional Hagen papers are also at Winterthur among Collection 56, the R T Haines Halsey Papers.

4 Kent, H W & Levy, F N 1909 *The Hudson-Fulton Celebration*, vol 2, *Catalogue of an Exhibition of American Painting, Furniture, Silver, and Other Objects of Art, MDCXXV–MDCCCXXV*. New York, ix–x. Previously, some of Hagen's research was published in newspapers and magazines, 'Old New York Furniture', *The New York Sun*, 12 August 1894 and 'The Cost of Furniture a Century Ago', *The House Beautiful* 17, no 5 (April 1905): 47; however, neither possessed the *cachet* nor reached an audience comparable to those who toured the Hudson-Fulton Celebration at the Metropolitan Museum of Art.

5 Marshall, J C 'Duncan Phyfe, American Cabinet Maker', *Country Life in America* 27, no 6 (April 1915): 48–50; Dyer, W A, 'Duncan Phyfe Furniture', *House Beautiful* 37, no 4 (March 1915): 120–5; Dyer, W A, *Early American Craftsmen*. New York, 1915; Dyer, W A, 'Rare Old Furniture of Duncan Phyfe', *Country Life* 39 (January 1921): 71–2; Charles Over Cornelius, *Furniture Masterpieces of Duncan Phyfe*, New York, 1922; Metropolitan Museum of Art, *Loan Exhibition of Duncan Phyfe Furniture*, New York: Metropolitan Museum of Art, 1922. Charles Over Cornelius, 'The Distinctiveness of Duncan Phyfe (1757–1854?)', *The Magazine Antiques* 2, no 5 (November 1922): 205–8; and Charles Over Cornelius, 'Furniture from the Workshop of Duncan Phyfe', *The American Magazine of Art* 13, no 12 (December 1922): 521–8.

6 Cited from an original draft of Ernest Hagen's 'Duncan Phyfe notes' courtesy of the Winterthur Library: Joseph Downs Collection of Manuscripts and Printed Ephemera, Collection 32, Ernest Hagen Papers.

7 Ormsbee, T H 'Phyfe né Fife', *The Magazine Antiques* 16, no 6 (December 1929): 496–9.

8 Nancy Vincent McClelland, *Duncan Phyfe and the English Regency, 1795–1830* (New York, 1939); Nancy McClelland Papers, Cooper-Hewitt National Design Museum, New York.

9 Ibid, 92–9, 318–19. I am indebted to Carole Wilson for updating this research at the National Archives of Scotland HM General Register House, Edinburgh. The earliest records from the Contin Kirk Sessions, which includes the area of Loch Fannich, do not date before 1993. Contin Parish is within the Presbytery of Dingwall and records housed at the National Archives of Scotland (NAS) span from 1649 to 1928. While not all of the minute books survive, those for 1760–2 and 1774–87, CH2/92/7 & 8 were checked, but there was no mention of the Fife family. The NAS does not house any monumental, or graveyard, inscription records for Contin Parish.

10 Familysearch.org provided the geneaology for surveying the surname Fife in Scotland.

11 The earlier baptismal record is for Duncan Phyfe's older brother, John (1767–1827): '97 John lawful Son … John Fife and Isobel Grant his Spouse in Lynmer of Go? born the 1st baptized [*sic*] the 25th October 1767 Alex. Cameron and Peter Grant in Croftmore witnessed.' Three years later the parish registered the baptism of his brother: '190 Duncan lawful Son to Donald Fife and Isobel Grant his Spouse in Croftroman of Garti(or e)more born the 27th baptized [*sic*] 29th April 1770 Duncan Grant in Fordmouth [*sic*] and Peter Grant in Cawstronan [*sic*] Witnesses.'

12 Familysearch.org has documented eighteen other marriages between 1750 and 1775 in which the surname of the groom is Fife and the bride's given name is Isobel.

13 The principal history and genealogy on the Clan Grant are found in Fraser, W, *The Chiefs of Grant*. 3 vols (Edinburgh, 1883); Sinclair, Revd A, *Reminiscences Historical and Traditional of the Grants of Glenmoriston with Selections from the Songs and Elegies of Their Bards* (Edinburgh, 1888); Grant, F J, *The Grants of Corrimony* (Lerwick, 1895); Earl of Cassillis, *The Rulers of Strathspey: A History of the Lairds of Grant and Earls of Seafield* (Inverness, 1911); I F Grant, *The Clan Grant: The Development of a Clan* (Edinburgh, 1955) and Lord Strathspey, *A History of the Clan Grant* (Shopwyke Hall, Chichester, Sussex, 1983).

14 Cameron, V R (ed), *Emigrants from Scotland to America, 1774–1775* (Baltimore, 1965).

15 Ibid, 30–4.

16 The Papers of the Ogilvy family, Earls of Seafield, hereafter cited as 'Seafield Papers', are on deposit at the National Archives of Scotland HM General Register House in

Edinburgh. This document, GD 248/473/6, is titled, 'Rental of Strathspey, 1773'. Other citations referring to Donald Fife include payment of a cess or land tax (1772), GD 248/144/1; and parish receipts, GD 248/144/1. Some monumental inscription records from the Abernethy and Kincardine area are housed at NAS, but none of these reference any members of the Fife family.

17 Cameron 1965, 57–60. While there simply is not sufficient detail to ascertain if this woman is indeed Duncan Phyfe's mother, her age is appropriate.

18 Ormsbee *op cit*, 497–8. Multiple references among the Seafield Papers identify members of the Clan Grant in Albany, New York: GD 248, Section 1, Castle Grant Mss, Boxes 49.1, 2 and 51, Francis Grant correspondence, Albany, New York, 1756–59; Box 52, 1, James Grant, 'measures to prevent emigration to America during present disturbances', July–December 1775; Recruiting in Strathspey for regiments going to America, April-July 1776; Box 53.4, news of war in America, November-December 1776; Box 54.4, 5, Capt. John Grant, New York, news of war, 26 June 1777; William Colquhoun, London, on his return from America, 22 August 1777; Box 55, Robert Grant, news of campaign and other Grants in America, 1777; Boxes 228.4, 235 and 244, executry of Capt. John Grant, commissary general at New York, 1781; 1779–81; 1782–8; GD 248/228/4, papers relating to the John Grant estate in New York.

19 Fearon, H B, *Sketches of America, A Narrative of a Journey of Five Thousand Miles through the Eastern and Western States of America; Contained in Eight Reports Addressed to the Thirty-nine English Families by Whom the Author Was Deputed in June 1817, to Ascertain Whether Any, and What Part of the United States Would be Suitable for Their Residence* (London, 1818): 24.

20 General Membership Meeting, Minutes of the General Society of Mechanics and Tradesmen of the City of New-York, vol 1, 1785–1802, 172. General Society of Mechanics and Tradesmen of the City of New-York, *List of Members of the Society from its Institution in 1785 to December 31, 1916* (New York, 1917): 4.

21 Duncan, W, *The New-York Directory, and Register, for the Year 1792 [i.e. 1793]. Illustrated with a new and accurate plan of the city and part of Long-Island, exactly laid down, agreeably, to the latest survey* (New York: T & J Swords, 1793): 51.

22 Duncan, W, *The New-York Directory, and Register, for the year 1794. Illustrated with a new and accurate plan of the city and part of Long-Island, exactly laid down, agreeably, to the latest survey* (New York: T & J Swords, 1794): 146.

23 Duncan, W & Tiebout, C, *The New-York directory, and register, for the year 1795. Illustrated with a new and accurate plan* (New York: T & J Swords, 1795): 168. For the next few years, Duncan Phyfe maintained his opposition to the Democratic-Republicans' politics.

24 Avery, K J, Shelley, M and Conway, C A, *American Drawings and Watercolors in the Metropolitan Museum of Art* (New York: Metropolitan Museum of Art, 2002): I, 112–13. Heckscher, M H 'Duncan Phyfe, revisitus',

The Magazine Antiques 151, no 1 (January 1997): 236–9. Carson, M S '"The Duncan Phyfe Shops" by John Rubens Smith, Artist and Drawing Master', *American Art Journal* 11, no 4 (October 1979): 69–78. Duncan Phyfe's real estate transactions and holdings are referenced in McClelland, 323–31 and Kenny et al 30, 47–9. A precise record of his properties is challenging to establish, for there are frequent discrepancies between New York City directory listing, tax rolls, and deed books.

25 *Minutes of the Common Council of the City of New York 1784–1831*, 4, 153; 8, 519 (New York, 1930).

26 Washington Benevolent Society in the City of New York, Membership List, 1810, Manuscript Collection, New-York Historical Society. [New York]; *American Citizen,* 23 February 1810; and *New-York Evening Post,* 1 June 1821 records Phyfe's commitment to serve as the Third Ward's representative for the Independent Republican Electors, the successor party to the Federalists.

27 A regular coastal trade began to develop by the second half of the eighteenth century. In addition to Annapolis and Savannah, other ports were Hampton, Lynchburg, Norfolk; and Richmond, Virginia; Edenton, Fayetteville, New Bern, Raleigh; and Wilmington, North Carolina; and Charleston, South Carolina, Newspaper files – exports, TS, Museum of Early Southern Decorative Arts.

28 The intricacies of the coastwise export trade are analysed and discussed in a number of sources, including Katherine Wood Gross, 'The Sources of Furniture Sold in Savannah, 1789–1815' (Master's Thesis, University of Delaware, 1967): 1–14; Forsyth M Alexander, 'Cabinet Warehousing in the Southern Atlantic Ports, 1783–1820', *Journal of Early Southern Decorative Arts* XV no 2 (November 1989): 1–42. Page Talbott, *Classical Savannah: Fine and Decorative Arts, 1800–1840* (Savannah, 1995): 82–3; McInnis and Leath: 142–50; Bradford L Rauschenberg and John Bivins, *The Furniture of Charleston, 1680–1820: Vol II, Neoclassical Furniture* (Winston-Salem, NC: Museum of Early Southern Decoratives Arts, 2003): 554–60.

29 Talbott: 126–9. Alexander: 29–36. Talbott publishes a detailed list of the cabinetmakers and chairmakers working in the vicinity of New York City who exported furniture to Savannah in the early nineteenth century, 165 n 3.

30 Kenny et al: 29, 39–40, 124–5; Marilynn A Johnson, 'John Hewitt, cabinet maker' *Winterthur Portfolio* 4 (1968): 192 n 21; Alexander: 30.

31 Mrs Charlton Theus, *Savannah Furniture: 1735–1825* (privately printed, 1967): 65–6; Alexander: 31; Talbott: 14, 19, 126, 136, 166 n 34, 167 n 55; Kenny et al: 40, 44, 60 n 86, 60 n 89, 61 n 105, 63 n 177. Shipments of furniture from Duncan Phyfe are recorded in the Inward Coastwise Manifests, Savannah, Georgia, Record Group 36, National Archives and Records Administration, Washington DC, Box 15, 15 December 1817; 27 March 1818; 30 April 1818; 16 November 1818; 21 January 1822; 11 March 1822; 8 April 1822; 11 May 1822; 16 December 1822; 9 January 1823; 2 December 1823, National Archives, Washington DC.

32 Each of Duncan Phyfe's three known labels is reproduced and discussed in Kenny et al, 30–1. While Phyfe is known to have conducted business in Charleston, South Carolina and New Orleans, Louisiana, those centres have not been researched and analysed as extensively as Savannah. For Charleston see, McInnis and Leath: 137, 146–9, 171 n 25; Kenny: 36, 39–40, 126, 128–9, 182–3; 202–4. By 1818, Duncan Phyfe had sent venture cargo to New Orleans, Johnson, 192 n 22, which quotes Allan Nevins, *Abram S Hewitt, With Some Account of Peter Cooper* (New York, 1943): 12.

33 McClelland: 320–1.

34 MacBean, W M, *Biographical Register of Saint Andrew's Society of the State of New York* (New York, 1922–5) II, 58–9, 162–3. Duncan Phyfe conducted business with other members including John Turnbull (d. 1839), the lumber merchant who was a partner to Phyfe's eldest son, Michael, and Edward Cairns Halliday, who with his partner, Edgar Jenkins, handled the dispersal of the remaining contents of the Phyfe shop in 1847.

35 Phyfe's receipt to George P McCulloch is dated 10 September 1806 and totalled $172 for eight pieces of furniture. The original is in the Winterthur Library: Joseph Downs Collection of Manuscripts and Printed Ephemera, MS. 54.37.33.

36 Haygood, P M and Thurlow, M A, 'New York Furniture for the Stirlings of Wakefield, Saint Francisville, Louisiana', *The Magazine Antiques* 171, no 5 (May 2007): 126–35.

37 Fenwick Lyell Ledger, 1800–13, 3, Monmouth County Historical Association Library and Archive, Freehold, New Jersey; Frelinghuysen, E L, 'Collector's Notes: Lyell, Slover, Taylor, Phyfe et al', *The Magazine Antiques* 97, no 1 (January 1970): 119–20.

38 Furniture craftsmen whose Scottish origins are documented include: Benjamin Crookshank (cabinetmaker, joiner and architect; b. 1723 at Aberdeen; active in New York City by 1785; d. 1819, New York; MacBean, vol I, 200–1); John Mowatt (cabinetmaker and chairmaker; b. 1740 at Montrose, Angus; d. 1830 New York; MacBean, vol I, 265); James Ronalds (cabinetmaker, joiner, carpenter, builder; b. 1752 at Paisley, Renfrewshire; d. 1812, New York; MacBean vol I, 248); Thomas Wallace (cabinetmaker; b. *c* 1758, Kilmaurs, Ayrshire, Scotland; active in New York City, 1789–90; Charleston, South, Carolina, 1790–1816; d. 1816, Charleston; Rauschenberg and Bivins, vol III, 1275–8); Andrew Gifford (cabinetmaker and lumber dealer; b. 1761 at Loanhead near Edinburgh, Scotland; active in New York City 1786–19; Charleston, South Carolina 1790; New York City 1791–1812; d. 1846; MacBean, vol I, 299; Rauschenberg and Bivins, vol III, 1029); Thomas Gibson (piano maker, b. *c* 1763 Scotland; active in New York 1801–43; d. 1858, New York; Spillane, *History of the American Pianoforte: Its Technical Development and the Trade*, 1890, 102); Hugh McDougall (cabinetmaker, gilder, painter and glazier; b. 1770 in Paisley, Renfrewshire; New York City, 1791–1802; Newark, New Jersey *c* 1799–1809; d. 1858; MacBean, vol I, 300; Johnson, 188 n 8); Robert Walker (cabinetmaker; b. 1772 at Cupar, Fife, Scotland; New York City 1793–5; Charleston, South Carolina 1795–1833; d. 1833, Charleston; Rauschenberg and Bivins, vol III, 1255–72); William Dove (cabinetmaker and upholsterer; presumably born in Scotland; active in New York 1798–1811; to Scotland 1811; d. 1824, Scotland; MacBean vol I, 360); James Ruthven (turner; believed to have been born in Edinburgh in 1783; MacBean vol II, 111–12); Thomas Gillespie (carver, b. Stirlingshire, Scotland; active in New York City 1817–18; Charleston, South Carolina 1824–30; Rauschenberg and Bivins, vol III, 1029–30).

39 The most detailed biographical portrait of Charles Watts appears in Rauschenberg and Bivins 2003, vol II, 583, 601–2, 747, vol III, 1290–6. Charles Watts accounts, 1802–15, 69 × 212cm and 81 × 15cm, Downs Collection, Winterthur Library. A cache of Watts papers are in the collection of the Patricia D Klingenstein Library at the New York Historical Society.

40 In addition to Lyell, Hewitt (see next note) and Watts, these include the cabinetmakers David Loring (Sikes, J E, *The Furniture Makers of Cincinnati, 1790 to 1849.* Cincinnati, 1976, 147–9). Loring's account book is now missing; however, photocopies of a portion of it are in the scholarship files, the American Wing, the Metropolitan Museum of Art; Elisha Blossom (Peter M Kenny, 'From New Bedford to New York to Rio and Back: The Life and Times of Elisha Blossom Jr, Artisan of the New Republic', *in American Furniture 2003*, edited by Luke Beckerdite, 238–69. Milwaukee, 2003); and Daniel Turnier, who noted a series of transactions with Duncan Phyfe in his bound copies of the 1796 and 1810 New York price books. This volume is in the collection of the Kitty King Powell Library and Study Center, Bayou Bend Collection and Gardens, Museum of Fine Arts, Houston. The daybook maintained by the turner, James Ruthven, dating 1792–1804, is in the collection of the New York Historical Society.

41 John Hewitt Cabinetmaker Records, 1800–14, Manuscript Group 84, New Jersey Historical Society, Newark. Hewitt's account book is discussed in Johnson, M A, 'John Hewitt, Cabinetmaker', *Winterthur Portfolio* 4 (1968): 185–205. See also, Kenny, P M et al, *Honoré Lannuier, Cabinetmaker from Paris: The Life and Work of a French Ébéniste in Federal New York*, New York: Metropolitan Museum of Art, 1998, 43–4, 84.

42 Mary Ann Apicella, *Scottish Cabinetmakers in Federal New York*. Hanover, New Hampshire, 2007.

43 Prominent among these are Rauschenberg and Bivins, and Hormor, William M Jr, 'A New Estimation of Duncan Phyfe', *The Antiquarian* 114, no 3 (March 1930): 36–40, 96; Kenny et al, 28, 37, 115–18, 158–65.

44 The receipt to John Jordan Morgan is dated 26 May 1823 totalling $229.25 for furniture and repair work. The original is housed in the manuscript collection of the New York Society Library, New York. A receipted bill for 12 March 1833, indicates that Luman Reed paid Phyfe for unspecified charges totalling $910. A photograph of this receipted bill (location of the original unknown) is in the Decorative Arts Photographic Collection (DAPC) at the

Winterthur Museum. A receipt book belonging to Oliver Wolcott notes payment for a wine cooler on New Year's eve, 1812. The volume, spanning 1803–14, is included among the Oliver Wolcott Jr Papers, Connecticut Historical Society, Hartford. A payment from the estate of Thomas Worthington for a coffin is dated 23 June 1827. The original is in the collection of the Ohio Historical Society, Columbus, Ohio.

45 Michael Phyfe's wife, Jane, died on 4 June 1831, and her husband's death occurred on 15 April 1836. Both are buried at Rahway Public Cemetery, Union County, New Jersey

46 For William Phyfe, see Kenny et al, 32, 58, 59 n 44, 62 n 154. For James Duncan Phyfe, see Kenny et al, 32, 51–2, 58, 246. The third son, Edward Phyfe (1808–87) may have suffered from physical or mental shortcomings, as he never worked. See Kenny et al, 30–2, 58, 63 n 178.

47 Letter from James H Hammond to Catherine E Hammond, 25 August 1840, James Henry Hammond letters, #305–z, Southern Historical Collection, The Wilson Library, University of North Carolina at Chapel Hill.

48 For an extensive examination and discussion of the prevailing French taste in New York, see Voorsanger, C H and Howat, J K (eds), *Art and the Empire City: New York, 1825–1861*. New York, 2000, 305–14.

49 Kenny et al, 52–3.

50 Voorsanger and Howat, 305, 306 n 135; *New Mirror*, 11 May 1844, 90.

51 *Peremptory and Extensive Auction Sale of Splendid and Valuable Furniture … at the Furniture Ware Rooms of Messrs. Duncan Phyfe & Son, Nos. 192 & 194 Fulton Street, West of Broadway, Embracing Their Entire Stock, and of Their Own Well Known Manufacture, of Fashionable and Seasonable Furniture*. Sale cat, Halliday & Jenkins, New York, 16–17 April 1847. This is the only known copy of this catalogue. Courtesy of the Winterthur Library: Joseph Downs Collection of Manuscripts and Printed Ephemera, Collection. (A more in-depth analysis of this booklet is published in Michael K Brown, 'Duncan Phyfe & Son's Peremptory and Extensive Auction Sale', *Antiques & Fine Art*, XI, no 6 (Summer 2012): 174–9.

52 Ibid, 17.

53 Ibid, 20.

54 For an extensive treatise of American and India exchanges, see Bean, S S, *Yankee India: American Commercial and Cultural Encounters with India in the Age of Sail, 1784–1860* (Salem, 2001). For examples of Indian furniture consult Jaffer, A, *Furniture From British India and Ceylon: A Catalogue of the Collections of the Victoria and Albert Museum and The Peabody Essex Museum* (London: 2001).

55 Contemporary publications describing the exposition include Cartensen, G and Gildemeister, K, *New York Crystal Palace, Illustrated description of the Building* (New York 1853); *Official catalogue of the New York Exhibition of the Industry of All Nations* (New York, 1853); Richards, W, *A Day in the New York Crystal Palace* (New York, 1853).

56 The inventory of Duncan Phyfe's estate is reproduced in McClelland: 332–9.

CHAPTER 7

Scotland crosses the Atlantic: evidence for eighteenth- and early nineteenth-century ceramic trade

GEORGE R HAGGARTY

This paper sets out to describe the extensive ceramic industry of Scotland and its development into a major exporter of delftware, white glazed stoneware, creamware and brown stoneware. This important refined ceramic industry grew up around the Forth and Clyde valleys in the Central Belt (illus 7.1a, 7.1b). Initially much of the ceramic trade was with Europe, the Baltic and the Mediterranean. Scottish ceramic exports of the eighteenth and early nineteenth centuries have been studied by collectors and unpaid researchers but they have been generally neglected by social and economic historians, who have not given them the importance they deserve. This trade preceded the later development of the huge[1] and diverse Victorian ceramic industry which exported worldwide (Bremner 1869: 390–403; Kelly 1994: 49–58; Dalgleish 2010: 202–12).[2]

One rich source from which the ceramic data for a five-year period, 1806–10, has been extracted is *The Clyde Commercial Advertiser*, a newspaper which contains lists of all departing and arriving shipping by port, along with their cargoes and destinations (Quail 1986).[3] George Gibb published three short notes based on his inspection of some Scottish east coast ports' Customs Accounts associated with the export of pottery (1979: 17–18; 1980: 55–8; 1981: 38–41). Importantly, the port books of Port Glasgow were examined and published by Peter Denholm for the years 1742 to 1773 (1979: 21–4; 1982: 71–80). However, as will become clear further on, problems with Scottish ceramic nomenclature mean that much of the data needs to be used with extreme care.

The Customs Records for the Kirkcaldy area have also been examined and a number of useful tables published. These show that small quantities of coarse brown earthenware[4] were being shipped across the Atlantic; to Martinique, for example, four

crates on 10 October 1776 and to Charlestown fifteen crates on 17 October 1790 (Bell 2006: 19). Later, on 19 May 1824, 4,000 pieces of earthenware were sent directly to Quebec. Probably more important was the export from Kirkcaldy of high-quality fire bricks and fireclay mainly to St Petersburg, but cargoes of bricks occasionally crossed the Atlantic. For example, in 1772 on 3 March 4,000 went to Grenada, and on 5 May in the same year 20,000 to Antigua on the *Adventurer* (ibid, 15). Direct shipping of small quantities from small ports on the Scottish eastern seaboard seems not to have been typical; most ceramic consignments crossing the Atlantic went via Leith on the Forth, or via Greenock and Port Glasgow on the Clyde (Quail 1986).

Delftware

Scotland was a late starter in the large-scale production of ceramics using a refined ceramic body. Although experiments had previously been conducted into the manufacturing of porcelain and almost certainly tin-glazed earthenware (delft) (Haggarty and Forbes 2004: 1–10) it was not until 1748 that a large-scale pottery manufactory was constructed on the shores of the River Clyde, at the Broomielaw in present-day Glasgow. Named Delftfield, it was initially for the production of tin-glazed earthenware (Kinghorn and Quail 1986). Erected by the Dinwiddie brothers, Lawrence and Robert, in partnership with Patrick Nisbet and Robert Finlay, its purpose was to supply Glasgow merchants trading mainly to the Caribbean and British colonies on the eastern seaboard of North America. Interestingly, this was at a time when elsewhere in Europe tin-glazed earthenware was fast becoming an outdated ceramic body, mainly due to the success of white salt-glazed stoneware, then creamware. Plagued with labour problems[5] and then the difficulty of finding a suitable clay source,

Illustration 7.1a and 7.1b
Map and inset showing Scotland's two important eighteenth- and nineteenth-century ceramic-producing areas: Firth of Forth, Firth of Clyde along with places mentioned in the text. [Terrain © OS Open Data, Crown Copyright]

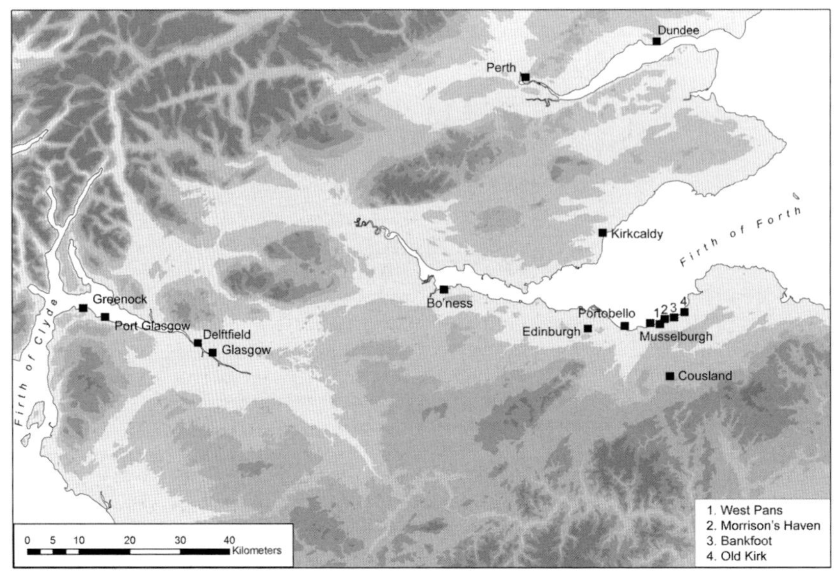

Delftfield, like many other British delft potteries on the western seaboard, began on 31 August 1748 to import calcareous clays from Carrickfergus[6] (NAS E504/28/3). The first explicit mention of delft being shipped from the Clyde was on 12 March 1749: '6cwt on the Duke of Cumberland' (ibid), although 'Parcels of Earthenware and Glass' and '300lb Glassware & Earthenware' had been shipped on 29 September 1748 and 7 March 1749.

It has been suggested that Delftfield may have still been producing its by now unfashionable tin-glazed earthenware until 1810 (Quail 1986: 1). This is unlikely, as is made clear in a letter dated 1781 from Gilbert Hamilton, senior trading partner at Delftfield, to James Watt detailing plans to dispose of their considerable stocks within a year.

Resolved to send out quantities of that ware to New York – Charleston etc … part has been taken & the rest will at least we hope bring prime costs so that by this means the stock of Delft ware is considerably diminished – we are still pursuing the same plan so that in another year I hope all our Delftware will be gone. (Hills 2001: 400)

Shipments of delft were still leaving the Clyde ports during the early years of the nineteenth century; for example, in March 1806, 8,000lbs to Trinidad and 16cwt to St Thomas, and a year later in March 1807, 2,000lbs to Antigua. Between 1807 and 1810, a few smaller cargoes of between 159 and 800lbs were also shipped to Trinidad, Jamaica, Grenada, Newfoundland and Quebec. However, it is entirely possible that this was trans-shipped continental wares.

Illustration 7.2
Cobalt decorated tin-glazed earthenware body sherds, Delftfield. [Courtesy AOC Archaeology]

131

The delft sherds excavated and published by Peter Denholm (1982: 39–84), combined with the study of a large ceramic assemblage recovered from more recent archaeological excavations carried out on the Delftfield kiln site by the AOC Archaeology Group, suggest that the cobalt decoration on its wares is generally unsophisticated (illus 7.2). Amongst other things, this evidence may put into doubt the attribution to Delftfield of a number of superbly decorated items including the Murray of Polmaise service[7] (illus 7.3)

(Haggarty and Gray: forthcoming 2013). Interestingly, although Watt was pleased with the profits from his investment in the Delftfield pottery, he did not think much of its wares. In a letter to his friend Small he wrote: 'Our pottery does well tho we make dam bad ware' (Hills 2001: 398).

A thorough search of the delft literature has been extremely disappointing in identifying, with any certainty, extant items matching the excavated Delftfield sherds. This is mainly due to the fact that,

Illustration 7.3
Tin-glazed earthenware plate from the Murray of Polmaise service.
[Courtesy Trustees of the National Museums Scotland]

Illustration 7.4
Sherds from two Delftfield tin-glazed earthenware bowls painted on their bases with a capital 'G',
possibly for Glasgow. [Courtesy AOC Archaeology]

apart from a few marked pieces, such as the painted letter 'G' (possibly referring to Glasgow) found on the base of two delft bowl sherds (illus 7.4), the majority of the decorative elements used, like those on rim sherds (illus 7.5), are in no way diagnostic; many were common to a number of potteries, especially those in London. To date, by far the best published evidence for Delftfield tin-glazed wares in the USA are sherds recovered from the numerous excavations carried out over the last eighty years at Colonial Williamsburg in Virginia (Austin 1994). Robert Dinwiddie, a partner in the Delftfield pottery, became Lieutenant-Governor of Virginia in 1752. The records of Robert Lang and his son William, both Glasgow merchants, give details of two shipments of pottery to Antigua from Delftfield in 1758–9 which help to illustrate the range of vessels available for export (NAS CS96/652:55; Turnbull 1997: 40–2).

Information contained in a letter from James Watt to Joseph Black, dated 15 February 1768 (Robinson and McKie 1970a: 8–9), showed that the renowned scientist and inventor had borrowed money to become a partner in the Delftfield pottery and had initially invested £244 4s 2d by 1764. Watt lived for a time with his new wife in the manager's house in Delftfield Lane. By 14 June 1772 his capital invested in Delftfield had risen to £474 4s 2d, an eighth share, giving him a handsome return (Hills 2001: 398). Importantly, Watt had significant contacts with Josiah Wedgwood (ibid, 381), and had certainly been heavily involved in developing new bodies and glazes for the pottery (Robinson and McKie 1970b: 8–12; Hills 2001: 387–92).[8]

Creamware and white salt-glazed stoneware

One important result emanating from the excavations by AOC at the Delftfield pottery was the recovery of a significant assemblage of eighteenth-century bisque creamware sherds.[9] Ongoing research on this material should increase enormously our knowledge of creamware production in eighteenth-century Scotland (Haggarty and Gray: forthcoming 2013) (illus 7.6).

Documentary sources, especially ships' manifests and newspaper advertisements in the period from 1750 to 1775, often give confusing and contradictory evidence for the production of both Scottish creamware and white salt-glazed stoneware. Despite the continuing problem of Scottish creamware terminology, Janine Skerry and Suzanne Findlen Hood (2009: 169–74) have attempted to clarify whether Delftfield, with Watt's help, did develop and produce a white salt-glazed stoneware body. Their conclusion, which suggests it did not, has been reinforced by a total

lack of such material being identified during a recent examination of all the excavated Delftfield sherds held by archaeological units, Glasgow Museums and the National Museums Scotland.

A number of other whiteware potteries were active in Glasgow during the final quarter of the eighteenth century (Quail 1982: 5–28; Haggarty and Gray: forthcoming 2013). At least one of these potteries is shown on a contemporary map as a 'delph house'. They are often classed in contemporary documents as delph or stoneware potteries, although what little evidence there is from a limited excavation (Quail 1982: 18, 22) and stray finds suggests that in all probability they were mainly producing a range of creamware and pearlware vessels. An advertisement of

1780 by the Glasgow potters Thomson and Robertson lists 'Queens Stoneware marble and enamelled ware', obviously a reference to the light–coloured creamware, christened Queensware by Josiah Wedgwood.

From the correspondence of James Watt with Joseph Black, the celebrated chemist and physician, we are made aware of Watt's research and experiments on glazes, kiln designs, fuels, delft and stoneware (Robinson and McKie 1970a). However, there is no mention of salt glazing, although he may have been dabbling with a porcelain body (Hills 2001: 383). As the following advertisement suggests, Watt was almost certainly giving advice early on and was instrumental in developing a new tin-glazed body. The *Glasgow Courant* of 2 May 1757 carried an advertisement by

134

the Delftfield Company stating that: 'by a compofition unknown to any Delft-houfe in Britain, they now make their WARE more STRONG and DURABLE than what can be had anywhere elfe'. It was also claimed that their ware would withstand boiling water and was 'equal in strength with Staffordshire stone-ware'.

Many of the Delftfield tin-glazed sherds recovered during the AOC archaeological excavations in April 1997, from a development known as Atlantic Quay, Glasgow, a gap site on the waterfront lying between York Street and James Watt Street, seem to support this claim. Although they are not true stoneware, the glaze does not spall from its body and those sherds,

which seem to be high-fired, 'ring' when tapped against similar examples. It is possible, given the archaeological evidence, that this improved tin-glazed body, along with cream-coloured earthenware, was being produced and may be what is being alluded to in 1772. In February of that year, in editions 13 to 20 of the *Glasgow Journal*, the pottery's new owners, Dinwiddie Martin & Company, advertised that they had 'now brought the STONE and DELPH Ware to the greatest perfection'.

John Gibson, writing his history of Glasgow in 1777, informs us that, for the year beginning 5 January 1771, exports from Port Glasgow and Greenock of delft and stoneware made in Glasgow amounted to

Illustration 7.6
Creamware sherds excavated at Delftfield. [Courtesy of AOC Archaeology]

Illustration 7.7

Large stoneware jug of outstanding quality dated 1858. Height 385mm. Decorated with classical chariots and figures, along with the Royal Arms of Scotland and Musselburgh. Impressed PROSPERITY TO SCOTLAND/ JAS BELL Esq/ LONG MAY THE THISTLE FLOURISH/ God Save The Queen/ 1858/ A Happy New Year/ MRS FANNY BELL/ 1858/ A GUID NEW YEAR AN' MONY O' THEM. (Courtesy Trustees National Museums Scotland) James Bell Esquire is almost certainly the Edinburgh solicitor who married a Fanny Chapman of Hawkfield South Leith on 22 June 1848. It is difficult to be sure which pottery produced the jug but it was possibly the Newbigging pottery in Musselburgh. This was leased to Andrew and Joseph Winkles of the North British pottery in Salamander Street, Leith, from 1857–60. From a surviving mid-nineteenth-century document we know that they were producing a range of stonewares. To date only a water filter 430mm high in a lilac purple glaze has been recorded from this pottery and that may be significant as it is possible that the jug is a one-off and that the sprigs were made for the production of filters. [Courtesy Trustees of the National Museums Scotland]

£5,000. He records 1,860 pieces of stoneware shipped to Boston, 2,600 delft items to Philadelphia, 10,720 pieces of earthenware to Maryland and, to Virginia, 12,828 pieces of delft, 37,526 pieces of earthenware and 25,078 pieces of stoneware (Gibson 1777: 226–8). A recent attempt to verify these figures was found to be impossible, as the cargoes were listed in pounds from Greenock (NAS E504/15, XV–XX) and by pieces or dozens from Port Glasgow. However, a survey of the Greenock Customs Account records from October 1767 through to January 1772, and Port Glasgow (NAS E504/28/3, XVII–XX), from July 1769 through to July 1772, confirmed that substantial quantities of stoneware were shipped to American ports and distinctions were made in many cargoes between delft, earthenware and stoneware (Skerry and Findlen Hood 2009: 182).

Brown stoneware

Although well out of date, what is still the best summary of the Scottish brown stoneware industry (Oswald et al 1982: Appendix 1, 223–42), states that brown stoneware in Scotland was mainly a product of the nineteenth century. Although this is true, its early development was firmly established during the last quarter of the eighteenth century. It may have been that the growth of the trade in whisky to the Americas from Scotland, and Glasgow in particular, was the catalyst for the establishment of a brown stoneware pottery at Coats, near Coatbridge on the Drumpellier estate. This estate had been purchased in 1735 by Andrew Buchanan, merchant, one of the celebrated Tobacco Lords and sometime Provost of Glasgow.

The Coats Pottery was constructed in the parish of Old Monkland, about eight miles east of Glasgow, where 'there was a salt glaze pot work built in the neighbourhood of the Monkland Canal in 1788 by Creelman, who, for ten years previous to that, was a tyle-maker in Millroad, Calton' (Neil 1912: 319–25; quoted in Forbes 1995: 17–19). The *First Statistical Account of Scotland* also informs us that in

> 1788 Mr Creelman commenced a pot work for making Salt ware … also called brownstone, or greybeard ware. It is … mostly exported to America and the West Indies. This branch was borrowed from the Dutch by the English and is the first of its kind in Scotland … About 70 people are employed at these works. (OSA: 91–9, vol 7, 382)[10]

Although some sources mention three generations of the family sequentially named Andrew Creelman, there is no documentary evidence in the Sasines to suggest that the potter at Coats, and later at Portobello, was any other than *William* Creelman.

However, it is possible that brown stoneware was also being made and shipped from elsewhere in late eighteenth-century Scotland, as an advertisement for a public roup in the *Edinburgh Gazette* of 1799 informs us that stoneware was being produced at Bo'ness on the Scottish east coast:

> To be SOLD by public roup, within the Pottery ware-house: at the east end of the town of Bo'ness, on Monday the 11th day of November, at 12 o'clock midday, and entered to at the term of Martinmas next. THE FOLLOWING SUBJECTS which belong to Thomas Cowan, merchant and manufacturer of stone ware in Bo'ness. The LEASE of that Valuable and Extensive POTTERY of STONEWARE, at the east end of the town of Bo'ness, 86 years of which are to run from the term of Martinmas next, with leases of sundry other subjects therewith connected.

With eighty-six years left to run, this might suggest that the pottery had been in operation for thirteen years by 1786, as it was usual to have a ninety-nine-year lease. This would be near the 1766 date, given by Kelly, with no reference for its founding (1999, 23). It would also be somewhat earlier than the date of 1784 given in the *Statistical Account* of *c* 1795 which goes on to state that

> the pottery had within three years been carried out on a much more extensive plan, and presently employs nearly 40 persons including men boys and girls. The clay for the stoneware is imported from Devon, the clay for the earthenware is found in the parish. Cream coloured and white stoneware plain and painted, and brown coloured earthenware are principally manufactured.

This pottery had almost certainly been built to produce creamware (Haggarty 2007a: 228–9) and just possibly white salt-glazed stoneware. However, by 1775 this had started to lose out to new ceramic bodies, and it is almost inconceivable that it would still have been in production at the end of the century. Either the pottery was producing brown stoneware or else this again demonstrates the problem with Scottish ceramic terminology.

On 12 July 1765 William Jamieson, an Edinburgh speculative builder and architect, leased his first plot, of three acres, at Portobello from William Mure, Baron of Caldwell (NAS 3/251 (2) f, 208 rd 2/631).

Illustration 7.8
Pearlware, cobalt painted sherds, West Pans. [Courtesy Historic Scotland]

Illustration 7.9
Pearlware sherds painted in Pratt colours, West Pans. [Courtesy Historic Scotland]

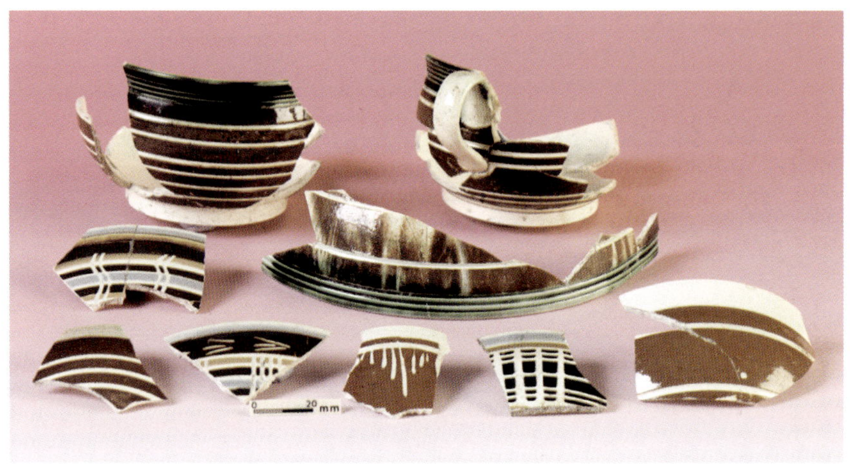

Illustration 7.10
Pearlware sherds dipped, lath cut and sgraffito decorated, West Pans.
[Courtesy Historic Scotland]

With his construction of a redware brick and tile works began what was to become a long ceramic history at the important potting area of Portobello. It is known that a number of potteries, including two or three for the production of refined whitewares, were constructed in the eighteenth century (Haggarty 2007a: 227–8). However, the first documentary evidence we have of the production of white wares on the west bank of the Figgate burn is not until 1784:

Import duty on flint and clay to be reduced to that of chalk as being raw material for pottery in the manufactory of William Jamieson. (ECA GB236 SL 1/1–15/12/1784)

A programme of documentary research is currently underway on the Portobello potteries, but already there is evidence to show that William Creelman, the stoneware potter from Coats, had settled in Portobello by 1812 (Forbes 1995: 17–19). At present it is unclear just what he was doing there, as it was not until later

Illustration 7.11
Marked polychrome decorated plate, Rathbone's Portobello *c* 1820.
[Courtesy Trustees of the National Museums Scotland]

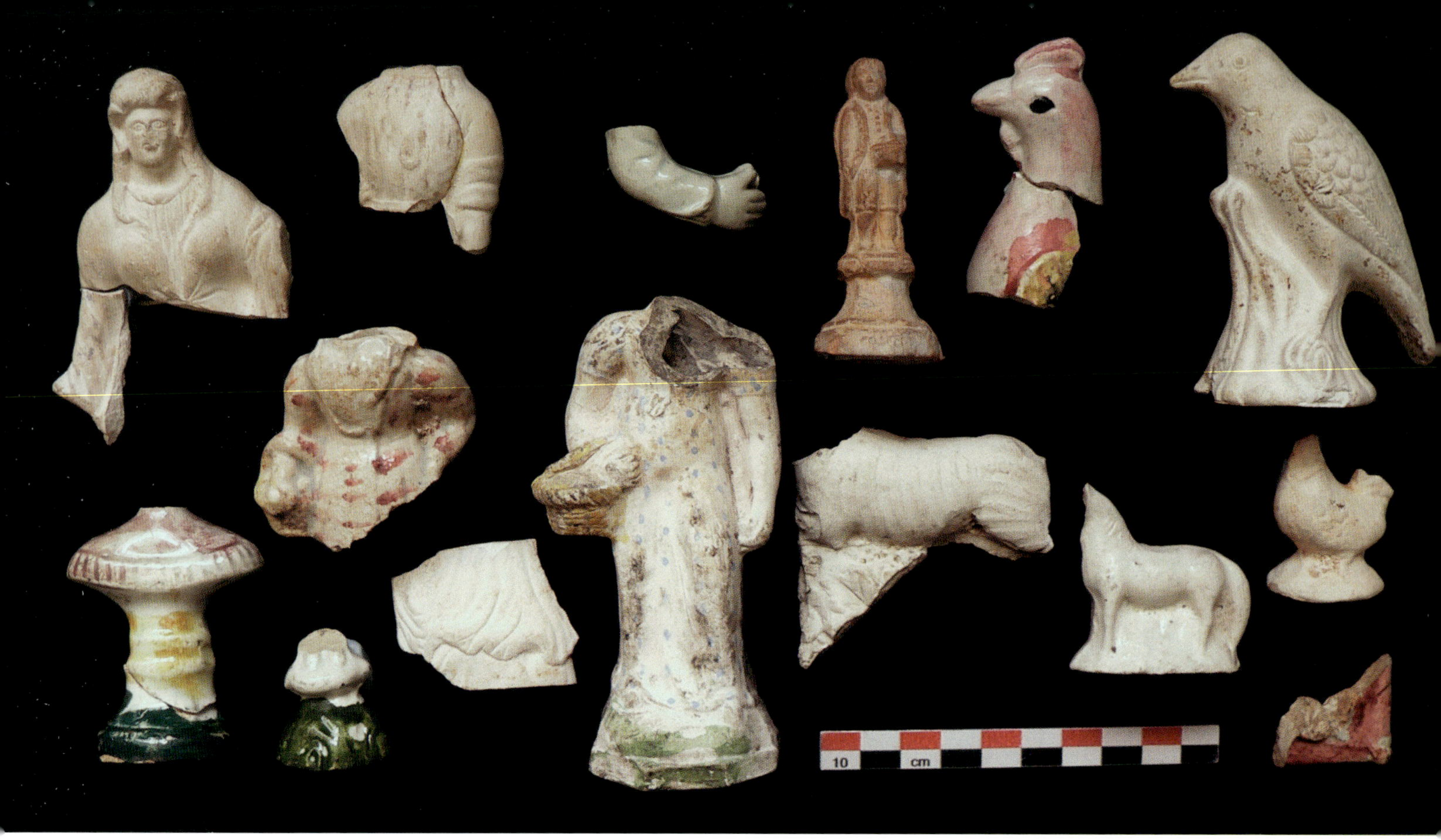

Illustration 7.12
Bisque sherds, George Gordon's Pottery, Bankfoot, Prestonpans. [Author]

that he was in charge of the Abercorn brick and tile works. Using the local red firing clay, Creelman diversified into architectural ceramics for gardens etc and in the process became wealthy, purchasing houses and ground around Portobello. This included the site of an earlier whiteware pottery. More interestingly, on his death aged seventy-five in 1830, he also bequeathed separately what is described as Creelman's Little Pottery (Sheila Forbes pers comm and NAS Sasine RS27/225/110–11). Although the location of this

Illustration 7.13a and 7.13b
Large white salt-glazed stoneware bowl inscribed 'Prestounpans 1754', Auld Kirk Pottery, Prestonpans.
[Courtesy City of Edinburgh Museums Service]

Illustration 7.14
Bat printed and painted creamware plate Old Kirk Pottery, Prestonpans.
[Courtesy City of Edinburgh Museums Service]

pottery has been identified, its date of construction remains unknown.

Certainly, in the early years of the nineteenth century there are records of stoneware being shipped from the nearby port of Leith to the Clyde for export, for example on 1 December 1806, 17cwt of stoneware was loaded for Jamaica. The Leith Customs Accounts are difficult to interpret, in that it is not possible to identify the ceramic manufacturers, the shippers being agents or independent exporting firms. Even more important than who was producing this stoneware is the fact that, for the first fifty years of all Scotland's production, we cannot identify one single example of what must have been a substantial output. Some later examples of Scottish stoneware are outstanding, suggesting an industry with a long history, which had developed to such an extent that it was capable of producing vessels of the very highest quality (illus 7.7).

During the period covered by George Gibb's survey of ceramic material shipped to the wider Americas from Leith 1742 to 1792, destinations included in America, Savannah (South Carolina), Edington (North Carolina), Portsmouth (New Hampshire) and Norfolk (Virginia). Other destinations included Antigua, Grenada, St

CORONAT FIDES

Illustration 7.16a
Moulded, Queen Caroline commemorative plate, West Pans. [Author]

Christopher (now St Kitts), Jamaica, Tobago and Barbados in the West Indies, farther south British Honduras and farther north to Quebec in Canada (1979: 17–18; 1980: 57). Gibb's research also showed

that William Cadell's goods were being trans-shipped via Perth and Dundee (1981: 38).

More than fifty brick, tile and pottery sites were in operation in the Forth littoral between 1700 and 1900, but, as far as can be determined, only a few were using large amounts of imported white firing clays prior to 1800. These are the Auld Kirk and Bankfoot potteries at either end of Prestonpans, the potteries at Morrison's Haven, West Pans (illus 7.8, 7.9, 7.10), Cousland, Portobello (illus 7.11) (where there may have been three) and Bo'ness, with the Gallatown pottery at Pathhead, Kirkcaldy,

Illustration 7.15
Porcelain coffee pot and cover, decorated with the arms of Pringle of Stitchell using polychrome enamels. There are also extensive traces of cold gilding over the usual streaky cobalt, West Pans. [Courtesy Trustees of the National Museums Scotland]

Illustration 7.16b
Details of a moulded border. [Author]

being problematic (Haggarty 2007a: 229–30; Bell 2006: 18).

While there is no archaeological evidence for the production of eighteenth-century white salt-glazed stoneware in the west of Scotland, both it and creamware were almost certainly being produced from 1750 at the Old Kirk pottery, Prestonpans, and slightly later at Bankfoot (Haggarty 2007a: 218–22). Only a few extant eighteenth-century ceramic items can, with any certainty, be attributed to the Old Kirk pottery and none to Bankfoot, although recent excavations have recovered an important group of nineteenth-century pearlware and bisque figure sherds (Haggarty 2010: 142–3) (illus 7.12).

Identifiable extant eighteenth-century Old Kirk stoneware consists of a very large grey/white salt-glazed punchbowl inscribed 'Prestounpans 1754', currently in the City of Edinburgh collections (accession number HH 3184/68) (illus 7.13a, 7.13b). The following entry in The Roll of Members (vol 1) held in Freemasons Hall, Edinburgh, shows that a stoneware bowl was originally presented by William Cadell of the Old Kirk pottery to the Edinburgh Masonic Lodge of St David (formerly Lodge Canongate in Leith): 'William Cadell having made a compliment to the Lodge of a most capacious Stone bowl which contains no less than 34 Scots pints or so' (Sheila Forbes pers comm). The other items are part of a 'Royal' pattern creamware dinner service, two plates of which are presently on display in the City of Edinburgh Museum (accession numbers HH 5764/1; 2/96). This dinner service, some pieces of which are marked (illus 7.14), and the majority of which now reside in a private American museum, was reputedly presented by William Cadell to his ward Anne Mocket on the occasion of her marriage to one James Cunningham on 3 August 1792, in Aberlady.

Lengthy and detailed ships' manifests and invoices contained in the Cadell of Grange papers (NLS ACC 5381), along with George Gibb's work on the Leith port books and ongoing research by the author and Sheila Forbes, show that in the eighteenth century the main markets for Scottish ceramics produced on the east coast were on the Continent. A large proportion was shipped to ports in Scandinavia and the Baltic

Illustration 7.17
Plate with central scene in pink lustre and oil drip border, Verreville.
[Courtesy Trustees of the National Museums Scotland]

regions, but distribution stretched from St Petersburg in the north to the then important Freeport of Livorno (Leghorn) in Italy (Haggarty: forthcoming 2013). Quail's research on the 1806–10 exports highlights a trade in earthenware from Leith, via the Clyde, to other destinations in the Mediterranean including Smyrna where 110 crates of earthenware were dispatched on 9 March 1810. Malta, Messina and Gibraltar were also by this time receiving regular supplies, and there is also evidence for the trade to the Portuguese port of Oporto (Skerry and Findlen

Hood 2009: 180–1) and the Spanish port of Cadiz which was almost certainly a trans-shipment point to South America (Spanish Indies) (McVeigh 1979: 170). By far the main western destinations for earthenware, from Leith, via the Clyde, at the beginning of the nineteenth century were Jamaica and Quebec (Quail 1986).

One of the most important excavations of a Scottish ceramic production site was carried out at the multi-period kiln site at West Pans (Lewis 2009: 333–76), where, for the first time, we see something of the range of eighteenth-century porcelain (illus 7.15) and nineteenth-century commemorative wares (illus 7.16a, 7.16b), being produced in Scotland. It comes as no surprise that many wares are somewhat identical to those being produced south of the Border (Haggarty 2006) and is a salutary lesson to those dealers and collectors who ascribe all British-made pottery to Staffordshire. Other extant examples include two plates impressed with the mark of the Verreville Pottery, Glasgow, which recently came to light in

Ireland (illus 7.17, 7.18), and there must be many more examples across the Atlantic.

Much more research is needed before Scotland's place in the history of Britain's refined ceramic tradition can be elucidated. There is no doubt that, given the importance of this trade in the late eighteenth and nineteenth centuries from the Clyde to the USA, Canada and Caribbean, much surviving documentation lies in the archives of countries other than Scotland.

Illustration 7.18
Plate decorated with polychrome hand painting, along with loose and cut sponging, Verreville.
[Courtesy Trustees of the National Museums Scotland]

Scottish Pottery Research Resource

Massive redevelopment of Scottish industrial kiln sites in the late twentieth and early twenty-first centuries led to the recovery of some large ceramic assemblages. In a bid to get these into the public domain, what has become known as the National Museums Scotland Sherd Programme was initiated. The efforts of a small team of volunteers working in the National Museums Scotland (NMS) have enabled large quantities of excavated sherd material to be made accessible on a series of CD-ROMs. These are not intended to be 'publications' in the accepted sense and should not be seen as such; they are merely research tools. Distributed in the *Journal of the Northern Ceramic Society*, funding for their printing has come from a number of sources, although predominantly from Historic Scotland. While this may not be the ideal solution, with minimal cost these CDs have put large amounts of information on Scottish ceramic fabric, decoration, form and functions into the public sphere. Assemblages from the east coast potteries of Newbigging, Musselburgh (Forbes and Haggarty 2002: 15–27; Haggarty 2005: 28), West Pans (Forbes and Haggarty 2004: 29–47; 2005: 5–22; Haggarty 2006: 110), Portobello, Morrison's Haven and Cuttle, Prestonpans, are now available for study (Haggarty 2005; 2006; 2008; 2009; 2010). Similarly, two assemblages from excavations on and near the large Verreville pottery in Glasgow are now published or accessible online (Haggarty 2007b; 2011a; 2011b), along with the nineteenth-century Campbellfield kiln site, also in Glasgow (Haggarty 2011c). A group of wares from a kiln site in Bo'ness and a second Portobello CD on late painted stoneware can also be accessed (Haggarty 2011d; 2011e). Cataloguing of the pottery from the eighteenth-century Glasgow Calton redware kiln site is ongoing.

Notes

1 To give some idea of the scale of this industry, the Barrowfield stoneware pottery had eighteen kilns, Bell's thirteen, Britannia twelve, Eagle twelve and Port Dundas thirteen, and by the 1870s Glasgow was Britain's largest stoneware-producing city, having totally eclipsed London and Bristol.

2 In his 2010 paper, George Dalgleish gives a brief overview of the nineteenth-century Scottish pottery export trade, looking at some of the wares exported, including the ubiquitous spongeware. It finishes with a detailed look at some of the specialist products aimed at the huge Canadian market, especially the work of the Britannia Pottery, Glasgow, originally built solely to supply the transatlantic market. Bremner states that there were at least fourteen potteries operating in Scotland, employing in excess of 5,000 people. With an estimated annual value of earthenware and porcelain exported in 1867 from Britain as a whole being £1,635,216, Scottish factories accounted for about £117,547 of this sum (a figure which Bremner says is an underestimate, as a great deal of Scottish pottery went first to England for subsequent export overseas).

3 This survey shows that ceramic exports included Bricks & Fire Bricks; Flat, Floor, Paving & Pan; Earthenware; Queensware; Delftware; Chinaware; Stoneware; Sugar Moulds; Apothecary Ware; Tobacco Pipes & Negro Pipes; Sugar Cones & Sugar Lump moulds: Kiln Heads(?). It is unclear exactly what apothecary ware is – most likely delftware. Most shipments were small, below 200lbs, except for a few in the 500–700lbs range and one of 2,086lbs to Rio de Janeiro. A much earlier reference to importation of apothecary ware into Scotland from Newcastle is contained in the Burntisland Customs Returns for 1666 (Blyth 1948: 112). Despite some research it is unclear what kiln heads are. The largest single shipment of earthenware was 80,800lbs or in excess of 36 tons, shipped from Port Glasgow on 25 September 1810, destination Havana.

4 Recent excavations in Scotland have identified a thriving late eighteenth-century redware industry producing moulded dishes decorated with joggled slip and a range of vessels with trailed slip decoration (Haggarty 2009). A programme of ICP chemical analysis has been carried out on a range of these wares from Scottish kiln sites (Haggarty, Hall and Chenery 2011). It is therefore entirely feasible for researchers working on redwares in the USA to pinpoint bricks and tile etc to Scottish production sites.

5 A large amount of information relating to the traumatic beginnings of Delftfield pottery is derived from a lengthy legal battle, the 'Delft-work Law Case' a 'Summons of Declaration and Payment', brought before Lord Erskine in the Court of Session in Edinburgh during 1748–9. The main facts relate to the dismissal of its manager, John Bird, a potter brought from London, who had agreed that local clay would be suitable followed by the subsequent realisation that it was not. These important papers were given to the Faculty of Procurators' Library in Glasgow by Dr Hill of Barlanark. This case was held to be so significant that a synopsis was published for the legal profession (Signet Library Edinburgh).

6 The first reference to clay being transported from Carrickfergus to Glasgow for use in the newly constructed Delftfield Pottery was on 31 August 1748 – 10 tons at £2 10s a ton, on the *Margaret* (Sheila Forbes pers comm). This was an exorbitant price and might suggest, as the documents imply, that somebody was on the fiddle. For the next few years all the clay came at five shillings a ton.

7 Included in this group is a number of other ceramic items, currently either being traded as Delftfield products or catalogued as such in museums.

8 The Boulton and Watt Archive and associated collections are amongst the most important held by Birmingham Archive and Heritage Services; it contains a number of letters and items which are of significant interest to ceramic historians.

9 A large number of bisque creamware sherds have been recovered from the excavations at the Delftfield site from plates with both feather-edged and Queen's patterns. Sherds from mugs, bowls and teapots all show extensive use of simple beaded rouletting while handles often have typical sprig-moulded terminals.

10 The figure of seventy includes those employed at the adjacent brick and tile works founded in 1785.

Acknowledgements

Without the research and continued support of my friends and museum volunteers, David Doxey, Sheila Forbes (especially for archival research), Jim Gray, Frances McLaren, Grant McMillan, Catriona and David Maisels, Ian Paterson, Susie Reid and Robert Stenhouse, there would be no Scottish sherd project and consequently no publications. For the sustaining of our work in the National Museums Scotland, I am indebted to a number of people in the Department of Scotland and Europe, David Caldwell, Jackie Moran, Lindsay McGill and especially George Dalgleish. I also wish to thank David Scarratt and Helen Edwards from the City of Edinburgh Museum Service, Mike Brooks from Historic Scotland, the AOC Archaeology Group, National Museums Scotland and a major Scottish private collector for images.

Documentary Sources

ECA: GB236 SL 1/1 – 15 December 1784: Edinburgh City Archives: Town Council Minutes.

National Archives of Scotland

NAS: CS96/643–653, 55: Business books, William Lang, 1717–68.

NAS: E504/15: Collector's Quarter Books, Greenock Customs Accounts.

NAS: E504/28/3: Collector's Quarter Books, Port Glasgow Customs Accounts.

NAS: 3/251 (2) f, 208 rd 2/631: Scottish Record Office: Feu, Baron William Mure to William Jamieson.

NAS: Sasine, RS27/225/110–11. 23 November 1860. Disposition presented by William Scott.

National Library of Scotland

NLS ACC 5381

Bibliography

Austin, J C 1994 *British Delft at Williamsburg.* Colonial Williamsburg Foundation.

Bell, J 2006 *Nine Potteries in Kirkcaldy: a history.* Fife Pottery Society.

Blyth, J J 1948 *Burntisland Early History and People.* Kirkcaldy

Bremner, D 1869 *The Industries of Scotland: Their Rise, Progress and Present Condition.* Edinburgh: A & C Black.

Dalgleish, G 2010 'The nineteenth-century Scottish pottery industry and its transatlantic exports', *in* Horning, A & Brannon, N (eds) *Ireland and Britain in the Atlantic World. Proc Irish Post-Medieval Arch Group* 2, 202–12.

Denholm, P C 1979 'Pottery exports from Port Glasgow to the Americas, 1747–56, from the Customs Registers', *Scottish Pottery Historical Review* 4, 21–4.

Denholm, P C 1982 'Mid-eighteenth-century tin-glazed earthenware from the Delftfield Pottery, Glasgow: excavations at the Broomielaw, 1975', *Post Medieval Archaeology* XVI, 39–84.

Forbes, S 1995 'William Creelman, Potter in Coats', *Scottish Pottery Historical Review* 17, 17–19.

Forbes, S & Haggarty, G R 2002 'William Reid's Newbigging Pottery, Musselburgh, 1800–1932', *The Northern Ceramic Society Journal* 19, 15–27. And Haggarty, G R 2005 'Newbigging Pottery, Musselburgh, Scotland', Ceramic Resource Disk, *The Northern Ceramic Society Journal* 21, 28.

Forbes, S & Haggarty, G R 2004 'The ceramic history of West Pans: Part I', *The Northern Ceramic Society Journal* 21, 29–47.

Forbes, S & Haggarty, G R 2005 'The ceramic history of West Pans: Part II', *The Northern Ceramic Society Journal* 22, 5–22.

Gibb, G 1979 'Leith Customs Accounts: a progress report', *Scottish Pottery Archive News* 4, 17–18.

Gibb, G 1980 'Slow progress on two fronts', *Scottish Pottery Historical Review* 5, 55–8.

Gibb, G 1981 'Customs accounts: some further information and some further thoughts', *Scottish Pottery Historical Review* 6, 38–41.

Gibson, J 1777 *The History of Glasgow, from Earliest Accounts to the Present Times.* Glasgow.

Haggarty, G R 2005 'Newbigging Pottery Musselburgh, Scotland: Ceramic Resource Disk', *The Northern Ceramic Society Journal* 21, 28.

Haggarty, G R 2006 'West Pans Pottery: Ceramic Resource Disk', *The Northern Ceramic Society Journal* 22, 110.

Haggarty, G R 2007a 'The evidence for eighteenth-century creamware production in the Forth littoral', *Creamware and Pearlware Re-examined. A collection of papers presented at a Colloquium held by the English Ceramic Circle at the Victoria and Albert Museum, 4–5 June 2005*, London, 218–30.

Haggarty, G R 2007b 'The Verreville Pottery, Glasgow: Ceramic Resource Disk', *The Northern Ceramic Society Journal* 23, 116.

Haggarty, G R 2008 'Portobello Potteries: Ceramic Resource Disk', *The Northern Ceramic Society Journal* 24, 24.

Haggarty, G R 2009 'A pottery assemblage from excavations at the Morrison's Haven kiln site near Prestonpans, East Lothian, Scotland: Ceramic Resource Disk', *The Northern Ceramic Society Journal* 25, 11–12.

Haggarty, G R 2010 'The Belfield Pottery Production Site: Ceramic Resource Disk', *The Northern Ceramic Society Journal* 26, 142–3.

Haggarty, G R 2011a 'Lancefield Quay, Verreville, Glasgow', Disk. National Museums Scotland. http://repository.nms.ac.uk/324/.

Haggarty, G R 2011b 'A deposit of ceramic kiln waste from the Britannia Pottery, Glasgow, recovered during archaeological investigations at the Broomielaw', National Museums Scotland. http://repository.nms.ac.uk/325/.

Haggarty, G R 2011c 'The pottery from excavations on the Campbellfield kiln site at Davy Street Glasgow', National Museums Scotland. http://repository.nms.ac.uk/329/.

Haggarty, G R 2011d 'Ceramic Resource Disk: Bo'ness Pottery', National Museums Scotland. http://repository.nms.ac.uk/326/.

Haggarty, G R 2011e 'A group of Buchan's stoneware from excavations at Portobello', National Museums Scotland. http://repository.nms.ac.uk/291/.

Haggarty, G R forthcoming 2013 'A ceramic trade, from Scotland to Livorno in the latter eighteenth century', *Journal Archeologia Postmedievale* 12.

Haggarty, G R & Forbes, S 2004 'Scotland: Lind and A-marked porcelain', *The Northern Ceramic Society Journal* 20, 1–10.

Haggarty, G R, Hall, D W & Chenery, S 2011 'Sourcing Scottish redware', Medieval Pottery Research Group Occasional Paper. Perth.

Haggarty, G R & Gray, J A forthcoming 2013 'English Ceramic Circle' Transactions.

Hills, R 2001 'James Watt and the Delftfield Pottery, Glasgow', *Proceedings of the Society of Antiquaries of Scotland* 131, 375–420.

Kelly, H E 1994 'The export trade of J & M P Bell & Co. and other Scottish potteries', *Scottish Pottery Historical Review* 16, 49–58.

Kelly, H E 1999 *Scottish Ceramics.* Atglen.

Kinghorn, J & Quail, G 1986 *Delftfield: a Glasgow pottery 1748–1823.* Glasgow Museums and Art Galleries.

Lewis, J 2009 'West Pans: excavations at a ceramic production site in Musselburgh, East Lothian', *Proceedings of the Society of Antiquaries of Scotland* 139, 333–76.

McVeigh, P 1979 *Scottish East Coast Potteries 1750–1840.* Edinburgh: John Donald.

Neil, J 1912 'The story of the Caledonian Pottery, Glasgow', *Transactions of the Old Glasgow Club*, vol 2, 319–25.

OSA: Old Statistical Account 1791–9, vol 7, 382. Old or West Monkland, County of Lanark.

Oswald, A, Hildyard, R J C & Hughes, R G 1982 *English Brown Stoneware 1670–1900.* London: Faber & Faber.

Quail, G 1982 'Four early Glasgow potteries', Glasgow Archaeological Society Occasional Paper 1, 5–28.

Quail, G 1986 'Ceramic exports from Scotland: 1806–1810', *Parks Canada* Research Bulletin 239. Canada: Ministry of Supply and Services.

Robinson, E & McKie, D (eds) 1970a *Partners in Science: Letters of James Watt & Joseph Black.* Cambridge MA, 8–9.

Robinson, F. & McKie, D 1970b *Partners in Science: James Watt & Joseph Black*, 8–12. London: Constable.

Skerry, J E & Findlen Hood, S 2009 *Salt-Glazed Stoneware in early America.* Colonial Williamsburg Foundation.

Turnbull, J 1997 'Delftfield wares for Antigua', *Scottish Pottery Historical Review* 19, 40–2.

CHAPTER 8

Kilmarnock carpets in the American colonies

VANESSA HABIB

In the context of leaving one home and travelling far to create another, textiles are perhaps nearest the heart. They are fragile, they wear out, they fade and then sometimes enjoy a second life, cut up and resewn. Often anonymous, often made by many hands, they form both necessities and the adornments of life. As people move from place to place they take with them the skills and knowledge of many generations, and this is an aspect of emigration which is sometimes overlooked.

For an area so rich in textiles, the wool trade of the west of Scotland is surprisingly little known, particularly the carpet manufacture for which Kilmarnock was renowned. During the eighteenth and nineteenth centuries, the woollen flat-weave carpets made there were used widely at home and exported to England, Europe and the American colonies. At the beginning of the eighteenth century, Kilmarnock was a modest town with around 4,000 inhabitants, lying on Kilmarnock Water and the River Irvine. Close to the port of Ayr, it was located about twenty miles south of Glasgow, and near the Atlantic trading ports of Port Glasgow and Greenock. The Clyde was not yet deep enough to make Glasgow a great port, and the main shipping route for freight and passengers lay from the westerly ports around the northern coast of Ireland and out across the Atlantic.

The rise of Kilmarnock

Two factors combined to change the fortunes of Kilmarnock: the Union between England and Scotland in 1707, and, contingent upon this, the Atlantic tobacco trade. Although the linen trade received the lion's share of government subsidy for industry through the terms of the Treaty of Union in 1707, some money was set aside for the coarse wool manufacture (Gulvin 1971: 50, 121–37). The wool lobby in the county of

Ayrshire was strong. The county was known for the fineness of its wool and a variety of cloths was made, including shalloons, blankets and serges, and tartans known as Ayrshire Plaids. There was a good market for serges in Holland, but in order not to compete with the English wool trade it had to devise new ways of working up the coarser wools to safeguard its traditional manufacture. Occasional, hazy references to the origins of carpetmaking in Scotland mention Kilmarnock, and in particular, the Earl of Kilmarnock as an early commercial pioneer, but the earl's name and endeavours were subsequently buried under the national policy to improve the linen trade after the Union (Durie 1979: 16). In fact, coarse woollen manufacture was initially supported in the Articles of Union, and after the establishment of the Board of Trustees for Manufactures in 1727, some effort was made to assist the wool merchants of Scotland. A letter from the 4th Earl of Kilmarnock to the Board (on behalf of a group of gentlemen) dating from 1743 refers to a new woollen manufacture which it is hoped the Trustees will support. The process involved using the coarsest wool from the fleece, and it was claimed that fifty-six looms and workhouses were already in a state of 'great forwardness'.[1]

The Earl of Kilmarnock, involved in the Jacobite cause, lost his life in 1746, but the woollen manufactory flourished; beginning with land at the Greenhead in Kilmarnock it soon extended to include a waulkmill in 1746. The Earl of Glencairn and his eldest son Lord Kilmaurs became partners in 1749. (McKay 1848: 92). In the *Glasgow Journal* of October 1752, the company advertised a variety of woollen goods including carpets. Merchants could apply to James Scot, merchant in Kilmarnock and sole manager of the company or to Archibald Coats, merchant in Glasgow with their commissions. Later, a warehouse in Greenock was added (illus 8.1). A furnishing

KILMARNOCK WOOLLEN
MANUFACTORY.

THAT JAMES WILSON and Co. of the
WOOLEN MANUFACTORY at Kilmarnock,
continue to manufacture all Kinds of CARPETS
and FLOOR-CLOTHS, both of the Scots and Wilton Kinds, after the very beſt Patterns, and of the
brighteſt Colours, alſo variety of BLANKETS,
raiſed and finiſhed in the Engliſh manner.

Which are to be ſold on the moſt reaſonable
Terms, either upon Credit or for ready Money, with
a ſuitable Diſcount, at the Company's Warehouſe
at Kilmarnock, and in Greenock at the Warehouſe
kept for them by DANIEL CRAWFORD Mercht.
there.

Commiſſions will be faithfully and punctually
anſwered.

Illustration 8.1
Kilmarnock Woollen Manufactory advertisement,
Glasgow Journal, September 1767

account from the Edinburgh upholsterer John Schaw to the Duke of Argyll for refitting his apartments at the Abbey of Holyroodhouse in 1753 included: 'A Kilmarnock Carpet 3 by 2½ yards £2 A Scots Carpet 2⅜ by 3 yards £1 3s'.[2] Matthew Dickie purchased '1 fine Carpet qt 5 yds square @ 6/- totalling £1 10s' from the 'Kilmarnock Woollen factory Co' for the use of Lady Saltoun in February 1756.[3] By the mid-eighteenth century these carpets also began to appear in the stock of upholsterers. In 1757 Archibald Bogle advertised amongst a long list of desirable furnishings 'Turkey, French, Whetton (Wilton) and Kilmarnock carpets, Persian bedsides, oil cloths and basses' (illus 8.2). Wilton carpets – carpets woven with a low velvety pile – were made in the Devonshire town of that name and also at Kidderminster and came early to Scotland via the busy shipping routes from Bristol to Whitehaven and Ayr. The Earl of Dumfries, who was furnishing his new house in Ayrshire at this time and who was able to commission the finest carpets and furniture from London, also purchased from James Wilson & Co. at the Kilmarnock Woollen Manufactory, 44½ yards of yard-wide carpeting in September 1766. A piece cut out for the hearth was included in the order as 'it may Answer for a Bedside'.[4] This was probably not put down in one of the state rooms but might have been ordered for a family bedroom.

The company had become extremely successful by this time, its stock in trade amounting to £6,150 according to Archibald McKay the historian of

Kilmarnock. James Wilson's advertisement in the *Glasgow Journal* in September 1767 stated that 'he continues to manufacture all Kinds of Carpets and Floor-Cloths, both of the Scots and Wilton Kinds, after the very best Patterns, and of the brightest Colours' which were sold at the company's warehouse in Kilmarnock and a warehouse in Greenock kept for them by the merchant Daniel Crawford, indicating that they were exported. When the Atlantic merchant Richard Oswald became a partner in 1765, the *Scots Magazine* commented that Scotch carpets were so popular both at home and in Europe and the American colonies, the demand for them could not be answered.[5] Two inventories from Maryland record Kilmarnock carpets. Household furnishings belonging to William Eilbeck from Charles County taken in November 1765 included '4 Kilmarnock carpets for floors, valued at £10, 2 small ditto for bed sides at 5s, an old painted floor cloath and two small old linen ditto at 3s'. Somewhat later, in May 1779, George Maxwell's inventory included '1 small plush carpet, 2 Kilmarnock carpets, another of the same, old, and 2 painted floor cloaths' amongst his household possessions. And in Fairfax County, Virginia, George Johnston, whose inventory was recorded in February 1767, owned two Wilton carpets valued at £9 and a Kilmarnock carpet valued at £4.[6]

Merchant princes

The emerging tobacco trade created a cycle of commercial activity from the American colonies and the Caribbean to Glasgow and back again, and had huge consequences for the wealth of Scotland. One man who typified this trade and one of the wealthiest merchants engaged in it was John Glassford, the son of a Paisley merchant. His fleet of twenty-five ships, the largest which crossed the Atlantic in the 1750s, 1760s and 1770s, carried principally tobacco one way and Scottish goods the other. With the profits he made, he supported almost all the leading manufacturing interests in Glasgow, including a huge tan works (in which James Wilson was a partner), a cotton and linen printfield and the Cudbear dyeing company. He was a partner in two banks, the Thistle Bank and the Glasgow Arms Bank, and involved in the cultural life of the city through his association with the booksellers and publishers Robert and Andrew Foulis, who were also printers to the University and set up the earliest, albeit short-lived, School of Design in Britain in 1753 (Devine 1975: 181).

One of the students at this Academy was Archibald McLauchlan who painted a portrait of John Glassford and his family in their town house. Their residence was said to be the finest house in Glasgow in the early eighteenth century, with extensive parks, gardens and hothouses, which can be glimpsed through the sash window (illus 8.3). Glassford had three wives and it was said of him that he 'lived high and married high'; his first wife was a merchant's daughter, the second a baronet's daughter (Anne, daughter of Sir John Nisbet), and the third an earl's daughter (Lady Margaret Mackenzie, daughter of the Earl of Cromarty). The luxurious carpet upon which the family is grouped,

ARCHIBALD BOGLE

Makes up all kinds of UPHOLSTRY FURNITURE at his ware-room in Gibſon's Wynd, ſuch as beds, couches, ſetters, chairs, feſtoon and ſpring window-curtains: He like-wiſe makes up marquies, tents, bell-tents, camp chairs, field-beds, matraſſes, &c.

And ſells all kinds of
Silk and worſted bed damaſks,
Morines, harratiens chineys, &c.
Checks, callicoes and chintzs,
Bed-laces, livery-laces, and ſhoulder-knots,
Counterpains, quilts, and Dutch bed-mantes,
Engliſh and Scots blankets,
Scots and Flanders bed tykes,
Bed bunts and white bolſter tykes,
Wool and hair matraſſes,
Demitys and fuſtains,
Turkey, French, Wetton and Kilmarnock carpets,
Perſian bedſides, oil cloths and baſſes,
Wax cloth for covers to tables and drawers,
Figured hair-cloth and leather for chairs,
Painted and flock paper,
Chineſe paper for room-hangings,
Mandareens and Indian flower pots for ſcreens,
Made up ſcreens,
Bells, bell-ſprings and cranks,
Clock pinns, caſteis, and curtain rings, with variety of other goods.
N. B. Workmen ſent to the country, to ſtuff chairs, make or put up furniture.

Illustration 8.2
Archibald Bogle advertisement, *Glasgow Journal*, April 1757

the exotic fruit, flowers and musical instrument suggest a man of cosmopolitan taste, accomplishment and considerable wealth (Macauley 1951: 14–16). The thick-pile carpet may reflect one of Glassford's own mercantile or manufacturing projects, for we know that they were made in Edinburgh and Ayr in the 1760s. The most popular carpets of this type were made by Thomas Whitty at Axminster in the south of England and Thomas Moore in London.

An Axminster carpet made by Whitty, dating from the 1750s, survives at Dumfries House in Ayrshire, not far from Kilmarnock. It shows a profusion of garden and hothouse flowers created in many shaded colours (illus 8.4). The central medallion, which is over eight feet in diameter, contains exotic flowers including aloe and a cactus in bloom (illus 8.5). This spectacular plant, native to the Caribbean and southern parts of America, was known as the Giant Torch Thistle and bloomed briefly at night. Lord Ilay, later Duke of Argyll, grew the Torch Thistle in his greenhouse at Whitton Park near Hounslow, along with other rare species. Ilay was a passionate botanist, and his gardens became a celebrated beauty spot. The composition of the Dumfries carpet, breaking with oriental convention and looking to the New World, cannot be accidental. Hand-knotted pile carpets were made locally but none have so far been identified, if they have survived at all. They used a great deal of wool, especially coarse wool, and could be knotted by women and children or those who had not been apprenticed to any craft (Habib 2005: 259–72).

Consumers and comfort

As money flowed into the economy from trade and manufacturing there were opportunities for more people to purchase the latest furnishings and domestic comforts. These were often imported but increasingly attempted at home. The School of Design set up in Glasgow in 1753 was followed in Edinburgh by the Trustees Drawing Academy in 1760, a principal aim of which was to teach the principles of good design to the apprentices of linen printers, damask weavers, carpetmakers, painters, sculptors and so on. Prizes were awarded for the best patterns or compositions produced each year. The Edinburgh Society for Encouraging Arts, Sciences, Manufactures and Agriculture, established in 1755, also offered annual prizes as an encouragement to Scottish manufacturers. The Resolutions of the Society noted:

Illustration 8.3
'Portrait of John Glassford and his family' by Archibald McLauchlan *c* 1767, oil on canvas, 78 x 87in (1980 x 2210mm).
A black enslaved servant, who may subsequently have been painted out, stands to the left of the group.
[Courtesy of Glasgow Museums, Copyright © Culture and Sport Glasgow]

Carpets are made in several places in this country: to encourage the manufactures to vie with each other, it was resolved, that a reward be allotted for the best-wrought carpet, and of the best pattern and colours, made within a certain time.[7]

Five guineas were offered for the 'Best Carpets as to work, pattern, and colours, of at least forty-eight yards' and four guineas for the next best. The length could be divided into any number of carpets not exceeding six and the 'patterns may be varied or not at the pleasure of the artist'.[8]

Illustration 8.4
Dumfries House, Cumnock, Ayrshire.
Thomas Whitty carpet. [With kind permission of the Great Steward of Scotland, Dumfries House Trust]

The winners' names were published. Thomas McCulloch & Co. from Kilmarnock gained the first prize and John Mackie from Dunfermline the second. These carpets were the flat and pileless kind which came to be known as Scotch carpets. Reviewing the results of the competition, the *Scots Magazine* commented:

> In particular, it is said, the carpet manufacture has risen 1000*l* this last year; and so great a rise is thought to be owing to the premiums given by the society, which, though of small value, have had the effect to excite a spirit of emulation amongst the manufacturers.[9]

The Premiums for 1756, therefore, included several classes of carpets, rather ambitiously as it turned out – Scotch, Damask figure, Wilton and Turkey. No Wilton or Turkey carpets were produced, but for the best Scotch carpet making forty-eight square yards, divided into any number of carpets, 'the firmest and best made, best figure, best colour and border, five guineas were awarded to the Hawick Carpet Manufactory in the Borders. David Hunter & Co. at Kilmarnock were runners up. For an all wool carpet of the best damask figure, best colour and border, four guineas were awarded to William Gilchrist at Kilmarnock'.[10] In subsequent years James Wilson & Co. at Kilmarnock were frequent winners.

No Scotch carpets from this early period have survived but a pileless woollen double cloth coverlet

Illustration 8.5
Detail of the central medallion of the Thomas Whitty carpet.
[With kind permission of the Great Steward of Scotland, Dumfries House Trust]

Illustration 8.6
Detail of the reverse of the Storrar Coverlet. [With kind permission of the owners]

Illustration 8.7
Storrar Coverlet (face). [With kind permission of the owners]

dated 1729 and still in the possession of the owners resembles the flat woven carpets we now know as Scotch. It may be an example of what was often called in weavers' daybooks a 'carpet coverlet' (illus 8.6) It is woven in one piece, in two colours, red and yellow-green, with a pattern of birds and chequered at each end. It is about five feet six inches by four feet and is reversible (illus 8.7).

The drawing master at the Trustees Drawing Academy was expected to produce designs for the manufactures each year. On the death of William DelaCour the Trustees wrote to the architects Robert and James Adam in London in 1767 about the appointment of a replacement. Although the principal role of the Academy was to 'improve the Taste of the young manufacturers of the Country', the university was much frequented and many young ladies were in Edinburgh for their education; consequently they said, 'the use of this establishment extends far beyond the purposes of Manufacture and becomes part of polite education, very ornamental and much in request here'. DelaCour, it seems 'understood Ornament and Landscape pretty well – He was defective in Architecture, in designing the human figure and Animals'. The Trustees asked the Adam brothers to look for a successor in London, though the artists there were known to have 'grown extravagant'. If not successful they were to look in Paris, perhaps at some of the designers working for the Gobelins Manufactory.[11] In the event, John Baptist Jackson, a designer of wallpapers and calico prints in London, was appointed for a salary of £100 a year.

Colours, patterns and dyes

In the absence of examples of the earliest Scotch carpets, records of carpet weavers, wool merchants and the growing profession of upholsterers reveal a considerable amount about how the carpets were made, the colours chosen and who purchased them. Occasionally, family papers, especially those families with manufacturing interests on their estates, give details of spinning and weaving projects. For example, James Paterson's account (dated 1744 to 1749) for dyeing wool for Lady Milton of Saltoun, for her carpets is quite detailed:[12]

June 2 1744	£	s	d
To dying 18 lb Carpet yarn Red @ 4d	0	6	0
To D° 21 lb ¾ Do Black @ 3d	0	5	5
To D° 5 lb Red fresh dip't @ –	0	0	5
To Scouring 16 lb Black yarn @ –	0	0	4

August 20 1746			
To Scouring 1 Stone White Wooling yarn –	0	0	8
To dying 12 lb D° Blue @ –	0	6	0
February 11 1748			
To dying 9 lb Hemp Yarn @ 10d	0	7	6
April 9 1748			
To 39 Yds Shalloon for 38 ½ yds @ 1s 4d	2	11	0
May 24			
To dying 46 lb Carpet yarn @ –	0	0	8
the ½ Red & the ½ Green	1	9	8
January 15 1749			
To dying a Piece hempen Cloath a Dark Chocolate Colour @ –	0	4	6
To dying 16 lb Carpet yarn the ½ Red And ½ Green @ –	0	10	8
To Spinning 56 lb Carpet yarn @ 3d	0	14	0
To Teasing & twining the yarn	0	3	0
To three Pints oyle	0	3	6
To Spinning 17 lb Carpet yarn @ 5d pr Pound twining Included	0	7	11½
To oyle to D° –	0	1	0
To 6 Stone Course Wool for the Carpet yarn @ 3s	0	18	0
February 20			
To dying 20 Yards Course harn Cloath a Logwood Blue Wt 16 lb @ 2½d	0	3	4

One company in Stirling, a town similar to Kilmarnock associated with serge weaving at the beginning of the eighteenth century, left very detailed daybooks. Many of their carpets were consigned to a Glasgow merchant, probably for export; some went to upholsterers in Edinburgh and others to England, Holland and Sweden. The carpets made by Gilfillan & Co. were reputedly known for their fine colouring. A detailed company ledger dating from the 1760s gives dye recipes. Some of their carpets were clearly very colourful; one woven in June 1767 was black, yellow, green, red and white (Habib 2000: 130, 795–807). Others were a substantial size and woven in a variety of widths which were sewn together and bound to make a complete carpet. Many of these patterns would have been geometric in composition and some of them were extremely striking with clearly defined areas of colour where the cloths interchanged (illus 8.8). Sometimes Gilfillan's customers provided their own yarn. For example, Lady Campbell of Gargunnock ordered a

Illustration 8.8
Scotch carpet, possibly made at Stirling.
[Courtesy John Claridge, Selkirk]

carpet eight and a half by six yards with a border in 1769. She supplied the yarn which Gilfillan dyed green and white. By far the most popular colours woven by Gilfillan were a simple two- colour combination of black and yellow, but he also dyed yarn red with madder and the more expensive cochineal for ingrain red. A loose letter in their ledger, dated 1 November 1769, discusses an order going abroad:

> Sir
>
> You'll please make a Common Carpet 16½ Feet Square or 5½ yards by 5½ with all Dispatch the Best Colours possible it is for a Gentn. Going abroad & must be Done Directly or will Lose the Ship. I show'd him N. 167 which pattern he pitches upon Pray be quick – Your obed Servt J Simpson

Another carpet weaver who left records of his business was Robert McLean of the village of Crookedholm, now a suburb of Kilmarnock. Towards the end of 1763 McLean, together with James and William Stevens, dyers in Crookedholm, and Hugh Wylie, merchant in Kilmarnock, agreed to carry on a trade of weaving woollen carpets, each of them contributing £20 to the company. A contract was drawn up but never signed, because initially the partners wanted to see how trade would progress.[13] The company prospered for a little more than four years but was dissolved in acrimony after a dispute over who owed money to whom. McLean accused James Stevens of overcharging for dyestuffs: 'the Whole Dye Stuffs to the Wooll Yarn Dyed Manufactured by the Company is Charged at Supposed rates far above the Real Value & Price of first Cost Particularly Yellow Wood Double Price it is Charged and alum in the same Manner'.[14] He also accused Hugh Wylie of owing him money for carpets sold. The dispute rumbled on for several years. Unfortunately, McLean, claiming 'ignorance and rusticity' in his defence, lost his case, the general view being that his business books had been 'cooked up recently'. However, his accounts do show the range of carpets which he made and the colours he wove. His stock included carpets in various sizes, carpet bed covers and twilled bed covers.[15] The carpets were sold through Hugh Wylie in Kilmarnock and to several of the principal upholsterers in Edinburgh, including Alex and William Bruce, Alex Beverly and Messers Russell and Gillespie. He used fewer colours than Gilfillan, principally black, red, yellow and green, occasionally 'brown sinimon'.[16]

'You find them in every house from the highest to the lowest': the spread of Scotch carpets

The writer Edward Topham, residing in Edinburgh in the 1770s and describing Scottish Manufactures in one of his letters, remarked:

> The sale which these Carpets meet with in England is astonishing: you find them in every house, from the highest to the lowest, as they are calculated to suit that class of people who wish for the conveniences of life, but who cannot afford the extravagant prices of Wilton, Axminster and other more extensive manufactories. They have been, in a great measure, the means of rendering the houses here so comfortable, and are the best securities against stone buildings, stone stair-cases and a cold climate. As yet their artists have not arrived at much elegance in the design or brilliancy of colour: but these improvements follow of course; the embellishments of art and luxury always succeed to convenience. In some pieces that I have seen, which have been made by particular orders, great taste has been shewn: a proof that an idea, as yet, probably in its infancy, has been started of improvements in this article. When those improvements take place, and the period will not be far distant, this manufactory may be as much distinguished for its elegance, as it is now for its goodness. (Topham 1776: 175).

Dalkeith Carpet Manufactory.

THat JOHN CLERK, WILLIAM HUME, and COMPANY, at Dalkeith, who have gained the premium for several years by-past, have a large assortment of the very best SCOTS CARPETS, both ingrained and common colours; also, coverings of all kinds for the navy or hospital beds; and they propose to serve both Merchants and others, upon as reasonable terms as any in this country can do; and for the conveniency of country commissions, there will be a large quantity at said William Hume's warehouse, opposite to the City-guard, Edinburgh: Where also will be sold, at the lowest prices, all sorts of houshold furniture, painted paper, and looking glasses.

Upholstery work performed in the neatest and best manner.

N. B. Commissions from the country, will be punctually answered, and proper discounts given for ready money.

Illustration 8.9
Dalkeith Carpet Manufactory advertisement,
Caledonian Mercury, April 1763

Topham felt strongly that the Scots should develop the manufacture of carpets. They had no competitors, and although the linen trade was subsidised and supported nationally, they might face threats from the linen manufacture in Ireland. Aided by a bounty on the quantities of coarse wool manufactured into cloth, numbers of Scottish wool merchants were persuaded to try weaving carpets and coverlets. Manufactories flourished in Glasgow, Lanark, Hawick, Stirling, Dalkeith, Edinburgh and many other smaller centres (illus 8.9).[17] It is recorded that weavers from Dalkeith had been encouraged to settle in Kilmarnock to develop manufacturing there. Sometimes carpets were

the woollen manufacturers made a procession through the town, representing all the different branches of that useful manufacture from the wools being taken from the sheeps back to the finishing it in all the different kinds of Carpets, Blankets, and Cloths made here, a specimen of each kind being exhibited to public view, the workmen were all clothed in the proper dress of that part of the work performed by them carrying their implements in their hands and accompanied with Drums, Violins, and other musical Instruments: they made a fine appearance, there being a very great number of hands young and old employed in that business here, it showed a better representation of the Spirit of industry; than any thing of the kind ever seen in this place.[18]

Illustration 8.10
Advertisement for Robertson's Carpet Store in New York.
[Courtesy of The Winterthur Library: Joseph Downs Collection of Manuscripts and Printed Ephemera]

James Wilson, a partner in Wilson Gregory & Co., regularly gained prizes in the Board of Trustees annual competitions which were designed to encourage Scottish manufacturing. The company already had trading links with the American colonies. In the 1760s the son of the partner William Gregory, also named William, was sent from the company of Scott Mitchell & Lennox in Glasgow to act as a clerk in Fredericksburg, Virginia. Later, he formed a partnership with another Kilmarnock man, William Glen, in New Haven, Connecticut, to import and export various goods to and from the West Indies. He kept a journal of a trip he made from Fredericksburg to Philadelphia and back again in the autumn of

woven by individual weavers working in their own workshops as part of the varied stock of a handloom weaver. An early publication, the *Housewife's Guide: or The Young Weaver's Instructor,* even gave printed directions about making them (Rutherford 1767: 34). Being made without a pile and in various widths they were comparatively easy to pack and transport. By the mid-eighteenth century there were at least five carpet manufacturers in Kilmarnock: William Gilchrist, John Wylie, John Murchland, David Hunter and, perhaps most importantly, James Wilson. A report from the Kilmarnock fair on 31 July 1768 describes the increase in manufacturing in the town:

1765, noting opportunities for trade: 'Went to the London Coffee house (in Philadelphia) and drank Punch. There you see everything that is done, or to be done – arrival of vessels, when, where and from what place. . . . I went and took a view of the Shipping. I never saw so many vessels at one time, at one Port I dare say there may be 250 vessels that go to sea.'[19] But with the outbreak of the War of Independence Gregory and Glen returned to Kilmarnock, Gregory becoming a partner in his father's carpet business. Wilson Gregory & Co. continued to weave Wilton and Brussels carpets but they were chiefly known for the flat two-ply Scotch type and in 1781 won joint first prize in the Board of Trustees competition.

The judges, the upholsterer William Hamilton in Edinburgh and the carpet manufacturer Robert Young in Stirling, commented:

> Under this article there were four parcels presented, and we found two of them to be preferable, the parcel marked B for the strong substance of the Cloth, and the parcel marked C, for the elegance of the patterns, and we were therefore of the opinion the Premium ought to be divided. On calling for the Sealed notes we found the parcel marked B were the manufacture of William Robertson & Company at Hawick, and the parcel marked C the manufacture of Wilson Gregory and Compy at Kilmarnock.[20]

In addition, the judges felt that the manufacture of Scotch carpets was now so buoyant that there was no longer any need for official encouragement. By the time the Statistical Account came to be written in the early 1790s, the annual value of carpets manufactured in Kilmarnock alone was thought to be £21,400.[21]

Carpets in the American colonies

In 1765 Benjamin Franklin's wife wrote to her husband, then in England, describing the new house which she had built: 'In this room, the little south one, is a carpet I bought cheap for its goodness, and nearly new. The large carpet is in the blue room. In the parlour is a Scotch carpet which has had much fault found with it (and) in the north room where we sit, we have a small Scotch carpet ... If you could meet with a Turkey carpet, I should like it' (Cole and Williamson 1941: 3). One can

Illustration 8.11
Three-ply carpet at Newhailes House, Midlothian. [With kind permission of the National Trust for Scotland]

Illustration 8.12
Carpet at Mellerstain House, Kelso. [With kind permission of the Earl and Countess of Haddington]

imagine the neatness and comfort of the various patterns of the carpets in her home and her wish for the glowing colours and soft pile of a Turkey carpet. Although she was critical of the Scotch carpet in the parlour, it was this kind which first became generally available to the colonists. A very early trade card has survived which advertised 'Carpets and Carpeting, English & Scotch, Ingrained & Common' at Robertson's Carpet Store in New York. There is an indistinct receipt on the back for carpeting at £1 15s per yard, signed by Robert Robertson & Son and dated 1756 (illus 8.10).

In the years following the War of Independence, however, Americans were able to develop their own manufactures for the first time, free from colonial demands to export raw materials and import finished goods from overseas. Weavers of Scotch carpets may have set up in business as early as 1775, in New York, Washington and Philadelphia,[22] but it was an English-man who is credited with being the first to manufacture Axminster carpets in America. Peter William Sprague, who was related by marriage to Thomas Whitty,

emigrated to New Jersey in the 1780s, moving later to Philadelphia. In September 1787 he advertised in the *Pennsylvania Gazette* under the company name of the Philadelphia Carpet Manufactory:

> Orders received by Peter William Sprague of Burlington, New Jersey, for any figure, size, shape of American made floor and bedside carpets, wove after the Axminster mode, which for softness, warmth and duration, exceed anything of the kind ever attempted in this country. (Sherrill 1996: 245)

His wealthier customers would have seen, if not purchased, genuine Turkey carpets and Axminster carpets on their travels in Europe but Sprague claimed that his carpets were 20 per cent cheaper than the imported ones and almost as cheap as Wilton carpets, since he employed, as Thomas Whitty had done in the 1760s, unskilled labour, usually women and children, to make them.

Sprague is celebrated for two important commissions in Philadelphia: one a carpet for George Washington's large dining-room at 190 High Street

and one for the Senate at Congress Hall. Neither of these carpets has survived but the Senate House carpet has been rewoven from contemporary accounts and description for the bicentennial celebrations. In size twenty-two feet by forty feet, it was apparently executed 'in a capital stile with rich bright colours' which gave a very fine effect with the mahogany desks, red leather chairs and crimson silk damask curtains provided for the Senators in a neoclassical style (Anderson 1978: no pagination). There is some uncertainty about what kind of carpet Sprague actually made for this chamber, as it was large for an Axminster and was seemingly made in strips. The decoration of the House of Representatives, however, was a more sober scheme, and the floor was covered with a flat weave ingrain carpet.

Washington was perhaps looking for something a little more distinguished for his own residence. His secretary Tobias Lear wrote to Sprague in February 1790: 'The President wishes to get a Carpet of the best Kind, for a room 32 feet by 22. We can get no carpet in New York to suit the room – Carpeting of the best kind – Scotch Carpeting is almost the only kind to be found here. If you will be so good as to inform me if anything of the above description can be found in Philadelphia, you will oblige me.'[23] There was certainly wealth in Philadelphia. 'Luxury', a French traveller observed 'already appears: they have carpets, elegant carpets; it is a favourite taste with the Americans; they receive it from the interested avarice of their old master, the English' (Brissot de Warville 1797: 317). For the majority of citizens, however, Scotch carpets were an attractive and comfortable addition to their homes and many handloom carpet weavers came to settle in Philadelphia as the city grew. Local manufacturing was aided by tariff duties on imported carpets which rose steeply from 1785 to 1816. The Pennsylvania Society for the Encouragement of Manufactures and the Useful Arts was established in 1787. The first American patent was issued in 1790.

Illustration 8.14
The White Mill at Enfield, Connecticut, demolished 1902.
[Courtesy of the Enfield Historical Society, Enfield, Connecticut, USA]

In Scotland technological change in the late eighteenth century helped to overcome the immediate effects of the tariffs. The introduction of the barrel loom, devised by Thomas Morton of Kilmarnock, a wheelwright and mechanic, lowered costs and considerably increased production, enabling patterned carpets to be woven without the aid of a drawboy. The weaver was able to lift the figuring threads himself by operating a pegged barrel mounted above the loom. This freed the drawboy, frequently a young boy or apprentice, from the drudgery of standing by the side of the loom, lifting the heavy worsted warp threads in the correct order (Anderson and Spivak 1990: 197). Morton made an exclusive agreement with the Kilmarnock manufacturers to use his barrel attachment, which proved to be especially effective in weaving small patterns.

Morton was also credited with popularising a three-ply flat weave carpet with the designer Thomas Barclay, a founding member of a drawing academy which was established in Kilmarnock.[24] This kind of carpet was thicker and softer than the two-ply, made by interweaving three layers of cloth. More colours could be introduced and even with single colours in each set of warps and wefts, many intricate shaded details could be created. The Jacquard figuring mechanism, which came into general use in Britain in the late 1820s, was used extensively

for these carpets. It greatly extended the potential width and depth of a pattern repeat by controlling individual warp threads with a system of punched cards, which in theory could be limitless. A bedroom carpet at Newhailes House in East Lothian, the home of the Dalrymple family, shows a three-ply carpet. In subdued tones of olive green, straw colour and black the three layers of cloth display many strongly modelled highlights and shadows in the drawing of the flowers and foliage, and in contrast, an intricate broken ground (illus 8.11). A carpet made for and laid in the Manchineel bedroom at Mellerstain House near Kelso in the Scottish Borders shows how a large pattern could extend fully across the width of the thirty-six-inch carpet strip with an elaborate pattern of trailing tendrils and garlands of fruit and flowers. Part of the coloured striped woollen binding tape still survives at the edge of the carpet (illus 8.12). The Mellerstain carpet, which is complete though worn and faded in some parts, also shows the characteristic multicoloured striped wefts which were a feature of earlier Scotch carpets (illus 8.13). In this case the stripes have become more prominent where some of the dyed yarns have faded. With the Jacquard mechanism attached to the loom, bigger patterns were much easier and faster to weave

Illustration 8.15
The Black Mill at Enfield, Connecticut, built in 1832–3.
[Courtesy of the Enfield Historical Society, Enfield, Connecticut, USA]

and for a while seriously competed with the more expensive Brussels and Wilton carpets. The width also became standardised and pattern matching between the strips less of a problem.

The *New Statistical Account* reported in 1845 that in the carpet factories in Kilmarnock 'about 1,200 are employed in weaving Brussels, Venetian, Turkey and Scotch carpets and rugs, the quality and patterns of which are not surpassed by any in Britain. The annual value of this branch of trade is about £150.000'. It added that in 1831 the company of Gregory Thomson & Co. had been awarded a large premium of £150 for four Turkey carpets, that is, hand-knotted pile carpets, with an extra prize of £30 by the Board of Trustees for Manufactures in their annual competitions. The Judges noted: 'The four carpets of the Turkey fabric ... the judges thought deserved most particular notice; that they are of a splendid description, and form an important addition to the Scottish manufactures, and fully entitle the spirited manufacturers to the liberal premiums adjudged to them.'[25] These most luxurious carpets could be ordered to fit a room but were very slow to produce and this is perhaps what led Richard Whytock and Alexander Templeton to experiment with making pile carpets in different ways in the 1830s, the former in Edinburgh with the printed Tapestry carpet, the latter in Glasgow with the Chenille carpet (Bartlett 1978: 12).

Scottish weavers in Enfield, Connecticut

Many of Gregory Thomson & Co.'s extensive range of carpets were purchased by James Elnathan Smith, the European buyer for the specialist carpet importers Andrews Thompson of New York. As protectionist trade tariffs, which were designed to support the home manufacture of carpets and restrict the import of British carpets, rose in America, Orrin Thompson, one of the partners, began to consider how to manufacture these carpets at home. Although he was a successful businessman, the problem lay in acquiring the technical skill and equipment to weave the carpets in America. For these he turned to Scotland and in 1828 formed a joint venture with Gregory Thomson & Co. to spin yarn in Kilmarnock and weave it at Enfield, Thompson's home town in Connecticut, on Scottish looms and with Scottish workmen.

A site had been found with sufficient water power to drive the machinery (Ewing and Norton 1955:

38), and initially twenty weavers were contracted to work for the Thompsonville Carpet Manufactory, as it was later known, for two years. The American partners paid for their passage on the understanding that money would be deducted from the weavers' wages on a weekly basis as work began. On their arrival at Enfield, however, the weavers discovered that the mill had not been built, and that they had no permanent accommodation. The Scots, therefore, had to set about building a row of cottages for themselves, known thereafter as Scotch Row.[26] They then turned their attention to the building of the mill, a three-storey frame building painted white, with the river running below, known as the White Mill, completed in the spring of 1829 (illus 8.14). On the top floor were housed the looms and below them, the carding engines and spinning frames.

Later in the year the weavers were joined by a second group of workmen. These included a spinner, a dyer and the previous owner of a carpet factory in Kilmarnock, Robert Thomson, who had married Mary, the daughter of William Gregory senior. Robert Thomson became the superintendent of the new mill. He was joined by two Kilmarnock brothers, Alexander and James Mitchell, who had already settled in New York and were familiar with the mechanism of the barrel loom and who could act as wrights. Alexander Mitchell had been apprenticed to Thomas Morton in Scotland and he began the production of two-ply carpets at Thompsonville and also began to spin the wool for the carpet yarn at the Mill. The so-called Black Mill, a four-storey brick and stone building, was begun in 1832 specifically for the weaving of three-ply carpets (illus 8.15). A fine example of this kind of carpet survives from the Crawick Carpet Company at Sanquhar near Kilmarnock (illus 8.16). Known for their bright fast colours, the carpets were exported, particularly to Russia, North America, South America and England.

Continuing links with Scotland ensured that the latest designs could be sent to America and woven on the Thompsonville Company looms before their competitors could import them: 'the designers, Scotsmen all, were readying the patterns. Customers supplied some of the ideas, Smith sent others from

Illustration 8.16
Detail of a three-ply carpet made at
Crawick Mill, Sanquhar, near Kilmarnock.
[Courtesy of Sanquhar Tolbooth Museum]

Europe. So prompt was he in forwarding three-foot copies of the latest patterns and styles that the Thompsonville line was ordinarily in the market ahead of other producers, both domestic and foreign' (Ewing and Norton 1955: 51).

Conclusion

Scotch carpets, of which the Kilmarnock carpet is a regional variation, became ubiquitous in the American home. Examples can still be seen in the many paintings of American interiors of the colonial period. Being made entirely of wool, they were tender and most have not survived, but a few have been rewoven for country houses and museums. They were colourful, made in strips of various widths with no pile and therefore easy to transport and fit to any size of room. They were as practical as a floor mat but as colourful as a Brussels carpet.

Thompsonville was perhaps not the first carpet mill to spin and weave ingrain carpets in America. Scottish workmen were also involved with the Medway Carpet Manufactory in Massachussetts, set up by the Boston merchant Frederick Cabot with the Scots mechanic Alexander Wright (Ewing and Norton 1955: 8). In 1826 Wright obtained three looms and twenty workmen from Scotland, including the designer Peter Lawson. This company was later absorbed into the Lowell Manufacturing Company. Wright was described as a man gifted with both administrative and technical proficiency, 'outstanding in three roles: initiator, adapter and organiser' (Ewing and Norton 1955: 12). Also at Tariff in Connecticut a carpet-weaving venture began in the 1820s. A notice in the *Boston Daily Advertiser* of 5 December 1826 commented:

> we have just seen a piece of Carpeting woven at Tariffville … it appears that carpets can be made there of any colours, and to any pattern, durable, cheap and elegant. Colouring can be done as well in this country as in any other, and the weaving by this loom is of the right sort. The public will in a short time become acquainted with their carpets, and we only claim the credit of being the first to mention them.

Some of the company weavers came from Kidderminster in England and many came from other parts of Europe, each community bringing its own particular skills and customs to a new and challenging homeland. Thompsonville was a largely Scottish enterprise, especially in the early days, known as a 'wee Kilmarnock, a Scottish village in the heart of Connecticut', which continued to celebrate a boisterous Hogmanay and whose families brought with them the sturdy independence of their forbears (Graham typescript). Perhaps William Gregory's story is not untypical. He went home to Scotland in 1784 and died a Burgess of Kilmarnock in 1817. His eldest son William, however, returned to America and settled in Alexandria, Virginia, becoming a successful merchant and banker in his new homeland.

Acknowledgement

This work was supported by a grant from the Society of Antiquaries of Scotland.

Notes

1 NLS Saltoun Mss 17560 f144 Letter from Lord Kilmarnock to Lord Justice Clerk, 27 October 1743.
2 NLS Saltoun Mss 17623 f60 Account from John Schaw to the Duke of Argyll, 8 August 1753.
3 NLS Saltoun Mss 16881 f26 Account from the Kilmarnock Woolen Factory Co., 23 February 1756.
4 Dumfries House 1766 4872DD Account from James Wilson & Co. to the Earl of Dumfries, 22 September 1766.
5 *Scots Magazine* 25, 1763, 654.
6 George Mason University, Virginia, Gunston Hall Plantation, 'Probing the Past', Probate Inventories from the Chesapeake region of Maryland and Virginia 1740–1810. Online database.
7 *Scots Magazine* 17, 1755, 126.
8 *Scots Magazine* 17, 1755, 129.
9 *Scots Magazine* 18, 1756, 48.
10 *Scots Magazine* 18, 1756, 107.
11 NAS NG1/3/10, 94. Letter Books of the Board of Trustees for Fisheries Manufactures and Improvements, 17 April 1767. Letter to Robert and James Adam from the Board of Trustees.
12 NLS Saltoun Ms 16874, f102. James Paterson's Account to Lady Milton, 1744–9.
13 NAS Court of Session Papers, CS21/22/6/1776.
14 NAS Court of Session Papers, CS21/22/6/1776. McLean's Evidence.
15 NAS Court of Session Papers, CS96/3175 10.
16 NAS Court of Session Papers, CS96/3175 19.
17 NAS NG1/3/3c, 5. Letter Books of the Board of Trustees, Instructions to William Cruikshank, Inspector of the Coarse Wool Manufacture, 9 April 1746. Quantities of wool and the amount of the bounty offered changed over time.
18 *Glasgow Journal*, 27 July to 3 August 1769.
19 'William Gregory's Journal, from Fredericksburg, Va., to Philadelphia, 30th of September 1765 to 16th October 1765', Omohundro Institute of Early American History and Culture 1905. *The William and Mary Quarterly* 13(4): 224–9.

20 NAS NG1/1/23, 9, 24 January 1781.

21 *Old Statistical Account of Scotland*, vol 2, 1792, 88. Parish of Kilmarnock.

22 Cole and Williamson, 11. William Calverly was said to have made carpets in Philadelphia as early as 1775. Peter Kennedy was said to have produced the first ingrain carpeting in Washington, 8.

23 Anderson 1978.

24 McKay, 229. Kilmarnock Drawing Academy was founded in 1831.

25 *New Statistical Account of Scotland*, vol 5, 1845 Parish of Kilmarnock, 551.

26 Much of the information in this section is taken from an article written by Barbara Graham, *Kilmarnock Carpet Weavers in America*, 33–41. Publisher and date unknown. Scotch Row was ultimately demolished as the carpet factory expanded in the early twentieth century.

References

Unpublished sources

National Archives of Scotland (NAS) Board of Trustees for Fisheries, Manufactures and Improvements, NG1/1 Minute Books, NG1/3 Letter Books.

National Library of Scotland (NLS) Saltoun Mss.

Bibliography

Anderson, C S & Spivak, S M 1990 'A re-examination of American antebellum handloom technology for weaving fancy coverlets and carpets', *Textile History* 21(2): 181–201.

Anderson, S H 1978 *The Most Splendid Carpet*. Philadelphia: National Park Service, US Department of the Interior, Washington. Online version.

Bartlett, J N 1978 *Carpeting the Millions: the growth of Britain's carpet industry*. Edinburgh: John Donald.

Brissot de Warville, J P 1797 *New Travels in the United States of America: Performed in 1788*.

Cole, A H & Williamson, H F 1941 *The American Carpet Manufacture: a history and an analysis*. Cambridge: Harvard University Press.

Devine, T M 1975 *The Tobacco Lords: A Study of the Tobacco Merchants of Glasgow and their Trading Activities, 1740–90*. Edinburgh: John Donald.

Durie, A J 1979 *The Scottish Linen Industry in the Eighteenth Century*. Edinburgh: John Donald.

Ewing, J S & Norton, N P 1955 *Broadlooms and Businessmen*. Cambridge: Harvard University Press.

George Mason University, Fairfax, Virginia 'Probing the Past, Gunston Hall Plantation Inventories from the Chesapeake region of Maryland and Virginia, 1740–1810. Online database.

Glasgow Journal.

Graham, B *Kilmarnock Weavers in America*. Typescript. No date and place of publication.

Gulvin, C 1971 'The Union and the Scottish Woollen Industry 1707–1760', *Scottish Historical Review* 50, 121–37.

Habib, V 1997 'Scotch carpets in the eighteenth and early nineteenth centuries', *Textile History* 28(2): 161–75.

Habib, V 2000 'Scotch Carpets at Stirling: Thomas Gilfillan's Cash Book and Ledger 1764–1770', *Proceedings of the Society of Antiquaries of Scotland* 130, 795–807.

Habib, V 2005 'Axminster carpet manufacture in Edinburgh in the mid-18th century', *Proceedings of the Society of Antiquaries of Scotland* 135, 259–72.

Loch, D 1778–9, 2 *Essays on the Trade, Commerce, Manufactures, and Fisheries of Scotland: with Notes and Observations concerning their Trade, Manufactures, Improvements Etc*. Edinburgh: Ruddiman.

Macauley, W J 1951 'A Scottish conversation piece', *Scottish Art Review* 3(4): 14–16.

McKay, A 1848 *The History of Kilmarnock*. Kilmarnock: Archibald McKay.

New Statistical Account of Scotland.

Old Statistical Account of Scotland.

Rutherford, J 1767 *Housewife's Guide: or The Young Weaver's Instructor*. Charleton Factory, near Richmond, Yorkshire.

Sherrill, S B 1996 *Carpets and Rugs of Europe and America*. New York, London and Paris: Abbeville Press.

Topham, E 1776 *Letters from Edinburgh in 1774 and 1775*. Edinburgh,

The influence of Scotland in American cabinetmaking

STEPHEN JACKSON

To attempt to summarise the influence of Scotland in American cabinetmaking is a risky undertaking at this stage of our scholarly understanding of the subject. I intend to focus on a number of documented geographical areas and assess them from the point of view of someone who looks at Scottish furniture extensively but at American furniture very seldom. This is therefore largely a critical commentary on the work of others, and I am clearly conscious of the great value of that work. My aim is to consider parameters for debate and suggest productive questions that might be kept in mind during fieldwork or documentary research. I hope that the result will not appear too random. The selection of illustrative images is weighted towards the Scottish, rather than the American, in order to increase awareness of the former material.

In this survey, relatively superficial design details are of greater interest than intricate technical analysis since ultimately the influence of Scotland on American cabinetmaking may rest as much with the consumer as with the maker. It is not solely about economic history – trade relations – it is also about cultural identity. It is about expressing who you are through your material culture, or at least using your material culture to reference your identity. Scottish identity is very dear to millions of people but we are still rediscovering exactly what it meant to feel Scottish, and to express Scottishness, in the seventeenth, eighteenth and early nineteenth centuries.

Our first difficulty is that some of the most familiar Scottish names in American furniture history were either born in America or emigrated at a young age. Duncan Phyfe, for example, was apprenticed to an Albany cabinetmaker at the age of fourteen. Nevertheless, it is also the case that skilled journeymen did often emigrate during their early twenties in order to better their prospects. James Honey, a journeyman wright, left Perth between 1773 and 1776 to settle at

Williamsburg. He was twenty-three in 1773 (Petznick 1999: 118). Henry Lamond left Edinburgh in his early thirties for Robeson County, North Carolina, where he continued to sign his work 'Henry Lamond, Cabinet Maker, from Edinburgh, N[orth] B[ritain]' (Doares 1994: 20). Men such as Lamond, who lived in an area of Scottish settlement, undoubtedly felt Scottish.

A second difficulty arises in characterising Scottish furniture, particularly in the period before 1800 and at the genteel level. Many forms of Irish furniture are instantly and uniquely identifiable but Scottish furniture offers far more subtle variations of the British tradition. A model of what one might hope to establish for Scotland in America is Ronald Hurst's work on the Irish presence in Virginia's Rappahannock River Basin (Hurst 1997). The Rappahannock evidence shows that it was natural for European craftsmen to continue making in a style that was little modified by the move to America, particularly where newly settled patrons existed to share in that style. Hurst identifies some unambiguously Irish traits in Rappahannock work of the third quarter of the eighteenth century: trifid feet, pillar feet and slipper feet, alongside deeply moulded knee scrolls. Found only sporadically in England, these features are also unique to the Rappahannock within the *corpus* of Virginian furniture. The form of a chest on a stand with drawers and cabriole legs, not exclusively Irish and yet strongly characteristic of Ireland, also crops up in this part of Virginia. The makers of this furniture are unidentified but Baltimore was one of the main ports of entry for the Irish, who arrived in large numbers after 1760.

Similar scenarios, therefore, should apply for Scotland. Not only was there an established trading presence in America but there were also significant levels of immigration after 1760. Advertisements in the Edinburgh newspapers offering free passage in return for a short period of indentured service begin in 1713,

Illustration 9.1
High chest of drawers by John Dunlap, for Jean Walker,
Bedford, New Hampshire, 1782.
[Courtesy New Hampshire Historical Society]

that journeymen could hope to better themselves by emigrating. Yet the contexts in which they might end up could differ considerably and some of the examples which follow demonstrate this variation in experience.

In 1994 Philip Zea of Historic Deerfield, in conjunction with Donald Dunlap, wrote an influential book about the Dunlap cabinetmakers of New Hampshire (Zea and Dunlap 1994). Archibald Dunlap emigrated from Ulster to New Hampshire at some point before 1741. He was a farmer and linen weaver but five of his sons were workers in wood, including John, who established a cabinetmaking dynasty when he moved to Bedford in 1777. The context is full of Scottish names both personal and geographical, but what about the furniture? Zea is careful to point out that there was no Scots-Irish enclave in New Hampshire and that where there were large numbers of Scots-Irish settlers, they were living alongside English neighbours. Nevertheless, ethnic groups did stick together in certain ways. Of more than forty people who bought furniture at a sale held by John Dunlap in 1771, nearly all had Scots-Irish surnames and of the patrons named in John Dunlap's account book for the period 1768 to 1789, 60 per cent had identifiably Scots-Irish names (Zea and Dunlap 1994: 14). The name Dunlap itself emanates from County Tyrone in Ulster and is probably an alteration of Dunlop, the Ayrshire parish from where the ancestors of Archibald and John were most likely transplanted during the seventeenth century.

Zea summarises the ethnic identity of Dunlap furniture in the following terms: 'The Dunlaps began to make furniture in the 1760s when memories of the first settlers were fading but before their ethnic pride surfaced in the 1820s. Rather than being ignorant of Anglo-Boston ways, some Scots-Irish preferred designs that reinforced the memory of their cultural past. The Dunlaps answered not with eccentricity but with continuity and a reactionary combination of features, refined by repetition, that were selected from the ancient vocabulary of Scottish design' (Zea and Dunlap 1994: 38).

What were these features, and more significantly, how ancient were they? Were they already in circulation in the Americas before the mid-eighteenth century? Zea relates certain carved details in the Dunlap *corpus*, specifically shells, rosette finials and basket-weave fretwork (illus 9.1), to a chair made in 1695 by Robert Rhea of Freehold, New Jersey (illus 9.2). Rhea, a joiner and persecuted Quaker, left Aberdeen in 1685 and his chair is now apparently one

first to Maryland and later to Virginia and other colonies. On 19 July 1748, for example, the *Edinburgh Evening Courant* carried a notice inducing two cabinetmakers and a chairmaker to travel to Charleston (Pryke 1989: 55). Along the Rappahannock, the Scottish-born furniture maker, Robert Walker of Port Royal, bought the indenture of his compatriot, Alexander Scott, only for Scott to abscond in 1755 (Leath 2008). It is clear that furniture makers were in demand and

London cabinetwork of the 1730s, as well as in Dublin tables carved at a similar date. The rosette embellished scroll can be seen in London cabinetwork of the 1740s onwards, although it is also prevalent in Edinburgh between 1750 and 1780, as in the American South. The basket weave galleries reference nothing directly comparable in British furniture, unless perhaps mid-eighteenth-century Irish carving. Moreover, both fans and rosettes have a place elsewhere in New England furniture.

The Dunlaps were trained in American workshops, under masters of unknown ethnicity, and produced forms which are quintessentially American, such as the chest on chest. If Scottish features were present, perhaps it was the clients who requested them. And if this were so, to what degree were such

Illustration 9.2
Chair by Robert Rhea, Freehold, New Jersey, 1685.
[Courtesy Monmouth County Historical Association, USA]

of only two surviving *caqueteuse* chairs to have been made in America.[1] The *caqueteuse* form enjoyed a distinctive popularity in eastern Scotland throughout the seventeenth century (illus 9.3) but died out around 1700, just as artistic commerce between London and Scotland entered a new phase. The *caqueteuse* was not a common form in western Scotland or Ulster, although it is not the form of Rhea's chair, which Zea compares with the work of John Dunlap, but rather the decorative devices. Could ideas common in seventeenth-century Scottish furniture have migrated in any way into the mid-eighteenth century? They did not do so in Scotland and, moreover, the motifs under discussion are not exclusively Scottish. The shell, or fan, although common in seventeenth-century Scottish joinery, features also, as marquetry, in

Illustration 9.3
Chair recording the marriage of William Chalmers and Isabella Forbes, Aberdeen, 1667.
[Courtesy Glasgow Life]

features considered to be Scottish and not simply normal or traditional? We can, of course, postulate a course of development in which Scots, or other ethnic groups, did consider certain decorative forms to be their own but only within the American context. This might reconcile any apparent disconnection between American and Scottish furniture with apparent similarities occurring in furniture made by men of Scottish origin in geographically separated parts of America. Zea does begin to suggest this when he asks whether certain anonymous pieces

Illustration 9.4
Chair, probably Fife, *c* 1800.
[National Museums Scotland]

from parts of New Jersey and Tennessee populated by the Scots-Irish bear comparison with the supposed eccentricity of the Dunlaps (1994: 40). Zea rightly rescued the Dunlaps from being seen as a bizarre solecism. However, one does not need to connect to a past across the ocean in order to do this. Vernacular makers constructed their own artistic vocabularies in response to a varied range of influences and through sheer originality. Some clients may have sought to dictate forms and decoration but it was often artisans who introduced customers to a particular article or novel fashion.

American furniture scholars fully realise that comparing sub-genteel American furniture with widely published high-style London pieces runs the risk of failing to encounter divergent or 'non-standard' regional forms. These forms, however, can be English as well as Scottish and there is variety within Scotland. British scholars are still mapping the divisions and connections at the local level. Identical chairs with hollow-seats (concave across the width) and button decoration (three small balls between stay rails) are found in East Anglia and Fife, two East coastal regions, one English, one Scottish (Cotton 1990: 220; Jones 1992: 6) (illus 9.4). Items of Welsh and Cumbrian form crop up in Galloway. In most respects the work of the Dunlaps, looked at cold from North Britain, resembles what it is: New England furniture. Zea is able to demonstrate very accurately the degree to which the cabinet furniture of the Dunlaps conforms to, and departs from, the norms of New Hampshire and Massachusetts. The high chest format flourished in Britain between 1710 and 1740, whereas it continued in demand in New England until the early nineteenth century. The form is not known to have been produced in Scotland at all. Does any part of the Dunlap *oeuvre* then reference Scottish or Ulster form and decoration?

One formal and functional characteristic described by Zea as an 'apparent Scots-Irish preference' is the 'Scotch Chest' upper drawer configuration of paired small drawers to either side of a single square drawer (1994: 38) (illus 9.5). This pattern was first described to the world of furniture scholarship by David Jones (1988). Zea cautiously noted that it is also found in the Connecticut River valley between Hartford, Connecticut, and Greenfield, Massachusetts (1994: 198, n 118). This observation was taken a step further when Mary Ann Apicella proposed that the Scotch Chest had been taken from Connecticut to Scotland (Apicella 2000). The Scotch Chest itself is not firmly documented on Scottish soil until 1825, the year in

Illustration 9.5
Scotch chest, probably south-eastern Scotland, *c* 1840.
[National Museums Scotland]

which James Mein of Kelso made one for Mellerstain House in Berwickshire. Other examples may predate this but the pattern is not given in the Edinburgh price books and so the 'reverse' migration hypothesis is attractive. Early nineteenth-century New York examples exist but there is no question that the drawer arrangement first appears on high chests in New England. The interesting question is how this tradition could have influenced Scottish cabinetmaking. One of the earliest examples uncovered by Apicella (its whereabouts currently unknown) bears an inscription 'Made by Joshua Read, Norwich [Connecticut] in the year 1752' (Apicella 2000: 93). Most examples,

however, date from the last two decades of the eighteenth century, by which time the high chest had become a chest on chest, and the 'Scotch' drawers had moved up river to southern New Hampshire. Parts of the Connecticut Valley had significant Scots-Irish populations and there were Scottish merchants in the area by the late eighteenth century, some recorded as having taken furniture from New England to the Caribbean. Apicella is even open to the possibility that Loyalists, deported to Nova Scotia and New Brunswick, could have transferred the Scotch Chest form to Canada, from where it eventually took root in Scotland.

Other routes of transmission are also possible. Among the New England prototypes for the Scotch chest is a chest-on-frame at Historic Deerfield dated to around 1769 and probably made by Benjamin Munn for a member of the Hoyt family (Lewis 1994: 14; Ward and Hosley 1985: 223). The square-faced central drawer is described by Michael Lewis as a 'bonnet drawer', the depth of the interior being ideal for hat storage. This same purpose gives rise to the later nineteenth- century Scottish term 'lum chest', the lum (chimney) referred to being a 'stove pipe' top hat of the 1850s (Jones 1998: 38). The Hoyt chest-on-frame is one of a number of examples cited by Lewis to provide evidence for the transmission of design characteristics from New England to the Carolinas in the decades immediately before the Revolution. Centres such as Newport exported large shipments of furniture to places like Charleston. Makers apprenticed along the North Carolina coast then took these influences with them when they moved to the backcountry to better themselves. One such journeyman, Jesse Needham, left a trail of furniture which documents this transfer of New England working including the absence of dustboards and the chest-on-frame form. Furniture preferences may even have migrated directly to the backcountry with New Light Baptists, of Scots-Irish descent, from the Connecticut River Valley. On the evidence of Lewis's study of the Hoyt chest, the bonnet drawer might well have escaped the Americas from the south, either as a familiar idea in the mind of someone settling in Scotland, or as a clever novelty witnessed by a Scottish traveller.

A final twist can be added to this inconclusive narrative. A black walnut chest of drawers in the Colonial Williamsburg collection, dated to around 1800 and made in either Mecklenburg County or Halifax County, Virginia, is described by Ronald Hurst and Jonathan Prown as 'highly unusual by American standards' (Hurst and Prown 1997: 356). It has a prospect door, concealing small drawers and pigeonholes, set between two deep drawers, the fronts of which are both moulded to appear as two graduated drawers. A dozen similar chests have been recorded in the Mecklenburg County area and the origin proposed for the form is East Anglian, on the evidence of a very similar chest of drawers in an English private collection (Hurst 1997: fig 112.2, 356). Artisans from Norfolk and Suffolk are known to have emigrated to Virginia in the late eighteenth century, and unusual tripartite drawer arrangements are found in other types of furniture from Norfolk. Linen, or napkin, presses with

square-fronted drawers flanking two central drawers of equal width were made in Norwich, perhaps as early as 1730 (Stabler 2006: 56; Gilbert 1991: 55). Although these presses are an entirely different fuctional form, imitation of the drawer arrangement adds a further hypothetical design migration, from England to America and then onwards to Scotland.

The reputation of John Shaw of Annapolis has been studied by furniture historians since the 1930s, largely because of a *corpus* of labelled, dated and initialled items, principally of the 1790s. Glasgow merchants controlled around one-third of Maryland's tobacco trade by the 1770s and Shaw's birth, in 1745, has been traced to Glasgow (Bartlett and Elder 1983: 13). He had arrived in America by the age of eighteen, so it is difficult to assess the degree to which any training he received in Glasgow affected his design work. By 1772 he had ceased to work as a journeyman and was in partnership with another Scot, Archibald Chisholm. This partnership did not last but subsequently both men were successful. In 1790 7.6 per cent of the population of Maryland were recorded as having been born in Scotland, while a further proportion would have been second-generation Scottish settlers (Brock 1982: 13). However, other identified Annapolis cabinetmakers have remarkably English, or American English, names (Gilbert Middleton; Gamaliel Butler) and advertisements placed in the Annapolis *Maryland Gazette* point to London as the source not only of luxury goods but also of labour. Henry Crouch, carver, arrived 'from London' in 1760 and in 1774 the importation was announced 'from London, ... [of] a parcel of healthy indented servants, among which are some valuable tradesmen, consisting of carpenters, cabinet makers ... [etc]' (Bartlett and Elder 1983: 38, 42).

Shaw's work is somewhat plain, and relative simplicity is a singular characteristic of Scottish furniture. This characteristic does not by itself, however, signal Scottish identity and William Voss Elder conjectured that before the Revolution, Annapolitan taste was neat and utilitarian, with exuberance limited to the transatlantic purchases of the rich (Bartlett and Elder 1983: 38–9). Shaw's case furniture is not incompatible with Scottish taste but in appearance it could equally stand in for well-made, economical London furniture. His desk and bookcases, dating from the late 1790s, are not consistent in all their features although the pierced fretwork and scroll pediments with inlaid rosettes can be read as relating to recorded Edinburgh cabinetmaking. His sideboards, however, exhibit no recognisable Scottish characteristics.

It is those features of a design that were readily recognisable to the consumer, and conformed to an idea of what was acceptable, that may prove key in establishing Scottish traits in American furniture. The evidence of workshop practices in construction, which can so usefully relate together groups of items, is not so relevant to the question of identity. Clients were not aware of how a leg was fastened to a rail and did not care. Shaw's cabinet wares are a good example of British-influenced construction. In common with the established practice in Charleston, Philadelphia and New York, he used three-quarter or full-depth dustboards (partitions), for example, in contrast to the nailed-on drawer runners of urban New England and parts of the rural South. Yet not only was this normal throughout Great Britain, Shaw could have learned it in Annapolis. Dustboards, or their absence, are a constructional feature that some consumers would have noticed but other similar features may simply be indicative of individual skill or the client's budget, and not regionality.

Elder and Bartlett wrote, in comparing desks with slant lids labelled by Joseph Middleton and John Shaw, that 'the homogeneous aspect of regional cabinetmaking is underlined by the fact that while construction details differ on the two desks, this was not as important a feature of regional cabinetmaking as were stylistic similarities' (1983: 74).

There was far more in common than at variance between Middleton and Shaw. What evidence there is of difference suggests that Shaw's shop produced slightly better goods. Elder and Bartlett continued: 'The relative simplicity of the Annapolis interpretation of the desk with slant lid as compared with the execution of the form in England and other cabinetmaking centres in America is also an example of local taste.'

Such a localised taste might have antecedents but might also be subconscious and not necessarily part of an ethnic self-identity. In general, written sources reveal surprisingly little about how people in the eighteenth century responded to the styles of other nations and places, unless in terms of fashion, the *cachet* of exclusive novelty.

One visible feature of Shaw's chairs and tables is a form of tapering leg which, although found on English chairs, was particularly common in Scotland. This is fundamentally a rhomboid-sectioned leg tapering along the three inside edges (illus 9.6). The outer edge

is plumb, with the innermost edge tapering to a greater degree than the two intermediate edges. In section, the external corner is slightly acute to conform to a trapezoidal seat plan. The fundamental reason for this design appears to be stability, and a range of minor variations are identifiable, although apparently not susceptible to analysis across time or space.[2] This leg form is notably prevalent in chairs from the American South. One such example was purchased in 1775 at the sale of the effects of the last colonial governor at Williamsburg, Lord Dunmore. The authors of the Colonial Williamsburg Collection catalogue consider that the chair was probably shipped in from London

Illustration 9.6
Dining chair, unknown maker, southern Scotland, *c* 1830.
[Private collection]

on the grounds that not only is it embellished with neoclassical decoration but also that constructional details, such as the size and placement of the corner braces, do not fit Williamsburg practice for the early 1770s (Hurst and Prown 1997: 119). The contents of Dunmore's Palace did indeed include items brought from London in 1768 by the previous occupant, Lord Botetourt. However, Dunmore was a Scotsman and the Ambler family who bought this chair in 1775 also bought a Glasgow-made long-case clock on the same day (Hurst and Prown 1997: 541). Could this chair, with Scottish legs, not therefore be Scottish?

There are many chairs of indisputably American origin with this form of leg. One difficulty with the Scottish leg hypothesis, however, is that other features of these chairs are dissimilar from each other. The introduction of the leg by Scottish-trained makers might therefore have been followed by a very general circulation of the idea across many colonies by men of different ethnicities, trained in America. A further difficulty is that the form is not Scottish in an identifiable way. In both America and Scotland it was favoured for its own qualities: presumably practical, perhaps also aesthetic. It could have been used more frequently in England but was not. Our sources, documents and artefacts, do not permit us to account for this apparently random distribution of adoption.

In contrast to this, another feature of the Scottish cabinetmaking tradition does bear a direct relationship to Scottish modes of living and was very clearly imported to America. Many Charleston sideboards, from the late 1780s into the early 1800s, incorporate a demonstrably Scottish stage top (Rauschenberg and Bivins 2003: 619). This feature, designed for storage as well as for the display of plate on special occasions, was uniquely Scottish and would have been recognised as such by an attentive late eighteenth-century observer. The Scots were notably conservative in their dining habits, resisting, for example, the incremental advance through the eighteenth century of the hour at which the principal meal was taken (Gow 1996: 143). It seems logical that Scottish clients in South Carolina would go to a Scottish cabinetmaker for a Scottish sideboard. For while there existed a near universal aspiration to live fashionably, where Scottish manners differed from the English such differences would be jealously maintained.

Charleston's post-Revolutionary fondness for British fashion is often noted. In 1802 the Governor of South Carolina, John Drayton, observed that 'Charlestonians sought in every possible way to emulate the life of London society. They were too much enamoured of British customs, manners and education to imagine that elsewhere anything of advantage could be obtained' (Fleming 1997: 343).

Elizabeth Fleming's in-depth analysis of the account book of the London merchant James Douglas illustrates this behaviour in action. During the 1780s and into the 1790s Douglas assembled speculative shipments of household articles including floor coverings, ceramics and metalwares. Between 1784 and 1786 he bought

Illustration 9.7
Lady's closet by George Riddell, for Sir John Clerk of Penicuik, Edinburgh, 1722. [Private collection]

furniture from eight London cabinetmakers to sell on to two Charleston-based mercantile firms, Cochran & William McClure and James Gregorie. What is so interesting about this trade is that all four names on both sides of the ocean are Scottish, but that the trade

is out of London. This might suggest that 'London-made' was not just a guarantee of fashionability for the purchaser but that Scottish merchants could make more profit by establishing themselves in London. Many of the articles that Douglas exported were of middling value, emanating from the wholesale warehouses and second-hand dealers of Broker's Row in Moorfields. An exception was William Fleming of Chandos Street who, interestingly, is the only maker in this group with any known link to Scotland, bearing as he does a Scottish name and having fulfilled a small order for the Marquess of Lothian at Hopetoun House in 1775 (Beard and Gilbert 1986: 304).

If buying from London was a guarantee of fashion, what properties could Scottish products have held? David Dobson, studying direct Scottish trade with Charleston, found regular small-scale shipments of furniture from east and west coast ports but nothing on the scale of London imports during the same period (Dobson 2009: 39). It is possible that such consignments had nothing to do with mercantile trade and represent the carriage of either existing possessions or bespoke commissions. In general, few goods have such a strong identifiable quality that substitutes made elsewhere are not acceptable. Tartan cloth, for example, the recognised product and emblem of a particular place and people, was exported from Leith to Charleston, although not in such quantity as to rival linen (Dobson 2009: 27). Some goods of Scottish origin may have had a comforting and familiar quality that was just as desirable, in a different way, to the fashionable gewgaws of London. And yet, further research is required. Although tartan, to continue with that example, was already highly emblematic by 1750, the tartan cloth exported to North America was fundamentally a colourful low-grade woollen used for blanketing and even more useful to clothe slaves or to trade with Native Americans.

Well-to-do Scottish customers for fine furniture did exist in the Carolinas. Alongside the poor farmers from Ulster and the numerous tradesmen were the merchants, clergy, doctors and a small number of planters (Dobson 1994: 160). Moreover, it may be that Scottish-born furniture makers were able to sell 'Scottish' furniture to colonists of English extraction. In addition to the stage-top sideboard, the uniquely Scottish form of the lady's closet is thought to have inspired a singular cabinet on chest made in Charleston in the early 1750s (illus 9.7, 9.8). The architectonic carving is attributed to Henry Burnett, who advertised his arrival from London in the *South Carolina Gazette*

Illustration 9.8
Cabinet on chest, attributed to Robert Deans, the carving attributed to Henry Burnett, Charleston, *c* 1755.
[Museum of Southern Decorative Arts, USA]

in April 1750 (Rauschenberg and Bivins 2003: 199, n 31). Burnett is a Scottish name (suggesting origins in Kincardineshire or Lanarkshire) and Robert Leath has drawn attention to Burnett's association with Robert Deans, who similarly advertised himself in January 1750 as a 'joiner from Scotland' (Rauschenberg and Bivins 2003: 963; Leath 2007: 155). Deans is recorded making furniture for Lord Milton in Edinburgh in 1749 (Pryke 1995: 290) and travelled to England in 1764, never to return (Rauschenberg and Bivins 2003: 963; Dobson 1994: 41). The pineapple-topped cabinet was apparently made for a member of the English Smith family. Rather than responding to instructions from his client, therefore, did Robert Deans provide something which he felt would answer his or her needs, possibly even unaware that the single mirrored door was something peculiar to Edinburgh?

John Shearer, who inscribed the fact of his departure from Edinburgh in 1775 on several pieces of work, used to be viewed as anywhere between eccentric and mad. Elizabeth Davison's recent study of his *oeuvre*, comprising over thirty items, successfully contextualises his loyalist patriotism and the vernacular character of his cabinetwork. Shearer was a typical rural joiner, in possession of wide-ranging, although ultimately limited skills, making do with the materials and tools available, and working to a budget for clients with a variety of expectations. In 1997 Hurst and Prown challenged previous assumptions of aberration with reference to 'Shearer's ethnic origins'. The backcountry, they wrote, was a 'culturally vibrant area' where Scottish, Irish, Welsh, German and Swiss settlers all arrived with their own 'ethnic craft conventions'.

'When considered in a more balanced cultural context, Shearer's wares emerge as the logical expressions of a Scottish-born furniture maker initially working in the ethnically diverse Shenandoah valley, and ... they inform modern observers ... about the needs and desires of patrons in the backcountry' (Hurst and Prown 1997: 443).

The primary difficulty with analysis of Shearer's work is that too much Scottishness is anticipated. Just as his British loyalism was a product of the backcountry, so in truth was the blending of 'ethnic' features in his furniture. Shearer's furniture does not look like Scottish furniture any more than it resembles

Illustration 9.9
Linen press, attributed to Francis Brodie, for Jean Carfrae, Edinburgh, 1786.
[National Museums Scotland]

work from Philadelphia, the Rhineland, Newport or London.

Moving forward in time, and northwards once again, to Federal New York, the *New York Revised Book of Prices* for 1810 invites comparison with Edinburgh's price books of 1805 and 1811. In his introductory essay to the reprinting of the Edinburgh price books, David Jones discerns only broad similarities between the Edinburgh and New York specifications (Jones 2000: 35). Mary Ann Apicella, by contrast, regards the books' small number of identical, non-London details as critically significant (Apicella 2007). For example, while New York had no specific stage-top sideboard, its 'French' sideboard had a loose framed plinth along somewhat similar lines. Jones, however, makes the point that not all New York work conformed absolutely to the price books, Duncan Phyfe's Edinburgh-manner, truss-legged lobby tables being one example.

Apicella's fundamental methodology is to compare features of proven or presumed Scottish work with pieces found in New York, and sometimes elsewhere in America. It is challenging material to control, however, and conclusions are elusive. She connects John Shaw's small inlaid ovals, framed within hollow-cornered rectangular mouldings, to the same pattern in work from New Jersey. It is difficult, however, to relate the pattern either directly or exclusively to Scotland, where large ovals are just as prevalent. Nor is it easy to eliminate London as a design source, for differentiating between London and provincial British centres for this period is often a close call. Design historians know that the contents of Sheraton's *Drawing Book*, or of Ince and Mayhew's *Universal System*, do not equate with what actually came out of cabinet shops, and caution must also be employed in regard to price books. Although, in contrast to engraved designs, price book entries originated in the market, some specifications, and particularly certain decorative details, were simply not commonly called for. Apicella notes that out of forty-eight glazing patterns drawn in the London price books, six offered lancet patterns compared with Edinburgh's ratio of four out of twelve. And yet not only are many of these designs never encountered, the lancet is arguably not as prevalent in Edinburgh practice as Apicella believes (ibid, 76).

Apicella's argument is overstated and a far wider sampling is required before concluding the validity of her general hypothesis for individual features. A press with pierced and scrolled pediment (illus 9.9), traditionally associated with Jean Carfrae of the

Canongate, Edinburgh, and attributed to either Francis or William Brodie, is certainly important not only in relation to New York but also to the work of Deans and Burnett in Charleston, to Shaw in Annapolis, and to Shearer in the Shenandoah Valley. Apicella notes that the rule joint used on the doors of this press crops up in Petersburg, Virginia (ibid, 74; Prown 1992: 33).

Illustration 9.10
Secretary bookcase, John Biggar, Edinburgh, *c* 1805.
[National Museums Scotland]

Illustration 9.11
Secretary book case, S James Nesbit, New York, *c* 1805.
[Courtesy Bernard and S Dean Levy Inc. New York]

relation to this form of pediment is similar and clearly describes something alike. Edinburgh's book of 1805 lists 'a small pedestal at each corner, and a square tablet in centre … with hollows between' while New York for 1810 has 'two eliptic hollows … tablet on the front' (Apicella 2007: 106). A further feature connecting Nesbit and Biggar, which Apicella considers to be widely shared between Scotland and New York in the period, is the large oval set into cross-grained veneers, mitred in the corners. She also suggests that another shared preference is for eight drawers over eight pigeonholes, as found in the work of both John Biggar and Richard Allison of New York. These insights are important although further research is necessary.

Although the presence in New York of many Scottish-born cabinetmakers may have had a subtle impact on the details of late neoclassical design in that city, the significance of that impact is open to question. If a characteristic exists, what does it tell us? Is lancet glazing really 'evidence of a choice rooted in a Scottish sensibility' (ibid, 77)? Consumers in early nineteenth-century New York could draw upon an unprecedented range of cultural options, and specific decorative details were likely to become rapidly less identifiable in such a melting pot. Apicella's attempts to find sporrans in the reeded forms of Connecticut chests, or echoes of annular brooches on Brodie's Carfrae press, are too far-fetched (ibid, 82–3).

From what we know of the adoption and retention of regional characteristics in furniture within Britain during this period, it is legitimate to conjecture that while immigrant groups to America at times exercised preferences, perhaps even expressing identity through those choices, over time exchange and amalgam were inevitable. The relationship between tradition and fashion was always complex, and ethnicity was one of many component influences on taste and behaviour. One conclusion can be reached, however: that Scottish cabinetmakers formed a vital part of the eighteenth-century artisanal labour force in America and prospered from their endeavours.

However, it can also be found on work by Gillow's of Lancaster (Stuart 2008: 48).

David Jones first drew attention to strikingly similar block-and-hollow pediments on secretaires of around 1805 by John Biggar of Edinburgh and S James Nesbit of New York (Jones 2000: 38). The overall broad massing of these pieces (illus 9.10, 9.11) contrasts with London work of the same period, while the Biggar secretaire employs a glazing pattern that is found in price books for Edinburgh and New York but not in the London book. The language of the price books in

Notes

1 Chinnery 1979, 249, fig 3:41. This chair, of maple and oak, is now at the American Museum, Bath, England. I am grateful to Lee Ellen Griffith, Executive Director of the Monmouth County Historical Association, for discussion about the Rhea chair.

2 Joiner-made chairs of the nineteenth century tend to exaggerate the feature, at times thrusting the leading edge

outwards so that the leg bears its load diagonally. The earliest documented example of this leg form known to the author, by Gillows of Lancaster, England, dates from 1787. The earliest documented example from Scotland, made in 1789, is by George Sandeman of Perth. The form appears to have found favour in the north of England as well as in Scotland and is associated at the end of the eighteenth century with the brander back.

Bibliography

Apicella, M A 2000 'The Lum Chest: a Connecticut Yankee in Scotland?', *Regional Furniture* 14, 87–103.

Apicella, M A 2007 *Scottish Cabinetmakers in Federal New York*. Hanover.

Bartlett, L & Elder, W V 1983 *John Shaw: Cabinetmaker of Annapolis*. Baltimore.

Beard, G & Gilbert, C 1986 *Dictionary of English Furniture Makers, 1660–1840*. Leeds.

Brock, W R 1982 *Scotus Americanus*. Edinburgh.

Chinnery, V 1979 *Oak Furniture: the British tradition*. Woodbridge.

Cotton, B D 1990 *The English Regional Chair*. Woodbridge.

Davison, E A 2011 *The Furniture of John Shearer, 1790–1820*, Lanham.

Doares, R 1994 '"That They May Long Remember Me … Henry Lamond, Cabinetmaker From Edinburgh, North Britten"', *Journal of Early Southern Decorative Arts* 20.1, 1–44.

Dobson, D 1994 *Scottish Emigration to Colonial America, 1607–1785*. Athens.

Dobson, D 2009 *Scottish Trade with Colonial Charleston, 1683–1783*. Glasgow.

Fleming, E 1997 'Staples for genteel living: the importation of London household furnishings into Charleston during the 1780s', *American Furniture* 5, 342–57.

Gilbert, C 1991 *English Vernacular Furniture, 1750–1900*. New Haven.

Gow, I 1996 'The Dining Room', *in* Carruthers, A (ed) *The Scottish Home*. Edinburgh, 125–54.

Hurst, R 1997 'Irish influences on cabinetmaking in Virginia's Rappahannock River Basin', *American Furniture* 5, 170–95.

Hurst, R & Prown, J 1997 *Southern Furniture 1680–1830: The Colonial Williamsburg Collection*. Williamsburg.

Jones, D 1988 'Scotch Chests', *Regional Furniture* 2, 38–47.

Jones, D 1992 'The laburnum tradition in Scotland', *Regional Furniture* 6, 1–9.

Jones, D 2000 *The Edinburgh Cabinet and Chair Makers' Books of Prices 1805–1825*. Cupar.

Leath, R 2007 'Many hands, many voices: southern furniture at MESDA', *The Magazine Antiques*, January 2007, 151–9.

Leath, R 2008 'Servitude and splendour: the craftsmen and carved furniture of the Rappahannock River Valley, 1740 to 1780', *The Magazine Antiques*, May 2008.

Lewis, M 1994 'American vernacular furniture and the North Carolina backcountry', *Journal of Early Southern Decorative Arts* 20.2, 1–37.

Petznick, W 1999 'James Honey: a wright from Perth in Colonial Williamsburg', *Regional Furniture* 13, 117–22.

Prown, J 1992 'A cultural analysis of furniture-making in Petersburg, Virginia, 1760–1820', *Journal of Early Southern Decorative Arts* 18.1, 1–113.

Pryke, S 1989 'A study of the Edinburgh furnishing trade taken from contemporary press notices, 1708–1790', *Regional Furniture* 3, 52–67.

Pryke, S 1995 *The Eighteenth-century Furniture Trade in Edinburgh: a study based on documentary sources*. Unpublished PhD thesis, University of St Andrews.

Rauschenberg, B & Bivins, J 2003 *The Furniture of Charleston, 1680–1820*. Winston-Salem.

Stabler, J 2006 'A dictionary of Norfolk furniture makers, 1700–1840', *Regional Furniture* 20, 1–254.

Stuart, S 2008 *Gillows: Of Lancaster and London, 1730–1840*, vol II. Woodbridge.

Ward, W R & Hosley, W N 1985 *The Great River: Art and Society of the Connecticut Valley, 1635–1820*. Hartford.

Zea, P & Dunlap, D 1994 *The Dunlap Cabinetmakers: a tradition in craftsmanship*. Mechanicsburg.

CHAPTER 10

The 'Raeburn craze' in Philadelphia

JENNIFER A THOMPSON

Portraits by Sir Henry Raeburn are ubiquitous in American museums. Almost every large municipal, small regional or college art museum in America boasts at least one canvas by Scotland's noted Enlightenment painter. Strong representations of work by Raeburn can be found in the British painting collections at the Philadelphia Museum of Art (thirteen), the Metropolitan Museum of Art (twelve), the National Gallery of Art in Washington DC (nine), and the Huntington Museum and Library in California (eight), but there are also seven Raeburns in Indianapolis, five in San Francisco, and a handful each in Boston, Chicago and Minneapolis. More regional collections like the Currier Museum of Art in Manchester, New Hampshire; the Mildred Lane Kemper Art Museum at Washington University in St Louis, Missouri; and the Memorial Art Gallery at the University of Rochester, New York, each have two Raeburns. The Memphis Brooks Museum in Memphis, Tennessee, the Joslyn Art Museum in Omaha, Nebraska, and the Ball State Museum of Art in Muncie, Indiana, have one apiece. In total, there are well over a hundred Raeburns in public collections in the United States, and auction records suggest that many more may be found in private ownership.[1]

Few Scottish artists were as prolific as Raeburn. He is thought to have painted over a thousand canvases in his lifetime so it is perhaps no surprise that his portraits have migrated around the globe. What is remarkable, however, is that works by Raeburn were known, exhibited and copied in America during his life and throughout the rest of the nineteenth century. A particularly strong interest in Raeburn was demonstrated by Philadelphians who accumulated more works by the Scottish painter than individuals in any other region of the country.[2]

Born in 1756 in Stockbridge, then on the outskirts of Edinburgh, Raeburn grew up amidst the Scottish Enlightenment, a period of great optimism in which thinkers and philosophers made important contributions to the fields of science, education and political thought in Scotland and around the world.[3] Educated at George Heriot's Hospital and apprenticed at age sixteen to the Edinburgh goldsmith James Gilliland, Raeburn received a thorough training in the drawing, design and engraving skills of the jewellers' trade before concentrating on painting around 1778. His marriage in 1779 or 1780 to the affluent widow Ann Edgar provided him with financial security and allowed him to travel. He may have gone first to London where he reportedly met Sir Joshua Reynolds, then President of the Royal Academy of Arts. In 1784 Raeburn left for Rome where he spent two years studying the works of the Old Masters. On his return to Edinburgh in 1786 he established a portrait painting practice and, from a studio on George Street in Edinburgh's fashionable New Town, produced portraits of local gentry and intellectuals. He regularly sent pictures for exhibition at the Royal Academy in London and was made an Associate Member of the Academy in 1812 and a full Academician in 1815. In 1822 King George IV awarded Raeburn a knighthood in recognition of his artistic contributions, and a year later he was named His Majesty's Limner and Painter in Scotland. Raeburn died in 1823 before being able to enjoy the distinction and benefits of this office, but it is a sign of the vibrancy and prosperity of Scotland in this period that he was able to conduct his entire career there.

Raeburn never travelled to the United States, though he was in contact with American artists and collectors. The first of his paintings to be shown publicly in America was probably 'Portrait of a Gentleman' loaned by the scientist James Renwick in 1817 to an exhibition at the American Academy of Fine Arts in New York, an association of connoisseurs who hosted annual exhibitions of paintings and sculptural casts.[4] The portrait belonging to Renwick may have sparked American interest in Raeburn, since the same year the artist was made an honorary member of the American Academy and in appreciation presented to them a portrait of a young New Yorker, Van Brugh Livingston (1792–1868). Raeburn wrote to the Academy's secretary, the Scottish-born miniature painter Alexander Robertson, on 10 August 1819 to explain that he desired 'to send along with my acknowledgement some small specimen of my own painting; and that it might have an interest with you beyond anything that I could give it, I wished it to be the portrait of some gent'm of your own country on which account it might be held in some estimation. And I have had at last the good fortune to meet with a young gent'm Vanbrugh Livingston Esq, who during the short time he was here augmented the good will, esteem and respect of every person who had the honour of his acquaintance …'.[5]

Livingston had spent two years travelling Europe, following his graduation from Columbia University. On his return from Scotland, where he visited relatives and met Sir Walter Scott, among others, Livingston became a diplomat and was later appointed Minister to Ecuador by President James K Polk.[6] His portrait by Raeburn arrived in New York in the autumn of 1819, accompanied by a second version which was intended for his mother. The Academy's painting was displayed in their gallery in the New York Institution building on the north side of City Hall Park and was included in annual exhibitions at the Academy from 1820 to 1828 and again in 1841.[7] Although the Academy ceased to operate in 1842, Raeburn's portrait remained in public view; it was purchased by subscription for the Wadsworth Atheneum in Hartford, Connecticut, and entered the collection there in 1855.[8] Mrs Livingston's version of the portrait was acquired by the Lenox Library in 1889 and later incorporated into the New York Public Library where it remains on display today.

The first Raeburn to arrive in Philadelphia may have been a portrait of the philosopher Dugald Stewart which was presented in 1825 by Dr Philip Tidyman to the Pennsylvania Academy of Fine Arts where 'it would be most suitably placed for the benefit of artists and the gratification of the largest number of Americans and strangers'.[9] The Raeburn was a much prized and copied painting until 1845 when it was destroyed in a fire in the Academy's building on Chestnut Street. Among the copies was one commissioned by the donor, a physician in South Carolina and former

student of Stewart. Tidyman hired the Philadelphia-based painter Thomas Sully (1783–1872) to make a replica of the portrait for the Academy of Fine Arts in Charleston, South Carolina; Raeburn had been named an honorary member of the newly founded southern academy in 1821.[10] The Stewart portrait was also copied by James Read Lambdin (1807–99) of Philadelphia who showed a 'Portrait of Dugald Stuart, LLD, FRS, from the original by Sir Henry Raeburn' at the American Academy of Fine Arts in New York in 1839 and at the Artist's Fund Society in Philadelphia in 1845.[11] Lambdin's entry was noted in the New York exhibition catalogue as being for sale, and it later became part of the collection of the Pennsylvania Academy where Lambdin was a member of the board of directors.[12]

Lambdin was not alone in exhibiting a copy after a Raeburn portrait; John Wesley Jarvis (1781–1840) showed a copy of a 'Portrait of Sir Walter Scott' in New York in 1824.[13] Raeburn's portrait of Van Brugh Livingston was copied by Sully between 19 August and 7 December 1828[14] and shown in Philadelphia three years later, perhaps inspiring others to follow suit since copies after Raeburn were exhibited there in 1831 by Hugh Bridport, in 1835 by John Neagle, and in 1841 by George G Heiss.[15] Raeburn clearly appealed to nineteenth-century American portrait painters who must have found resonance with his direct painterly style.

In addition to these artist copies, several Raeburn paintings belonged to Philadelphia collectors and were publicly displayed there in the 1840s and 1850s. James Gibson (1769–1856), a Philadelphia lawyer and founding member of the Pennsylvania Academy of Fine Arts, owned at least four Raeburn paintings that he loaned to the Pennsylvania Academy in 1848. They included portraits of Sir Walter Scott, Sir David Baird, Sir Ralph Abercrombie and a Head of Cupid.[16] These works never became part of the Academy's painting collection, and it is not clear what happened to them at Gibson's death in 1856. Another Philadelphia resident and businessman, Samuel Bradford Fales (1808–80), owned Raeburn's 'Portrait of Lord Galloway' by 1855, the year he loaned it to a Pennsylvania Academy

Illustration 10.1
'Portrait of William MacDonald of Saint Martin's', Henry Raeburn, *c* 1803. Oil on canvas 78 x 60in (1981 x 1524mm). Purchased with the W P Wilstach Fund, W1895-1-9. [Philadelphia Museum of Art]

exhibition.[17] Following Fales's death, it was auctioned by Thomas E Kirby & Company in New York for $100, according to the Philadelphian John G Johnson's annotated copy of the sales catalogue.[18]

Despite the notable presence of Raeburn portraits in Philadelphia in the mid-nineteenth century, British paintings do not seem to have attracted the interest of area collectors again until the end of the century. Contemporary works by the pre-Raphaelites and others were shown in 1858 at the Pennsylvania Academy in the 'American Exhibition of British Art: Oil Pictures and Watercolours', which saw modest interest by local collectors but deeply influenced artists. In 1876, at the Centennial Exposition in Philadelphia, the Great Britain section of the art gallery was praised as being one of the fullest and best of its kind.[19] Earl Shinn, an American art critic writing under the name of Edward Strahan, particularly admired the pictures loaned by the Royal Academy of Arts, including John Constable's 'The Lock' and David Wilkie's 'Boys Digging for Rats'. He noted the presence of portraits by Sir Thomas Gainsborough and George Romney, and declared Sir Joshua Reynolds' self-portrait the most important picture in the foreign exhibits.[20] Among the paintings loaned to the exhibition was Raeburn's 'Portrait of Alexander, the Fourth Duke of Gordon', belonging to the Duke of Manchester, though it escaped the notice of reviewers.[21]

In 1895 a new round of Raeburns was purchased by Philadelphia collectors, sparking a buying trend which would last over twenty-five years and bring almost twenty additional Raeburn portraits to the city. In December 1895 the 'Portrait of William MacDonald of Saint Martin's' was purchased for the Wilstach Gallery (illus 10.1). One of the earliest public art collections in Philadelphia, the Gallery was the legacy of merchant and leather manufacturer William P Wilstach (1816–70) and his wife Anna (1814–92), who left the city of Philadelphia more than 150 paintings and a generous fund for additional purchases. Acquired from the Grafton Gallery in New York, Raeburn's portrait of the engaging Perthshire lawyer shows MacDonald, a seventy-year-old man, seated in front of a window lined with voluminous yellow curtains. Raeburn first painted MacDonald in 1803 for the Royal Highland and Agricultural Society of Scotland, a charity for which he had served as treasurer for twenty years. The Wilstach picture with its comfortable domestic setting was a second portrait made for MacDonald's home of Saint Martin's Abbey in Strathmore, but it was sold by his heirs in Edinburgh in June 1893 before

making its way to America.[22] Reginald Cleveland Coxe, in a 1908 article on the Wilstach Collection in *Scribner's Magazine*, highlighted the Raeburn portrait, noting that it 'calls for a fuller notice than the others in this article, because this great painter of portraits is not well known to us; though comparatively a modern, his works are difficult to obtain and there are few important ones in this country'.[23] Coxe praised the Wilstach picture, stating that Raeburn 'shows his power in its strongest form' and commended his ability to translate his sitter's personality to canvas with dignity.

The acquisition of the 'Portrait of William MacDonald' with public funds was a bold step, suggesting Raeburn's rising popularity among a new group of American collectors. The Wilstach Collection was managed by a committee of local leaders who selected and voted on works to be purchased and displayed in a designated gallery in Memorial Hall in Fairmount Park. In 1895 the Wilstach Committee, which included collectors such as Alexander Cassatt, John G Johnson and P A B Widener, made thirteen acquisitions in the fields of American, British and Dutch art: the Raeburn portrait; an early Gainsborough landscape; a painting of Montclair, New Jersey, by the American artist George Inness; a Jacob van Ruisdael waterfall; and James Abbott McNeill Whistler's 'Arrangement in Black: Portrait of Lady Archibald Campbell', among others.

The Philadelphia institutional interest in Raeburn was not unique; the Metropolitan Museum of Art acquired its first Raeburn in 1896 as a gift of Arthur Hearn, and in 1901 the Worcester Art Museum made its very first purchase a portrait by Raeburn. This collective American rediscovery of Raeburn is associated with a group of diverse social and political factors that led to the artist's increased visibility in auction rooms and print publications.

A series of agricultural depressions in Great Britain and the introduction of death duties in 1882 meant that there were rising numbers of British portraits on the market at a time when American collectors were eager to acquire them.[24] Gradually turning their attention away from French painting, Americans began to

Illustration 10.2
'Portrait of Lady Belhaven', Henry Raeburn, *c* 1790.
Oil on canvas 36⅛ x 27⅞in (918 x 708mm).
The John Howard McFadden Collection, M1928-1-21.
[Philadelphia Museum of Art]

emulate the collecting tastes of Baron Ferdinand de Rothschild and Edward Cecil Guinness, the 1st Earl of Iveagh, both of whom had assembled remarkable collections of British portraits in the 1870s and 1880s. *The New York Times* in 1895 described the trend: 'when the group of Fountainebleau men had been fully exploited and prices for their best work made them almost prohibitive, it came about naturally that they [American collectors] turned to the canvases of Englishmen, known of course to us here, but in truth never fully understood or properly appreciated save by a few. Here were pictures of ancestors, of our own race, painted ingenuously and frankly, drawn with knowledge and skill, aping no special school, but executed with honesty of purpose and naive in treatment.'[25] Less sympathetically, an editor of the London-based *Burlington Magazine for Connoisseurs* called this 'the American invasion' of the European art market since wealthy Americans were bidding up prices at auction, thereby encouraging hard-pressed European families to part with heirlooms.[26] The American pursuit of European Old Master painting was further supported by the Payne-Aldrich Tariff bill of 1909 which repealed heavy tariffs on the importation of works of art over a century old.

Reynolds, Gainsborough and Raeburn were among the British painters most sought by American collectors, but Raeburn was the first to break the £20,000 mark at auction in 1911 and within two years his portraits were fetching over £30,000.[27] Raeburn's prominence in the art market of the early twentieth century was partly due to the scores of his portraits which were suddenly available. The historian H C Marillier wryly noted in 1926 that 'everyone knows that of recent years enormous prices have been paid for the portraits by Gainsborough, Reynolds, Romney, Raeburn, Hoppner and Lawrence, and so long as the demand for them in America continues unsated there is no likelihood of the prices coming down ... family portraits do not come into the market before the fourth generation of their possessors. A man will not sell the portrait of his mother, nor even as a rule the portrait of his grandmother; but when he needs the money, or finds there is a high value attached to it, he will part with the portrait of his great-grandmother, whom he could not by any ordinary possibility have known.'[28] The influx of Raeburn portraits of great-grandparents in the 1890s was paralleled by a series of biographies and newspaper articles on Raeburn that brought him to the attention of collectors, underlining the sense

that they had discovered an accomplished and under-appreciated painter.

Beginning in 1876, *The New York Times* printed a series of articles on Raeburn, arguing that 'we do not think that in the United States the work of Raeburn is given the credit it deserves'.[29] The articles reviewed recent exhibitions of Raeburn's paintings and biographies of the artist such as Edward Pinnington's *Sir Henry Raeburn, R.A.* (1904) and contain statements like 'portraits by Sir Henry Raeburn are in great demand' or 'the value of a Raeburn has been immensely augmented of late years, for in 1903, £14,700 was paid for one of them'.[30] This habit of introducing Raeburn, commenting on his life, and expressing surprise at the current prices being paid for his paintings was described by the writer R S Clouston in 1907: 'whenever a portrait by Raeburn fetches a higher price than usual in one of our salesrooms, someone always writes to the daily papers on "the Raeburn craze"'.[31] The craze even extended to biographies of the artist, as in February 1913 when *The New York Times* noted that a record price of $250 had been paid for Sir Walter Armstrong's 1901 publication on Raeburn.[32]

Perhaps the most dedicated collector of Raeburn portraits in America was John Howard McFadden (1850–1921) of Philadelphia who amassed eight Raeburns, more than any other single collector in the United States. Born in Philadelphia to an English mother and an Irish father, McFadden and his elder brother George managed an international cotton trading business called George H McFadden & Brother that had been established by their father. Responsible for the overseas interests of the corporation, John Howard McFadden lived aboard, mainly in London, from 1871 to 1904. While there, he began to devote his free time to philanthropic interests such as funding for cancer research and collecting art. His painting collection would grow to include more than forty-five paintings by significant British artists such as Gainsborough, Raeburn, Romney, Reynolds, William Hogarth, George Stubbs, John Constable and J M W Turner.

In May 1895, shortly before the Wilstach Collection acquired its Raeburn, McFadden purchased

two female portraits by Raeburn from the London art firm of Thomas Agnew & Sons.[33] One of them, the shy and restrained 'Portrait of Lady Belhaven', had previously belonged to Lord Iveagh, whose model of collecting British portraits might have appealed to McFadden who also made his purchases through Agnew's (Lord Iveagh, however, only ever owned two Raeburns, including the one he returned to Agnew's) (illus 10.2). The other Raeburn, acquired on 20 May 1895, was the magnificent 'Portrait of Lady Elibank' (illus 10.3), one of the finest Raeburns in America, according to the *Philadelphia Inquirer*: '"Mrs. Elibank" by Raeburn remains the glorious example of this painter's work it has always been – a firm piece of flesh painting of a great epoch – a face full of expression – a pose full of character and a hand matchless in drawing and charm'.[34] McFadden would purchase six more paintings by Raeburn between 1902 and 1919, all of them from Agnew's and all bought in London, since he did not like to buy pictures sight-unseen. While the earliest collectors of Raeburn in America seem to have been attracted to portraits of men, particularly significant literary, cultural or military figures, McFadden was drawn to Raeburn's depictions of women and children, paintings which must have been selected for their aesthetic merits rather than a strict concern with the sitter's importance or accomplishments (illus 10.4). Contemporary collectors appear to have shared this preference, since portraits of women and children were often represented in twentieth-century American collections.

When he returned to Philadelphia in 1904, McFadden bought a residence at the corner of 19th and Walnut Streets on the north side of Rittenhouse Square where he hung his growing collection of British portraits and landscapes. They could be seen by interested parties, and the collection quickly gained recognition as one of the best representations of British art in America. By 1916 news of McFadden's latest acquisitions were being relayed to the Philadelphia papers by cablegram, and the arrival in the port of new paintings was announced in the local press. When McFadden sold the building on Walnut Street in 1916 to a real estate consortium that demolished it in order to construct a fifteen-storey apartment building on the site, the collection went on tour to the Pennsylvania Academy of Fine Arts, the Carnegie Art Institute in Pittsburgh, and the Metropolitan Museum of Art. It was heralded at one venue as 'the choicest collection of paintings by English artists of the eighteenth century in America'.[35] On completion of the new apartment

building, known as the Wellington, McFadden leased the thirteenth and fourteenth floors, where the papers reported that 'above the city dust line, and where there is no possibility of the light being cut off by the buildings' he showed his collection. The rooms were open each Wednesday when McFadden's daughter Alice served tea to visitors.[36] The public nature of the collection enabled McFadden's fellow Philadelphians to see his Raeburns and ensured that the Scottish artist continued to be well known in the city. The *Philadelphia Public Ledger* wrote of the collection after McFadden's death in 1921: the 'eight canvases by Raeburn unquestionably present this painter, the "Velasquez of Scotland", in a way unequalled in any gallery, since the very climax of portrait painting is beyond doubt reached in the "Sir Alexander Shaw" of the McFadden collection, if not in the equally beautiful "Gentleman in the Green Coat" or in the two famous women by Raeburn, "Lady Elibank" and "Lady Belhaven", which made the McFadden collection distinguished in its women' (illus 10.5).[37] McFadden's will stipulated that the paintings would be given to the city of Philadelphia if an appropriate museum facility was constructed to display them within seven years of his death. McFadden had served on the city's Museum Committee from 1914 to 1920 and was deeply involved in plans to construct a large museum building in the city, but he was equally cognisant of the many delays inherent in such a project. The seven-year timeline specified in his will was one of the driving forces behind the completion of the Pennsylvania Museum in 1928. Local papers during the construction period frequently fretted over the possible loss of the collection and spurred fundraising efforts. In March 1928 a handful of galleries devoted to British painting opened in the new building, including four period rooms that showcased the McFadden collection.

McFadden served on the Museum Committee alongside three fellow Philadelphia collectors who also acquired portraits by Raeburn: John G Johnson, P A B Widener and Edward T Stotesbury. Johnson and Widener, close friends, business associates and members of the Wilstach Committee, followed one

Illustration 10.4
'Portrait of Master John Campbell of Glensaddel', Henry Raeburn, *c* 1798. Oil on canvas 49¼ x 39⅜in (1251 x 1000mm). The John Howard McFadden Collection, M1928-1-24. [Philadelphia Museum of Art]

another in their pursuit of other Scottish artists: each owned landscapes by Patrick Nasmyth and added works by Raeburn to their growing painting collections around the turn of the century. The 'traction king' P A B Widener (1843–1915) of Lynnewood Hall owned a portrait by Raeburn of the actress Mrs Siddons in 1900, but it had left his collection by 1915 (his son Joseph later acquired Raeburn's distinguished portrait of David Anderson, now at the National Gallery of Art in Washington).[38] Johnson (1841–1917), a formidable trial lawyer and art collector with broad interests, purchased a half-length portrait then attributed to Raeburn sometime between 1892 and 1914.[39] It shows a young boy wearing a cap and holding a large bearded mask of an old man in his hands. The Philadelphia interest in Raeburn may partially be ascribed to William Roberts (1862–1940), an antiquarian bookseller, art historian and London *Times* critic who was considered an authority on British painting and wrote catalogues of the McFadden, Johnson and Widener collections. It is not clear precisely what role he played in the formation of these collections and whether he suggested purchases to collectors. Roberts has a reputation today for supporting dubious attributions, and in the case of Johnson and Widener's Raeburns, these have not held over time, a sign of the prestige and value associated with a Raeburn attribution in the early twentieth century.[40] It should be noted that one of McFadden's purchases, 'Portrait of a Gentleman' acquired in 1910, is now considered the work of a follower of Raeburn.[41]

Edward Townsend Stotesbury (1849–1938), an investment banker who was a partner of Drexel & Company in Philadelphia and its sister firm J P Morgan & Company in New York, was not to be outdone by his peers. Stotesbury entered the Raeburn field in a magnificent fashion in 1912 when he purchased Raeburn's portrait of Mrs Andrew Hay from the London dealer Joseph Duveen for the record price of £22,260.[42] The painting hung in Stotesbury's home at 1925 Walnut Street in Philadelphia while he constructed Whitemarsh Hall, a vast 150-room Palladian-style house designed by Horace Trumbauer. At Whitemarsh Hall, which was decorated with a superb collection of eighteenth-century British portraits, ceramics and furniture, the Raeburn hung in Mrs Stotesbury's Library, the room in which she managed the couple's affairs and properties.[43] Twenty years after its purchase the 'Portrait of Mrs Hay' was still being heralded as one of the finest portraits in Stotesbury's collection: 'for perfection of arrangement and refinement of colours, it confirms one's feeling that in Raeburn the greatest heights in British portraiture were reached'.[44] The Stotesburys owned at least two other Raeburns, a 'Portrait of Mrs David Moneypenny' and a 'Portrait of James Harrower of Inzievar with his Wife and Son', which was purchased from the Galerie Heinemann in Munich in 1913. Stotesbury must have been familiar with McFadden's Raeburns, which were only a few doors away on Walnut Street, and he served in the company of Widener and Johnson, as the President of the Fairmount Park Commission, the titular head of the Wilstach Collection, from 1912 to 1938.

Members of the Elkins family purchased three Raeburn portraits between 1911 and 1920. Related by marriage to the Wideners and supporters of the efforts to construct a new museum in Philadelphia, the Elkins family spawned several generations of notable collectors with a shared inclination for British and American portraits. George W Elkins (1858–1919), a financier and philanthropist, his daughter Louise (Mrs Wharton Sinkler), and his grandson George D Widener Jr (1889–1971), all acquired female half-lengths by Raeburn with distinguished records of exhibition and publication. George W Elkins bought the 'Portrait of Mrs John McCall of Ibroxhill' from the dealer Scott & Fowles in New York around 1911 (illus 10.6), and his daughter Louise acquired the charming but vaguely similar-looking 'Portrait of Jane Ann Catherine Fraser', which had been illustrated in Clouston's 1907 volume on Raeburn, from Knoedler Gallery in New York in February 1920. Her nephew George D Widener followed his Elkins and Widener grandfathers by adding Raeburn's 'Portrait of Mrs William Stewart of Summer Bank, Perth' to his collection around 1913.[45]

These acquisitions were nearly the last Raeburns to come to Philadelphia, since in the 1930s sales of works by Raeburn and of British portrait paintings in general dropped precipitously with the American stock market crash, and they never fully recovered. John Howard McFadden Jr, no doubt inspired by his father's example, acquired two Raeburns in the

Illustration 10.5
'Portrait of Alexander Shaw', Henry Raeburn, *c* 1810–15.
Oil on canvas 30 x 25⅛in (762 x 638mm).
The John Howard McFadden Collection M1928-1-27.
[Philadelphia Museum of Art]

Illustration 10.6
'Portrait of Mrs John McCall of Ibroxhill', Henry Raeburn, *c* 1820. Oil on canvas 30 x 25in (762 x 63mm).
The George W Elkins Collection, E1924-4-23. [Philadelphia Museum of Art]

1940s that he displayed in English interiors in his home in Memphis, Tennessee. In the 1970s a few new Raeburns were brought to the city by a private collector, but these lacked the fanfare and excitement of the period from 1895 to 1920 when Philadelphians seemed to be engaged in a competition to outdo or at least keep up with one another in their Raeburn acquisitions.

Of course, Philadelphians were not the only Americans to acquire works by Raeburn. Henry

Huntington of San Marino, California, Andrew Mellon of Pittsburgh and Washington DC, and Henry Clay Frick of New York, among others, were also avid collectors of British portraits and owned several Raeburns apiece.[46] Unlike the closely linked collectors in Philadelphia, these gentlemen did not inspire others in their respective cities to acquire great numbers of portraits by Raeburn.

It is something of a surprise that Raeburn appealed so strongly to Philadelphia collectors. Few of them were of Scottish descent, and they did not otherwise show a strong preference for Scottish art or history. The constant presence of Raeburn paintings in Philadelphia from the 1820s onward may have encouraged local collectors to build a taste for his portraits. The Pennsylvania Academy of Fine Arts with its active art school and annual exhibitions provided an eager and receptive audience for Raeburn, whose work was shown there in greater numbers in the nineteenth century than any other British painter. In the period from 1820 to 1860 six Raeburns and numerous copies after Raeburn were shown at the Pennsylvania Academy, while only four paintings by Reynolds, two by Gainsborough, and one each by Romney and John Hoppner were exhibited.[47]

One must assume that it was the paintings themselves that spoke most to collectors. Raeburn's sitters represented the intelligence, ingenuity and prosperity of the Scottish Enlightenment and as such appealed to conservative and Protestant tastes in the Quaker city. The healthy, rosy-cheeked Scottish merchants and their wives and children in Raeburn's portraits have an honesty, earnestness and familiarity which make them appropriate 'ancestors' for one's walls. For men such as the Philadelphia financier George Elkins, whose father had started his career stocking shelves in a grocery, it might have seemed fitting to own Raeburn's portrait of Mrs John McCall of Ibroxhill, the lively daughter of a Glaswegian sugar merchant. Raeburn's appeal may equally have been his timelessness, since writers compared him to Diego Velazquez and suggested that he was a precursor to modern artists: 'Of the great triumvirate of British portrait painters of our great century, Raeburn survives as the most modern, and among all his contemporaries, dates the least ... his figures live for us to-day as beings of flesh and blood, free from self-consciousness, abnormality or sophistication.'[48]

Notes

1 My thanks to Alexandra Olsman for her assistance in tracking down more than 115 Raeburns in American museums.

2 In the course of preparing this conference paper for publication, I learned that Robyn Asleson has written an essay on Raeburn's reception in American for a volume on Raeburn, edited by Viccy Coltman and Stephen Lloyd (*Henry Raeburn: Context, Reception and Reputation*, Edinburgh University Press, 2012), and that Jordan Mearns, a doctoral student at the University of Edinburgh, is also researching American collectors of Raeburn.

3 For an outline of Raeburn's life and its historical context, see essays by Duncan Thomson, Nicholas Phillipson and David Mackie in Duncan Thomson et al, *Raeburn: The Art of Sir Henry Raeburn 1756–1823*. Edinburgh: Scottish National Portrait Gallery, 1997. Arthur Herman, *How the Scots Invented the Modern World*, New York, Three Rivers Press, 2001, provides a lucid overview of the Scottish Enlightenment.

4 James Renwick (1792–1863) was a professor of chemistry at Columbia University and a director of the American Academy from 1818 to 1822. He was the son of Jean Jaffray Renwick, the 'blue-eyed lassie' of Robert Burns's 1788 poem, suggesting that the Raeburn may have been a family painting. Mary Bartlett Cowdrey et al, *American Academy of Fine Arts and American Art-Union*, New York: New York Historical Society, 1953, 293.

5 Mabel C Weaks, 'Works by Raeburn in America', *Connoisseur* 1936, vol 97, 276.

6 *The National Cyclopaedia of American Biography*, New York: J T White Company, 1906, vol 13, 177.

7 Cowdrey, 293.

8 I am grateful to Eric Zafran for sharing material from the Wadsworth Atheneum's curatorial file with me.

9 Robert Walsh, *Didactics: Social, Literary, and Political*. Philadelphia: Carey, Lea & Blanchard, 1836, vol 2, 252.

10 Edward Biddle and Mantle Fielding, *The Life and Works of Thomas Sully (1783–1872)*. Philadelphia: Wickersham Press, 1921, 279, no 1649. Sully's copy was later given by Tidyman to the St Andrew's Society of Charleston, South Carolina.

11 Cowdrey, 220. Anna Wells Rutledge, *Cumulative Record of Exhibition Catalogues: The Pennsylvania Academy of the Fine Arts 1807–1870, The Society of Artists 1800–1814, The Artists' Fund Society 1835–1845*. Philadelphia: The American Philosophical Society, 1955, 176.

12 Godfrey T Vigne, 'Six Months in America', *Waldie's Select Circulating Library*, vol 1, no 6, 21 November 1832, 82.

13 Cowdrey, 207.

14 Biddle and Fielding, 214, no 1107. Henry James Brown (1811–54) painted in Sully's Philadelphia studio and made a copy of Sully's copy after Raeburn's 'Portrait of Van Brugh Livingston'. Brown's painting now belongs to Sweet Briar College, Virginia. Lucille McWane Watson, 'Virginia planter-painter Henry James Brown', *Antiques*, October 1971, vol 100, no 4, 592–93.

15 Rutledge, 176.

16 Rutledge, 176.

17 Rutledge, 176.

18 Thomas E Kirby & Co., New York, Chickering Hall, 9 November 1881, lot 97. Johnson's marked copy is in the Philadelphia Museum of Art library.

19 J S Ingram, *The Centennial Exposition, Described and Illustrated*. New York: H W Bishop, 1876, 327.

20 Edward Strahan (ed), *The chefs-d'œuvre d'art of the International Exhibition*. Philadelphia: Gebbie & Barrie, 1878, 71, 123, 131.

21 United States Centennial Commission, *Official Catalogue*, Philadelphia: John R Nagle & Company, 1876, part 2, no 144.

22 Richard Dorment, *British Paintings in the Philadelphia Museum of Art*. Philadelphia, 1986, 265–67.

23 Reginald Cleveland Coxe, 'The Wilstach Collection', *Scribner's Magazine*, vol 43, May 1908, 637.

24 For a discussion of the American interest in British paintings in this period, see Shelley M Bennett, 'The Formation of Henry E Huntington's Collection of British Paintings', *in British Paintings at the Huntington*, Robyn Asleson & Shelley M Bennett. New Haven: Yale University Press, 2001, 1–15.

25 *New York Times*, 11 October 1895.

26 'The Consequences of the American Invasion', *The Burlington Magazine for Connoisseurs*, vol 5, no 16, July 1904, 353–5.

27 Gerard Reitlinger, *The Economics of Taste: The Rise and Fall of Picture Prices 1760–1960*. London: Barrie & Rockliff, 1961, vol 1, 416–17.

28 H C Marillier, *Christie's 1766 to 1925*. London: Constable & Company, 1926, 244.

29 *New York Times*, 27 August 1904.

30 *New York Times*, 23 March 1902 and 27 August 1904

31 R S Clouston, *Sir Henry Raeburn*. London: Newnes Art Library, 1907, vii.

32 Notice on the sale of the library of M C D Borden at American Art Galleries in the *New York Times*, 18 February 1913.

33 Today McFadden's eight Raeburns belong to the Philadelphia Museum of Art. See Dorment, cat nos 67, 69, 70, 72, 74, 75 and 76.

34 *Philadelphia Inquirer*, 15 July 1917.

35 John Frederick Lewis, President of the Pennsylvania Academy of Fine Arts, quoted in the *Evening Bulletin*, 23 October 1916.

36 Dorment, xv.

37 *Philadelphia Public Ledger*, 17 February 1921.

38 The portrait appears as a supplement in *Catalogue of paintings forming the private collection of P A B Widener, Ashbourne, near Philadelphia*. Paris: Goupil & Co., 1885–1900, no 160. A catalogue of the Widener collection published in 1915 does not include a Raeburn.

39 Philadelphia Museum of Art, John G Johnson Collection, cat 840. The painting does not appear in an 1892 catalogue of Johnson's collection, but it is included in W R Valentiner, *Catalogue of a Collection of Paintings and Some Art Objects*. Philadelphia: 1914, vol 3, 59.

40 See Brian Allen, 'Paul Mellon and scholarship in the history of British art', *in Paul Mellon's Legacy: A Passion for British Art*. New Haven: Yale University Press, 2007, 45.

41 Philadelphia Museum of Art, M1928–1–28. See Dorment, cat 79.

42 Reitlinger, vol 1, 194, 416.

43 Charles G & Edward C Zwicker, *Whitemarsh Hall: The Estate of Edward T Stotesbury*. Charleston, South Carolina: Arcadia Publishing, 2004, 49.

44 Henri Marceau, 'The Stotesbury Collection', *The Pennsylvania Museum Bulletin*, December 1932, vol 28, no 151, 21.

45 Today these three works are part of the Philadelphia Museum of Art: E1924–4–23, 1963–171–1 and 1972–50–3. Dorment, cats 78, 77 and 68.

46 For the range of Raeburns owned by private collectors in America, see Alfred M. Frankfurter, 'Painting by Raeburn in America', *Antiquarian*, 1930, vol 14, no 1, 32–5.

47 Rutledge, 78, 102, 180 and 186.

48 'A Hidden Masterpiece by Raeburn', *Connoisseur*, 1936, vol 97, 272.

Scottish high-style furniture: the key types, 1750–1850

DAVID JONES

The development of distinctive fashionable or high-style furniture in Scotland is best seen as part of the 'great improvement' of the country, in which lairds felt safe enough to quit their tower houses and build anew in a generous classical manner. Indeed, it is not possible to explain the rapid improvement of architecture and, correspondingly, furniture in Scotland after the mid-eighteenth century except in terms of an economic boom which, following in the wake of a secure internal peace, brought wealth to the landed classes in the eighteenth century and to the urban *bourgeoisie* in the next. This is when the country reached a new cultural maturity, developing a material culture that was adapted to genteel, but very particular ways of living in both town and country.

A late-developing piece, but probably the signature high-style furniture type in the Scottish furniture maker's repertoire, and often the most striking item of display in a country house or New Town dining-room, is the stage-top sideboard table. This has origins in Scotland that date from around 1770[1] and the closest analogies are to be found in France. The stage, like the *étage* on a French *buffet* of the mid-eighteenth century, was primarily intended for the display of plate, and it is interesting to note that Edinburgh silversmiths, when advertising their wares, would sometimes use 'sideboard full of plate' as a collective term.[2] Few stage-top sideboards survive today in their original purpose-built niches, but the effect of such an ensemble, in a candle-lit room with lights from candle branches reflecting from plate, and glass tiered upon an elevated stage, must have provided an eye-catching spectacle.

The earliest stage-top sideboards in the country were open-framed tables, designed to be arranged *en suite* with separate cellaret and urns on pedestals; they had fixed stages that were simply platforms for display. This type was known as a 'Straight Front Sideboard Table', the most basic specification in the *Edinburgh Cabinet Makers' Book of Prices* (illus 11.1).[3] The type most commonly seen today, however, is the 'Straight Front Celleret [*sic*] Sideboard' (illus 11.2), which has integrated cellaret drawers and a stage designed for both storage and display. Drinking glasses were usually stored inside the baize-lined stage, but deeper bottle wells for spirits were features of Glasgow sideboards.[4] The *Edinburgh Cabinet Makers' Book of Prices* (1811) has over twenty pages of sideboard specifications and lists stages separately in five different shapes with either drawers, tablets (plain rectangular panels), sliders (sliding panels) or tambour (fillets of wood glued to canvas) on the front. This last feature, again, is taken from French furniture design.[5] Within Scotland regional differences are noticeable; Glasgow sideboards, for example, were usually longer than their Edinburgh counterparts and could be ordered with a stage that wrapped around three sides of the top, as seen in the engraving of Cleland Jack Paterson's Trongate wareroom (illus 11.3).[6]

The stage top was definitely the type of preference within Scotland to the extent that it was requested as a special extra when English cabinetmakers were engaged to provide furniture. For example, in 1795 Mrs Robert Gordon of Cairness, Aberdeenshire, specifically asked Thomas Seddon of London for a stage top on a sideboard as part of her furnishing scheme supplied by this firm.[7] The stage top was an enduring feature that characterised Scottish sideboards from the eighteenth to the early twentieth centuries. George Walton, for instance, adapted it for his progressive designs of 1902 to 1912, in particular his *Brussels* sideboard (illus 11.4), to the bewilderment of critics in the London-based *Studio* magazine, who, clearly, had never seen such a feature.[8]

The first recorded mahogany furniture made in Scotland dates from the early 1660s, but high-style pieces in expensive imported timbers such as this were

Illustration 11.1
'Straight front' stage-top sideboard, c 1780. [Courtesy, The Earl of Moray]

not executed in quantity until the following century.[9] Prior to the 1740s much of the high-status housing in the countryside was of the tower house type, difficult to furnish with large pieces such as sideboards and case furniture, because of the relatively small proportions of the rooms, asymmetrical window arrangements and narrow turnpike stairs that connected the vertical stacks of apartments. This meant that furniture, especially case items, had to be small. Edinburgh cabinetmaker Francis Brodie's *Lady's Closet* of 1753 is a good example (illus 11.5). Made for the old house of Liefnorris, Ayrshire, for the Earl of Dumfries, it was a fashionable

Illustration 11.2
'Straight front celleret' sideboard table with silver, Pitlour House, Fife.

Illustration 11.3
From R Chapman, *The Picture of Glasgow or Stranger's Guide*, 1812. [National Library of Scotland]

piece, with cavetto cornice, stylish 'Roman' bracket feet and brass stringing detail. Its proportions are quite miniature, and it is made from padouk, a high-status cabinet timber imported from the Andaman Islands. The design of the small folding flap on the lower section appears to have been developed from the French *bureau brise* ('broken' bureau) form.[10] The Dumfries *Lady's Closet* was ordered with a similarly space-saving and classically detailed corner cupboard in walnut, also with brass stringing.

The acquisition of such small but luxurious pieces of furniture brought a focus of modernity into otherwise old-fashioned castles. Further attempts to classicise tower houses can be seen in the enlargement of first-floor windows to create a more obvious *piano nobile* (good examples can be seen at Kellie, Fife, and Craigievar, Aberdeenshire) and the placing of pier tables between the new openings.[11] Francis Brodie provided such pier table ensembles; the gilt eagle pier table was a signature piece that figured prominently on his billhead, and the smaller versions are recognisable as pieces made for seventeenth-century buildings.[12]

But many of Scotland's key types of the eighteenth century were not gilded showpieces like Brodie's eagle pier table; they were neat and plain pieces developed for particular practical function. One such design that is found only in Scotland and countries where its cabinetmaking traditions have taken root is the

Illustration 11.4
George Walton, 'Brussels' sideboard with stage top and tambour. Illustrated in Walter Shaw Sparrow,
The British Home of Today, 1904. [National Library of Scotland]

'bedroom table'. Its identifying feature is a single long flap that hangs down the back of the table when it is not open.[13] Examples can be found with or without a drawer in the frieze, and they are usually made from solid mahogany with a square-edged top and rule joint. The Edinburgh cabinetmaker Alexander Peter made these in 1759, calling them 'square mahogany tables, one leaf' (illus 11.6), and by the end of the century they were being made with newly fashionable tapered legs instead of cabriole legs and pad feet. The bedroom table was used for writing or taking meals in the bedchamber and is similar in design to the most simple dining table. The narrow top and deeper single flap give the table a space-saving quality, enabling it to be placed against a wall, or even behind a door, when not in use. These slim proportions have caused bedroom tables to be used in other places where space is limited, such as small parlours,[14] ante rooms and corridors, where they can still be found in many Scottish houses.

A related type is the traditional Scottish kitchen table (illus 11.7, 11.8), usually made from fir and also with one leaf and one drawer. When opened up, this was not used for writing or dining like its bedroom cousin, but for baking or food preparation. Although rather plain and anonymous-looking, the Scottish bedroom and kitchen table form has perhaps been one of the most influential types in the repertoire. The earliest cabinetmakers' price book in America, for instance, printed in Philadelphia in 1772, specifies the design.[15]

Scottish furniture was, of course, subject to the impulses of international fashion. The rococo style was perhaps slow to be assimilated by furniture makers but, once established, it certainly developed national characteristics. The Earl of Dumfries was particularly ambitious in commissioning a number of rococo parade pieces for his new Ayrshire mansion in 1757–9, and amongst these is a useful spectrum of Scottish work (around 200 pieces) that illustrates the distinctive nature of the style in this country.[16] They range from the relative simplicity of Alexander Peter's sofa for the family parlour (illus 11.9), with its ramped-up scrolled arms and gently humped back (comparable to American rococo examples),[17] to the flamboyant personality of William Mathie's carved and gilt frames. Mathie's picture frame for the dining-room at Dumfries (illus 11.10) is perhaps the best representative of high-style, mid-century Scottish rococo. It features the same elements as Thomas Chippendale's contemporary carved work, scrolls, floral trails and Ho-Ho birds, but these are realised with greater delicacy and are naturalistically observed. There is plenty of 'fresh air' around the different elements of Scottish rococo works such as this.

Alexander Peter's dining chairs made in 1759 for Dumfries House are a striking instance of the fashionable modernity of Edinburgh production.[18] Built using very dark Jamaican mahogany of the sort favoured by mid-century Scots cabinetmakers, and upholstered in Scottish-made 'Osenburgh' cloth (a loose-weave flax fabric), they represent Peter's response to the stimulus of rococo designs in the first edition of Thomas Chippendale's *Gentleman and Cabinet Maker's Director* (1754). Peter's design was probably inspired by chairs in plate XII of the pattern book, but the fan-back enrichment of carved wheatsheaf, acanthus fronds and rosettes is Peter's own (illus 11.11).[19] The acquisition of new furniture of this type accompanied the 'great rebuilding' of Scotland's antiquated country houses, a phenomenon that affected the Highlands as well as the more prosperous Lowlands. Replacement of a vertical tower house with a spacious and symmetrical residence influenced by Italian architectural style, often situated very near or even adjoining the old place, was a practice repeated throughout the country. Ayrshire could be cited as a very good example, because it contains notable clusters of new Palladian houses built between 1755 and 1765.[20] All were newly furnished at varying expense,[21] but the contents of most have been dispersed. The twenty-four mahogany dining chairs made by Peter for Dumfries in 1759, for which the full bill remains in the family archive, represent perhaps the best surviving

Illustration 11.5
Francis Brodie, Lady's closet, 1753 (open). [Courtesy of Christie's and Great Steward of Scotland, Dumfries House Trust]

Illustration 11.6
Alexander Peter, bedroom table, 1759. [Courtesy Great Steward of Scotland, Dumfries House Trust]

Scotland's involvement in the neoclassical movement determined the design of key furniture types from the late 1760s. Architect designers such as James Stuart, William Chambers and Robert Adam had come into contact with the international *avant garde* coterie while studying ancient remains in Rome or visiting Paris. In 1764 Adam designed the first suite of furniture in the 'Antick' manner for wealthy Edinburgh patron Sir Lawrence Dundas.[22] By 1767 the fully neoclassical plan for the capital's New Town had been prepared by architect James Craig. A large number of the New Town houses were rented, often by families living outside Edinburgh who came to the city for the education of their children, or for business, or simply for the social season. The furniture for these spacious new houses was usually hired, often in a complete package of house and contents offered by an entrepreneurial cabinetmaker. These particular social circumstances, along with the universal use of cabinetmakers' price books, encouraged uniformity in the city's furniture, and the dominant style was neoclassical.

Many of the houses were designed for entertainments, mainly supper parties and dances, so they had large and impressive lobbies, more than one drawing-room, and, where they were not flatted dwellings, a downstairs dining-room with a niche for the sideboard. Newspaper advertisements and household

repertoire of this 'new furniture'. In the same house is a set of twelve related chairs, of slightly smaller proportions, not enriched with carved detail but plainly constructed from Scots elm (*ulmus glabra*) (illus 11.12). These chairs, made for the backstairs areas of the house, could be described as 'common' rather than high-style furniture because they were made using native timber and were intended for everyday use by the working staff. The crestings are subtly enriched with 'rollers', that is backward-scrolling mouldings that resemble tightly rolled paper. These are an identifying feature on Scottish chairs of this period. Although the chairs are a deliberate simplification of a genteel or high-style model, made by a fashionable Edinburgh maker and not by a country wright, they are nevertheless part of a spectrum of furniture design across the social scale in Scotland (illus 11.13).

Illustration 11.7
Scottish kitchen table, with single flap, nineteenth century.
[Fife Folk Museum]

Illustration 11.8
Scottish kitchen table, showing frieze drawer, nineteenth century.
[Fife Folk Museum]

inventories dating from between 1800 and 1830[23] confirm that the furnishing formula of these rented houses, with their hired furniture, differed only in small details. Little thought would need to be given to individual items because the cabinetmaker or hirer could supply the whole complement of furniture *en bloc*.

Even the architectural arrangement of the houses made the use of standard items of furniture obligatory. No lobby was complete without its lobby table and chairs, and a dining-room would have looked unfurnished without its stage-top sideboard. The popular dining chair choice was the brander back, a geometric design featuring plain or reeded banisters (illus 11.14). It was markedly different from the rococo Chippendale derivative that had been so common in Scotland in the mid-eighteenth century. The distinctive neoclassical pattern of the brander back was frequently executed in mahogany, but also in the more regionally specific timber of Scots laburnum (*laburnum alpinum*).[24]

A substantial number of the city's cabinetmakers can be seen to have used the Edinburgh price books as straightforward pattern manuals. For example, items such as card tables appear in identical form with different makers' stamps or labels. Typical of card table design around

Illustration 11.9
Alexander Peter, sofa, 1759.
[Courtesy Great Steward of Scotland, Dumfries House Trust]

1800 was the D-shaped tea/card table (illus 11.15). The distinctive Scottish feature is the frieze drawer fitted with three 'cannisters' for teas and sugar. Like several other table types of its time, the piece is multipurpose.

Drawing-room games, and the culture of the card table, were an important part of life in the Edinburgh home, perhaps of more significance than in other cities. Constant features of the cabinetmaker's repertoire during the late eighteenth and early nineteenth centuries were the various 'entertainment tables' including billiard, bagatelle, trou madame, drawing, quartetto, screen writing, deception and fly, draught and cribbage. One of the most unusual was the 'polyterpic' that functioned as a card table but contained a zograscope and camera obscura.[25]

The rising popularity of needlework and spinning as a drawing-room distraction is well recorded in early nineteenth-century views of both New Town house and suburban villa interiors by artists such as John Harden and Alexander Carse, but it is reflected, also, in the number of work tables surviving in private collections and on the antiques market. The most distinctive Edinburgh type was the 'French' work table, with characteristic semi-circular ends. An example can be seen clearly in Alexander Carse's watercolour of the drawing-room at Midfield Cottage, Lasswade, painted in 1807 (illus 11.16). The French model from which this design was borrowed was the eighteenth-century *tricoteuse* that had semi-circular ends and a capacious central section for storing wool; examples are known to have been made by top Parisian makers such as Martin Carlin. In Edinburgh they were

Illustration 11.10
William Mathie, picture frame, 1759. [Courtesy Christie's and Great Steward of Scotland, Dumfries House Trust]

Illustration 11.11
Alexander Peter, dining chair, 1759.
[Courtesy Great Steward of Scotland, Dumfries House Trust]

relatively common household item only in the early nineteenth century. Its distinguishing feature was the row of three drawers across the top, later modified to one large square drawer flanked by two pairs of smaller ones. This formula, which was applied also to 'secretaries' or desks and book cases, came from France, like the sideboard stage top, and remained as an enduring signature of Scottish pieces until the beginning of the twentieth century.[26]

The cabinetmaker and property tycoon who achieved greatest prominence in Edinburgh in the early nineteenth century was William Trotter (1772–1833) whose forbears Young, Trotter and Hamilton had relinquished their loyalty to the Old Town by setting up a new wareroom on Princes Street in 1772. They were the first to move out of the Old Town to a position that was eminently convenient for the first 'colonists' of the New Town (illus 11.19). As can be seen in the engraved view of 1804, the

manufactured by cabinet firms who were beginning to cluster around the edge of the expanding New Town, ready to catch the market for *bourgeois* drawing-room items.

Makers of the table in illustration 11.15, Bruce and Burns, retailed a varied selection of small furnishings from elegant warerooms on the South Bridge, Edinburgh, but not all tradesmen followed this example. The maker of the 'Scotch chest' (illus 11.17, for example), John Biggar, did not operate from a wareroom on a main street, but from a builder's yard in a narrow wynd. He was a builder and cabinetmaker who represented the close association that existed between architecture and furniture in the city at that time (illus 11.18). After the stage-top sideboard, the Scotch chest was the next most ubiquitous furniture type in the country's list of key types, but it seems to have become a

Illustration 11.12
Alexander Peter, chair, 1759.
[Courtesy Great Steward of Scotland, Dumfries House Trust]

Illustration 11.13
'Cottage Interior with a Seated Woman Darning', 1830. Drawing by Walter Geikie, DD 4427/17.
[Courtesy National Galleries of Scotland]

wareroom façade was designed to look like a spacious New Town house, but the façade disguised top-lit furniture and upholstery galleries behind. In terms of leadership in taste – the fashion stakes – their break did not come until 1796, when they were called in by HM Exchequer to furnish apartments in Holyrood Palace for a new resident, Charles Philippe, Comte D'Artois, later Charles X of France. This furniture, which took four months to supply, at a cost of £2,613 13s 9½d, was in a smart neoclassical idiom that reflected the type of items the company supplied to customers in the New Town. Certain features, such as large let in ovals of crotch veneer, contrasting timber colours and 'stump' feet, are characteristic of Edinburgh furniture of the period, and Trotter's repertoire in particular. William Trotter, whose career at the head of his family firm from 1805 to 1833 corresponded with

Illustration 11.14
George Sandeman, laburnum dining chair, 1789, Perth.
[Courtesy Mr and Mrs George Waterston]

Illustration 11.15
Bruce and Burns, 'round cornered' card table with elliptic front, *c* 1805.
[National Trust for Scotland]

the evolution of an idiosyncratic Greek Revival style in the 'Northern Athens'[27] was concerned almost exclusively with the supply of fashionable furniture. His domestic pieces, for lobby, dining-room, drawing-room and bedroom, developed from price book specifications while deriving some decorative ideas from London and Paris, helped to establish the notions of formality that came to characterise the New Town house. But to see Edinburgh furniture of the early nineteenth century as being completely standardised would be a false impression indeed. Two examples of individually adapted Edinburgh furniture types can be cited in support of this view. First is a 'picture viewing sofa' that was designed by William Trotter for the purpose-built gallery at Paxton House, Berwickshire,

Illustration 11.16
Alexander Carse, 'Mr and Mrs Campbell with Lady Molesworth and Miss Brown in the
Drawing Room at Midfield Cottage, Lasswade', 1807. [National Portrait Gallery, Edinburgh]

Illustration 11.17
John Biggar, chest of drawers, *c* 1805. [S Henderson Esq]

had been initiated by George IV at Carlton House, London, and Brighton Pavilion, but he was adapting this whimsical taste to Edinburgh types.[31]

Returning to classical revival tropes, the key chair designs of the nineteenth century were of Greek and Roman derivation. The so-called 'Edinburgh' chair, named because it had an enduring influence in the capital and its orbit, was based on the Grecian tablet back with 'klismos' legs. It developed into the familiar 'yoke'-shaped pattern after 1825 and is well represented in Chair Makers' price books. During the later nineteenth century it became the model for the most common type of kitchen chair in eastern Scotland, popular until the Second World War.

The 'Roman' chair, on the other hand, had a continuous back and arms that surrounded the sitter and was perhaps designed for less formal use than its 'Grecian' counterpart. Edinburgh examples are recorded by makers such as Richard Clark & Son of Leith Walk, but a similar specification was used by makers in Glasgow. The firm Cleland & Jack of Virginia Street, Glasgow, for example, supplied 'eight Roman chairs covered with fine Crimson Moreen brass ornaments and strong brass castors' at a cost of £5 each, to the new Hunterian Museum in September 1809.[32]

Specialist items amongst seat furniture in eighteenth- and nineteenth-century Scotland are diverse, but it will serve the purpose of this chapter to select two from a large range. 'Hunter's' chairs

1814.[28] At seven feet eleven inches long, the seat is of a much larger scale than the standard Edinburgh 'Grecian' sofa, but its design corresponds with the Edinburgh Chair Makers' *Book of Prices* specification of 1825 which describes bolsters 'sunk' into scroll ends. The unique feature of the sofa is its specially raked back that allows the connoisseur a reclining view of pictures hung high on the gallery walls, at the 'ideal' distance of 22 feet, recommended by the painter Henry Raeburn.[29]

Second is a 'clothes press with wings' made for Lord Gray at Kinfauns Castle, Perthshire, in 1825. This type of wardrobe was very much part of the Edinburgh cabinetmaker's repertoire in the early nineteenth century, and although the Kinfauns example is an unusually exotic version, it nevertheless corresponds with the specification given in the *Edinburgh Book of Prices for Manufacturing Cabinet Work*, 1821: 'A CLOTHES PRESS WITH WINGS. Seven feet long, seven feet six inches high, veneered on deal, cock beaded, the wing doors to open from top to bottom, backs all framed, loose cornice and plinth'.[30] Lord Gray was following the fashion for chinoiserie that

Illustration 11.18
Detail of John Biggar's chest of drawers (Illustration 11.17) showing his trade label inside the central drawer.

Illustration 11.19
Detail from 'Register House, Edinburgh', etched by James Fittler after a drawing by J C Nattes, 1804,
showing the Ware-room of Young, Trotter & Hamilton

appear consistently enough in the country house context to be considered a key Scottish type. The 'Lounging or Hunters chair' is a generously proportioned armchair with the option of an additional square frame at the front for resting the legs. Its robust construction and hard-wearing upholstery was specifically designed to accommodate the fatigued hunter just returned from the chase. The square easy chairs with 'saddle tree cheeks' that appear to have been made in Scotland until the twentieth century are of interest because they seem to reflect eighteenth-century traditions. These are armed chairs with draught-averting straight rectangular 'cheeks' set at a slight angle from the back, resembling the construction of a boarded wooden arm used to store saddles when not in use.

Specific types of music chair are a consistently noted Scottish preference, too. Harp (or *clarsach*) playing became a drawing-room craze in Edinburgh following the release of James Macpherson of Balavil's 'translations' of the Gaelic epic poems *Fingal* and *Temora* and the small book *Fragments of Ancient Poetry*.[33]

Accordingly, the music chair designed for this purpose had an adjustable seat rising on a wooden screw and a very straight back to accommodate the strictly upright posture adopted by players of the new versions of the old Celtic harp (illus 11.20).

Illustration 11.20
James Mein, Kelso, music chair, *c* 1825.
[Courtesy of the Earl and Countess of Haddington]

Scottish-made chairs were sold in the home market, being supplied to customers on the mainland and the offshore islands, but the 'Extra work in chairs for exportation' specified in the *Edinburgh Book of Prices for Manufacturing Cabinet Work* suggests that they were sent farther afield. The extra work involved either strengthening the frames, or constructing them with dovetails and tenons instead of glued pins. The use of dry joints enabled the chairs to be knocked down so that they could be exported safely in component form. Makers in ports with an established export trade, such as Greenock, on the River Clyde, are known to have requested price books from Edinburgh,[34] which would support the theory that some chairs made in the West, for export to Ireland and across the Atlantic, were made to Edinburgh specifications.

Notes

1 One of the earliest dated examples is that made by Edinburgh cabinetmaker James Russell. It is now at Duns Castle, Berwickshire.

2 *Edinburgh Evening Courant*, 10 August 1822.

3 *Edinburgh Book of Prices for Manufacturing Cabinet Work*, 1805, 12.

4 The Scottish stage-top sideboard in the Temple Newsam collection, Leeds (catalogue no 340), which has bottle wells beneath the stage, is a good provenanced example of this variant.

5 Mid-eighteenth-century French pieces use sliding panels of timber 'reeds' stuck to a backing of canvas in cases where no great strength or security is needed; for example, in night tables and pot cupboards. The adaptation of these 'sliders' to sideboard stages appears to be a peculiarly Scottish variant.

6 Interior view, warerooms of Messrs Cleland, Jack, Paterson & Company, Trongate, Glasgow. R Chapman, *The Picture of Glasgow or Stranger's Guide*, 1812. Sideboard tables made in Ulster are also known to have featured a three-sided stage. See David Jones and Fergus Purdy, 'Irish Sideboards', *Regional Furniture*, vol XIX, 33–43.

7 Mrs Gordon of Cairness required a sideboard that was to be longer than the standard English specification and to have a stage, as was Scottish practice. Thomas Seddon Senior wrote to her on 7 March 1795 confirming the request: 'the one you saw in my wareroom was 7ft 9in and yours is to be 8ft 8ins Besides the addition of a Shelf Behind for Waiters &c.' Mrs Gordon also found the chairs rather pinched and ordered a larger size. Aberdeen University Library, Gordon of Cairness Papers, MS1160/28/4.

8 Reviewing Walton's stage-top dining-room sideboard in the 1903 Arts and Crafts Exhibition at the New Gallery, London, the *Studio* critic wrote: 'the recess furnished by Mr Walton at once attracts attention to its beautiful dresser

in dark, unpolished walnut. Extremely plain and free from added ornament, its grace of proportion and its variety of line and form make it an ample decoration for a room, and at the same time a joy to the eye of the housewife by reason of its spacious and convenient parts'. *The Studio*, vol XXVIII, no 119, February 1903, 36.

9 The prominent example is the Fleshers chair, dated 1661, from Trinity Hall, headquarters of the Aberdeen Incorporated Trades. See David Learmonth, 'The Trinity Hall Chairs, Aberdeen', *Furniture History*, vol XIV, 1978, 1–8.

10 The Lady's closet is a most idiosyncratic Scottish furniture type that most probably evolved from the tower room, or closet, off a bedchamber, in which a lady of the house could keep her precious things. Seventeenth-century inventories such as that of Leuchars Castle, Fife, 1696, describe such rooms as Lady's closets and their contents as being almost identical to those of the later padouk wood Lady's closet by Francis Brodie, at Dumfries House. Thanks to Sarah Medlam for first bringing my attention to the *bureau brise* form.

11 The new drawing-room made at Kinnaird Castle, Brechin, in the late seventeenth century is a very good example of the classicisation of an older house. Two large sash windows were inserted to make a new central wall pier, against which a pier table (and probably looking-glass and attendant candlestands), could be placed. See David Jones, 'A seventeenth-century inventory of furnishings at Kinnaird Castle, Angus', *St Andrews Studies in the History of Scottish Architecture and Design*, vol I, 1988, 49–64.

12 A design for a pier table on eagle pedestal can be seen on the billhead of Francis Brodie (1708–82), for example, Account to the Duke of Gordon to Francis Brodie, 1739, NAS GD44/51/465/1/34, in which the ensemble can be seen at the top right.

13 The basic specification for the bedroom table can be seen in *The Edinburgh Book of Prices for Manufacturing Cabinet Work*, 1811, 60.

14 A very good illustration of a bedroom table in use is William Douglas, *The Chaplain's Room, Trinity College Hospital, Edinburgh*, 1845. There are good examples of bedroom tables in corridors in country houses such as Newhailes, Midlothian.

15 The Philadelphia version was to be executed in pine rather than fir. See *The Philadelphia Furniture Price Book: A facsimile/with an introduction and guide by Alexandra Alevizatos Kirtley*. Philadelphia Museum of Art, 2005, 21.

16 There are fifty rococo pieces by Thomas Chippendale the Elder in the house and over 200 rococo pieces by Edinburgh luxury makers Alexander Peter and William Mathie.

17 Morrison Heckscher and Leslie Greene Bowman show comparable examples from Philadelphia in *American Rococo: Elegance in Ornament*. Yale, 1992.

18 The chairs were supplied by leading Edinburgh furniture maker Alexander Peter on 5 July 1759: 'To 24 Mahogy.

Dining room chairs wt carving on ye front & feet buff'd over seats osenburgh covers at 30s. £36 0s 0d.'

19   The wheatsheaf was a favoured adaptation of pattern book designs used in Scotland. It appears to have been more attractive to Scottish wrights than the esoteric classical ornaments that were available.

20   Around Cumnock, for example, are Dumfries House, Auchinleck and Ballochmyle, all built and fitted up around 1760.

21   In her *Diaries of a Duchess, Extracts from the Diaries of the First Duchess of Northumberland (1716–76)*, Hodder & Stoughton, 1936, 225, Lady Elizabeth Percy writes (in 1760), that 'Auchinlech' is 'just built', that Ballochmyle is a 'new house very neatly fitted up and finish'd', and she visits the newly completed and expensively furnished Dumfries House, Cumnock, where she parties with the Earl.

22   Thomas Chippendale made the seat furniture and invoiced Dundas on 9 July 1765 for: '8 large Arm Chairs exceeding Richly Carv'd in the Antick manner … £160' and '4 large Sofas Exceeding Rich to match the Chairs … £216'. Robert Adam charged £5 for the design.

23   Letting advertisements appear in *The Edinburgh Evening Courant* from 1800 to 1830.

24   See David Jones, 'The laburnum tradition in Scotland', *Regional Furniture*, vol VI, 1992, 1–10.

25   There is an example made by John Buchanan of Greenock, 1817, in the collection of the National Museums Scotland, Edinburgh. 'Polyterpic' referred to the multi-purpose use of the table and a zograscope was a device for viewing prints through a magnifying lens.

26   Designs for three-in-a-row top drawers can be seen in plates 513 and 637 of Pierre Antoine Leboux de La Mesangere's *Collection de Meubles et Objets de Gout*, published as a supplement to *Journal des Dames et des Modes* in Paris from

1797. 'Scotch' chests of this type are still made for the New Zealand market, but have passed out of fashion in Scotland itself.

27   The popular name 'Athens of the North' was adapted from the widely distributed illustrated book by John Britton, with engravings by Thomas Shepherd, *Modern Athens! Displayed in a series of views: or Edinburgh in the nineteenth century; exhibiting the whole of the new buildings, modern improvements, antiquities, and picturesque scenery, of the Scottish metropolis and its environs.* Jones & Co., Edinburgh, 1829.

28   This gallery, called the 'Picture Drawing Room', the first purpose-built picture gallery in Scotland, was designed by the celebrated New Town architect Robert Reid (1776–1856) and constructed between 1811 and 1813.

29   Letter from Henry Raeburn to John Forbes of Callander, NAS/GD/71/26/35.

30   Reprinted in David Jones, *The Edinburgh Cabinet and Chair Makers' Books of Prices 1805–25*. Cupar: Kirk Wynd Press, 2000.

31   As well as providing a rare insight into the resolution of design problems by Trotter's, the Kinfauns commission is, amongst all their surviving documented projects, perhaps the best indicator of the sheer range and versatility of the company's operations. From their Edinburgh shop, they were able to supply all the customer's needs, including japanned furniture, sumptuous upholstery materials, and even an artist able to imitate Chinese painting.

32   Celine Blair and David Jones, 'Furnishing the Hunterian Museum, Glasgow Style, 1809', *Regional Furniture*, vol V, 1991, 86–92.

33   See Hugh Cheape, 'The culture and material culture of Ossian, 1760–1900', *Scotlands* 4.1, 1997, 1–2.

34   Ian MacDougall, 'The Edinburgh Branch of the Scottish National Union of Cabinet and Chair Makers, 1833–1837'. *Book of the Old Edinburgh Club*, vol XXIII, 1969–72, 17.

CHAPTER 12

Collecting Scottish weapons

DAVID H CALDWELL

The Scots have a proud martial tradition and anyone attempting to understand this is sooner or later bound to want to know about Scottish weapons. They are well represented in museums in Scotland and elsewhere, but this does not mean that collecting and studying them are solely matters for professionals. As with so many other areas of archaeology and history, important contributions have been, and remain to be made, by amateur collectors. This paper aims to provide some clues for those with an interest in, but not much experience of Scottish weapons.

Early evidence for collecting

The impulse to collect antique Scottish weapons goes back a long way. Often this was not motivated by an appreciation of their beauty or effectiveness but was because of their associations. Thus King James IV owned a sword he believed had belonged to the great patriot, William Wallace, and had it refurbished (Caldwell 2007a: 170). The desire to keep such relics was often greater than the evidence for their authenticity. Indeed, in the late sixteenth and early seventeenth century, inscriptions were added to sword blades to link them with heroes of previous centuries or worthy ancestors, like the sword long in the possession of descendants of Sir James Douglas who was a companion of King Robert Bruce in the early fourteenth century (illus 12.1). The decoration includes initials for both the king and Douglas, a heart, and verse instructions by the former to the latter to take his heart after his death for holy burial (at Christ's Sepulchre in Jerusalem) (Paton 1890: 33). It must be assumed that some owners knew full well that the attributions they sought to confirm were at best wishful thinking if not new inventions. Such must be the case with a long gun that belonged to Sir John Grant, 6th Laird of Freuchie (1596–1637), its lock-plate marked 'AP' (for Andrew Philp, Dundee?) and dated 1635 (illus 12.2). A silver strip along the barrel is engraved in Latin: 'Sir John Grant Sheriff of Inverness had me made in Germany in 1434.' This barrel might be a few years earlier than 1635 but certainly not 200 years. Perhaps there was a political

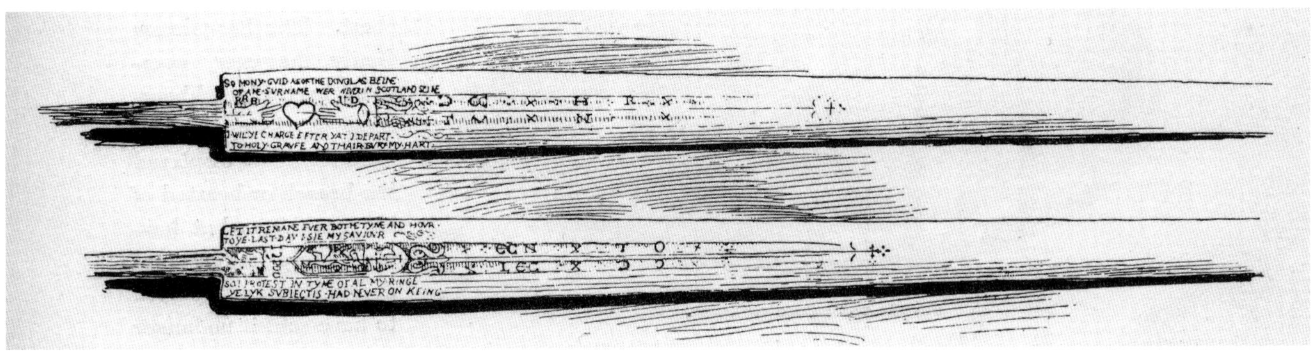

Illustration 12.1
The blade of the 'Douglas Sword', late sixteenth century, but with inscriptions relating to Sir James Douglas in the early fourteenth century. After Paton 1879, figs 36 and 37

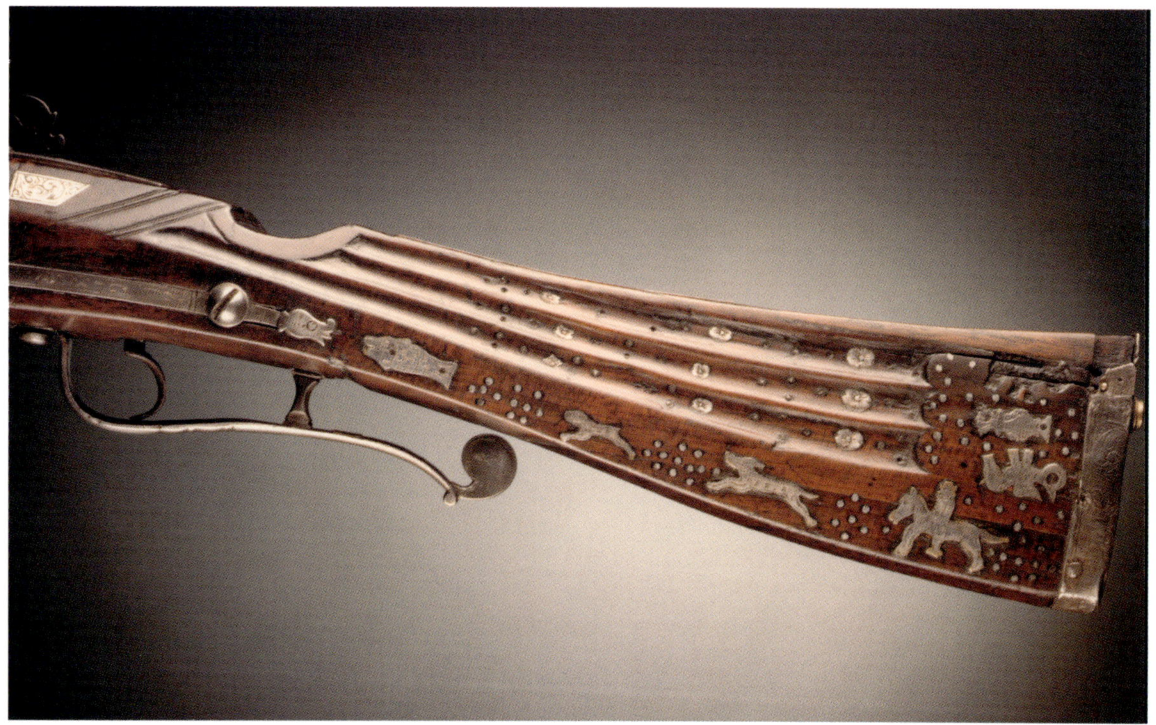

Illustration 12.2
The stock of a long gun, inlaid in silver with a hunting scene, probably made by Andrew Philp, Dundee, 1635.
It belonged to Sir John Grant of Freuchie. The barrel is decorated with a spurious inscription indicating
it is German work of 1434. NMS: H.LNA 24. [Copyright © Trustees of the National Museums Scotland]

imperative to back-date an ambition for sheriffship. Whatever else, these examples should teach caution in accepting dates, marks and traditions at face value.

A few surviving inventories, like those for plenishings in the houses of the lairds of Glenorchy in the late sixteenth and early seventeenth century, demonstrate how some nobles had private armouries, including weapons for sport, ancestral pieces and equipment for use in war (Innes 1855: 319–90). From the nineteenth century aristocratic owners of some great houses used weapons as wall decoration. An early example can still be seen at Culzean Castle in Ayrshire (National Trust for Scotland) where the 12th Earl of Cassillis used weapons purchased in 1812 from the Office of Ordnance to decorate the hall (Moss 2002: 113).

Collecting and research by antiquaries and scholars

The amassing of collections of weapons in Scotland purely from antiquarian interest has its roots in the eighteenth century. The catalyst was the foundation of the Society of Antiquaries of Scotland in 1780 at the instigation of David Steuart Erskine, 11th Earl of Buchan. Within a year Buchan had gifted to the society's museum a close helmet (NMS: H.LN 25) and a guidon with its lance (NMS: H.LF 1) which related to the regiment of dragoons raised in 1688 by his ancestor, Lord Cardross (Caldwell 1990). Early printed catalogues of the museum, like that of 1863, show that other Scottish weapons were collected, many of them stray archaeological finds, but there were practically none of the archetypal weapons — basket-hilted swords, dirks, targes, all-metal pistols, etc — considered so collectable today. They are first in evidence in the printed catalogue of 1892 (illus 12.3).

The society was, in the words of Sir James Simpson's anniversary address in 1861 (reproduced in the preface of the 1892 catalogue), primarily interested in making a collection of 'ancient Archaeological and Historical Memorials of our native Land'. This definition seems to a large extent to have excluded examples of applied art and *objets d'art* of the eighteenth and nineteenth centuries, perhaps because the antiquaries considered that this would be the field of interest of the Industrial Museum of Scotland (later renamed the Royal Scottish Museum) founded in 1854. It acquired in 1904 the collection of arms and armour put together by the successful painter, Sir Joseph Noël Paton, which included many typical Scottish pieces (Paton 1879; Norman 1972), but otherwise did not make further collecting in this field a priority.

Until the mid-twentieth century the study and collection of Scottish weapons was largely in the hands of gifted amateurs. Interest in and the availability of such weapons was greatly increased by the visit of

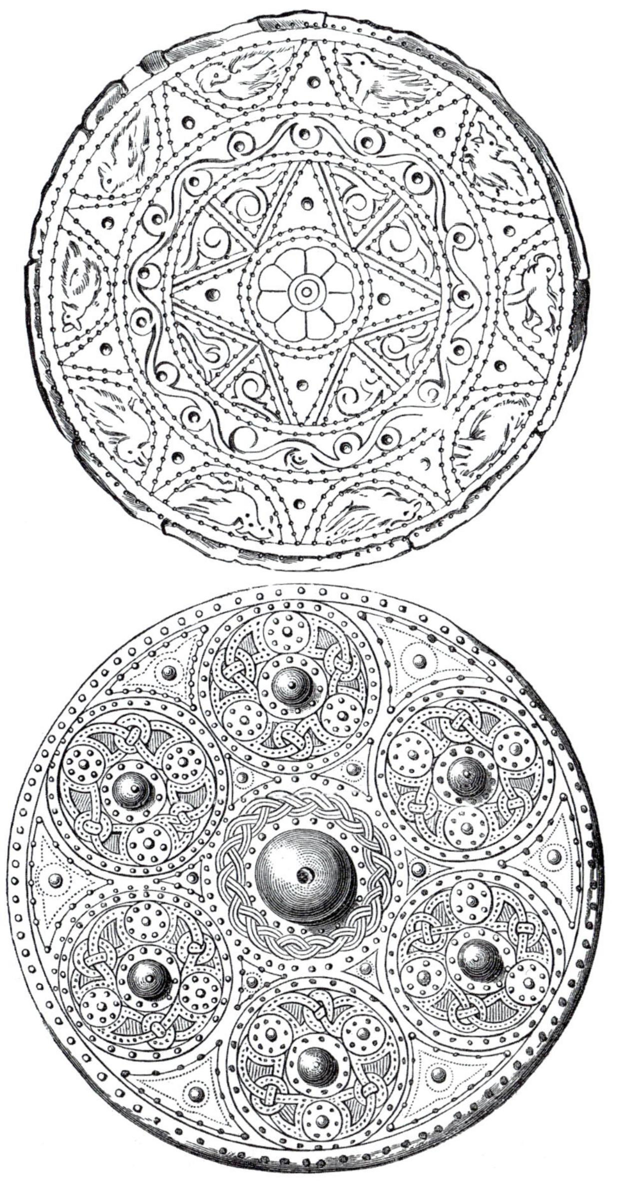

Illustration 12.3
Two late seventeenth-century Highland targes (H.LN 34 and H.LN 35) illustrated in the 1892 printed catalogue of the National Museum of Antiquities of Scotland.

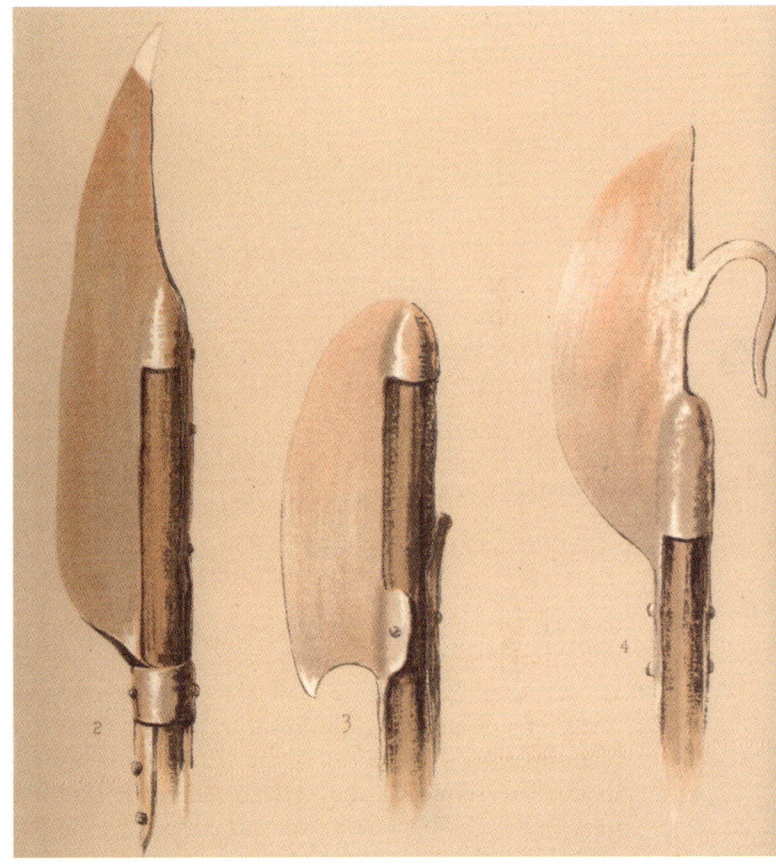

Illustration 12.4
Illustrations of long shafted weapons by James Drummond. The one on the right is a typical example of a Lochaber axe. [From Drummond 1881, pl XXXII]

King George IV to Edinburgh in 1822, which under the stage-management of Sir Walter Scott saw the recreation of clan armies as a major element in the proceedings (Caldwell 2009). Another artist who took an interest in the subject was James Drummond, who on his death in 1877 left an almost finished series of coloured illustrations of weapons and other iconic

Scottish objects (illus 12.4), published in 1881 with an introduction and notes by Joseph Anderson, custodier of the National Museum of Antiquities and a truly great scholar (Drummond 1881). Anderson's introduction is still worth reading, though he was greatly hampered by his lack of information on the individual weapons and their whereabouts. The book is held in high regard by collectors nowadays but there should be more awareness that the illustrations are often artistic rather than accurate, and include several pieces which are either not Scottish or of doubtful authenticity.

Other nineteenth-century works should also be used with caution, none more so than Lord Archibald Campbell's study of *Highland Dress, Arms and Ornament* of 1899. Already by that date, however, the study of Scottish weapons was being put on a sound basis by a young Scottish collector, Charles Whitelaw, to whom

all interested in the subject continue to be deeply indebted. Whitelaw's scholarship can first be seen in his contributions to two major exhibitions in Glasgow, the Glasgow International Exhibition in 1901 (Paton 1902: 234–42) and the Scottish Exhibition of National History, Art, & Industry in 1911 (Glaister 1911: 303–45). He went on from there to contribute a treatise on Scottish hand firearms to a work on European guns (Jackson 1923: 52–108). There were other important papers on signed basket hilts, dirks and gun locks (republished in Whitelaw 1977: 302–9), and the indispensable dictionary of Scottish arms and armour makers, eventually published in 1977, long after his death in 1939, through the efforts of Sarah Barter and others.

Whitelaw's great gift, however, was his thoroughly documented, large and comprehensive collection

218

of Scottish weapons which he bequeathed, part to Glasgow Museums and part to the National Museum of Antiquities of Scotland. The gift to Glasgow joined a magnificent collection of European arms and armour and related books created by the Greenock shipbuilder Robert Lyons Scott, which he left to the museum on his death in 1939 (Joubert 1924) and which itself included a number of rare and fine Scottish pieces. The two bequests together form the basis of Glasgow's internationally renowned collection of arms and armour.

The Whitelaw gift to Edinburgh included many outstanding pieces: for example, the pair of all-brass pistols, signed 'IL' (James Low, Dundee?) and dated 1611 (illus 12.5), from the collection of King Louis XIII of France. It provides the backbone of a truly comprehensive national collection which has now expanded to include weapons of all types made and used in Scotland, from medieval times to the present day. Significant large-scale additions have included the important collection of Scottish weapons put together by Norman Colville, purchased in 1932 by the Scottish United Services Museum in Edinburgh Castle (now part of NMS) and transferred to the National Museum of Antiquities in 1949. To a large extent this has complemented the Whitelaw bequest. Then in 1977 the museum acquired the collection of the Earls of Seafield, a unique surviving private armoury with

Illustration 12.6
Group of traditional seventeenth-century long guns from the collection of the Earls of Seafield.
Much of the work on them appears to have been done by the Grant family's armourer, William Smith.
[Copyright © Trustees of the National Museums Scotland]

Illustration 12.7
Late seventeenth-century Highland targe and dirk, along with a broad sword with ribbon basket hilt. It was this combination of weapons that brought success to Jacobite armies on several battlefields.
[Copyright © Trustees of the National Museums Scotland]

Collectable Scottish weapons

Scottish weapons regularly appear in the catalogues of auction houses and the shops of antique dealers in Europe and North America, and are sought after by specialist collectors. The main focus of collecting is often on weapons of a type and date to have been used in the Jacobite uprisings of the seventeenth and eighteenth centuries (illus 12.7). In fact, authentic Scottish medieval weapons very rarely turn up, and study of them is largely based on early documents and representations in art. The medieval sculpture of the West Highlands is a particularly rich source (Steer and Bannerman 1977; Caldwell 2007b). Traditional Scottish weapons are often richly decorated with engraving, inlaid metal and carved detail in wooden stocks. There are often clear differences in the repertoire

an exceptional series of seventeenth-century long guns (illus 12.6). These have curved, fluted butts, and are richly decorated. Much of the work on them appears to have been done by a smith retained by the Grant family, William Smith, whose repertoire of designs betrays his Highland heritage. The guns themselves may mostly have been used for hunting.

Since the 1970s the identification and acquisition of numerous individual weapons for the national collection has been made easier by the research output of a small group of museum professionals and collectors who have based much of their output on the collection itself. Amongst many works of continuing use we should mention here the study by John Wallace of swords and dirks (Wallace 1970), the 1979 book by the author and the papers on weapons and fortifications published two years later (Caldwell 1981a), the 1995 study of firearms by Claude Blair and Robert Woosnam-Savage, and the book on basket hilts published that same year by Cyril Mazansky. There are also several useful contributions to the subject in journals and magazines, including the *Proceedings of the Society of Antiquaries of Scotland*, the *Journal of the Arms and Armour Society*, and *The Park Lane Arms Fair*.

Illustration 12.8
A claymore, the type of two-handed sword used by Highlanders in the sixteenth century. NMS: H.LA 105.
[Copyright © Trustees of the National Museums Scotland]

two-handed cross hilt swords, characterised by drooping quillons (guards) with quatrefoil terminals (illus 12.8). Second, there are the so-called Lowland swords, often with side rings and long straight guards with down-turned terminals ending in buttons (illus 12.9). Third, there are the swords with guards described in early documents as 'clam shellit' since they each have two upright guards, rather like shells, protecting the grip (illus 12.10). Several of these two-handed swords have been preserved as 'bearing swords' for ceremonial use.

The most collectable Scottish swords are single-handed and mounted with basket hilts, the earliest

Illustration 12.9
Two-handed sword of the type used by Lowlanders
in the sixteenth century. NMS: H.LA 6.
[Copyright © Trustees of the National Museums Scotland]

of designs used, on the one hand by armourers, cutlers and smiths based in the towns, and on the other hand by craftsmen based in the Highlands (Caldwell 1985). The motifs employed by the former include strap-work, foliage and flowerheads while interlace patterns and spotted animals are often characteristics of the latter.

There are, however, a significant number of two-handed swords still in private hands. The fashion for fighting with large swords grasped in two hands took hold in Scotland in the sixteenth century, and three types can be distinguished. First, the claymores used in the Highlands (Caldwell 2005), the great

Illustration 12.10
A 'clam shellit' two-handed sword of the late
sixteenth century. NMS: H.LA 172.
[Copyright © Trustees of the National Museums Scotland]

221

Illustration 12.11
Ribbon basket hilt of the late seventeenth century, still with
its original japanned and gilt finish. NMS: H.LA 142.
[Copyright © Trustees of the National Museums Scotland]

(illus 12.14). Glasgow was another important centre of manufacture in the eighteenth century with some armourers, like John Simpson father and son, marking their hilts with their initials and a 'G' for Glasgow. The vast majority of basket hilts, however, are not marked, and are difficult to date closely or assign to a maker or town.

By and large the blades of Scottish swords were imported; mostly, it is believed, from the German blade manufacturing centre of Solingen. For unknown reasons, the Scots came to respect the name Andrea

Illustration 12.12
Basket hilt of the mid-eighteenth century,
signed by Walter Allan of Stirling. NMS: H.LA 125.
[Copyright © Trustees of the National Museums Scotland]

dating to the late sixteenth century. Not all basket-hilted swords are Scottish, and there were many varieties made for use by units of the armed forces. Their origins, possibly in Scotland or elsewhere in the British Isles, are considered in an article by Claude Blair (1981a). Many Scottish basket hilts of the seventeenth century were made of ribbons of iron, hence 'ribbon hilts' (illus 12.11) while those generally considered the finest were made in Stirling in the middle of the eighteenth century, principally by an armourer called John Allan, and his son Walter (illus 12.12). We know this since they have marked their hilts with their own initials and an 'S' for Stirling (illus 12.13). The very best are inlaid with silver or copper

Ferara as that of a maker of quality blades, and this name was obligingly copied on to blades for sale in Scotland by several swordsmiths in Solingen. There was an Italian swordsmith of that name in the sixteenth century but none of his work has been identified in Scotland. The blades are mostly 'broad', sharpened on both edges, or 'back blades', sharp on the forward edge only.

Knives or daggers were carried by many Scots from medieval times onwards. In 1963 John Wallace and Claude Blair identified as Scottish a group of fine late sixteenth- and early seventeenth-century daggers (illus 12.15), mostly with slender wooden

Illustration 12.14
Basket hilt inlaid with designs in copper,
fully signed and marked by John Allan (senior)
of Stirling, 1731. NMS: H.LA 157.
[Copyright © Trustees of the National Museums Scotland]

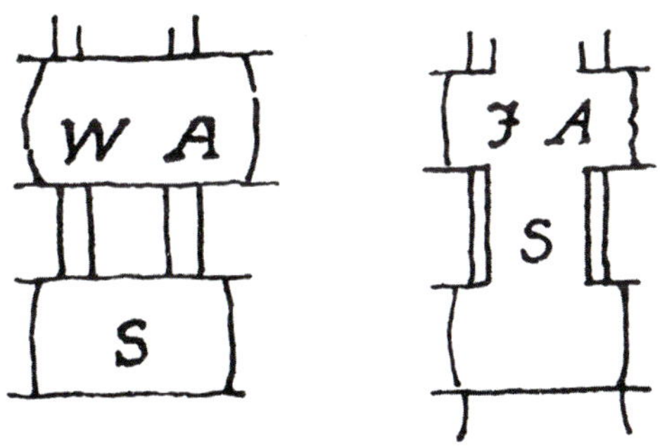

Illustration 12.13
The marks of Walter Allan and John Allan (junior) of Stirling,
as found on the undersides of their hilts.
[After drawings in Whitelaw 1977, 309]

hilts and diamond section pointed blades gilt and etched with heraldic and other decoration (Blair and Wallace 1963). It is now known that they were called whingers and were manufactured in Edinburgh (Caldwell and Wallace 2003). Better known are the dirks, often associated with Highlanders, several of which survive from the late seventeenth and eighteenth centuries. Dirks have long pointed back blades, sometimes cut-down sword blades, and short hilts, normally with prominent haunches and a flat-topped pommel. Most are carved from wood and are decorated with interlace designs (illus 12.16). Some have grips of brass and bone. There is some evidence for dirks being made by smiths and armourers based in the Highlands, including one MacNab who was working at Dalmally in mainland Argyll in the late eighteenth century (Faujas de St-Fond 1799: vol 1,

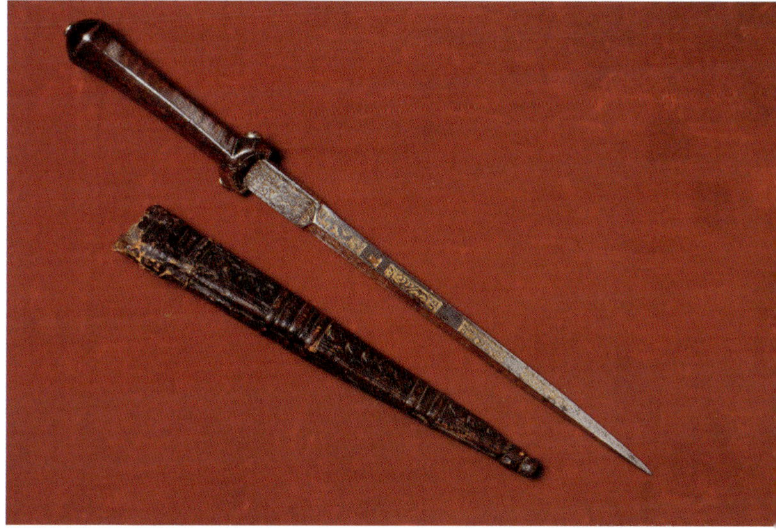

Illustration 12.15
Whinger with gilt and etched decoration on its blade,
dated 1612; probably made in Edinburgh
or Canongate. NMS: H.LC 111.
[Copyright © Trustees of the National Museums Scotland]

290–4). Others were undoubtedly manufactured in burghs like Inverness and Perth.

Guns first made an appearance in Europe at the beginning of the fourteenth century but the Scots were slow to utilise this new technology. King James III, however, was already having bronze cannon

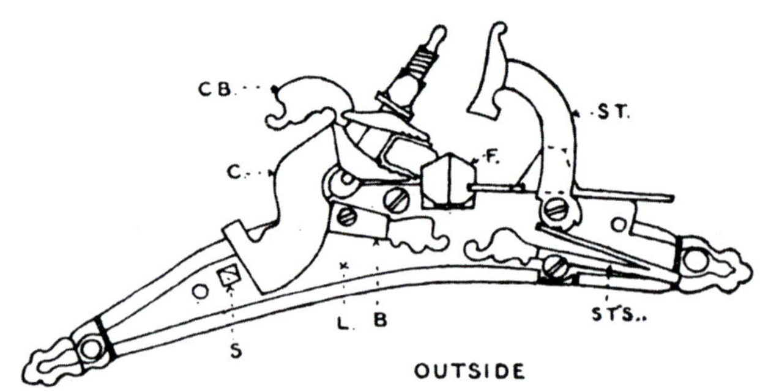

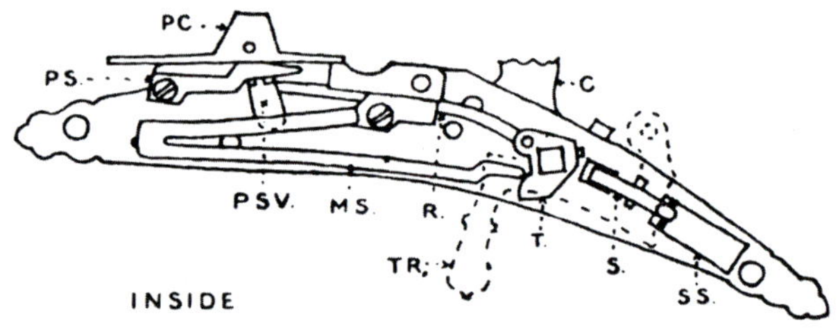

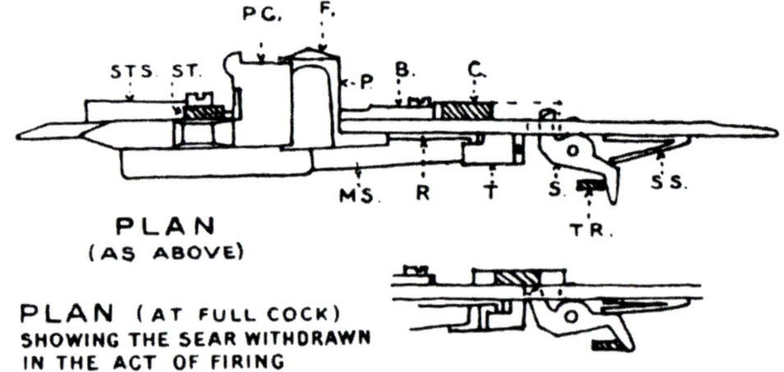

Illustration 12.17
Diagrams by Whitelaw (Jackson 1923, 61) of the working of the early Scottish snaphance. T = tumbler, S = sear. It is the in and out, horizontal operation of the sear which is the defining characteristic of this type of mechanism. When the lock is 'cocked', the sear holds the tumbler. Pulling the trigger releases the tumbler and causes the flint in the jaws of the cock to strike sparks against the steel over the powder pan

Illustration 12.16
Highland dirk, late seventeenth century. The blade is inscribed: THY KING AND COUNTRIES CAUSE DEFEND THOUGH ON THE SPOT YOUR LIFE SHOULD END, and A SOFT ANSUER TOURNETH AWAY WRATH. NMS: H.LC 14.

cast in the 1470s, and in the first half of the following century there was a cannon foundry operating in Edinburgh Castle (Caldwell 1983). Some of the smaller pieces made there still survive, including one in the collections of Glasgow Museums with the arms and initials of King James V. In the mid-seventeenth century the Scots developed an idea tried out in Sweden and produced 'leather guns' – lightweight pieces bound with cord and covered in leather – which were suitable for limited action in battle as field guns

(Stevenson and Caldwell 1977). The Scots had eagerly adopted firearms by the end of the sixteenth century, and a gun industry was established, particularly in Edinburgh and neighbouring Canongate, and also at Dundee (Caldwell 1987). The surviving pairs of pistols produced in those centres in the first three decades of the seventeenth century are a high point in the story of Scottish weapons, and the few that appear on the market fetch large sums of money. They invariably have a firing mechanism known as a snaphance, a predecessor of the flintlock; they are fitted with belt-hooks but lack trigger guards. Their wooden stocks are decorated with engraved metal mounts, and many have stocks totally of metal, mostly brass. This is a characteristic of the traditional Scottish gunmaking industry.

To understand and appreciate firearms it is necessary to have some interest in how they worked (illus 12.17). The Scots were amongst the first to adapt the snaphance lock for use with pistols. It was a relatively cheap and reliable mechanism that caused the powder in the pistol barrel to explode through the ignition of a secondary charge in a pan alongside, lit by sparks from a flint. This process was to remain standard for firearms until the nineteenth-century invention of the percussion lock, also by a Scotsman – discussed below. In the intervening years, however, traditional Scottish gunsmiths were very conservative, making locks which were little different from snaphances although from the late seventeenth century dressed up on the outside to look like the more advanced flintlocks used elsewhere. Some appreciation of these developments

Illustration 12.18
Wooden-stocked lemon butt pistol, probably by Robert Mosman of Canongate, 1625 and an iron pistol with globular butt, probably by James Gray of Dundee, 1627. NMS: H.LH 283 and H.LH 324.
[Copyright © Trustees of the National Museums Scotland]

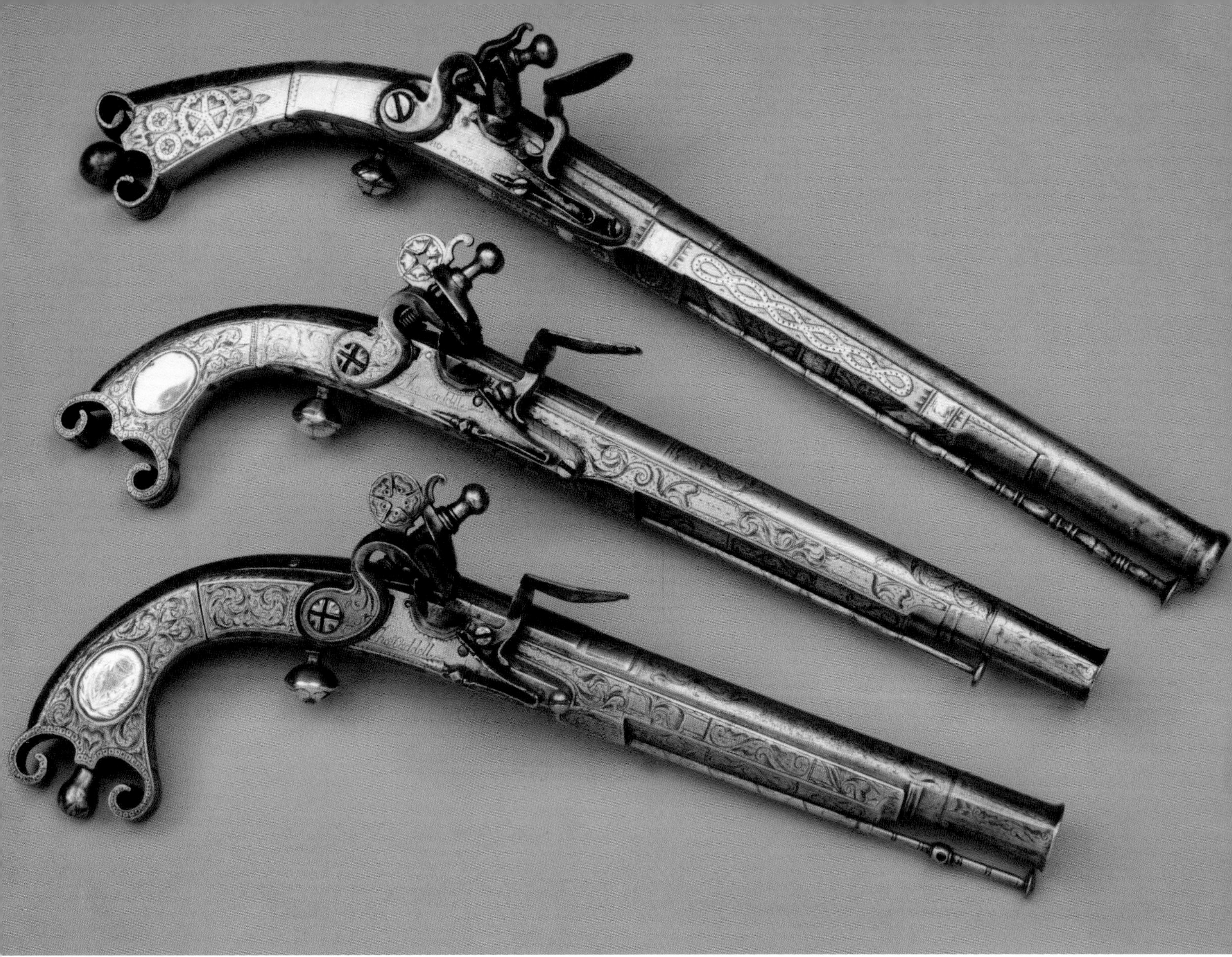

can be gained from a study of the drawings by Charles Whitelaw (Jackson 1923: 61, 67; Whitelaw 1977: 316–17).

Early seventeenth-century pistols either have fishtail, lemon or globular-shaped butts (illus 12.5, 12.18). By the second half of the century pistols were almost all made of iron, and the butts had developed heart-shaped and scroll forms. Many gunsmiths set up in towns near the Highlands, the source of much of their business. Doune in Stirlingshire was a particularly famous and prolific centre, producing richly decorated iron scroll butt pistols. Most of them have full signatures on their lock-plates of the gunsmiths who made them, including four

generations of a family called Caddell, all christened Thomas (illus 12.19). There were also Campbells, Murdochs and Christies. Apart from the outstanding collection of long guns in National Museums Scotland (illus 12.6) there are almost no traditional Scottish long guns with curved fluted butts surviving anywhere (Woosnam-Savage 1992).

Although not actually weapons, the powder horns made in the north-east of Scotland in the late seventeenth and early eighteenth century are often sought after by collectors (Caldwell 1989). They are made from flattened cow horns and decorated all over with geometric and foliage designs, and sometimes animals (illus 12.20). Of similar date are the targes or

Illustration 12.20
Powder horn of the late seventeenth century with Highland-type decoration. NMS: H.LK 43.
[Copyright © Trustees of the National Museums Scotland]

targets that were such an important part of the kit of the Highlanders who fought in the Jacobite uprisings (illus 12.3, 12.7). These circular shields were fitted with straps and handles to enable them to be carried on the left arm to parry bayonet and sword strokes. They are made of wooden boards covered with leather, tooled with interlace and other designs, and decorated with studs and bosses. A few have evidence of having been fitted with a spike or dagger blade in a central boss. In others the central boss could be unscrewed to serve as a drinking cup (Blair 1981b).

The manufacture of traditional Scottish weapons received a severe knock-back with the rigorously enforced Act of Parliament of 1746 requiring Highlanders to disarm. Swords, pistols and dirks, however, continued to be manufactured, perhaps largely for army officers (Caldwell 1998). Many of the finest Stirling-made hilts and Doune-type pistols clearly date to after 1746. Doune-trained gunsmiths moved to other towns including Perth, Stirling and Leith to seek new business. As a result of the great success of the visit by George IV in 1822 it became fashionable for Scots from all regions and walks of life to wear Highland dress and to carry pistols, dirks and sgian dubhs (Gaelic for black knives) as costume accessories. In the past, these weapons have been

overlooked, or even despised, by collectors, but they include many of very considerable craftsmanship and design. The pistols, which continue the tradition of

Illustration 12.21
Two sgian dubhs, both by W Robb of Ballater, *c* 1920.
NMS: H.LC 93 and H.LC 94.
[Copyright © Trustees of the National Museums Scotland]

those made in Doune, albeit with updated flintlock and percussion firing mechanisms, are often by the best gunsmiths operating in towns like Edinburgh and Perth. The dirks, made or retailed by town-based goldsmiths, are more richly decorated than their Highland predecessors, often with silver mounts and large crystals or citrines set in their pommels. Small decorative knives known as sgian dubhs were, and still are, manufactured for wearing in the top of a stocking (illus 12.21).

Also deserving of more attention by collectors are the products of the gunsmiths who set up in business in the towns from the late eighteenth century, principally to provide shotguns and rifles for sporting purposes. The work of the best of them, including James Innes in Edinburgh, Gunmaker to his Majesty in the early nineteenth century (illus 12.22), and Thomas

Elsworth Mortimer (illus 12.23), based in Edinburgh from the 1830s to the 1870s, is of a very high standard, comparable to that produced in other European centres. We might also note Alexander Forsyth, a Scottish minister who in 1805 invented the percussion lock (illus 12.22), one of the greatest leaps forward in the history of firearms. The company he set up to manufacture guns with the new firing mechanism was based in London.

Some of the weapons issued to the rank-and-file of Highland regiments are of recognisably Scottish type, albeit mass-produced by English manufacturers, like the late eighteenth-century all-metal pistols by Isaac Bissell and John Waters of Birmingham and the basket-hilted swords by Nathaniel Jefferys of London. Some nineteenth-century dirks bear the insignia and battle honours of Scottish regiments (illus 12.24).

Illustration 12.22
Early Forsyth 'scent bottle' percussion lock, made by James Innes of Edinburgh, *c* 1814. NMS: H.LH 220.
[Copyright © Trustees of the National Museums Scotland]

Illustration 12.23
Double-barrelled fowling piece by T E Mortimer, Edinburgh, mid-nineteenth century. NMS: H.LH 274.
[Copyright © Trustees of the National Museums Scotland]

Authenticity and identification

One of the major challenges facing the collector of Scottish weapons is the problem of authenticity. Museum curators can sometimes offer helpful opinions on specific items, but it is impossible for them to provide a regular, overall service. Anyone collecting Scottish weapons is well advised to attain sufficient knowledge and understanding of the weapons themselves prior to acquiring them. Much can be learned from the publications mentioned in this article and listed at the end, but there is no adequate substitute for close examination of good weapons in museums and other significant collections, even if only through the glass of a display case. Regrettably, there are several Scottish weapons of recent manufacture which pretend to be of earlier date or which have bogus associations and provenances. There are others of a genuinely early date – say pre-1750 – but which have been inappropriately cleaned and restored.

Of course, any weapon of date is most unlikely to have retained its original pristine condition. Apart from the ravages of corrosion or damage by living organisms, alterations and additions are likely to have been made during the weapon's lifespan, and pieces may also have been lost. Some weapons have only survived because they were put to alternative use, like the targes used as barrel lids or the dirks adapted for

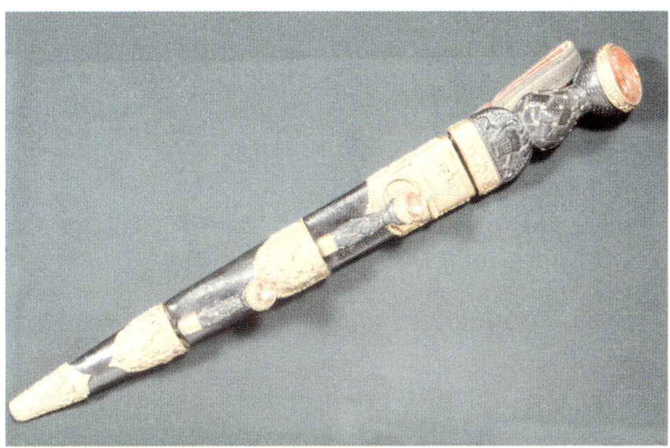

Illustration 12.24
Dirk with the battle honours of the
71st (Highland Light Infantry), c 1835–82. NMS: H.LC 95.
[Copyright © Trustees of the National Museums Scotland]

229

use as butchers' knives. Weapons may show signs of such use.

With the help of Whitelaw's *Scottish Arms Makers* it is sometimes possible to identify makers' marks and to find out a great deal about the makers of Scottish weapons in general. Increasingly, the focus of interest is turning towards the study of how these weapons were used in battle and their effectiveness rather than as examples of craftsmanship or art. The way that basket-hilted swords, dirks, guns and targes were used by Highland armies from 1644 to 1746 has long been a subject of fascination. Writers from Stewart of Garth in the early nineteenth century onwards (Stewart 1822: vol 1, 69–74) have understood how this combination developed into a winning tactic known as the Highland Charge, and how it was used against regular drilled armies. Some re-enactment groups are looking at the use of swords and how armies were drilled.

Of course, the surviving weapons, and in particular those deemed as collectable, are not representative of the whole range used by generations of Scots in battle. These are most likely to have included axes, spears and bows. A few axe-blades, spearheads and arrowheads have survived in excavated condition, and there is a considerable body of more recent long shafted weapons used for ceremonial functions by town officers and the like (Caldwell 1981c). They include halberds and Lochaber axes. The latter are generally identified as having relatively long axe-blades backed by a hook, but we should be wary of assuming that this was always the form of such a weapon, which may have changed over time or developed local variations. An interesting challenge is the almost total absence of armour from Scotland of sixteenth-century or earlier date. It is known from documentation and representations, mostly funeral effigies and grave-slabs and there were French armourers working at Holyrood Palace in the 1530s, making quality armour (Caldwell 1981b: 86–7). If any of it survives it would probably be indistinguishable from armour assumed to be made in France. Nevertheless, there is at least a small hope that continuing interest and growing knowledge in the subject will lead to more Scottish discoveries being made.

Scottish weapons can be viewed in museum and other collections in a number of different countries. The best collections are, not surprisingly, in Scotland. Apart from National Museums Scotland and Glasgow Museums, there are good collections in local museums like Aberdeen and Stirling, and in great houses like Inverary Castle, the home of the Dukes of Argyll, and Blair Atholl Castle, the home of the Dukes of Atholl. The Royal Armouries in Leeds have good collections, and the most significant ones in North America are in the Metropolitan Museum in New York and the Royal Ontario Museum in Toronto.

Bibliography

Blair, C 1981a 'The early basket-hilt in Britain', in Caldwell 1981a, 153–252.

Blair, C 1981b 'A type of Highland targe', in Caldwell 1981a, 391–8.

Blair, C & Wallace, J 1963 'Scots – or still English?', *Scottish Art Review*, special number, *Scottish Weapons* 9/1, 11–15.

Blair, C & Woosnam-Savage, R 1995 *Scottish Firearms*. Bloomsfield, Ontario: Museum Restoration Service.

Caldwell, D H 1979 *The Scottish Armoury*. Edinburgh: Blackwood.

Caldwell, D H (ed) 1981a *Scottish Weapons & Fortifications 1100–1800*. Edinburgh: John Donald.

Caldwell, D H 1981b 'Royal patronage of arms and armour making in fifteenth- and sixteenth-century Scotland', *in* Caldwell 1981a, 73–93.

Caldwell, D H 1981c 'Some Notes on Scottish Axes and Long Shafted Weapons', in Caldwell 1981a, 253–314.

Caldwell, D H 1983 'The Royal Scottish Gun Foundry in the Sixteenth Century', in O'Connor & Clarke 1983, 427–49.

Caldwell, D H 1985 'The art of Scottish firearms', *Man at Arms* 7/1 (Jan/Feb 1985): 26–30.

Caldwell, D H 1987 'The Lutiger Gun Barrel and the Manufacture of long guns in 16th-century Scotland', *The Fourth Park Lane Arms Fair*, D A Oliver (ed) (Apollo Magazine Ltd), 16–19.

Caldwell, D H 1989 'Scottish Powder-horns', *The Sixth Park Lane Arms Fair*, 21–4.

Caldwell, D H 1990 'The Guidon of Lord Cardross's Dragoons', *Dispatch* 122, 15.

Caldwell, D H 1998 'Traditional Scottish Weapons: The Last Phases', *The Fifteenth Park Lane Arms Fair*, D A Oliver (ed) (Apollo Magazine Ltd), 35–42.

Caldwell, D H 2005 'Claymores – the two-handed swords of the Scottish Highlanders', *The Spring 2005 Park Lane Arms Fair*, D A Oliver (ed) (Apollo Magazine Ltd), 47–53.

Caldwell, D H 2007a 'The Wallace Sword', in Cowan 2007, 169–75.

Caldwell, D H 2007b 'Having the right kit. West Highlanders fighting in Ireland', in Duffy 2007, 144–68.

Caldwell, D H 2009 'The re-arming of the Clans, 1822', *Review of Scottish Culture* 21, 67–86.

Caldwell, D H & Wallace, J 2003 'Ballocks, Dudgeons & Quhingearis. Three Scottish daggers recently acquired by the National Museums', *History Scotland* 3/6 (Nov/Dec 2003): 15–19.

Campbell, Lord A 1899 *Highland Dress, Arms and Ornament*. London: Constable.

Cowan, E J (ed) 2007 *The Wallace Book*. Edinburgh: John Donald.

Drummond, J 1881 *Ancient Scottish Weapons*. Edinburgh and London: Waterston.

Duffy, S (ed) 2007 *The World of the Galloglass: Kings, Warlords and Warriors in Ireland and Scotland, 1200–1600*. Dublin: Four Courts Press.

Faujas de Saint-Fond, B 1799 *Travels in England, Scotland and the Hebrides; undertaken for the purpose of examining the state of the Arts, the Sciences, Natural History and manners in Great Britain*, 2 vols. London: James Ridgway.

Glaister, J (convener) 1911 *Palace of History. Scottish Exhibition Glasgow*. Glasgow: Dalross.

Innes, C (ed) 1855 *The Black Book of Taymouth*. Edinburgh: Constable.

Jackson, H J 1923 *European Hand Firearms of the 16th, 17th & 18th Centuries*. London: Martin Hopkinson.

Joubert, F 1924 *Catalogue of the Collection of European Arms and Armour formed at Greenock by R. L. Scott*. Glasgow: David Robertson.

Mazansky, C 1995 *British Basket-Hilted Swords: A Typology of Basket-type Sword Hilts*. Woodbridge: Boydell.

Moss, M 2002 *The 'Magnificent Castle' of Culzean and the Kennedy Family*. Edinburgh: Edinburgh University Press.

Norman, A V B 1972 *Arms and Armour in the Royal Scottish Museum*. Edinburgh: HMSO.

O'Connor, A & Clarke, D V (eds) 1983 *From the Stone Age to the 'Forty-Five*. Edinburgh: John Donald.

Paton, J N 1879 *Private Catalogue of Armour, Weapons and Other Objects of Antiquity in the Collection of Sir Noël Paton*. Edinburgh: privately printed.

Paton, J (ed) 1890 *Scottish National Memorials*. Glasgow: MacLehose.

Paton, J (ed) 1902 *Scottish History & Life*. Glasgow: MacLehose.

Steer, K A & Bannerman, J W M 1977 *Late Medieval Monumental Sculpture in the West Highlands*. Edinburgh: RCAHMS

Stevenson, D & Caldwell, D H 1977 'Leather guns in Scotland and other light artillery of the mid-seventeenth century', *Proceedings of the Society of Antiquaries of Scotland* 108, 300–17.

Stewart, D 1822 *Sketches of the Highlanders of Scotland*, 2 vols, 2nd edition. Edinburgh: Constable.

Wallace, J 1970 *Scottish Swords and Dirks*. London: Arms and Armour Press.

Whitelaw, C E 1977 *Scottish Arms Makers*. London: Arms and Armour Press.

Woosnam-Savage, R 1992 'Some short notes on Scottish long guns in Scotland's public collections', *The Tenth Park Lane Arms Fair*, D A Oliver (ed) (Apollo Magazine Ltd), 24–32.

Index